CWSP™

Certified Wireless Security Professional™
Official Study Guide

(Exam PW0-200)

FIRST EDITION

Planet3 Wireless

McGraw-Hill/Osborne
New York Chicago San Francisco Lisbon London Madrid
Mexico City Milan New Delhi San Juan Seoul Singapore Sydney Toronto

McGraw-Hill/Osborne
2100 Powell St. 10th Floor
Emeryville, CA 94608
U.S.A.

To arrange bulk purchase discounts for sales promotions, premiums, or fund-raisers, please contact McGraw-Hill/Osborne at the above address. For information on translations or book distributors outside the U.S.A., please see the International Contact Information page immediately following the index of this book.

CWSP Certified Wireless Security Professional
Official Study Guide (Exam PW0-200) First Edition

1234567890 JPI JPI 019876543

ISBN 0-07-223012-6

Publisher	**Editorial Director**	**Indexer**
Brandon A. Nordin	Gareth Hancock	Jack Lewis
Vice President &	**Technical Editors**	**Computer Designers**
Associate Publisher	Joel Barrett	Scott Turner
Scott Rogers	Berni Gardiner	
Acquisitions Editor	**Copy Editor**	**Illustrator**
Timothy Green	Kevin Sandlin	Scott Turner
Project Editor	**Proofreader**	**Series Design**
Devin Akin	Kevin Sandlin	Scott Turner

CWNP™ Certification Program

The Certified Wireless Network Professional Training & Certification Program is intended for individuals who administer, install, design, and support IEEE 802.11 compliant wireless networks. Because the CWNP program is vendor neutral, candidates who achieve the different levels of CWNP Certification will be trained and qualified to administer and support many different brands of wireless LAN hardware. Although there are many manufacturers of wireless LAN hardware, the technologies behind the hardware – Radio Frequency and Local Area Networking – are the same for each piece of gear. Each manufacturer approaches these technologies in different ways.

The CWNP program consists of 4 levels of certification:

Administrator (CWNA) – Site survey, installation, and management of 802.11 compliant wireless LANs

Security Professional (CWSP) – Design and implementation of 802.11 security techniques, processes, hardware, and software

Integrator (CWNI) – Design, management, QoS, advanced site surveying, advanced RF theory, and vertical market analysis of 802.11 compliant wireless LANs

Expert (CWNE) – Wireless LAN packet analysis and troubleshooting using the latest software tools

We at Planet3 are humbled by God's awesome grace. Every day we ask, "What about today Lord?" and every day He provides. The success of Planet3 Wireless stands as a message to all that nothing is impossible with God for those who have a willingness to participate in His plan for their lives. Through no strength or wisdom of our own has this company been built, but rather God has made straight our path and given us the tools to accomplish His will.

Luke 1:37 "For nothing is impossible with God."

Acknowledgements

Planet3 Wireless, Inc. would like to acknowledge and thank the following people for their contributions to the CWSP Study Guide:

Devin Akin, Author: Devin's never-ending drive to learn the very latest technologies, solutions, problems, hardware, software, and implementation methods is the primary ingredient in the content of the CWSP Study Guide. Devin is the Chief Technology Officer of Planet3 Wireless, Inc. Devin has over seven years of IT experience and has held Cisco's CCNP and CCDP certifications since 1999. Devin helped shape Cisco's wireless specializations and also holds CWNA, CWNT, MCSE, and Master CNE certifications. Devin was the primary courseware, study guide, and exam subject matter expert for the CWNA certification. Devin has previously worked as a Senior Network Access Design Engineer with Earthlink and BellSouth, and a Senior Systems Engineer for Foundry Networks and Sentinel Technologies. Devin is the principal courseware architect and subject matter expert for the CWSP Exam, CWSP Study Guide, and Official CWSP Courseware.

Joel Barrett, Technical Editor: Thank you to Joel for his willingness to take on this project over and above his enormous responsibilities at Cisco. Joel's excitement about this content and attention to detail gave us constant encouragement to finish this project strong. Joel is a Channel Systems Engineer and Enterprise Wireless LAN Technology Leadership Program (TLP) member with Cisco Systems, Inc. Joel has over fifteen years of IT experience and has attained Cisco's CCNP, CCDP, and wireless specializations as well as the CWNA, MCSE, and Master CNE certifications. Joel handles Cisco's channel partners in Georgia and is also responsible for assisting Cisco's wireless developers throughout the southeastern United States. Joel is the principal technical editor for the CWSP Study Guide and one of the subject matter experts who helped develop the CWSP courseware. Joel contributed the Wireless Security Policy template found in Appendix A of this text.

Berni Gardiner, Technical Reviewer: Berni has been in the computing industry for 25 years starting her career in System Design and Integration.

Over the past 14 years she has focused on the telecommunications industry in a combination of roles ranging from Network Manager to Dial Product Architect to VP of Technology and Integration. Over the past 6 years, Berni has also been active in the training sector, designing and delivering courseware and lab content for Cisco CCNP courses and CWNA courses. Her specializations include voice over data technologies and wireless networking. Berni has earned Cisco's CCSI and CCNP certifications and the CWNA and CWNT certifications.

Contents at a Glance

Contents

Forward

Ask ten IT managers for their opinion on the greatest challenges associated with wireless LAN (WLAN) deployment and security will be at the top of most every list. It's understandable. Weaknesses in the underlying 802.11 security capabilities have been widely documented and a range of freely downloadable applications are now available, allowing relatively unsophisticated users to exploit these vulnerabilities. Stories about war driving are common in the popular press, and plans for how to modify a Pringles potato chip can for use as a high-gain directional antenna have found their way into e-mail in-boxes worldwide. And if you think Denial of Service (DoS) attacks are a serious problem on the Internet, wait until you see how the combination of a simple signal generator and antenna can affect a wireless LAN system.

While wireless LAN security problems are indeed quite serious, many organizations have been able to implement wireless LANs in a manner that meets even the most stringent security policies. But doing so usually comes at a high price, not only in the cost of add-on software and hardware, but also in the more hidden cost of increased complexity. For many IT managers, wireless LAN infrastructure is already viewed as a somewhat exotic technology that introduces many inherent and unique management challenges. Alas, it's the cost of doing business in the wireless world, so be prepared to make some substantial investments to achieve the elusive goal of "secure wireless LAN."

Designing, implementing, and managing secure WLANs requires careful planning from the start. Few organizations can afford to take a "learn as you go" approach to security. Sorting out the many security-related issues requires a systematic approach and a substantial level of expertise. In most organizations, the wireless gurus – if there are any – don't have a strong security background, and the security experts often lack a detailed understanding about how radio-based networks operate. The industry is hungry for experts who combine these two skill-sets. The industry is hungry for wireless security professionals, and proper training is the key.

Wireless Industry Viability

How the industry deals with these security concerns will largely determine the future viability of enterprise wireless LANs. There's no silver bullet, just lots of work to do designing more secure systems from the start, preferably without resorting to proprietary implementations. The IEEE pioneers who brought us 802.11 insist that the security provisions included in the original specification – most notably the WEP encryption technology – were never intended to serve as the foundation for a truly secure network environment. Instead, they were intended to provide security equivalent to that provided on wired networks. In essence, that's an indictment of the relatively primitive security implemented on many enterprise Ethernet networks, where it's relatively easy in many organizations to find a port, plug in your notebook, and with just a little bit of effort, gain access to central systems. Judged by that standard, wireless LANs may indeed have security equivalent to wired systems.

The bar for wireless security has to be set higher, and most enterprise IT professionals understand this. While layer-2 switching and layer-3 routing technologies helped to mask some of the underlying security vulnerabilities of traditional shared-media Ethernet systems, with wireless, we're witnessing a return to the "ether," an environment where packets are literally flying through the air, just begging to be intercepted, and where session hijacking and denial of service attacks are relatively simple to implement. Predictably, the standards bodies have reacted to the fact that their image has been tainted and they are determined not to let that happen again. The end result is a painstakingly slow march towards open security standards. Lest you forget, it took the IEEE seven years to develop the original 802.11 specification. We can't afford another seven years for robust security.

Outside the formal standards bodies, the industry has reacted to the wireless LAN security problem in many different ways, often exacerbating the problem. Many enterprise IT professionals have adopted the "mini-max" principle, where they seek to minimize their maximum regret by prohibiting any use of any wireless LAN technology whatsoever. While such an approach certainly addresses the security problem, it also makes it impossible for those organizations to recognize the obvious productivity benefits associated with wireless technology. It's also worth noting that banishment doesn't mean you don't have to learn about wireless LAN security. You'll still need to have some mechanism for monitoring internal policy compliance.

Wireless LAN vendors have also taken a variety of approaches. A sub-segment of the wireless industry has been launched specifically to address wireless LAN security problems and a few vendors have been able to sell enough security overlay products to maintain their business viability. Others have spent so much time publicizing the vulnerabilities, in hopes of selling their high-priced solutions, that they have further discouraged adoption, not only because they create fear but also because in tight budget periods, they've made it convenient for CIO's to just say "we can't afford wireless, regardless of the benefits."

The lack of acceptable security standards has also led some vendors to develop proprietary solutions, making them easy targets for criticism. But in their defense, you can hardly blame them for trying to solve their customer's deployment problems. Industry associations like the Wi-Fi Alliance understand this market need and they have reluctantly stepped in to fill the standards void, with solutions like Wi-Fi Protected Access (WPA), which provides a security framework that meets most enterprise needs.

Finally, there are those who advocate the use of existing security technologies to solve the problem, the logic being that even if it's not the ideal tool, a big enough wrench can be used to hammer a nail. While standards-based VPN technology surely plays an important role in the wireless LAN industry (providing secure access from hotspots, for example), it isn't the most flexible security solution for wireless because it wasn't designed to support mobile devices, which hop from access point to access point and often experience moments of disconnected operation.

The Patience to Do The Right Thing

A poorly designed wireless LAN is often far worse than none at all. Poorly funded wireless LAN pilot-projects often create expectations that cannot be met in a production system. And IT professionals can't just look the other way, either. Wireless LAN technology is so inexpensive that it's likely to find its way in the back door, just like PC's did 20 or so years ago. And a "just say no to wireless" is likely to be about as successful as other similar initiatives designed change complex human behavior using overly simplistic solutions.

What's needed now more than ever is education. The industry needs rigorous programs that allow IT professionals to learn what needs to be learned in order to implement secure wireless LANs. This is not an easy challenge for a relatively immature industry. But that's the challenge that the folks at Planet3 Wireless took on in creating their Certified Wireless Security Professional (CWSP) program, one of the key elements of a broader initiative to promote a vendor-neutral technical certification program for Certified Wireless Network Professionals.

Experienced IT professionals understand that implementing effective network security requires a multi-faceted approach. First, you need to understand the security challenges, including the various types of intrusions and the tools available to monitor organizational vulnerabilities. Second, organizations need to assess their level of risk tolerance, balanced by the potential benefits of wireless technology, and establish sound policy to drive wireless technology adoption and support. And finally, information professionals need to understand the specific wireless security solutions available on the market, and their relative costs and benefits.

Is the material included in the CWSP program perfect? Probably not. Technologies are rapidly evolving, so while the designers of this program have gone to great effort to be comprehensive in their approach, passing the CWSP exam does not guarantee total competence. Instead, it establishes a foundation of knowledge, based both on advanced technical understanding and also on proven hands-on competence. As an educator at a large University, I've learned through experience to better appreciate the delicate balance needed between theory and practice. The designers of the CWSP program understand that balance as well.

-Dave Molta,

Senior Technology Editor, Network Computing Magazine

Preface

Hacking a wireless LAN

Wireless hacking is easy…if you know how wireless LANs work, what tools yield what results, and how to attack certain scenarios step-by-step. It is purely a matter of memorization and resourcefulness. Anybody can learn to be a wireless hacker on their own given some free time, a high-speed Internet connection, and Google.com. The tools are out there, and most are cheap. Let's be honest, most malicious hackers don't pay for software anyway, and instead use cracks, other people's serial numbers, warez (copied software), keygens (key generators), etc. What we've tried to do with the first part of this book is to show you the tools and how hackers use them, as well as how security auditors use them. We discuss the tools (Wintel tools if you can believe that), the techniques, and even what happens if the bad guy gets caught. We're not trying to encourage hacking – in fact, it's just the opposite. We know that only an adept hacker can prevent intrusion and catch other hackers in the act. This book is by no means a "Wireless Hacker's Bible", but we hope that it gives the reader sufficient information to prevent intrusion and to do penetration tests on his or her own network.

Wireless LAN Security Policy

How can anyone like policy? That's the sentiment of most engineers and even some IT managers, but without good network security policy, no security solution is going to do the trick of keeping the bad guys out. Once you know how to create, implement, and enforce (that's the hard one) a quality security policy, you become a much more valuable resource to your employer.

There are simply too many wireless LAN security holes to plug for any one piece (or one hundred pieces) of hardware or software to be complete. How can a VPN server prevent a help desk person from giving out a username and password to an intruder by mistake? It can't, of course. When a rogue access point is found on the network, an administrator's first instinct is usually to confiscate it and start screaming at employees, right? How about taking a look at those access point association tables to see who's connected? And what about those log files...think there's anything good in there? As you can see, there are many things covered in policy that you might not think of.

The Policy section in this book is a comprehensive list of, "Don't forget this, and don't ever do this, and when this happens, you must do that!" There's even a security policy template for you in the back of the book that should serve as a solid starting point for your new security policy that will include wireless. Many consultants lose out on additional revenue after a site survey, an install, or a security consulting project. By not helping an organization with their lack of wireless security policy, consultants do themselves and their clients a disservice. Most companies don't know they even need anything new for wireless.

Wireless LAN Security Solutions

Solutions? You mean a wireless LAN can be secure? Absolutely. There are so many wireless security solutions on the market now that it is mind-boggling. From software for almost any operating system platform to security appliances, there are solutions of every kind. There are layer 2 solutions like proprietary VPNs and 802.1x/EAP; there are layer 3 solutions like tried-and-true VPN technology; and there are even layer 7 solutions like SSH2 and secure applications. If you're not familiar with the OSI model, have a quick – but thorough – review before starting this book because we reference OSI layers constantly.

We will discuss the solution technology, but not the vendors that implement the technology for the most part in this book. An example of an exception is Cisco's LEAP, for which their implementation is proprietary, but popular (especially with the new Cisco Compatible Extensions program) and interoperable enough to be considered a generic type of solution. The bottom line for this section is that there are so many great new solutions on the market, that after reading this book, not only will you be eager and able to get some hands on experience with the gear, but also you will be able to jump right into it because you understand the technology behind any wireless security solution. Understanding the technology is always the first step, but even that will not help you land a great job until you can configure and install any security software and hardware necessary to keep hackers out of your network.

After reading this book, you should be able to talk the talk, walk the walk, dance circles around all of your wireless friends, and scare the heck out of anyone considering a new wireless implementation. You will find much in this book that you cannot find anywhere else. We have taken the time to read manufacturer's manuals, scour hundreds of great whitepapers, talk with leading engineers at manufacturers, and get authors and engineers with various backgrounds involved in offering information on the topics covered in this book. I like to use the wireless Kerberos implementation native to Windows 2000 Active Directory as an example. Do you understand 802.1x? How about Kerberos v5? How about Active Directory? What about IPSec? We have sections that explain how each of these plays a part in a complete solution and how it all works together.

It's not enough to know all of the pieces individually because a wireless security solution is made up of authentication, encryption, network access control, and many other moving parts all fitting together into a single engine of sorts. Some of the sections, like IPSec, are discussed briefly compared with just how in depth they could be discussed because our intention is to show you how it fits into wireless LANs. There are other books on IPSec and topics of that nature that go into extreme detail. We encourage you to read one or two of them in your spare time.

We are sure that this book, followed by hands on experience with various security solutions and hacking tools, will both prepare you for a wonderful career in wireless security and for the CWSP exam. We hope that when you finish this book your brain hurts as much as ours did when we finished writing it. Have fun, and we wish you the best in your IT career!

-Devin Akin

Author, CWNA and CWSP Study Guides

Introduction

In early March 2003, only days prior to the publication of this book, NIST, the National Institute of Standards and Technology (http://www.nist.gov/), released a draft paper titled Wireless Network Security, 802.11, Bluetooth™ and Handheld Devices. On page 38 of that document, in section 3.5.1, is the following statement:

"Another management countermeasure is to ensure that all critical personnel are properly trained on the use of wireless technology. Network administrators need to be fully aware of the security risks that WLANs and devices pose. They must work to ensure security policy compliance and to know what steps to take in the event of an attack. Finally, the most important countermeasures are trained and aware users."

It is directly to the final point in the paragraph above that we have created the CWSP certification, instructor led class, and official study guide. It is the firm position of the CWNP program that no piece of hardware or software can secure any wireless network without the oversight of a properly trained wireless security professional.

The CWSP Official Study Guide is intended to help you in two ways. First and foremost, this book will teach you the ins and outs of enterprise wireless LAN security. Second, the book will play a major role in your preparation for the CWSP certification exam. This book, along with your hands-on experience designing, implementing, and troubleshooting wireless LAN security solutions, will help prepare you for the CWSP exam. In addition to this study guide, IT professionals seeking the CWSP certification should also take advantage of the following resources as preparation for the CWSP exam:

- Official CWSP instructor led training
- Official CWSP practice exams
- The 802.1x, 802.11i, and WPA standards
- Books and other resources of network security solutions such as IPSec, VPNs, VLANs, firewalls, and other related solutions that are prevalent in the wired networking world but still fairly new to wireless LANs

But, above all, hands-on experience will be the most important item of preparation for CWSP.

Learning how to implement wireless LAN security, not just *about* wireless LAN security, will set you apart from the vast majority of IT professionals today. Security is a very hot topic in the IT world, and even hotter in the wireless LAN sector because of the very fact that 802.11 wireless networks are not inherently secure. This book is your first step toward learning how hackers approach wireless networks and how you can defeat those hackers' attempts by implementing the proper solutions, policies, and practices to lock down your wireless network.

In order to more fully comprehend the two components in this book – wireless LANs and security – it is required that any candidate who seeks the CWSP certification first earn the CWNA™ certification, and recommended that all CWSP candidates have a solid understanding of computer and network security. Such an understanding can be gained through study and achievement of such certifications as:

- ISC2 CISSP (www.isc2.org)
- Security Certified Professional (www.securitycertified.net)
- CompTIA Security+ (www.comptia.org)

While these security certifications are not required to earn CWSP, they will build a foundation of security knowledge that makes understanding how wireless LANs can be secured much easier.

The wireless LAN market continues to grow at an incredible pace, even several years after the solidification of the 802.11b standard caused the Wi-Fi sector to begin its remarkable growth. Inherent in that growth is the need for qualified IT professionals who understand how to use the dozens of hardware and software products that are flooding the market as "security solutions." From this book and from the CWSP instructor led training course you will learn that, no matter how much money your organization invests in the best wireless LAN security hardware and software, if there is not a qualified individual to implement and manage these solutions, the solutions are not worth their weight in plastic antennas.

How is this book organized?

This book is divided into three major units: Intrusion, Policy, and Solutions. Intrusion takes a detailed and enlightening look from the intruder's point of view at how simple a wireless LAN can be compromised. The tools that are available today can enable any experienced networking professional to break into or shut down almost any wireless network, and these tools are readily available and easy to use. In the hands of a malicious person, these tools can cost an enterprise millions of dollars and thousands of hours of resources to repair damage that costs only a few hundred dollars and a few minutes to prevent.

The Wireless Security Policy unit examines all of the DOs and DON'Ts that will challenge even the most experienced security professional, and also offers a complete security policy template for your organization to use in implementing a wireless LAN security policy.

The final section, Wireless LAN Security Solutions, digs deep into hardware and software solutions that exist throughout the OSI model layers. Wireless VPNs, Kerberos, 802.1x/EAP versions, TKIP, SSH2, Wireless Bridging security, enterprise wireless gateways, enterprise encryption gateways, and layered security solutions are all systematically explained in this one-of-a-kind unit about how to implement secure wireless LAN solutions.

The combination of first learning how your worst enemy – the hacker – can get into your network, then discovering how many attacks can be thwarted by simple policy, and topping it off with a double helping of the very latest technologies driving wireless LAN security provides a thorough foundation for securing the wireless LANs of today and the future.

Each chapter of each of the three units has review questions that not only cause you to think about what you just read, but can also serve in your preparation for the CWSP exam.

Why should I pursue the CWSP certification?

While this book will go far in helping IT pros develop secure wireless networks, it will also provide the next learning challenge after CWNA to those who choose to learn a skill and measure their knowledge in a high stakes testing environment.

How many people do you know today who know how to secure any enterprise wireless network? It is a rare person indeed who can talk intelligently not only about layer 2, 3, & 7 hardware and software solutions for wireless LANs, but also completely view the world through the best hacker's eyes to find holes in their own wireless security solution. Even rarer still is the IT professional who can address what brand of wireless LAN hardware will perform best as part of an overall security solution. Then there are the elite who will learn all of these topics and put their own knowledge to the test in a proctored exam environment for 90 painful minutes to prove to all that they really do know their stuff.

There is no other advanced, vendor neutral, wireless LAN security certification in the world, period. CWSP is the first of its kind, and earning this certification tells the world that you have endured the reading, staging, testing, breaking, and hacking your own networks using multiple vendors' equipment so that you can handle any wireless LAN security scenario that may raise its head.

How do I earn the CWSP certification?

Prior to taking the CWSP certification exam, the candidate is required to earn the CWNA certification. Details about the CWNA certification can be found at http://www.cwne.com.

Once you have obtained the CWNA certification, you are ready to build upon that base of wireless LAN knowledge by earning your CWSP certification, #2 on the way to earning the brass ring CWNE certification. This book and the Official CWSP Practice test at www.cwne.com are the official self-study tools for the CWSP exam.

The best method of preparation for the CWSP certification is to attend a Wireless LAN Security course, the official course for preparing for the

CWSP exam. There is only one substitute for the 12 hands-on intrusion and solution labs that are performed during the 45 hours of CWSP learning, and that is real-world, hands-on experience in the same situations that are developed in these lab exercises. Many of the questions on the CWSP exam come directly from the solutions that are learned and demonstrated in these labs, and can also be learned by designing, implementing, troubleshooting, and "auditing" these solutions in the wild.

Once you are prepared to sit for the CWSP exam, you must purchase a CWSP exam voucher at www.cwne.com. You will use this voucher to register at either www.2test.com or by calling Prometric directly at 1-800-639-3926 for exam # PW0-200. On the CWSP exam, you will see 60 exam items, some of which will be interactive items requiring drag and drop, point and click, or other interactive functionality. All other questions will be multiple choice and multiple answer questions. The subject matter of the questions is divided according to the CWSP Exam Objectives, which are covered in the next section of this book, and are also available on the CWNP Program web site at http://www.cwne.com.

Who is this book for?

This book builds upon the knowledge that is gained through preparing for and earning the CWNA certification, so many of the concepts that are explained in this book assume a certain amount of RF and networking knowledge. This book is intended for three main audiences: CWNAs, IT Security Professionals, and wireless LAN integrators.

For CWNAs, this book represents a starting point towards the next level of certification within the CWNP program: CWSP. For those who have set themselves apart by proving their knowledge of the foundations of 802.11 wireless networks, the next logical step is to progress onwards toward CWNE by learning how to secure the very same networks that they have learned to install and manage.

For IT Security Professionals, this book may or may not represent an opportunity to achieve another certification. Either way, the CWSP Study Guide means a wealth of new knowledge about the fastest growing segment of the computer networking industry, and how to apply their security skills to wireless.

For wireless LAN integrators, working to implement high-end wireless LAN infrastructures in hospitals, warehouses, WISPs, and other mobile environments, the CWSP Study Guide offers an in-depth handbook for what not to do, what to do, and how to do it. Additionally, it provides a template for creating a thorough wireless LAN security policy, something that few organizations today have even considered.

Exam Objectives

The CWSP™ certification covering the 2003 objectives will certify that successful candidate understands the weaknesses inherent in wireless LANs, the solutions available to address those weaknesses, and the steps necessary to implement a secure and manageable wireless LAN in an enterprise environment. The CWSP candidate must have obtained the CWNA certification prior to attending a CWSP class or taking the CWSP certification exam.

The skills and knowledge measured by this examination are derived from a survey of wireless networking experts and professionals from around the world. The results of this survey were used in weighing the subject areas and ensuring that the weighting is representative of the relative importance of the content.

This section outlines the exam objectives of the CWSP exam.

Wireless LAN Intrusion – 20%

1.1.   Explain how intruders obtain network access through analysis, spoofing, and information theft including the following methods:

   1.1.1.   Monitoring & obtaining data sent in clear text or with weak encryption

   1.1.2.   Use of wireless LAN protocol analysis and site survey tools

   1.1.3.   WEP Decryption

   1.1.4.   MAC address spoofing and circumventing filters

   1.1.5.   Active intrusion techniques (connecting, probing, and configuring the network)

1.2.   Explain how the following types of Denial of Service (DoS) attacks can occur in a wireless LAN and identify the tools that can be used to perform these attacks.

   1.2.1.   RF jamming

   1.2.2.   Data flooding

   1.2.3.   Client hijacking

1.10. Describe weaknesses in and identify and configure the appropriate security-related controls for each of the following:

    1.10.1. SSIDs

    1.10.2. SNMP security (alarms, strong strings, disabling)

    1.10.3. Output power settings

    1.10.4. MAC filters

    1.10.5. Manufacturer's default settings

    1.10.6. Strong passwords

    1.10.7. Secure access to wireless infrastructure devices

1.11. Given the following wireless LAN hacking hardware & software, explain how an intruder could gain access to a network

    1.11.1. Password gathering software

    1.11.2. Protocol analysis software

    1.11.3. Session reconstruction software

    1.11.4. Enumerating software

    1.11.5. Rogue hardware

    1.11.6. Directional & Omni antennas

1.12. Summarize the following legal issues that apply to wireless LANs, and how they apply to computers and intellectual property:

    1.12.1. U.S. Federal laws regarding information security and illegal intrusion

    1.12.2. U.S. State laws regarding information security and illegal intrusion

Wireless LAN Security Policy – 20%

2.1. Explain the purpose and goals of the following wireless LAN security policies

    2.1.1. Password policy

    2.1.2. User training

    2.1.3. On-going review (auditing)

    2.1.4. Acceptable use & abuse policy

    2.1.5. Consistent implementation procedure

2.11. Given a set of business requirements, design a scalable and secure wireless LAN solution considering the following security tactics:

2.11.1. Wireless LAN segmentation

2.11.2. Wireless DMZ configuration

2.11.3. Use of NAT/PAT

2.11.4. NAT/PAT impact on secure tunneling mechanisms

2.11.5. Redundancy

2.11.6. Wireless LAN equipment staging & deployment

2.11.7. Wireless LAN cell sizing and shaping

2.11.8. Scalability

2.11.9. Appropriate use of different antenna types

2.11.10. Operational verification

2.12. Secure equipment configuration and placement

2.13. Describe appropriate installation locations for wireless LAN hardware in order to avoid physical theft and tampering, considering the following:

2.13.1. Security implications of remote placement of devices

2.13.2. Physical security for remote infrastructure devices

2.13.3. Secure remote connections to wireless LAN infrastructure devices

2.14. Implement physical security measures and describe why they are essential to prevent the following:

2.14.1. Hardware theft

2.14.2. Access to secure consoles

2.15. Security solution interoperability and layering

2.15.1. Explain the benefits of interoperable wireless LAN security solutions

2.15.2. Design and implement co-existing wireless LAN security solutions

2.16. Security management

2.16.1. Explain the necessary criteria for regular wireless LAN security reporting and documentation

2.16.2. Implement and conduct timely and consistent reporting procedures

3.3. VPNs

    3.3.1. Implement, configure, and manage the following VPN solutions in a wireless LAN environment:

        ○ PPTP

        ○ IPSec

        ○ L2TP

    3.3.2. Explain the importance and benefits of session persistence in a wireless VPN environment

    3.3.3. Explain the differences, strengths, and limitations of each of the following as a wireless VPN solution

        ○ Routers

        ○ VPN Concentrators

        ○ Firewalls

    3.3.4. Describe benefits of mobile VPN solutions

3.4. Enterprise Wireless Gateways

    3.4.1. Understand the functionality of enterprise wireless gateways

    3.4.2. Recognize strengths, weaknesses, and appropriate applications for an enterprise wireless gateway

    3.4.3. Describe common security features, tools, and configuration techniques among enterprise wireless gateway products

    3.4.4. Install and configure an enterprise wireless gateway, including profiles and VPNs

    3.4.5. Manage and recognize scalability limitations of an enterprise wireless gateway

3.5. RADIUS and AAA

    3.5.1. Explain the wireless authentication and association processes

    3.5.2. Explain the purpose, location, and scalability of RADIUS and AAA solutions

    3.5.3. Describe the wireless standards supported by RADIUS

    3.5.4. Implement scalable RADIUS/AAA user authentication and auditing solutions

3.12. Describe the following types of intrusion detection methods and tools for wireless LANs

    3.12.1. 24x7 centralized, skilled monitoring

    3.12.2. Honey pots

    3.12.3. Professional security audits

    3.12.4. Accurate, timely reporting

    3.12.5. Distributed agent software

    3.12.6. Security spot checking

    3.12.7. Available wireless LAN intrusion detection software and hardware tools

3.13. Given a list of wireless LAN configuration and security requirements, select and implement the appropriate type of authentication from among the following

    3.13.1. Kerberos

    3.13.2. EAP / LEAP / PEAP

    3.13.3. WEP / TKIP

    3.13.4. VPN

    3.13.5. Certificates

    3.13.6. 2-factor & 3-factor authentication

    3.13.7. PAP / CHAP / MS-CHAP-v2

    3.13.8. LDAP / Directory Services

    3.13.9. RADIUS / AAA

Contact Information

We are always eager to receive feedback on our courses, training materials, study guides, practice tests, and exams. If you have specific questions about something you have read in this book, please use the information below to contact Planet3 Wireless, Inc.

Planet3 Wireless, Inc.
P.O. Box 412
Bremen GA 30110
866.GET.CWNE
866.422.8354 fax
http://www.cwne.com

Direct feedback via email:
feedback@cwne.com

Wireless LAN Auditing Tools

CWSP Exam Objectives Covered:

❖ Explain how intruders obtain network access through analysis, spoofing, and information theft including the following methods:

- Monitoring & obtaining data sent in clear text or with weak encryption

- Use of wireless LAN protocol analysis and site survey tools

- WEP Decryption

- MAC address spoofing and circumventing filters

- Active intrusion techniques (connecting, probing, and configuring the network)

❖ Locate & identify wireless LANs within and around a facility

- War Driving

- War Chalking

❖ Given the following wireless LAN hacking hardware & software, explain how an intruder could gain access to a network

- Password gathering software

- Protocol analysis software

- Session reconstruction software

- Enumerating software

- Rogue hardware

- Directional & Omni antennas

In This Chapter

Wireless LAN Discovery tools

Password Capture & Decrypt Tools

Share Enumerators

Network Management & Control Tools

Wireless Protocol Analyzers

Antennas & Other Wireless LAN Equipment

Securing a wireless network is not an easy task, and once a wireless LAN has been secured it must be thoroughly tested for vulnerabilities. As a part of the security policy for a company, the network should be audited periodically for any changes that may introduce security holes in the network. There is an extensive list of software and hardware tools that can be used to perform the task of auditing a network. For the network administrator or auditor, these tools will provide valuable insight into how, when, and where a network could be exposed to outside attack. However, hackers can use these same tools to find and exploit the vulnerabilities in a network. This is to say that if an auditor is to find holes in the network, the auditor must think and attempt intrusions like a hacker would.

This chapter will cover in detail the many types of audits that should be performed on wireless networks, and the types of vulnerabilities each audit can expose. Each audit describes why a security administrator or consultant should perform the audit, and how the hacker exploits the security holes that can be found from each audit. The following auditing tools are discussed in this chapter.

- Wireless LAN Discovery Tools
- Password Capture & Decrypt
- Share Enumerators
- Network Management & Control
- Wireless Protocol Analyzers
- Manufacturer Defaults
- Antennas & WLAN Equipment
- OS Fingerprinting & Port Scanning
- Application Layer Analyzers
- Networking Utilities
- Network Discovery Tools
- RF Jamming Tools
- Hijacking Tools
- WEP Decryption Tools
- Operating System Exploit Tools
- Homeplug Devices

Wireless LAN Discovery Tools

Most wireless LANs in use today are Wi-Fi® compliant DSSS networks. Many discovery tools on the market are focused on finding these types of networks. However, the wireless security professional should not be fooled into thinking that intruders would limit themselves to only the latest Wi-Fi gear for penetrating a wireless network.

NetStumbler

Written by Marius Milner, NetStumbler is a free Windows-based software utility, usually installed on a laptop computer, for locating and interrogating wireless LANs. War drivers, war walkers, war flyers, and war chalkers (all terms for individuals that roam about locating wireless LANs) love using NetStumbler to locate wireless networks because it is simple to use and supports a wide variety of wireless network interface cards (NICs). After locating these wireless networks, war drivers occasionally try to gain unauthorized access to the wireless LAN using other networking tools, or, at the very least, get free high-speed Internet access for a time.

 Someone using NetStumbler may just be a curious about wireless networks and not necessarily trying to cause damage or harm to your company. There are no statistics on what percentage users are using NetStumbler for the purpose of breaking into a network with bad intentions. State laws differ on what defines breaking into a network, as well as the penalties for doing so.

NetStumbler operates by scanning the 2.4-2.5 GHz frequency range used by IEEE 802.11b compliant wireless devices and locating any access points or peer-to-peer networks. When NetStumbler finds an access point, it displays the following information, as shown in Figure 1.1

- MAC Address
- SSID
- Access Point name
- Channel
- Vendor

- Security (WEP on or off)
- Signal strength
- GPS coordinates (if GPS device is attached)

FIGURE 1.1   Sample output from NetStumbler

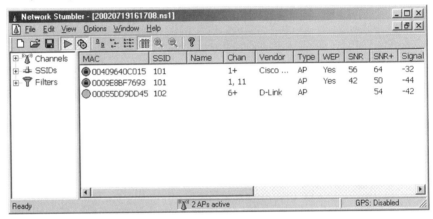

Usage

NetStumbler is first installed on a laptop computer equipped with a WLAN card. The most common type of card used by both auditors and hackers is Proxim's Orinoco Gold Card. This card has an external antenna jack whereby, using a pigtail cable, a high gain omni or a directional antenna can be attached to the card. Using external antennas of this nature, range and focus can be easily enhanced. The same can be done with Cisco's 350 series PC Cards provided the correct firmware and driver are used. Some Cisco cards have an external antenna jack also. The Cisco card can be configured to produce 100 mW output (variable) whereas the Orinoco is fixed at 32 mW. It is common for hackers to install magnetically mounted omni antennas on the roofs of their cars and then drive around looking for wireless networks, as illustrated in Figure 1.2.

FIGURE 1.2   War driver scanning for wireless LANs using NetStumbler

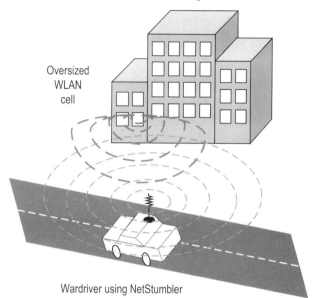

Oversized
WLAN
cell

Wardriver using NetStumbler

Functionality

There is always debate on how NetStumbler functions and how to keep
NetStumbler from finding your network. This debate is usually taken up
by those who think that security through obscurity (hiding the unsecured
network) is the best approach. NetStumbler sends probe request frames
that cause, according to the 802.11 standard, all access points to respond
with information about themselves, including the SSID. When using the
"closed network" feature available in some access points, NetStumbler
will not see the access point provided the access point does not respond to
probe request frames using "broadcast SSIDs." "Broadcast SSID" means
that the SSID field in the probe response frame is blank (empty) and has a
byte length of zero. Contrary to popular belief, NetStumbler does not get
its information from passive scanning (listening to beacons). This
functionality of NetStumbler can be verified using a packet analyzer.

SSIDs occur in the following frames:

- Beacon Management Frames
- Probe Request Frames
- Probe Response Frames
- Association Request Frames
- Reassociation Request Frames

Broadcast SSIDs

The method that 802.11 vendors use to hide the wireless LAN's SSID is to use the Broadcast SSID in the beacons. For the station to join or roam in a wireless LAN, it sends an *Associate* or *Reassociate* request to the access point. The *Associate* and *Reassociate* frames always contain the SSID. If the station were to use the Broadcast SSID, there would be no restrictions on which stations can join the wireless LAN. If the SSID in these frames does not match the SSID configured in the access point, the access point rejects the association. There is no reason code in 802.11 standard for 'Invalid SSID'; thus, the most likely reason code will be 'Unspecified reason'. A Broadcast SSID can be used in any of these frames. However, it is difficult to operate a wireless LAN if *Probe Response* frames contain the Broadcast SSID. Thus, practically speaking, only the Beacons and *Probe Request* frames can use the Broadcast SSID, meaning the wireless LAN's SSID is regularly exposed.

Normal Operation

The normal operation of a wireless LAN is for all the access points to transmit Beacons at approximately 10 times per second with the wireless LAN's SSID included, along with the time, capabilities, supported rates, and PHY parameter sets. Stations configured for that particular SSID would then measure the signal strength of each access point and select the best access point for association. This is called passive scanning. The station sends an *Association Request* with the SSID to start its connection with the access point. If the station roams from one access point to another, it may use a *Reassociation Request* with the SSID, but most stations send an *Association Request* even when roaming. Beacons permit a station to easily find the strongest signal for the wireless LAN and minimize bandwidth consumption for management. This behavior pattern allows for efficient operation of the wireless LAN, particularly in the presence of other wireless LANs - at the cost of announcing the network name (SSID).

Some access points provide a software switch to exclude the SSID from the Beacon. Beacons are still sent, providing the timing, channel, data rates, and other capabilities. This is done to *hide* the wireless LAN's identity, its SSID. When this is done, the station cannot directly discover the wireless LAN and MUST be configured with the SSID. In actuality, the access point is using the Broadcast SSID in the Beacon, and this forces the stations to use active scanning to find their wireless LAN (since the station does not passively detect any Beacons with its SSID). For a station to join a wireless LAN, it sends Probe Request frames on all channels with its SSID and listens for Probe Response frames, also with SSIDs. The station uses Probe Responses, as it would Beacons, to select the strongest signal among available wireless LANs. Normal Association Requests are then used to join the wireless LAN.

Finding the SSID

From this, it would appear that wireless LANs can be effectively hidden because Probes, Associations, and Reassociations, which carry the SSID, should be infrequent and missed by a war driver. However, there are two situations that actually make SSIDs appear more frequently in a wireless LAN. For a station to roam, it needs to discover an access point with a strong, quality signal. Roaming happens both with mobile stations and when stations are receiving weak signals from multiple access points. A station can be forced to roam when the environment around it changes, for example when additional stations start up, or interference starts (RF jamming, signal blockage, or environmental interference like a microwave oven). A station preparing to roam in a wireless LAN whose Beacons do not carry the SSID, but rather the Broadcast SSID, has to actively scan for access points. The station sends out Probe Requests sequentially on all channels with its SSID and listens for Probe Responses. The station may do this channel scanning every 50 milliseconds as it attempts to discover a stronger signal. In some configurations, stations have been observed to *bounce* between access points, spending only minutes on one access point and then switching to another based on signal strength. Thus, a wireless LAN that has stations with weak signals from the access points will readily expose the SSID in all the Probe Responses and Association frames.

The excessive Probe Requests and Responses in this configuration have the potential to negatively impact wireless LAN performance - particularly when there are many stations roaming. And again, roaming does NOT require the station to physically move. A station with a weak signal (including one whose reception is weakened due to local interference) or located between two access points may continually attempt to roam.

The 802.11 Standard & Active Scanning

When a station sends a Probe Request, ALL access points that receive it MUST send a Probe Response with the SSID even if the Probe Request contains the Broadcast SSID. Some access points have a switch to disallow this standard behavior. That is, they will only send a Probe Response if the Probe Request had a matching SSID. This switch is typically a different switch from the Beacons SSID disable switch, and is rarely set even if the Beacon is set to hide the SSID. Attackers can readily use this to discover the SSID of a *hidden* access point that will respond in the standard way.

Additionally, there is a relatively simple method for an attacker to learn the SSID of a *hidden*, but active, wireless LAN. The attacker sends a spoofed *Disassociate* message for an active station to the station's access point (there are simple software tools for this). This will force the station to rejoin the wireless LAN. The station will first cycle through Probe Requests and then associate. This will occur within a second after the Disassociation attack. This method to force a hidden wireless LAN to reveal its SSID could take less than a second when launched against a station actively transmitting data.

Finally, Ad Hoc wireless LANs work the same as Infrastructure WLANs, with the following caveat. All stations can send Beacons and/or Probes. So the same mechanisms exist to find the SSID of Ad Hoc wireless LANs as in Infrastructure WLANs. As with Infrastructure wireless LANs, excessive Probe Requests and Responses will negatively impact performance. Since Broadcast messages are sent out as unicast messages to all stations in an Ad Hoc wireless LAN (as compared to being sent twice in Infrastructure wireless LANs), Ad Hoc wireless LANs almost always suffer from poor performance.

Auditor Uses

Auditors can use NetStumbler's output to check for rogue access points in a given coverage area. NetStumbler also shows if any of the access points have security turned off when the access point should have security turned on. When scanning for rogue devices using NetStumbler, one must be careful, again, not to be fooled when one finds no rogue access points in the 2.4 GHz ISM frequency band. A rogue access point could be in the 900 MHz ISM or 5 GHz ISM or UNII frequency bands, neither of which is covered by NetStumbler.

Hacker Uses

Hackers will use NetStumbler's output to find access points that do not have any security implemented on them and those access points that are still configured with the manufacturer's default configurations. These access points will be likely targets for attacks if the hacker's intent is illegal activity. An access point with basic security such as WEP installed is much less appealing to a hacker, because the time investment to break into this type of network is much greater than an open network without security. Open networks are everywhere, and hackers will naturally be attracted to easier targets.

NetStumbler.com

Netstumbler.com is a large source of information about the use of NetStumbler and war driving. Many forums exist detailing the very inexpensive hardware setups that can be used to locate wireless networks. When used for war driving, NetStumbler can output the results of the access points that are found. These results can then be uploaded to a national database of open access points. Auditors that have not used security in their wireless LAN may find themselves listed in the national map of open wireless LANs. NetStumbler.com is not the only website of this nature.

MiniStumbler

MiniStumbler is the first cousin of NetStumbler, and runs on the PocketPC platform. This program is more commonly used when war walking, because it does not require the user to walk around with a heavy laptop to gather information. Both NetStumbler and MiniStumbler offer the same functionality.

Kismet

Written by Mike Kershaw, Kismet is an 802.11 wireless packet analyzer. Kismet runs on the Linux operating system and works with most wireless cards that are supported under Linux. Kismet offers similar functionally to NetStumbler with a few features that are not available in NetStumbler. Some features available in Kismet are:

- Multiple packet sources
- Channel hopping
- IP block detection
- Cisco product detection via CDP
- Ethereal/tcpdump compatible file logging
- Airsnort-compatible "interesting" (cryptographically weak) logging
- Hidden SSID decloaking
- Grouping and custom naming of SSIDs
- Multiple clients viewing a single capture stream
- Graphical mapping of data (gpsmap)
- Cross-platform support (handheld Linux and BSD)
- Manufacturer identification
- Detection of default access point configurations
- Detection of Netstumbler clients
- Runtime decoding of WEP packets
- Multiplexing of multiple capture sources

More information about Kismet can be found at www.kismetwireless.net. There are far more hacking tools on the market for Linux than for Windows. Many of today's talented hackers are also proficient with Linux.

dstumbler

Written by David Hulton, dstumbler runs on BSD (Free, Net, Open) using the *wi* driver. *dstumbler* includes many of the same features as NetStumbler including GPS support.

Proactive Measures

The following are some of the options available for reducing the effectiveness of discovery tools. Some of these options, such as the intermediate and advanced security solutions, will be discussed in much greater detail in later chapters.

Fake Access Points

Software such as Black Alchemy's FakeAP for Linux generates thousands of counterfeit beacons. This functionality allows regular wireless LANs to hide in plain sight among "Fake APs". As part of a honeypot or as an instrument of your site security plan, FakeAP confuses war drivers, NetStumblers, script kiddies, and other undesirables. This software can be run on a regular PC or a laptop as long as a wireless card is in use. When the software is executed, it sends out information that fools programs such as NetStumbler and Kismet into believing there are dozens or hundreds of access points on the network. Because a hacker would not be able to easily determine which one is the real access point, in theory, the would-be intruder would most likely not invest any time into figuring out which information belonged to the real access point.

Advanced Security Solutions

The basic 802.11b security options, including MAC filters, WEP, and closed system for hiding SSIDs, are not useful in thwarting a determined hacker's efforts in gaining access to a wireless network. Advanced solutions such as 802.1x/EAP or VPNs are much more effective, and will be discussed in detail in the Solutions section of this book.

Awareness

Employees and security personnel should be educated to recognize potential hackers in the vicinity of the premises. When employees see someone with a computer and an antenna walking around the facility, it should be cause to immediately contact security.

Password Capture & Decrypt

Most of today's computer security is based on passwords. Weak passwords are one of the most serious security threats in networking, for obvious reasons. Intruders easily guess commonly used and known passwords, such as "password", "admin", etc. Short words or strings of characters are often at risk from a brute force password attack program, and passwords made from words found in the dictionary can easily be circumvented using dictionary attacks.

All of this information is common knowledge to security administrators, but what is not commonly considered is that passwords flow from client to server across unsecured networks all the time. In the past, there was a common misconception that wired networks were secure, but wireless LANs have opened the eyes of many administrators and attackers that networking systems using passwords passed in clear text across any medium are unsecured. For this reason, password encryption has become very popular along with security mechanisms, such as Kerberos, that implement such encryption. Two auditing tools often used by administrators and hackers alike to view clear text passwords are *WinSniffer* and *ettercap*.

WinSniffer

WinSniffer is a password capture utility capable of capturing FTP, HTTP, ICQ, Telnet, SMTP, POP3, and NNTP, and IMAP usernames and passwords in a shared medium networking environment such as wireless APs or wired hubs. WinSniffer is installed on a Windows-based computer, usually a laptop being used to audit wireless networks. In a switched network, WinSniffer can only capture passwords that originate from either the client that sent the password or the server that sent the client the information directly. WinSniffer can be used to capture your own passwords (when saved in applications) when you forget them. Sample output from WinSniffer is shown in Figure 1.3.

FIGURE 1.3   Sample password output from WinSniffer

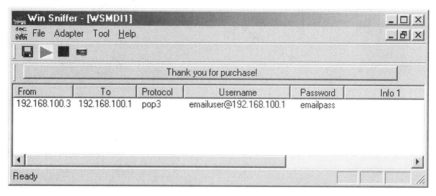

Consider Figure 1.4 in which the user is checking email over an unencrypted wireless LAN segment. An attacker is scanning the wireless segment using a password sniffer and picks up the user's email login information and the domain from which the user is checking the email. The attacker now has access to the user's email account and can read all of the user's email.

FIGURE 1.4   Obtaining passwords from unsuspecting users

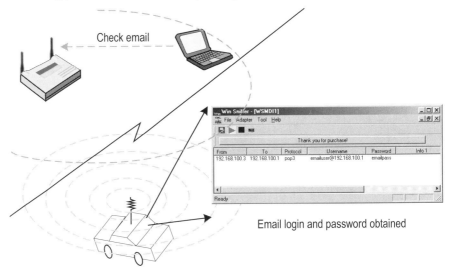

Public access wireless networks (Hotspots) such as those found in airports or in metropolitan areas are some of the most vulnerable areas for user attacks. Users that are not familiar with how easy it is to obtain their login information through a peer-to-peer attack unknowingly check their email or access their corporate network and end up giving access to their accounts to a hacker. Once the hacker obtains a valid login to a corporate account, they are now well equipped to try to obtain further access into the network to locate more sensitive information.

ettercap

Written by Alberto Ornaghi and Marco Valleri, ettercap is one of the most powerful password capture and auditing tools available today. ettercap supports almost every operating system platform, and can be found at http://ettercap.sourceforge.net. ettercap is capable of gathering data even in a switched environment, which far exceeds the abilities of most other audit tools. ettercap uses *ncurses* as a menu style user interface, making it more user friendly for beginners. Some of the features available in ettercap are:

Character injection into an established connection: A user can inject characters to a server (emulating commands) or to a client (emulating replies) while maintaining a live connection.

SSH1 support: A user can analyze usernames and passwords, and even the data of the SSH1 connection. ettercap is the first software capable of analyzing an SSH connection in full-duplex mode.

HTTPS support: A user can sniff HTTP-SSL data even if the connection is made through a Proxy.

Remote traffic through a GRE tunnel: A user can analyze remote traffic through a GRE tunnel from a remote router

PPTP broker: A user can perform man-in-the-middle attacks against PPTP tunnels

Plug-ins support: A user can create your own plug-in using the ettercap's API. Many plug-ins are included in the base package.

Password collector for: TELNET, FTP, POP, RLOGIN, SSH1, ICQ, SMB, MySQL, HTTP, NNTP, X11, NAPSTER, IRC, RIP, BGP, SOCKS-5, IMAP4, VNC, LDAP, NFS, SNMP, HALF LIFE, QUAKE 3, MSN, & YMSG

Packet filtering/dropping: A user can configure a filter that searches for a particular string (even hex) in the TCP or UDP payload and replace it with a new string or drop the entire packet.

OS fingerprinting: A user can fingerprint the operating system of the victim host and its network adapter

Kill a connection: From the connections list, A user can kill all the connections he or she chooses

Passive scanning of the LAN: A user can retrieve information about any of the following: hosts in the LAN, open ports, services version, host type (gateway, router, or simple host) and estimated distance (in hops).

Check for other poisoners: ettercap has the ability to actively or passively find other poisoners on the LAN

Bind sniffed data to a local port: A user can connect to a port on a client and decode protocols or inject data

L0phtCrack

In many cases, operating systems implement password authentication and encryption at the application layer. Such is the case with Microsoft Windows file sharing and NetLogon processes. The challenge/response mechanism used by Microsoft over the years (and over several operating system and service pack upgrades) has changed from LM (weak), to NTLM (medium), to NTLMv2 (strong). Before NTLMv2, tools such as L0phtcrack could easily crack these hashes. This evidence makes a strong case for keeping service packs on Windows operating systems up to date. It is also important to properly configure your Windows operating system to use NTLMv2 and not to use the weaker versions. This process must be accomplished manually, and instructions can be found at www.technet.com.

L0phtCrack, also known by the newer name LC4 (short for L0phtCrack version 4), is a password auditing and recovery tool created by L0pht Heavy Industries, now owned by @stake. L0phtCrack is used to audit passwords on Windows operating systems. There are many different ways that L0phtCrack can capture password hashes, but two in particular that auditors frequently attempt are file share authentication and network logons. L0phtCrack can capture these challenge/response conversations and derive the password. The stronger the challenge/response mechanism used, the more difficult it is for L0phtCrack to crack them. The output of a password recovery session is shown in Figure 1.5.

FIGURE 1.5   Sample password auditing output from L0phtCrack

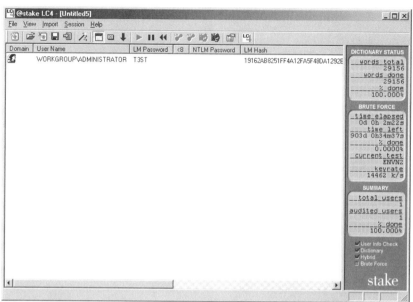

Once the intruder has captured the targeted password hashes (as many as deemed appropriate in a given audit), the hashes are imported into LC4's engine, and a dictionary attack automatically ensues. If the dictionary attack is unsuccessful, a brute force attack automatically begins thereafter. The processor power of the computer doing the audit will determine how fast the hash can be broken. L0phtCrack has many modes for capturing password hashes and dumping password repositories. One mode allows for 'sniffing' in a shared medium (such as wireless), while another goes directly after the Windows Security Access Manager (SAM).

Windows 2000 service pack 3 introduced a new feature called "SysKey", which is short for System Key. This feature, implemented by running the syskey.exe executable file, encrypts the SAM such that L0phtCrack cannot extract passwords from it as was possible before it was encrypted. L0phtCrack has the capability of letting the auditor know that he or she is auditing a SAM that has been encrypted so the auditor will not waste waste much time attempting to extract that password.

L0phtCrack is often one of the first tools a hacker will use in an attempt to gain access to a network. Once administrative level account information is obtained, many of the other tools discussed in this section become quite useful.

LRC

Proxim Orinoco PC Cards store an encrypted hash of the WEP key in the Windows registry. The Lucent Registry Crack (LRC) is a simple command line utility written to decrypt these encrypted values. The problem is getting these values from another computer – one that has the WEP key that the hacker wants to obtain installed. This task is accomplished through a remote registry connection. The attacker will make a remote registry connection to the target computer using the tools in Window's Registry Editor on his own computer. Once the hacker is connected, the hacker must simply know where the key is located in the registry in order to copy and paste it into a text document on his or her computer. These encrypted strings are stored per profile, as shown in Figure 1.6.

FIGURE 1.6   Orinoco WEP key in encrypted form stored in the Windows Registry

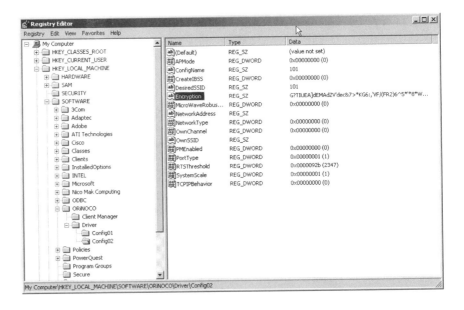

LRC can then be run against this encrypted string to produce the WEP key. The decryption process takes about 1-2 seconds. Once the attacker has the WEP key, it is a simple matter of plugging it into his or her computer to gain access to the network. For this reason, wireless end users should implement peer attack safeguards such as personal firewall software or IPSec policies. The LRC operation process is shown below in Figure 1.7.

FIGURE 1.7   LRC cracking the encryption used for safeguarding WEP keys

Share Enumerators

File sharing in general is seen as a major benefit of networking. The risk in file sharing arises when a PC, workstation, or server is improperly configured and data is exposed. Share enumerators are software programs that can scan a Windows subnet for open file shares. Open file shares are directories on a windows network that are available to users for browsing. A Windows file share will provide access to a particular directory on a computer, allowing anyone with access to the share to obtain data from it. Once shares are located on the network, they can be cracked (the password, if one is in place, can be circumvented) or their properties can be changed (in the Windows registry). A common attack is to access another computer's Windows registry (peer-to-peer attack through the access point) and redefine the properties of a file share from something like, "c:\misc\myshare" to just "c:\". After a reboot, the file share still looks to the user like the original, but now when a hacker browses the share, the file share shows the entire contents of the C drive. Locating shares across a large subnet takes time unless you have a utility that can do it very quickly.

Legion 2.1

Legion 2.1 is a popular freeware program that quickly scans a subnet and lists all open file shares. Because of the speed that Legion provides, an auditor can quickly determine what file shares are available for access on a network. Sample output from this software is shown in Figure 1.8.

FIGURE 1.8 Sample share enumeration output from Legion

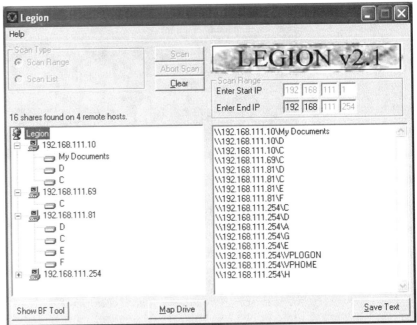

Proactive Measures

If network shares are found on the wireless segment, they should be disabled or secured. Peer-to-peer file sharing should be limited or disabled according to corporate policy. If a node on the wireless segment has open file shares, those shares are then directly exposed to any intruder that has gained access to the wireless network.

Network Management & Control

There are inexpensive tools available that allow for remote access and management of Windows servers and workstations. This software can be executed on an inexpensive laptop computer using wireless network connectivity with almost no performance issues. Two such applications are Hyena (www.systemtools.com) and LANBrowser (www.firestormsoftware.com). While there are many other such tools, these two are quite popular with network auditors. Both allow most every function on Windows based computers to be remotely managed. Hyena goes a step further allowing integration of VNC, a popular remote control program. Hyena can push the VNC executable file to another computer and remotely execute VNC to have complete remote control over that computer. It is not difficult to see how this could be a dangerous combination in the hands of a malicious intruder in an open wireless environment. Each of these management utilities can shut down services on remote computers, including:

- email servers
- firewalls
- virus protection
- ftp servers
- web servers
- intrusion detection systems

To use these tools, an auditor would need to have administrative access to control the Windows network. An auditor could obtain administrative access through the password recovery procedures as discussed in the L0phtCrack section above or through social engineering. Remember that close to 80% of all network security breaches come from inside the organization, by authorized users.

FIGURE 1.9 Sample Hyena output

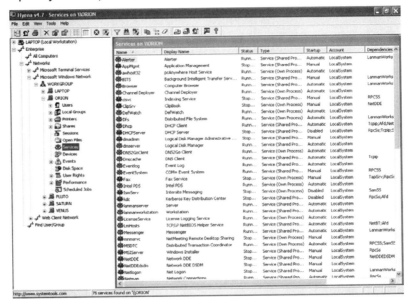

FIGURE 1.10 Sample LANBrowser output

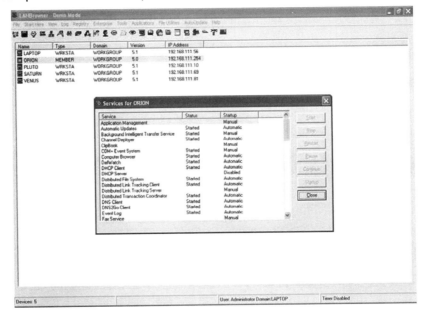

Considerations

If an attacker is able to gain administrative privileges on the network, the worst-case scenario should always be assumed. Using tools such as Hyena and LANBrowser (shown above in Figures 1.9 and 1.19), the attacker could quickly and easily circumvent security measures, disable network services, and remotely install malware – all from the parking lot or the building next door.

Alert protection should also be added to the network where appropriate. Some programs (firewalls and intrusion detection systems for example) may include features that notify an administrator any time they are shut down. Intruders would likely shut down the firewall or intrusion detection system before proceeding to any more valuable targets.

Wireless Protocol Analyzers

Wireless protocol analyzers, can capture, decode, and filter wireless packets in real-time (depending on the product in use). Many products in this market support multiple frequency bands such as those used in 802.11b and 802.11a networks. Protocol analyzers operate in RF Monitor mode, capturing the packets transmitted across the medium, as shown in Figure 1.11. Protocol analyzers do not attempt to connect or communicate with access points or other wireless peers in any manner while in this mode.

FIGURE 1.11   Sample output from Wildpackets AiroPeek

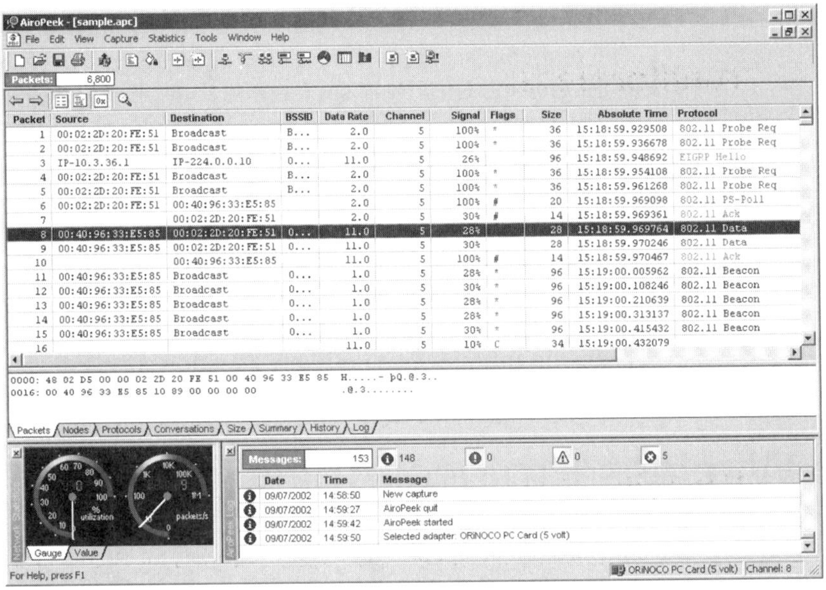

Vendors

There are many vendors in the protocol analyzer market space, such as:

- Wildpackets Airopeek
- AirMagnet
- Fluke WaveRunner Wireless Tester
- Ethereal
- Network Associates Sniffer Pro Wireless
- Network Instruments Observer
- Ephiphan CEniffer
- Tamosoft Commview

Not all wireless packet analysis tools have the same functionality. For example, some do not offer real-time packet decodes, but instead make the user capture packets and export them to a reader utility. Some analyzers decode layers 2-7 protocols, while others decode only layer 2 frame headers. Some run on only x86 Windows platforms while other run on Windows, Windows CE, Linux, and custom platforms. There are times when a combination of these tools is helpful to the network administrator because of platform support or analysis features.

Auditor Uses

A network administrator will use a wireless packet analyzer to spot security risks such as:

- unencrypted wireless traffic
- rogue wireless hardware or software
- oversized RF cells
- misconfigured security features (such as closed system)
- exposed Network Layer information (such as IP addresses)

Proactive Measures

Layer 2 or 3 encryption prevents hackers from gathering sensitive network traffic. Solutions to prevent an intruder from gathering sensitive data might include:

- Static or Dynamic WEP
- IPSec or GRE
- SSH2

Implementation of these solutions will be covered in the Solutions unit.

Manufacturer Defaults

The most common mistake among administrators implementing new wireless setups is NOT changing any of the defaults included by the manufacturer. When changing manufacturer default configurations, the following items should be addressed.

- IP address & subnet range
- Device login information
- WEP keys
- SNMP strings
- SSID

Infrastructure devices are a very common point of attack. Many enterprise devices support SNMP, Telnet, Serial Console Ports, HTTP, HTTPS, and others. Devices with these types of ports usually come with no login requirement configured or with the manufacturer's default settings, which are published in the user's manual. When left in this default configuration, hackers can access and manage them just as easily as the authorized administrator can.

A common attack is to find a single access point that is unsecured and then secure its settings, such as login password, WEP keys, SNMP strings, etc. After securing the device with passwords that only the attacker knows, the hacker uses a management utility that is built into many enterprise units. This utility allows one access point to push its configuration to all other access points using the same SSID. This functionality effectively locks legitimate users and the network administrator out of the access points and gives over control of the entire wireless network to the attacker.

This same attack also works well with wired devices such as PoE switches. Imagine if the attacker were able to log into your PoE switch via Telnet and just as he was pushing firmware from one access point to all others, the hacker terminated the power to all access points. The result of such an act might very well necessitate sending all of the access points back to the manufacturer for repair.

Preventing such attacks is as simple as reconfiguring the defaults during the staging process. There are websites on the Internet that list all manufacturers' default settings from user manuals and store them in one text file for hackers. Such sites save hackers time in accumulating this information. As a wireless security professional, one must assume that every hacker is already well equipped to attack any organization's wireless network.

Antennas & Wireless LAN Equipment

The tools used for auditing a wireless network include antennas, wireless cards, a portable computer, and specialized software. All of these "tools" are legal, available, and affordable. In most cases, the combined cost for a wireless radio card, antenna, and a pigtail cable can be as little as $125. Most auditing software is freely available on the Internet through open source, freeware, or through copyright violation. To the administrator, this bit of information means that anyone who has the desire can afford to eavesdrop on an organization's wireless network.

Antennas

Antennas that are magnetically-mounted to the top of a car, antennas made from pineapple juice cans or Pringles chips cans, Orinoco or Cisco pigtail cables, and all sorts of connector contraptions are used by war drivers to locate wireless LANs. Administrators should use both omni and strong yagi or patch antennas when performing their security audits. Figure 1.12 below illustrates a war driver using a roof-mounted omni antenna.

FIGURE 1.12   Using an omni antenna to locate WLANs

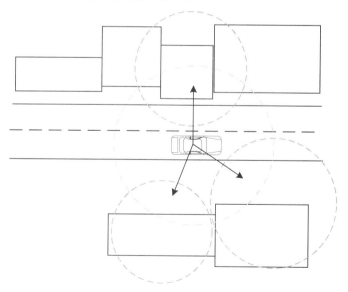

On both sides of the street there are offices and buildings, three of which have installed access points on their networks. The war driver will be able to determine the network names, WEP usage, and the GPS coordinates of the units located. Once a wireless network is found, a directional antenna such as a patch or Yagi can be used to focus the beam and listen at greater distances without the worry of trespassing on a corporation's property. A directional antenna also hears much fainter signals than an omni antenna and allows the intruder to establish a better quality link at greater distances. The use of a directional antenna is shown in Figure 1.13.

FIGURE 1.13 A directional antenna to obtain a stronger signal and avoid trespassing

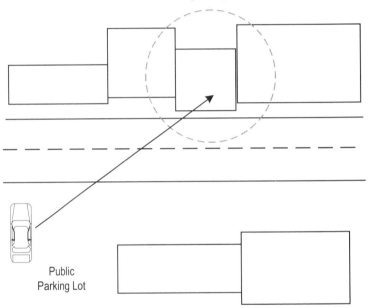

In the figure above, the war driver has returned to where he or she originally found an access point with an omni antenna. Instead of trespassing on the company's property or parking their vehicle in a conspicuous area, the war driver has parked in a public parking lot down the street from the network that he or she is attempting to hack. The directional antenna will allow a quality connection from this location provided the access point is putting out enough power to reach this location.

Wireless Cards

The three most popular PC cards used by auditors and hackers are:

- Lucent Gold PC Card
- Cisco 350 PC Card
- Symbol LA-4121 PC Card

These cards are the cards of choice for many auditors and war drivers because:

- They are inexpensive
- They are popular so they can be easily obtained on eBay
- They allow an external antenna (depending on the model) to be connected to the device
- Pigtail cables, connectors, and homemade external antennas are inexpensive and readily available
- Most auditing software supports these card's radio chipsets
- Each card comes with site surveying utilities that make them useful for more than just intrusion audits

What one card doesn't support, the other does, and together, they support most of the latest security features on the market today. The reason for the Lucent Gold instead of Silver is for 128-bit WEP support. Suppose that you, as an auditor, wanted to try to guess your client's WEP key. If they are using 128-bit, as most organization's will do given the choice of 40 or 128, then you will need to be able to enter a 128-bit WEP key into your wireless client utility software.

OS Fingerprinting & Port Scanning

Operating System fingerprinting and port scanning are two of today's most common beginnings for full-blown intrusions. Hackers must start out by finding what operating systems and open ports are on the network. After this information is gathered, weaknesses in the network can be exploited. Programs such as LANGuard Network Security Scanner (www.gfi.com) can quickly and thoroughly scan and fingerprint an entire network. LANGuard is customizable, and when an auditor purchases the full version, the reporting feature is added.

These programs begin fingerprinting a network by scanning an entire network within an IP range or even a single host, and can generate reports on:

- service packs installed on machines
- missing security patches
- network shares
- open ports
- services in use
- users and groups
- strength of passwords
- known vulnerabilities and where to find the exploit

A sample output from a network scan taken by LANGuard is shown in Figure 1.14. The report produces a significant amount of detailed data about a computer, and this report was only run against one computer.

FIGURE 1.14   Sample output obtained from LANGuard Network Security Scanner

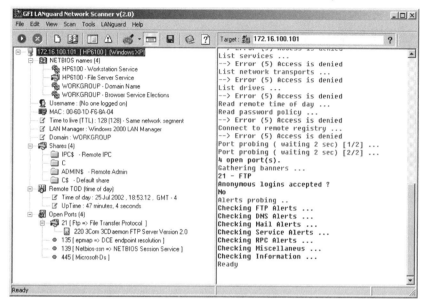

Considerations

If the wired network's resources (such as servers) are adequately protected from intruders using strong authentication, there is still a good chance that peer attacks are a possibility. For example, suppose that an attacker uses an RF jamming device, access point software, and DHCP server software on his laptop. When the intruder jams the authorized users, the client devices will roam to his laptop (which is also an access point), associate, and then automatically request an IP address. Remember, this roaming functionality is exactly what a wireless client device is designed to do. Once the hijacked wireless clients have an IP address provided by the laptop's DHCP server, the hacker could then use LANGuard against the client computers in a peer-to-peer attack to locate exploitable security weaknesses.

Application Layer Analyzers

Application layer analyzers are programs that capture and then reassemble data packets into their original application format for use by the auditor. For example, consider two users having an instant messaging conversation over a wireless LAN. An application analyzer can capture the packets transmitted in both directions and reassemble them into the actual instant message session of each user. The same is true for other applications such as:

- Instant messenger conversations
- Email, *including* attachments
- Login information (usernames & passwords)
- HTML pages and websites visited

Figure 1.15 below displays output from Iris, an application analyzer

FIGURE 1.15   Sample output from Iris, an application analyzer

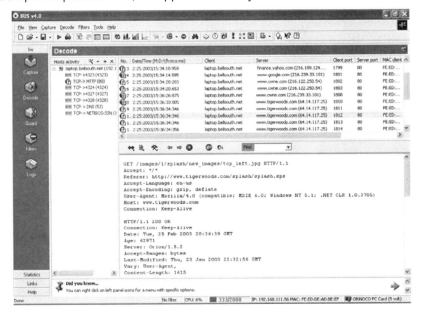

There are several manufacturers of application layer analyzers on the market, but again, these utilities are not all created equally. Some allow for real-time decoding while others require capture/save/import/decode as separate steps.

Auditors would typically use the information gathered by an application layer analyzer to present to a corporate executive as proof of the need of a wireless LAN security solution. For example, suppose that a government employee uses an intranet website to access sensitive government information over an unsecured wireless link. The auditor could capture both the IP address of the intranet website plus the login information for that user. All traffic sent by the server back to the user could likewise be captured and stored for later use in a report.

Networking Utilities

Most intrusion attempts start with a scan of the network. In order to find out what resources are on the network, one must find out what computers are on the network. To gather this information, the client needs to obtain a valid IP address either through DHCP or by statically assigning one. The next step is to use a network utility software package such as WS_Ping ProPack (www.ipswitch.com) or NetScanTools Professional (www.netscantools.com) that can perform functions such as ping sweeps (pinging every IP address in a subnet looking for active nodes), port scans for defined ports (FTP, POP3, SMTP, NETBIOS), and computer name resolution (Accounting, Human_Resources, Sales, Marketing). Once these tasks are performed, more detailed probes can be accomplished with tools such as LANGuard.

Once access point scans are accomplished using Netstumbler and ping sweeps are accomplished with networking utilities, the IP addresses of access points can be determined by comparing the laptop's ARP cache against NetStumbler's results. The ARP cache on the laptop is viewed by opening a command prompt window and typing "arp –a". This command will give you the IP addresses and MAC addresses of each node on the network. Figure 1.16 below depicts the output from a ping sweep using WS_Ping Propack.

FIGURE 1.16 Sample output of a ping sweep using WS_Ping ProPack

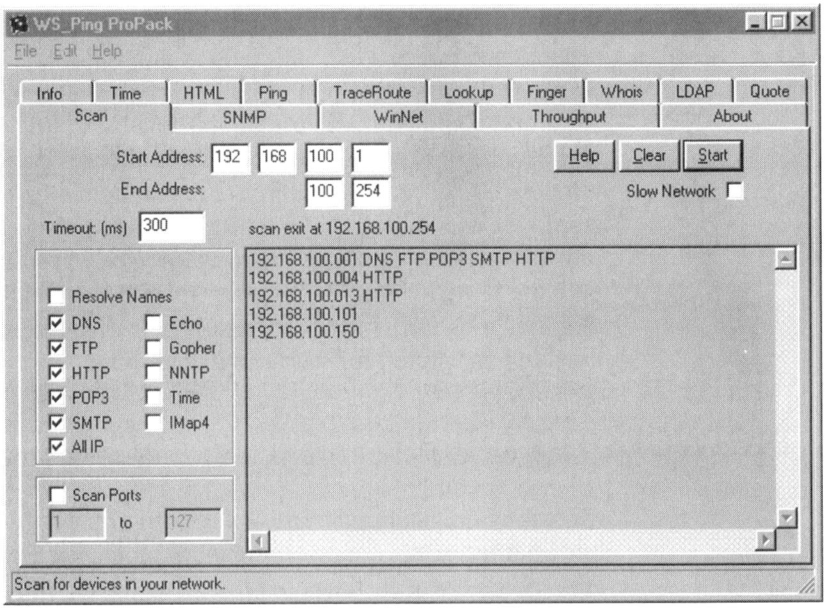

Proactive Measures

There are two practical measures against this type of attack. First, intruders should not be allowed to associate to an access point without first having been authenticated, and second, secure DHCP can be used. Secure DHCP is discussed in the Solutions unit. If layer 3 VPNs are chosen as a wireless security solution, the type of VPN technology being used will determine the exposure level to networking utilities such as the ones mentioned above. For example, PPTP builds a tunnel between two end points and uses IP addresses both for the establishment of the tunnel and inside the tunnel itself. The IP addresses that are used to initiate the VPN tunnel are exposed to port scans.

Network Discovery Tools

Many tools used for enterprise management also include features for network discovery. For example, management software package such as What's Up Gold (www.ipswitch.com), SNMPc (www.castlerock.com), and Solarwinds (www.solarwinds.net), have network node discovery tools that use SNMP to map their way through an enterprise. Once an attacker gains access to the network through the wireless LAN and steals some SNMP strings, the attacker can begin forming a map of the entire extended network using tools such as these.

Suppose that the intruder is breaking into a network at a branch office. The branch office is often connected to the central office through leased WAN lines. The management software will discover WAN subnets and computers on the other side of the WAN link as well as local nodes. This information could be valuable in breaking through security measures at the central office. For this reason, enterprises with distributed wireless LAN deployments should make sure that the wireless segment is secure at each and every location.

RF Jamming Tools

RF jamming tools allow auditors and intruders to do a number of things. The auditor may use an RF jamming device to force users to roam (for security function tests and application analysis) and to introduce interference to examine the stability of certain RF technologies such as FHSS in a noisy environment. Attackers may use RF jamming devices for DoS and hijacking attacks.

RF jamming devices are not cheap, but they are available to anyone who would spend a moderate amount of money on such a device. You won't find anyone selling an RF Jamming device by name because that might cause that company or person legal hardships if someone tried to defer the blame. Instead, wireless LAN test devices, such as YDI.com's PSG-1, that are used for testing antennas, cables, and connectors can easily become jamming devices when connected to an appropriate antenna. Devices such as this provide high-power, narrowband test signals that, when attached to an antenna with high gain, can jam a wireless LAN on a particular channel at a very long distance. A high-powered narrowband RF signal can completely disable a wireless LAN operating on the same channel as the narrowband transmission.

A spectrum analyzer shows narrowband and spread spectrum RF quite differently. Looking at Figure 1.17 below, you can see the high-powered narrowband RF signal on the left (around the channel 1 region), and the spread spectrum signal on the right (around the channel 11 region).

FIGURE 1.17 Spectrum Analyzer view of narrowband and spread spectrum RF

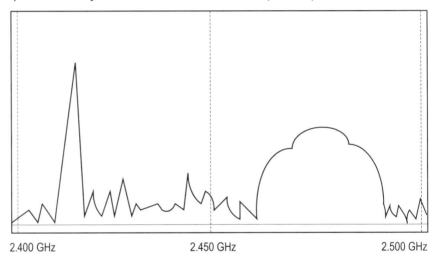

2.400 GHz   2.450 GHz   2.500 GHz

Hijacking Tools

Hijacked wireless LAN users become targets for enumeration, penetration, and snooping. A hacker can use a laptop running access point software to hijack unsuspecting wireless LAN clients. A hacker can jam the signal of a valid access point on the network, forcing the client device(s) to associate with the access point software running on the hacker's laptop. Running a DHCP server on the same laptop provides the client with a network to join to, allowing a hacker to attack the user's PC. The following are some of the programs available that provide software based access point functionality.

- ZoomAir AP (Windows)
- Cqure AP (Linux)
- Orinoco Client Utility (Base Station mode)

Proactive Measures

There are several measures that can be taken to prevent users from being hijacked by a rogue software access point. These include:

- Client side security (802.1x/EAP, VPN)
- User training
- Mutual authentication

WEP Decryption Tools

A great deal of media hype has been made about the vulnerabilities of WEP and the security risks its use poses. WEP decrypters are used to recover WEP encryption keys. These decrypters recover WEP keys by passively monitoring the data transmissions on a wireless LAN segment. After enough data has been gathered, these tools can compute the key used to encrypt the data. A significant amount of data – approximately 5-10 million packets – is required by WEP decrypters to determine the key in use. The second requirement of these utilities is to collect enough packets with "weak" initialization vectors. On a wireless LAN under a heavy traffic load, it could take from many hours to many days to gather enough packets that meet the criteria of "weak." On a SOHO or home wireless LAN it would take considerably longer, which is why SOHO networks would be much less likely targets.

Popular WEP crackers include:

- AirSnort
- WEPcrack

Both applications run in UNIX based environments such as Unix, BSD, or Linux.

Proactive Measures

Because it is still possible, although not very reasonable for most hackers, to crack WEP, the following security mechanisms can and should be enhanced to prevent such an occurrence:

- Physical security
- Use security solutions stronger than static WEP keys

Solutions beyond static WEP are discussed in detail in the Solutions unit.

Operating System Exploit Tools

There are so many operating system exploits for even a single operating system that tracking them all is a full time activity for many programmers at each operating system manufacturer. Security scanner tools, such as LANGuard, can point out operating system exploit opportunities for a hacker. One exploit in particular for Windows that stands out in a wireless environment is the default setting for the Windows registry to accept remote connections. Using the Windows registry editor on his or her local computer, an intruder can attach to another local computer's registry. An intruder with remote registry access can change application parameters, change file share properties, copy WEP key strings, and can even crash the computer by deleting critical data. Such attacks can be done in peer-to-peer fashion on the wireless segment when wireless clients do not adequately protect their computers.

Not all wireless cards store the WEP key in the registry. Some cards store the WEP key only in the firmware of the card. On UNIX-based systems, the same types of attacks can occur by obtaining the WEP keys from /etc/pcmcia/wireless.opts.

Proactive Measures

Desktop management software, such as Novell's ZENworks, can be used to push operating system updates, such as security patches, to all desktops in a single sweep. Another option is one of the new features available in Windows 2000 and Windows XP that allows automatic updates to be installed on desktop computers directly from Microsoft. Automatic updates are generally less desirable because of complications and conflicts that are possible from installing untested updates, but it remains an option nonetheless.

Homeplug Devices

There is a new type of device that was only recently released into the marketplace: Homeplug. Homeplug devices are devices that use a building's electrical wiring for data transmission. With the invention of Homeplug devices, rogue devices can now be even more dangerous because they can now be mobile.

For example, consider a Hospital as a place that rarely has extreme physical security. If an intruder were to place a Homeplug Ethernet bridge under a table into an electrical outlet in an unoccupied room, then run a short Cat5 jumper cable between the Ethernet bridge and the nearest live RJ-45 jack, the data would be extended onto the Hospital's power lines. Next, consider that this technology often has enough power to extend the data to buildings next door where another identical bridge can be placed to receive data from the first bridge. However, an intruder might look suspicious having a cable running from his laptop to the power outlet on the wall. Instead of this not-so-discreet solution, the hacker uses a Homeplug access point to connect his laptop wirelessly back into the wired network through the Homeplug Ethernet bridge across the power lines in the building.

If the intruder is now able to carry his rogue access point with him wherever he goes, we now have a case of a two-piece, mobile rogue access point where one piece can talk to the other from down the city block. An intruder might even label the Homeplug Ethernet bridge something like, "Security System Power Line Voltage Monitor" and place it on a power strip under a desk for camouflage.

An administrator should keep in mind that any Cat5 jack next to a power outlet is fair game, so regular sweeps should be performed, and intrusion detection systems should be used when possible.

Summary

The very length of this chapter alone should inform the reader as to the extent of both the availability and the capability of wireless LAN "auditing" tools that are on the market today. Anyone familiar with computers and somewhat familiar with networking can start off with an interface as simple as that of NetStumbler and quickly work his or her way up to summarily dismantling enterprise wireless networks with tools that won't cost them more than a few hundred dollars on the high end.

The wireless security professional must be intimately familiar with as many of these tools as possible. If a security professional does not know and understand what intruders are using to penetrate a network, there is no way that the hacker can be stopped.

These tools are just as readily available to the IT pros on the inside of the network as they are to the malicious intruders on the outside of the network. The list of tools in this chapter is by no means complete, but does provide an excellent starting point for the wireless security professional to get to know the types of tools that will be used to attack his or her network.

Key Terms

Before taking the exam, you should be familiar with the following terms:

application layer analyzers

brute force attack

Lucent Registry Crack

peer-to-peer attack

port scanning

OS fingerprinting

RF jamming device

share enumerator

system key

Review Questions

1. What security hole is left open when scanning a wireless LAN for rogue Wi-Fi access points using a discovery tool such as NetStumbler?

    A. RF jamming devices can only be located by FHSS scanners

    B. The frequencies covered by WLAN discovery tools are hardware dependent and may not show all rogue access points

    C. Wireless LAN discovery tools cannot see access points using WEP

    D. Wireless LAN discovery tools cannot see access points when VPN technology is being used

2. Why is using WEP, MAC Filters, and a "closed" network a reasonable deterrent for keeping war drivers out of a wireless LAN?

    A. When used together, they are sufficient security for any wireless network

    B. When used together, they make the wireless LAN invisible and impossible to detect

    C. When used together, they effectively prevent a wireless LAN from being penetrated by even the most adept hackers

    D. When used together, they are often sufficient security to cause war drivers to seek out an easier network to attack

3. How can employee training be used by an organization to deter or prevent war driving intrusion attempts?

    A. Train employees to prevent the success of war drivers by turning on a fake AP application whenever they see a war driver

    B. Train employees to shut down the wireless segment whenever they recognize a war driving attack

    C. Train employees to turn on IPSec on the wireless segment whenever they think a war driving attack is likely to occur

    D. Train employees to recognize a war driving effort and report it to security

4. Which one of the following is the most serious security hole in a wireless network?

    A. Unlayered encryption

    B. Wireless NIDS

    C. Default settings

    D. Weak MAC filters

5. Why are public access wireless networks (Hot Spots) a prime venue for attracting hackers?

    A. Peer-to-peer wireless attacks can be done without the victim's awareness

    B. Strong encryption and authentication techniques implemented at those locations allow hackers to hone their skills

    C. Many users do not understand the need for or the operation of wireless security solutions

    D. Because there is no technical support available at these sites

6. Where in the OSI model do most operating systems, as with Microsoft Windows file sharing and NetLogon processes, implement password authentication/encryption?

    A. Layers 1-2

    B. Layer 3

    C. Layer 4

    D. Layer 7

7. File sharing in general is seen as a major benefit of networking. What is the risk in file sharing?

    A. Once a file share is configured, anyone who can see the file share can access the data within it if it isn't adequately protected

    B. All file shares are open to the Internet by default once a computer is connected to the Internet

    C. Many users do not use personal firewall software to protect against inbound service requests from attackers

    D. Most firewalls allow NetBIOS packets through in both directions by default

8. If a hacker were attempting to take advantage of a file share, where can the hacker change the properties (settings) of the file share?

    A. The properties of the file or directory being shared

    B. The Windows registry of the computer doing the file sharing

    C. The properties of the hard drive on the computer doing the file sharing

    D. The Windows registry of the domain controller through which the computer doing the file sharing is authorized to be part of the network

9. What would an auditor need to have to remotely manage and control a network from an organization's parking lot?

    A. Stable wireless connectivity to the network

    B. Administrative access to network resources

    C. A particular brand of wireless network interface card

    D. Network management software

10. Which of the following security risks would an auditor use a wireless packet analyzer to find?

A.   Unencrypted wireless traffic

B.   Rogue wireless hardware or software

C.   Oversized RF cells

D.   Misconfigured security features

E.   Exposed Network Layer information

Answers to Review Questions

1. B
2. D
3. D
4. C
5. A, C
6. D
7. C
8. B
9. A, B, D
10. A, B, C, D, E

Gathering Information

CWSP Exam Objectives Covered:

❖ Locate & identify wireless LANs within and around a facility:

- War Driving
- War Chalking
- War Flying

❖ Describe how intruders use profiling to select a target or gather information

- Searching publicly available resources
- Social engineering
- Wireless peer attacks to obtain corporate information

In This Chapter

Target Profiling

Tools, Traffic, & Social Engineering

In order to be an effective wireless auditor, one must learn to use more than just a few pieces of management and analysis software. There are many aspects of wireless LAN security, as we will discuss below, each of which brings you closer to the ultimate goal: complete wireless LAN security. Many more hours may be spent understanding the operations and intimacies of your customer than are spent trying to break into the network.

Conversely, the first step that a malicious intruder will take before attacking a network is to gather some information about the target network. Simply speaking, information gathering can be described as what a war driver does when he or she uses a discovery tool like NetStumbler to find open networks. This example is a simple one, but demonstrates the point that, by gathering certain pieces of information (SSID, open or closed network, WEP or no WEP, bandwidth), the intruder can make decisions about how to approach a target network. An intruder who attacks a wireless LAN that is protected by a thorough security solution, not armed with relevant and necessary information, is going to waste a considerable amount of time while obtaining nothing.

Target Profiling

Target profiling is a term that is demonstrated by the action of choosing a target for hacking, and then doing some research about that target. Because the Internet has made public information even more public and very easy to access, once a target has been identified, it can be a simple task to uncover a great amount of information – even personal information – on nearly any individual.

Target profiling is not for the casual seeker of free wireless Internet access, but rather, as its ominous name suggests, is done by professional hackers who usually aspire to attack targets because the target has, or has access to, something valuable to the hacker. Such high-level intrusion means that the *profiler* has a set of tools, plenty of time to carry out specific tasks, and a strong desire to acquire whatever it is that the target has.

Publicly Available Information

The Internet is a wonderful tool for finding most anything, including information about individuals, corporations, and even network security information. If it is public information, then it can likely be found on the Internet, and with just a little extra effort, a malicious individual can find:

- Who you are
- Names of family members
- Where you live and work
- If your work place has a wireless LAN
- What wireless security solutions are used by a particular company

Consider the fact that many individuals post their resumes on their homepages, which tells where they have worked, where they currently work, their home information, and much more. If the resume touts wireless LAN proficiency, it's a good bet that the person has one at home. If they have a wireless LAN at home, there is a good chance that this wireless LAN is not secured and information about their employer's wireless LAN may be accessible. It is even more probable that sensitive corporate data is exposed on the user's laptop or desktop computers. Thus, a small amount of personal information can expose much more critical data that could lead to a major security breach on a corporate network.

Public WLAN Maps

As mentioned in the previous section, NetStumbler is a very popular, although not the only, tool that can be used to sniff out wireless LANs just about anywhere. NetStumbler.com also offers a unique mapping of all the reported wireless LANs that NetStumblers (term used to define those that use NetStumbler) have found, as shown in Figure 2.1.

FIGURE 2.1   NetStumbler National Map

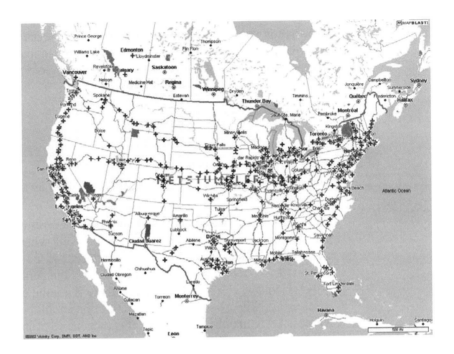

There are many other web sites that contain similar information. The point behind some of these sites is quick and easy location of *public* wireless Internet access. If a war driver can use a corporation's wireless LAN as *public* access, the wireless LAN may well be listed on one of these sites. As if the security on that particular network was not already bad enough, anyone can now make it public knowledge that there is free Internet access through that wireless LAN.

Again, the Internet contributes much needed information to malicious intruders, even down to whether or not a company has an open wireless LAN, where the network is located, and how to access the network. The Internet has made information gathering much, much easier both for good and bad purposes.

Search Engines

Have you ever been "Googled?" Search engines are the researcher's best friends. If something is out there, Google (www.google.com) has probably already found it and indexed it in a directory. It might be an interesting exercise to type your name, in quotes, into the Google search engine and see what the results are. Consider that any potential target of a hacker likely has or knows something of value to the hacker, so the hacker isn't going to target "John Smith" out of the phone book. More likely, the hacker will choose a high level target from a company that owns something that the hacker considers valuable. Doing a simple search on Google, or any other search engine for that matter, can turn up a plethora of information that can help a hacker figure out passwords, find out what type of security solutions are in place, etc.

Have you ever used a dog's name, birth date, anniversary date, or family member's name for any password? The truth is that most people do use these types of things for passwords because these things are easy to remember. Even when an employer has strong network password policies in place, there are still numerous combinations of birthdays and names that can be used to create unique passwords. Hackers think of these things, too. If a hacker found out a target's full name, spouse's name, dog's name, and all their birthdays, then it will just be a matter of time (a hacker has plenty of time) before the hacker figures out a password or two.

War Driving

Invented, or at least coined as a usable term, in late 2000, war driving has created many urban legends and some frightened wireless network administrators. For most of the people who actually use this technique for discovering open wireless LANs, it is simply a method of finding free high-speed Internet access and networks to practice their intrusion skills on.

In some cases, war driving is not a crime, but this depends on both where it is done and what is done. In some states, it is punishable by years in federal prison, depending on how the jury sees the damage, the intent, and how the legal statutes are written. There are federal and state laws against network intrusion and against intercepting communications between two or more other parties.

Using NetStumbler, Airopeek, a spectrum analyzer, or any number of other tools, anyone can drive through a city or neighborhood and easily locate wireless networks. Once a wireless LAN is located, tools like NetStumbler and Airopeek show the SSID, whether WEP is being used, what manufacturer makes the wireless equipment, IP subnet information, and what channel the network is using. Once a person has this information, they can either associate and use DHCP, or guess a static IP (from obtained subnet information) and join the network. Once on the network, free Internet access is the very least that the unauthorized person gains. Using simple auditing tools, a malicious attacker can scan a network for other devices or even use the VPN connection from the gateway into a corporate network!

Connecting and Trace Routing

War driving is handy for finding a wireless network, or many wireless networks. In a city or near an office building with potentially many wireless LANs, any number of wireless LANs in a building may be available. Using the trace route utility on any Windows computer can quickly give more information on a particular network connection. A trace route displays and resolves the name of all the hops between your computer and that of another host (a web server for instance). A casual war driver might not care which network is providing free Internet access, but a serious attacker might want to know the ISP to which the organization is connected. Perhaps the malicious attacker decides to spam (unsolicited bulk email) many people through the unsuspecting organization's Internet connection and include his own email address. Then, the attacker could report the company for email abuse, and have their Internet connection disconnected for violations of the ISP's policy on spam. Knowing which ISP the organization is using for Internet service would be an essential part of this type of attack. Trace routing gives the attacker a way to find out where he is logically located on the

Internet once connected to a wireless LAN that they cannot physically see.

War Chalking

If a network has been war chalked, that network has also been war driven or war walked. If a network has been war driven, that network has likely been hacked, or at least "borrowed" for free high-speed wireless Internet access.

War chalking is a relatively new term that originated from the practice of war driving, and is yet another way for hackers to help other hackers. There is a developing language of signs for those who practice war chalking, most of which can be found at www.warchalking.org. Sample war chalking symbols are shown in Figure 2.2. The practice involves marking a sidewalk or building near an accessible wireless network with chalk, notifying other war drivers that there is a wireless network nearby, and offering clues as to the structure of the network, such as:

- Is the network open or closed?
- Is WEP enabled on this network?
- What is the speed of the Internet connection?

FIGURE 2.2   War chalking symbol examples

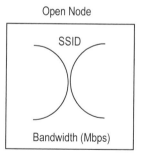
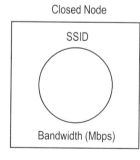
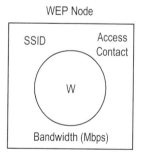

War chalking is a rudimentary form of public documentation, and its end result is faster, more efficient war driving. What one hacker accomplished on one simple war driving expedition is already completed for the next hacker, so the next hacker has documented progress and a much easier time of getting into and through the war chalked wireless LAN. When trying to break into a network, one of the biggest challenges that all hackers face, whether they are wireless LAN hackers or not, is time. The longer it takes to break into a network, the better the chance of getting caught. Fortunately, if they have taken the time to plan their steps carefully, the time spent on location will be more beneficial to them. War chalking is one of the many ways that hackers save one another time in getting into wireless networks.

From a criminal standpoint, war chalking could be considered the crime of vandalism, but since chalk is easily removable, it's questionable as to whether an organization could successfully prosecute offenders. As a network security professional, one should strive to avoid any of the possible signs that war drivers look for in a war chalking symbol: open wireless LAN, broadcast SSID, not using WEP (or TKIP if possible). If a war chalk drawing is found on your premises, it should be erased (washed off), and you should be alert for further possibility of intrusion.

Many pieces of networking equipment allow the administrator to change the 'greeting' that people view when they login, or attempt to login, to that network or that piece of equipment. It has been argued in court that having a "Welcome!" screen on the interface of a network router is legally an invitation to a hacker.

One anecdotal example of using this type of deterrent on a wireless LAN occurred when the administrator configured the SSID to "Do not attempt to associate to this WLAN". This message may have served as more of a challenge to any nearby war drivers, and the administrator probably would be better off by simply configuring the wireless network to be *closed* - not broadcasting any SSID at all.

Tools, Traffic, & Social Engineering

In Chapter 1, we discussed many types of networking tools used to gather sensitive information from an unsecured wireless network. These types of tools included discovery tools, packet analyzers, application layer analyzers, network utility applications, share enumerators, and more. As IT professionals learn how to design and build secure wireless networks, some of these tools will be rendered useless. Social engineering is typically the hacker's next approach.

Social engineering is a term for convincing someone to give you something that they should not give you. Successful social engineering attacks occur because the target might be ignorant of the organization's information security policies or intimidated by an intruder's knowledge, expertise, or attitude. Social engineering is one of the most dangerous and successful methods of hacking into any IT infrastructure. If defeating WEP has stumped the hacker, the hacker might try to trick an employee who is authorized to have the WEP key into giving up this information. Once the hacker has the WEP key, the hacker will plug it into his or her own computer and again use the tools from Chapter 1 to capture sensitive data in real time, just as though there was no security. For this reason, social engineering has the potential of rendering even the most sophisticated security solution useless.

Hackers are not always like they are portrayed in movies: the cigarette-smoking, caffeine-loaded teenager in a dark room in a basement with multiple high-speed connections to the Internet, loud music, and plenty of spare time. Many times the most successful and damaging network intrusion is accomplished in broad daylight through clever efforts of someone who walks into a business like they own it. In the very same manner, a hired professional security auditor should openly attempt intrusion as one tactic of testing security policy adherence.

There are some well-known targets for this type of attack:

- The help desk
- On-site contractors
- Employees (end-users)

The Help Desk

The help desk is in place to assist those individuals who need help with some aspect of a computer or network. It becomes quite awkward in many situations for the help desk *not* to provide answers to questions when the person on the other end of the line seems to know what they need. It is not an easy task to train help desk personnel not to be helpful in certain situations; nevertheless, this type of education is crucial to corporate network security. The help desk should be trained to know exactly which pieces of information related to the wireless network should not be given out without the proper authorization or without following specific processes put in place by security policy. Items that might be marked for exclusion are:

- SSID of access points
- WEP key(s)
- Physical locations of access points and bridges
- Usernames and passwords for network access and services (i.e. email)
- Passwords and SNMP strings for infrastructure equipment

The auditor should (and the hacker *will*) use two particular tactics when dealing with help desk personnel:

- Forceful, yet professional language
- Playing dumb

Both of these approaches have the same effect: getting the requested information. Help desk personnel understand that their job is to help people with their problems. They also understand that their manager will not be happy with them if their customers are not happy with the service they are receiving. By threatening to speak with, or write a letter to, the manager, the social engineer can get the help desk person to give over the requested information just to appease and settle down the social engineer. Some people are just naturally inept at handling personal conflict, and some people are easily intimidated by anyone with an authoritative voice. Both of these situations can be used to the advantage of the social engineer. The human factor has to be overcome with training, discipline, and repetitively following documented procedures.

Playing dumb is a favorite of many social engineers. The help desk person is usually disarmed and stops paying attention when they figure out that the person to whom they are speaking knows very little. This situation is exacerbated when the 'dumb' customer is overly polite and thankful for the help. It's important that a help desk person be alert to this tactic at all times. A social engineer is likely to call over and over, hoping to speak with different representatives, and taking different approaches with each.

Contractors

IT contractors are commonplace at many businesses today, and very few, if any, are put through organizational security training. Few are given a copy of the company security policy or required to sign privacy agreements. For this reason, and because IT contractors, like the help desk, are there to help, IT contractors can be especially good targets for social engineers. Contractors are privy to the exclusive details about network resources because they are often on-site to design or repair the network. In wanting to be helpful to their customer, contractors often give out too much information to people who are not authorized to have such information. For this reason, strong security solutions that rely on multi-factor authentication are recommended.

Employees

Since people spend many hours each day with each other at their work location, they often share private information – such as network login information – with one another. It is also common to see that same login information on sticky notes under keyboards and on monitors. Another problem is that most computer users are not computer network or security savvy. For this reason, they might not recognize spy ware, hack attempts, or social engineering.

Wireless technology is still very new to most organizations. Employees who are not educated about wireless security may not realize the dangers that unauthorized access via the wireless network can pose to the organization and to them personally. Specifically, non-technical employees who use the wireless network should be aware of the fact that their computers can be attacked in a peer-to-peer fashion at work, at home, or on any public wireless network. Social engineers take advantage of all of these facets and even engineer elaborate stories that would fool almost anyone not specifically trained to recognize social engineering attacks.

Traffic Pattern Analysis

Once an intruder has obtained access to a network, one type of information gathering is traffic pattern analysis. This type of attack might include an understanding of where the majority of the traffic on the network is going, how much traffic is going to these places, and what time of day certain types of traffic are being sent.

Suppose that an attacker wanted to gather login information and figure out what resources on the network were the most important. Beginning an attack on location at 8am, near enough to an access point to make a stable connection, an attacker could collect early-morning logins and, using a packet analyzer, figure out where most of the network's most important resources are located. This information would be especially important if there were honeypots on the network. Honeypots are software packages running on computers that emulate single or multiple computers on a network. Honeypots are used to attract hackers and, once the hacker attacks, collect information about the attack and the attacker. In order to avoid this type of trap, intruders may use traffic analysis techniques so that they know where *not* to direct a future attack.

Summary

As the first step in the intrusion process, information gathering is the foundation of any attack on a computer network. If the data behind the firewall is valuable enough to the intruder(s), the time spent to gather all of the necessary and pertinent information could be months. Professional intruders could use social engineering, traffic analysis, and packet and protocol analyzers to obtain whatever it is that they are seeking.

Wireless security professionals must think in these same terms as they create policies, solutions, and practices for securing the wireless network.

Key Terms

Before taking the exam, you should be familiar with the following terms:

NetStumbler

social engineering

target profiling

trace routing

traffic pattern analysis

Review Questions

1. Name 5 sources of information that could be used to gather information on your organization's executives or IT infrastructure.

    A. _____

    B. _____

    C. _____

    D. _____

    E. _____

2. Name 5 pieces of information related to the wireless network that should never to be given out without the proper authorization or personal authentication of the person requesting the information.

    A. _____

    B. _____

    C. _____

    D. _____

    E. _____

3. What are some common names, phrases, or other pieces of information that should NOT be used as the basis for creating network access passwords?

    A. _____

    B. _____

    C. _____

    D. _____

4. As a network security professional, what action should be taken when a war chalk drawing is located on your premises?

   A. Correct the drawing if it is wrong

   B. Contact the local wireless users group

   C. Erase the drawing & be alert for more intruders

   D. Contact the police

5. Explain why proper training on wireless LAN security is essential to preventing social engineering.

Answers to Review Questions

1. Multiple Answers

   A. Google.com

   B. Resume

   C. Press releases about technology

   D. Executive Bios

   E. Vendors or contractors

2. Multiple Answers:

   A. SSID(s) of access points

   B. WEP key(s)

   C. Physical locations of access points and bridges

   D. Usernames and passwords for network access and services (i.e. email)

   E. Passwords and SNMP strings for infrastructure equipment

3. Multiple Answers:

   A. Dog's name

   B. Birth date

   C. Anniversary date

   D. Family member's name

4. C

5. If employees are not aware of the risks of social engineering attacks, the entire organization becomes vulnerable to attack.

Unauthorized Access

CWSP Exam Objectives Covered:

❖ Explain how intruders obtain network access through analysis, spoofing, and information theft including the following methods:

- Use of wireless LAN protocol analysis and site survey tools

- Active intrusion techniques (connecting, probing, and configuring the network)

❖ Active intrusion techniques (connecting, probing, and configuring the network)

❖ Explain common points of attack:

- Default configurations

- Clear text data transmissions

- Rogue hardware

❖ Describe common non-secure configuration issues that can be the focus of an attack

❖ Describe weaknesses in existing security solutions

❖ Explain security vulnerabilities associated with public access wireless networks

❖ Explain how malicious code or file insertion occurs in a wireless LAN through the use of:

- Viral attacks

- Placement of illegal content

❖ Explain peer-to-peer hacking and how it can be prevented:

- Recognize wireless client exposure

- Identify detection and prevention mechanisms including IDS and personal firewall software

- Understand how corporate policy can be used to prevent use of corporate hardware on public networks

A "rogue" device is any device that is not authorized to be on the network. In wireless networks, it is common to see rogue access points, bridges, and Ad Hoc networks installed without authorization. A rogue access point or bridge, when discovered on the wired network, should be considered a security breach of the highest level. Whether an organization employs wireless LANs or not, the vulnerability of rogue access points exists and is very serious. A rogue access point is the same as running a Cat5 cable to a freely available hub in the parking lot. How auditors should proceed when testing networks for rogue equipment vulnerabilities is discussed below.

Once an intruder gains access, potentially through a rogue device, there are a number of actions the intruder might perform. The most common security risk mentioned is that of data theft; however, other actions, such as data insertion, peer attacks, and unauthorized network control, can have far more detrimental effects on a corporation and its network. These security risks and their effects are detailed in the following sections.

Rogue Devices

As a wireless security professional, one will likely have the responsibility of preventing and also discovering rogue devices on a network. The best way to go about discovering rogue devices is to learn how a professional intruder would go about placing a rogue device. If you are going to defeat intruders, you must become familiar with how intruders work. The best methods for placing rogue access points are those that allow a person to accomplish the goals of gaining the highest degree of access into and the highest degree of control over a network. Below is a list of items that an experienced intruder might consider when placing rogue access devices.

Access Points

Location

Rogue devices will be placed as if the device were designed to be there in the first place. An access point, for example, should not cause any disruption in service (interference) to the existing network, so that the rogue device will not be noticed.

WEP settings

Static WEP would be enabled if static or dynamic WEP were already being used on the wireless network on which the rogue is being placed. If an administrator is scanning the area with NetStumbler or Airopeek, he or she will be looking for unencrypted data packets as a sign of a rogue device. There is no way to tell the difference between the data packets that are encrypted with an intruder's WEP key and the data packets that are encrypted with the authorized network WEP key. An intruder will have to set a WEP key on his or her rogue access point that matches the WEP key on the intruder's computer.

Placement

Rogue devices will be placed near the edge of the building – the closer to a window the better. This placement allows for better coverage from outside the building. Intruders will try to place the rogue in a part of the building that has a physically unsecured outside perimeter, so that the intruder can be within range of the access point while not arousing suspicion.

Costs

Small and cheap access points are usually used. The chance of losing a rogue access point to an administrator is almost 100%, assuming the organization knows and cares about the dangers of rogue access points. For this reason, intruders would normally use an inexpensive SOHO model.

Visibility

Rogue devices will be well hidden. Many network administrators are reluctant to challenge upper management, so placing the rogue in the CEO or other executive's office behind his or her desk is ideal. This placement, however, would require a significant amount of social engineering. Most intruders have to settle for hiding it behind a plant or in a ceiling tile.

SSID settings

The SSID of the rogue will be set to match that of the existing wireless LAN implementation. This setting allows the rogue device to blend in with its surroundings. Also, 'closed system' features will be enabled so that NetStumbler and other discovery tools cannot detect the rogue device.

Frequency

Intruders may use 900 MHz units instead of 2.4 GHz (802.11b) or 5 GHz (802.11a) Wi-Fi compliant units. Almost no WLAN discovery tools can use 900 MHz equipment.

Spectrum Choice

Intruders may use FHSS technology like 802.11, Bluetooth, OpenAir, or HomeRF instead of DSSS. Almost no current WLAN discovery tools can use FHSS equipment.

Antennas

Horizontally polarized antennas are often used on the rogue and the client. This tactic will give the rogue a very small RF signature on any scanning devices. The rogue is not likely to be detected in a scan unless the administrator is physically very close to it.

Wireless Bridges

Placement

A rogue bridge is placed within the Fresnel Zone of an existing bridge link. The Fresnel Zone of a wireless bridge link may span several miles and be extremely broad, making rogue placement easier on the intruder and rogue detection tougher on the administrator.

Priority

A rogue bridge must be set to a very low priority so that the rogue does not become the root bridge, and thus give itself away as a rogue device.

MAC Spoofing

If MAC spoofing features are available in the bridge, the MAC address of an authorized non-root bridge can be spoofed.

Antenna Use

Intruders will use high-gain directional antennas to ensure a consistently high quality connection.

Costs

Remember that bridges, generally, are far more expensive than a SOHO access point, so the cost of being discovered is much higher, even though the chances of being discovered in the middle of a 3-mile point-to-point bridge link are much lower than inside a corporate office. Administrators rarely detect rogue bridges.

Summary

Rogue access points are serious security threats because the presence of unauthorized wireless access into a network represents 11 Mbps (802.11b) or maybe even 54 Mbps (802.11a & 802.11g) of bandwidth into and out of the network. An extreme amount of damage can be done in a very short time at those speeds. No matter what kind of network is deployed, proper security policy should require regular scans for and constant awareness of rogue access points.

Data Theft & Malicious Insertion

Often "getting hacked" is equated only with having some damage done or something valuable stolen from a computer network. It is easy to think through the possible damage that could be done when an intruder removes, copies, or deletes valuable corporate information, but what would the result be if an intruder obtained access to a network and deposited files on that network? High-speed wireless connectivity allows nearby intruders to pull large amount of data from a network very quickly, but it also allows an equal amount of data to be pushed *to* the network.

Illegal, Unethical, or Inappropriate Content

It is a common practice among the *warez* community (software piracy groups) to use open FTP servers on the Internet to store pirated software and illegally copied media. The same could be even more prevalent with wireless networks: intruders using an open wireless network to store many gigabytes of copyrighted software. Taken to the next level, what would be the result of a hacker depositing the secret intellectual property of one company on the files servers of that company's biggest competitor, and then alerting the press and/or legal authorities? What if tape backup systems had backed up the copied material for days or weeks before? Destroying such data to remove any trace of the data would be very difficult and time consuming.

Instead of targeting a corporation such as in the previous example, perhaps an attacker wants to target an individual employee (perhaps a former coworker). By gaining access to the network from the parking lot, the hacker could place pornographic material on the person's computer directly. This tactic would undoubtedly be a clear violation of corporate policy, which could result in the termination of the targeted individual.

Viruses & Spyware

There are many types of malware (malicious applications) that an intruder can place on a computer in order to obtain information that the intruder could not get just by having regular file access to the computer. The most common types of malware today are viruses and spyware. Viruses are capable of disabling desktop PCs, taking web sites down, and even overloading email servers. A wireless host connected to a public access network or on an unsecured corporate wireless network is a perfect place to put a virus. The unsuspecting authorized user would then take the virus into the corporation where it could do its intended harm.

Trojan Horse applications (often called just "Trojans") are specific types of viruses that pose a serious threat to network security. According to legend, the Greeks won the Trojan War by hiding in a huge, hollow wooden horse to sneak into the fortified city of Troy. In today's computer world, a Trojan Horse is defined as a "malicious, security-breaking program that is disguised as something benign." For example, suppose a user downloads what appears to be a movie or music file, but when the file is opened, a dangerous program is executed. This new executable erases the user's hard disk, sends their credit card numbers and passwords to a stranger, or lets that stranger hijack the user's computer computer to commit illegal DoS attacks.

Another specific type of virus is a *worm*. Worms self-replicate and self-proliferate creating a very large-scale problem in a very short period of time. Worms often come in the form of email worms that send themselves to everyone on a computer user's addresses book by disguising themselves as harmless attachments. Worms often do most of their damage well before they are ever noticed.

Most worms, trojans, and other types of viruses can be caught and disinfected before they do damage by using properly installed, configured, and updated virus scanning software. There are numerous virus scanning applications on the market, and it has recently been suggested that running two such applications simultaneously is worth while. Considering the high risk associated with wireless LANs, such a belt-and-suspenders approach is worth while to consider. Using at least one such scanning application should be required.

Another distinct, and relatively new, type of malware is spyware. Spyware typically comes as a multi-featured software package that can:

- Capture instant messenger traffic
- Capture email traffic
- Capture web site traffic and sites visited
- Capture keystrokes and passwords
- Be installed remotely and without an install dialog
- Automatically form and publish web-based (HTTP) reports

One of the most used spyware applications in a wireless environment is iSpyNow (www.ispynow.com). When combined with previously discussed utilities like Hyena and VNC that can push the spyware to unsuspecting hosts and remotely execute and control them, spyware can be a powerful tool for gathering information. A hacker can collect the gathered data by simply pointing his or her web browser to the authorized user's IP address and proper port number (defined by the spyware application).

There are many web sites dedicated to virus details, removing viruses, and avoiding re-infection by a virus. Two of the most popular such sources are www.symantec.com and www.mcafee.com Spyware is often not detected as a virus because spyware is an installed application that looks like any other authorized program. For this reason, companies have started making anti-spy software that works much like a virus scanner, but more specifically hunting down spyware. A popular anti-spy application, NetCop, can be found at www.anti-spy.com. Keep in mind that one can prevent malware from being placed on a wirelessly connected computer by using personal firewall software in most cases.

Peer-to-Peer Attacks

Peer-to-peer attacks are attacks instigated by one host aimed at another particular host, both of which are clients of the same network system. Targets that hackers commonly seek in peer-to-peer attacks are sensitive data files, password files, registry information such as WEP keys or file share properties, and network access information.

There are many ways to perform peer-to-peer attacks, some of which are listed below.

- *Spread spectrum RF* – using a compatible RF technology such as 802.11b, an intruder can directly attack a peer node either in ad hoc mode or through the access point in infrastructure mode.

- *Infrared* – many computers and operating systems have the infrared port enabled by default and users often forget to disable the infrared port when it is not in use. The infrared port is generally located on the back of the computer, so anyone sitting in front of the authorized user will be able to gain access to the computer through the infrared port without the authorized user's knowledge.

- *Hijacking* – in order to capture an authorized user's layer 2 and layer 3 connections, a rogue access point (hardware or software) and a rogue DHCP server can be used. Both of these are easily installed on a laptop computer. Once a user's connections are captured, the user can be directly attacked using the utilities discussed in chapter 1. In order to force a user to roam to the rogue access point, an RF jamming device will be needed as part of the attack.

Peer attacks are the most common type of wireless attack because client stations are left vulnerable far more than are corporate network infrastructures. New service offerings such as Wi-Fi Hotspots and hardware such as laptops with integrated wireless LAN radios are exacerbating the problem immensely. With the release of Intel's Centrino™ CPU, a new era of wireless intrusion will begin. This new CPU integrates a Wi-Fi radio directly into the CPU, and while such integrated technology can be a great convenience and cost savings to some, it opens the doors for hacking to others. Consider that even computers that do not connect to wireless networks will have wireless radios, which will allow intruders to invade a person's privacy quickly, quietly, and easily.

Unauthorized Control

Network Management Tools

Network management tools are powerful utilities for managing large enterprise LANs and WANs from a central point of control. Consider what could happen if an intruder gained sufficient access (administrative passwords) to control the network. (Remember also that 80% of all computer network attacks come from current or former employees) Using software packages such as Hyena, Solarwinds, What's Up Gold, and SNMPc, an intruder could take over an entire enterprise from a single mobile workstation. Most intruders only need to be familiar with one such software package in order to do substantial damage to individuals and to the organization.

Configuration Changes

Having an intruder take over the wireless infrastructure because of unsecured settings (i.e. default configurations) is a hazard that no administrator would want to encounter. For example, an intruder could do such mischievous things as reconfiguring one access point and having that access point push its configuration to all other access points on the wireless LAN. Further, the intruder could instruct the access point to push its firmware to all others on the wireless LAN. If the access point were first loaded with old firmware, the network-wide push could cripple the wireless LAN because of old bugs or incompatibilities. If the intruder first used Telnet to gain access to the unsecured PoE switch powering the access points, that intruder could start a firmware push between access points and terminate the power to all access points in the middle of the firmware push. Such an attack could damage or disable all access points indefinitely.

Another common type of attack over the wireless network is to reconfigure items for future intrusion, or "open the front door". For example, suppose that a small company were using a SOHO wireless gateway, and the administrator did not change the default login parameters prior to installation. This lack of attention to security would allow the attacker to add virtual server settings to the SOHO gateway, permitting the hacker to come back into the network via the Internet connection. Virtual servers are redirected port mappings that allow internal hosting of services behind a Port Address Translation router such as a SOHO gateway. Secondly, additional services that were not previously enabled, such as SNMP or Telnet, could be enabled on the gateway, though the opportunity for such a tactic is usually more available on enterprise access points. If an administrator had disabled SNMP but did not disable or secure Telnet, the intruder could use Telnet to re-enable SNMP and to change the HTTP administration password.

Third Party Attacks

Denial of Service and SPAM attacks originating from an unsuspecting network with an unsecured wireless LAN are commonplace. Many of yesterday's spammers were getting free AOL and MSN accounts for a month and using them to spam. With the rapid proliferation of wireless LANs, the same malicious individuals now have free high-speed wireless access with no account signup and cancellation. AOL, MSN, and others of course cancel accounts of known spammers, but spammers just go and get another account under a different name. Since the initial signup is free, the only real hassle is the slow speed. Borrowing someone's broadband Internet connection – especially a corporation with multiple T1s – makes spamming and other malicious acts much easier.

Additionally, the corporation can then be blacklisted and eventually disconnected from their ISP for spamming people. Such a result might even be the intruder's goal in the first place. If not, then the intruder simply moves to another unsecured wireless connection and performs the same act.

Spamming isn't the only way to attack someone using someone else's wireless LAN. Denial of Service attacks are easy to perform when the source network has a large Internet connection like a T1 or multiple T1s. The situation can be exacerbated when that unsecured wireless network belongs to an ISP or large corporation, which typically have multiple DS3 (45 Mbps) or OC3 (155 Mbps) lines to the Internet. These types of attacks commonly cause costly damage to target networks, and can result in legal action against the source – in this case, the unsuspecting wireless network owner.

Summary

The term "unauthorized access" may not sound very intimidating, but should be equated with "serious security breach." Consider each type of unauthorized access discussed above – rogue devices, data theft/insertion, peer-to-peer attacks, and unauthorized control – each has the potential to bring an entire corporate network to a standstill, either directly or indirectly. Each of these attacks has been possible with wired networks, and is now much more possible, less expensive, and easier to attempt with wireless networks.

It is vitally important that the person in charge of securing an organization's wireless network be intimate with the details of these attacks in order to prevent them, through policy, practices, and solution design strategy.

Key Terms

Before taking the exam, you should be familiar with the following terms:

hijacking

peer-to-peer attacks

rogue device

Spyware

Review Questions

1. Why would a hacker use a frequency hopping wireless access point as a rogue device?

    A. FHSS cannot be detected by a wireless packet analyzer

    B. Most wireless LANs today are Wi-Fi™, so FHSS may not be noticed by DSSS scanning software

    C. FHSS has better throughput than Wi-Fi, and allows better access to the network

    D. NetStumbler only works with FHSS

2. Why are third party attacks a problem with unsecured wireless LANs? Choose the two best answers.

    A. Legal implications of being the source of an attack on someone else's network

    B. Authorized email transmissions can be redirected to a different person other than the intended recipient by an intruder

    C. Smurf attacks can cause DoS on the unsecured WLAN

    D. Possible disconnection of Internet service by the wireless LAN owner's ISP for abuse of services

3. Why are insertion and/or theft of data more dangerous from a wireless network connection than from a typical Internet connection?

   A. Because the perpetrator does not need a physical connection to the network to conduct the attack.

   B. Most common Internet connections are part or all of a T-1 (1.544Mbps), whereas a wireless LAN connection may be 54 Mbps

   C. Certain pieces of data that can be transmitted over a wireless connection cannot be sent over the Internet

   D. An internet connected intruder cannot likely access protected servers, whereas a wirelessly connected intruder might be able to.

   E. A wireless intruder's connection cannot be tracked in order to identify him

4. Name four methods that can be used to conduct a peer attack using wireless LAN technologies.

   A. _____

   B. _____

   C. _____

   D. _____

5. Name three items that are needed to hijack a wireless LAN's associated clients both at layer 2 and layer 3.

   A. _____

   B. _____

   C. _____

Answers to Review Questions

1. B

2. A, D

3. A, B, D, E

4. Multiple answers:

    A. Ad Hoc (direct peer connection)

    B. Infrastructure (through the access point)

    C. Infrared

    D. Hijacking

5. Multiple answers:

    A. Access point

    B. DHCP services

    C. Jamming device

Denial of Service

CWSP Exam Objectives Covered:

❖ Explain how the following types of Denial of Service (DoS) attacks can occur in a wireless LAN and identify the tools that can be used to perform these attacks:

- RF jamming
- Data flooding
- Client hijacking
- Infrastructure misconfiguration

Denying authorized users access to their own network is a favorite past time of some attackers. There are many ways that this type of attack can be accomplished against a wireless LAN, including RF jamming, data flooding, and user hijacking. In the sections below are some insights into how and with what tools these types of attacks are accomplished.

RF Jamming

With some relatively inexpensive tools, jamming a direct sequence spread spectrum wireless LAN is quite simple, even at long range. Most of today's indoor wireless LANs operate at less than 100 mW, and DSSS wireless LANs only use 22 MHz of RF spectrum to transmit data. What this means is that, with an RF generator that can generate very low amounts of power (less than 1 Watt), antennas that can broadcast the signal at long distances (either directionally or in an omni-directional pattern), and a small power source, anyone can jam a wireless LAN with ease. While spread spectrum wireless LANs are known for their resilience in a noisy RF environment, few can function properly in the presence of an RF power source that produces a signal up to 40 times (4 Watts) more powerful, whether that signal is spread spectrum or narrowband. For example, a transmitter that can produce a 1 Watt narrowband signal attached to an antenna that has a 6 dBi gain is producing 4 Watts of radiated power (EIRP).

With that amount of generated RF signal, nearly any wireless LAN can be jammed, causing either a complete disruption in service to client devices on the RF channel being jammed, or forcing those users to roam to another access point. That other access point could be an intruder's access point, set to the same SSID as the authorized access point. This type of attack is known as hijacking, and is discussed later in this section.

Where can a person buy or get the parts to build such a jamming device, and how much do they cost? To answer this question, one must first understand that most RF generators are very expensive and used for their precision output power and frequency accuracy. Neither of these traits is important in finding or creating an RF jamming device. These types of generators, made by manufacturers such as Hewlett Packard and Anritsu, are made mostly for calibration lab or field instrumentation use, and are not designed for use as jamming devices. Since that is the case, one must look for high-powered, low-cost, lightweight (even more difficult to find) units that specifically have output frequency ranges in the ISM or UNII band(s) that an attacker is trying to jam. These criteria narrow the scope of such a search tremendously, and it is important to understand that no manufacturer makes "RF Jamming Devices" because of the possible legal implications. Instead, in order to find such a device, one must look for equipment used to test wireless LAN antennas, cables, connectors, and other accessories such as YDI's PSG-1 (Power Signal Generator), shown in Figure 4.1.

FIGURE 4.1   Power Signal Generator (PSG-1) from YDI (www.ydi.com)

There are sources other than a simple jamming device that can cause serious RF jamming problems in a wireless LAN environment. Microwave ovens, Bluetooth devices, other RF devices, and wireless LAN devices can all cause problems for a wireless LAN. When the jamming source is unintentional – as with a microwave oven – it can simply be removed from the environment, but when the source is an attacker using an RF jamming device, physical security is the administrator's only defense.

Data Flooding

Data flooding is the act of overwhelming an infrastructure device or computer with more data than it can process. In the case of wireless LANs, a data flooding attack does not require much data. 802.11b-compliant access points typically saturate at 5.5 Mbps or less because they are half-duplex devices. Wireless LAN client devices are also capable of the same amount of throughput, and each has the ability to saturate an access point. What this means to an attacker is that, with an application that can generate at least 5.5 Mbps of traffic, an access point can effectively be disabled. Attempting to send this much data through or to an access point will deny a reasonable quality of service to other users. Since wireless LAN devices use the CSMA/CA protocol, all nodes attached to an access point will receive some amount of time to transmit, but when a single node is transmitting so much data, the other notes can pass very little, if any, data. A data flooding attack on a network is illustrated in Figure 4.2 below.

FIGURE 4.2   Data flooding illustration

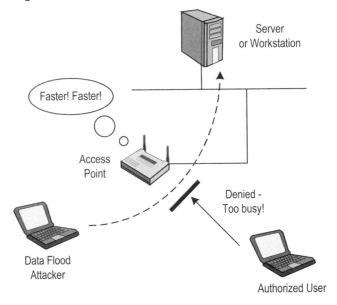

There are many methods of performing a data flooding attack. The first way is simply to pull a very large file from the Internet, but this method would require an FTP server, a very large Internet connection, and would be subject to security measures put in place by the organization that owns the wireless LAN. Basically that means that an attacker could not perform a data flooding attack any time he wanted. This scenario usually happens as unintentional flooding by authorized users who use the corporate wireless LAN to download their favorite music or movie files.

The second way is to pull or push a file to or from an internal server on the LAN. Again, this scenario would be subject to the security measures put in place by the organization that owns the wireless LAN – effectively preventing such an attack in many instances. The third method is to use a packet generator software package. There are several such applications, one of which is Tamosoft's Commview (www.tamosoft.com). The Commview interface is shown below in Figure 4.3 and 4.4. Commview is a low cost packet analyzer that has a native packet generator feature.

FIGURE 4.3   Tamosoft's Commview (Choosing the packet generator feature)

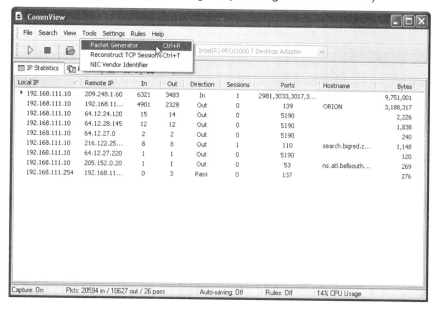

FIGURE 4.4   Tamosoft's Commview (Configuring the packet generator)

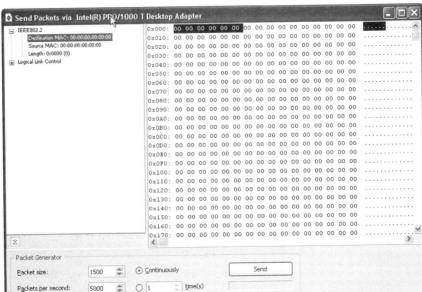

The packet generator is easy for a beginner to use, and can push more than enough traffic to saturate any wireless LAN. Packet size, packet rate, destination and source MAC addresses, and continuous transmission are all options that can be easily configured by the user. When the destination is configured for the access point itself, even the strongest security measure cannot prevent this type of attack. As the packet-generating node is transmitting, all others in range of the node that are on the same channel must stop transmitting because of the nature of any half-duplex environment. Second, when the access point hears the transmission and sees its MAC address, it recognizes that the transmission is destined to itself. The access point processes the frame, and subsequently drops it because the frame is not destined to any other node or the access point's own IP stack. This process takes processing cycles on the access point's CPU, and with enough of these invalid wireless frames, the access point becomes saturated and the wireless medium becomes unusable by other nodes. This type of attack is very similar to RF jamming except that it uses spread spectrum transmissions to accomplish the same result.

Hijacking

Hijacking is a situation in which an unauthorized user takes control of an authorized user's wireless LAN connection. In wireless, hijacking is done at layer 2 for denial of service and at layer 3 for attacking purposes. In order to hijack a wireless user, one must use an access point that replicates the functions being performed by an authorized access point. This task is usually accomplished in software running on an attacker's laptop. Using Proxim's Orinoco client software as an example, we can see in Figures 4.5 and 4.6 below that this wireless LAN PC card can be configured to operate as an access point.

FIGURE 4.5   Orinoco client base station setting

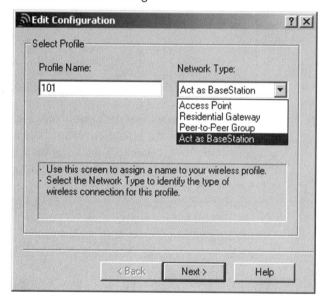

FIGURE 4.6 Orinoco client configured for a different channel

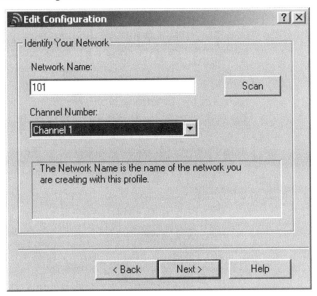

When configuring the rogue software access point, one must choose a channel that is not in use in a particular area. Then, when a jamming device is used to force users to roam (looking for a better connection), the client devices will roam off of the authorized hardware access point onto the rogue software access point as shown in Figure 4.7.

FIGURE 4.7   Forced roaming and hijacking

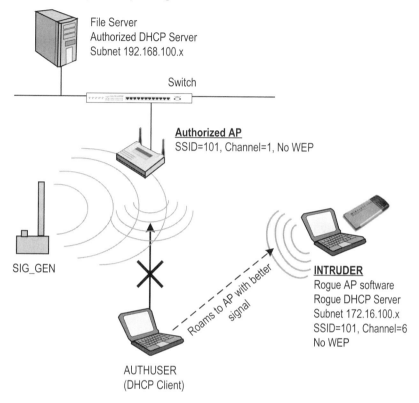

Once a user's layer 2 connection is hijacked, the next step is to allow the hijacked user to establish a layer 3 connection with the hijacker. The layer 3 connection is established by running a DHCP server on the same laptop as the access point software. An example of a low-cost, powerful DHCP server is Kerio's WinRoute (www.kerio.com).

FIGURE 4.8   WinRoute's DHCP server feature

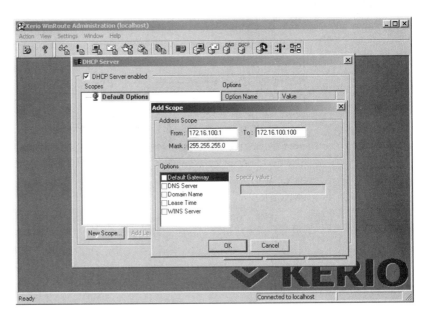

Windows NT based products such as Windows NT 4.0, Windows 2000, and Windows XP automatically renew their DHCP lease each time the layer 2 connection is broken, whether the connection is wired or wireless. This auto renew function is advantageous to the hijacker because no extra steps are required to assure the host under attack obtains an IP address. Once the IP address is obtained, the process of attack is as simple as checking the DHCP lease table in WinRoute and pointing scanning software such as LANGuard toward the IP address of the new client.

Summary

There are three main types of wireless denial of service attack: RF jamming, data flooding, and hijacking. For two of these three, RF jamming and hijacking, the best, and sometimes the only, defense is physical security: keeping the attacker away from the premises. The tools required to conduct any of these attacks are very inexpensive and very easy to acquire, but the damage to production, service, or end user productivity can be immense if these types of attacks are not prevented. The individual responsible for wireless LAN security must be aware of exactly how these attacks can and will be attempted on the wireless network, and know how to prevent or react to them.

Key Terms

Before taking the exam, you should be familiar with the following terms:

data flooding

half-duplex

hijacking

RF Jamming

Review Questions

1. RC4 is available in which of the following bit lengths?

    A. 56

    B. 64

    C. 128

    D. 192

    E. 256

2. RC5 is a _____ cipher?

    A. stream

    B. block

    C. chunk

    D. circular

    E. rotating

3. With the DES encryption algorithm, every 8th bit is a parity bit resulting in a _____ -bit key strength.

    A. 56

    B. 64

    C. 104

    D. 128

4. Triple DES is a block cipher that processes data in _____ -bit chunks.

    A. 56

    B. 64

    C. 168

    D. 192

5. AES is specified for use by US Government agencies for protecting sensitive (unclassified) information in what FIPS standard?

   A. 167

   B. 204

   C. 142

   D. 197

Answers to Review Questions

1. A, B
2. A, C, D
3. B, D
4. D
5. C

Legislation

CWSP Exam Objectives Covered:

❖ Summarize the following legal issues that apply to wireless LANs, and how they apply to computers and intellectual property:

- U.S. Federal laws regarding information security and illegal intrusion

- U.S. State laws regarding information security and illegal intrusion

In This Chapter

Acts of US Congress

State Laws

It is important that intruders, auditors, and administrators understand the legal ramifications of connecting to and penetrating a wireless LAN that does not belong to them. The legal consequences of illegal intrusion can far outweigh any gains, and many times the intruder considers what he or she is doing to be within the confines of the law when it is not. Legal statutes vary from state to state in the United States and from country to country abroad.

Some states prosecute offenders vigorously and have very strict codes on what constitutes a violation. In fact, many individuals may be breaking the law when they are not actually attempting a network intrusion because of how wireless network cards and Windows XP acts by default. Unless your wireless network card is disabled in the operating system, there is a good likelihood that it will automatically connect to the first unsecured access point it detects. In many states, this default action alone is considered intrusion. Certainly anything beyond this passive action, such as eavesdropping with a packet analyzer or port scans of servers on the network, would be considered an intentional breach of the network.

In order to make a legal case against an individual, intent must be proven. Suppose that a wireless security auditor was working for the ABC Corporation on the first floor of a high-rise office complex. When the auditor started a wireless packet analyzer on channel 1, it is possible that the packet analyzer may capture traffic both from this customer's wireless LAN and from a nearby office. While the FCC defines this behavior as eavesdropping, certainly it cannot be helped and there is no ill intent toward the neighboring business. If the auditor were to use the information gathered for personal gain or to damage the other company in some way, then that would be construed as illegal intrusion and abuse.

There are many new federal laws regarding computer intrusion, and many more on the way as the United States tightens home land security. Some of the existing laws are discussed below.

Acts of US Congress

Because of the rapid proliferation of wireless devices in and outside the U.S., lawmaking bodies must attempt to keep up with the growth of the industry and the legalities that arise as new technologies find new applications. Each new technology, especially those that apply to the wireless sector, can and usually does create many new opportunities for criminals to attempt to take advantage of the period of time in which there are no laws to restrict their actions. The U.S. Congress has been active in creating and maintaining laws that address wireless and the many different technologies that affect wireless.

Some of the specific Acts of the U.S. Congress that are used in prosecuting criminal trespassers in computer related cases are:

- 1998 Identity Theft and Assumption Deterrence Act
- 1986 Computer Fraud and Abuse Act
- 1986 Electronic Communications Privacy Act

Identity theft, computer fraud, and eavesdropping cost consumers and corporations millions of dollars each year. The fact that wireless networks, and wireless client computers, are even easier to compromise will aggravate this already bad situation. Therefore, it must be up to those IT professionals who manage wireless networks to step above and beyond what current laws require, because current laws will always lag behind the technology.

Identity Theft and Assumption Deterrence Act

Identity theft often seems unavoidable, undetectable, and unstoppable. Public concern over identity theft is understandably enormous, in part because it seems to be widespread and in part because the consequences can be devastating. Consumers feel particularly vulnerable knowing that, no matter how careful they may be, they may nevertheless become identity theft victims.

The 1998 Identify Theft and Assumption Deterrence Act was created to address the problem of identity theft in several concrete ways. It directed the Federal Trade Commission (FTC) to establish the federal government's central repository for identity theft complaints and to provide victim assistance and consumer education. This Act makes it a federal crime to:

> *"knowingly transfer or use, without lawful authority, a means of identification of another person with the intent to commit, or to aid or abet, any unlawful activity that constitutes a violation of Federal law, or that constitutes a felony under any applicable State or local law."*

The second way in which the Act addresses the problem of identity theft is by focusing on consumers as victims. In particular, the Act provides for a centralized complaint and consumer education service for victims of identity theft and gives the responsibility of developing this function to the Commission. The Act directs that the Commission establish procedures to: (1) log the receipt of complaints by victims of identity theft; (2) provide identity theft victims with informational materials; and (3) refer complaints to appropriate entities, including the major national consumer reporting agencies and law enforcement agencies.

A violation of the act is punishable by up to 15 years of imprisonment and $250,000 in fines. The law establishes that the person whose identity was stolen is a *true* victim. Previously, only the credit grantors who suffered monetary losses were considered victims. This legislation enables the Secret Service, the Federal Bureau of Investigation (FBI), and other law enforcement agencies to combat this crime, and it allows for the identity theft victim to seek restitution if there is a conviction.

In enacting the Identity Theft Act, Congress recognized that coordinated efforts are essential to best serve the needs of identity theft victims because these fraud victims often need assistance both from government agencies at the national and state or local level and from private businesses. Accordingly, the FTC's role under the Act is primarily one of facilitating information sharing among public and private entities. In order to fulfill the purposes of the Act, the Commission has developed and begun implementing a plan that centers on three principal components:

- *Toll-free telephone hotline.* The Commission has established a toll-free telephone number, 1-877-ID-THEFT, that consumers can call to report identity theft. Consumers who call the hotline receive telephone counseling from specially trained personnel to help them resolve credit-related problems that may have resulted from the misuse of their identities.

- *Identity theft complaint database.* Detailed information from the complaints received on the FTC's identity theft hotline is entered into the FTC's Identity Theft Data Clearinghouse. The information in the Clearinghouse is available to law enforcement agencies nationwide via the FTC's secure law enforcement website, Consumer Sentinel. Access to the Clearinghouse information supports law enforcement agencies' efforts to combat identity theft by providing a range of complaints from which to spot patterns of illegal activity.

- *Consumer education.* The FTC has taken the lead in coordinating with other government agencies and organizations the development and dissemination of comprehensive consumer education materials for victims of identity theft and those concerned with preventing this crime.

 The United States Government has a central website detailing both federal and state laws regarding identity theft: http://www.consumer.gov/idtheft/

Computer Fraud and Abuse Act

The 1996 Computer Fraud and Abuse Act was enacted to clarify the definitions of criminal fraud and abuse for federal computer crimes. This Act also removed the obstacles that had previously been in the way to prosecute violators of these crimes, and further defined the legal aspects of computer crime to eliminate any misunderstandings. Section 1030 of the Act was amended on October 26, 2001, by Section 202 of the USA Patriot Act anti-terrorism legislation to expand the ability of service providers to get government help with hacking, denial of service attacks, and related Computer Fraud and Abuse Act violations.

While the USA Patriot Act dramatically changed the Computer Fraud and Abuse Act, it did not change the requirement that there must be damage and loss. "Damage" still requires impairment to the integrity or availability of data, a program, a system or information. Normal port scanning, for example, is not likely to cause such impairments. However, the USA Patriot Act does make it much easier to meet the definition of "loss," which must exceed $5,000. Victims can now add nearly every conceivable expense associated with the incident to arrive at the $5,000 threshold.

The focus of this Act was to protect "government-interest" computers, such as those used by government agencies and their affiliates. If compromised, these computers pose great risk to national security and the viability of government function itself, and because no clear law existed at the time to prevent unauthorized access to government computers, this law was enacted.

The Act includes coverage for federal, state, county, and municipal systems; financial and medical institutions; and computers used by contractors supplying such institutions. Specifically, the law prohibits the use of "a program, information, code, or command" with intent to damage, cause damage to, or deny access to a computer system or network. The Act specifically prohibits even unintentional damage if the perpetrator demonstrates reckless disregard of the risks of causing such damage. Appendix B of this book contains the full text of title 18, part I, chapter 47, section 1030 for reference.

Electronic Communications Privacy Act

The Electronic Communications Privacy Act (ECPA) sets out the provisions for access, use, disclosure, interception, and privacy protections of electronic communications. The law was enacted in 1986 and covers various forms of wire and electronic communications. According to the U.S. Code, electronic communications means "any transfer of signs, signals, writing, images, sounds, data, or intelligence of any nature transmitted in whole or in part by a wire, radio, electromagnetic, photo electronic, or photo optical system that affects interstate or foreign commerce." The ECPA prohibits unlawful access and certain disclosures of communication contents. Additionally, the law prevents government entities from requiring disclosure of electronic communications from a provider without proper procedure.

The ECPA assigns fines and prison sentences for anyone convicted of unauthorized interception and disclosure of electronic communications such as phone calls through landlines or mobile systems and email. The ECPA specifically prohibits making use of an unlawfully overheard electronic communication if the interceptor knows that the message was unlawfully obtained. On the other hand, providers of electronic messaging systems, including employers, are permitted to intercept messages on their own systems in the course of their normal operations. The ECPA also prohibits access to stored messages, not just those in transit.

Appendix C of this book contains the full text of title 18, part I, chapter 119, section 2511 for reference. Appendix D of this text contains the full text of title 18, part I, chapter 121, sections 2701-2711 for reference.

State Laws

State laws differ greatly in their statutes on network penetration and intrusion. Some states do not consider it a crime for a hacker to penetrate a network while others consider it a felony offense punishable by hefty fines and years in prison. States without statutes on computer crimes are quickly enacting legislation to prevent such activity due to recent events with national security. Some states have laws modeled after federal statutes such as the Computer Fraud and Abuse Act where there are minimum damage threshold values – such as $5,000. Depending on the county, district, or other local municipality, some may not prosecute such a crime until damage has reached over $50,000 because of an extremely high caseload of crimes against persons and severe understaffing of the court system. State laws vary widely in their definitions of what a computer break-in is, as well as the fines and punishment for a violation.

As mentioned at the beginning of this section, the administrator, security auditor, and intruder should be familiar with the laws of whatever state or country in which his or her organization operates. Intruders should know what the risks are if they are caught, and administrators and auditors should know exactly what evidence and documentation will be required to make a case against an alleged intruder.

Summary

This entire book deals with security, a breach of which may or may not be a crime, depending on where, when, and how the breach occurred. This chapter specifically addresses the laws that are in place relative to wireless security breaches. It is meant not to teach the IT professional the law, but to make sure that the security professional understands that he or she must be familiar with the local laws. As part of policy and procedure, if a law is broken during a security breach, that information should be conveyed to executive management and legal authorities as appropriate during the reporting and documentation of any incident. If an IT professional is not familiar with the laws, that person cannot make any kind of judgment about whether a law has been broken. As a security professional in IT, being able to tell executive management *everything* about a security breach is part of the job.

Key Terms

Before taking the exam, you should be familiar with the following terms:

identity theft

minimum damage laws

Research Questions

1. What is the punishment in your local or state government for eavesdropping, intruding, or capturing information from a neighbor's computer?

2. What documentation are you prepared to present in the event that your organization is damaged by a hacking incident?

3. Research which U.S. states have the weakest laws concerning computer crimes and note what the implications of such weak legislation may be.

4. Why is it important to be familiar with the local, state, and federal laws regarding data theft and intrusion before you implement a wireless LAN?

5. How do the laws of your state or province differ from the national or federal laws regarding data theft and intrusion?

General Policy

CWSP Exam Objectives Covered:

❖ Explain necessary items to include in the creation and maintenance of a wireless LAN security checklist

❖ Describe and recognize the importance of asset management and inventory procedures for wireless LANs

❖ Explain the importance of including wireless LANs in existing change management programs

❖ Explain the purpose and goals of the following wireless LAN security policies

- Password policy

- User training

- On-going review (auditing)

- Acceptable use & abuse policy

- Consistent implementation procedure

- Centralized implementation and management guidelines and procedures

❖ Locate & identify wireless LANs within and around a facility:

- Explain the assets to be protected through securing a wireless LAN

- Explain and demonstrate the inherent weaknesses in wireless LAN security

- Given a wireless LAN attack scenario, explain and respond to the attack

- Given a wireless LAN configuration, explain and implement all the necessary steps to securing the wireless LAN

- ❖ Perform an impact analysis for a series of wireless LAN attack scenarios which may include the following methods of attack:
    - ▪ Analysis, spoofing, & information theft
    - ▪ Denial of Service
    - ▪ Malicious code or file insertion
    - ▪ Target profiling
    - ▪ Peer-to-peer hacking
    - ▪ Physical security
    - ▪ Social engineering
    - ▪ Wireless LAN hacking hardware & software
- ❖ Summarize risks to wired networks from wireless networks
- ❖ Summarize the security policy related to wireless public-access network use

When strictly followed and combined with effective technical solutions, wireless LAN security policies can reduce intrusions, risks, and costs associated with intrusion response and legal action. Where security policies are not strictly followed, gaping security holes exist that no technical solution can repair. There are so many security holes to plug with wireless LANs that nobody could be expected to remember them all. For this reason, these security holes should be well documented and resolution procedures should be implemented as part of an organization's comprehensive security policy.

Wireless LAN security policy falls into two categories: General and Functional. Both categories have multiple subcategories. General Policy describes the items taken into consideration that do not fall into a specific technical category. Much of what is addressed in General Policy covers a broad range of corporate networking because it is not technology specific – thus wireless is only one piece of the puzzle.

In this text, General Policy is broken down into the following categories:

- Getting Started
- Risk Assessment
- Impact Analysis
- Security Auditing

Security policies vary as widely as the organizations that implement them. How stringent a wireless LAN security must be is up to the decision makers at the organization, but due to legal risks alone, all organizations should implement at least some wireless LAN security policy, *even if the organization does not deploy a wireless LAN.* The more critical the security of the organization's data, the stronger and more detailed the wireless LAN security policy should be. It is important to note that even organizations with no wireless LAN in place need a section in their policy regarding the proper use of wireless LANs – even if it is only to say that wireless LANs may not be used. The reason for this requirement is that rogue (unauthorized) wireless LAN devices present a security hole for any organization and should be strictly policed.

Taking wireless LAN security seriously through implementation of strong and thorough policy represents a viable framework for mitigating risks and ensures that this emerging technology can be deployed throughout the workplace in a measured and responsible way. The primary issues addressed in a wireless LAN security policy are ownership and control of the wireless network, controlling access to the network, physical security of infrastructure hardware, encryption, auditing, and procedures for detecting and handling rogue devices.

Getting Started

A critical success factor in the effort of a wireless security policy is to obtain sponsorship within the organization. A high ranking executive, typically the CEO and/or the CIO, who understands and supports the value of the wireless LAN implementation project, is often needed to persuade others to see the benefit of the process. If only junior or mid-level employees support the policy, the network may continue to remain vulnerable. The bottom line is that security policy starts at the top and flows downward through the organization.

Every use of wireless technology within an organization should be done in accordance with a security plan. This plan must address at least the following three issues:

- *Resources* – controlled access prevents unauthorized users from consuming limited wireless network resources (bandwidth).
- *Privacy* – controlled access prevents unauthorized users from accessing confidential or sensitive data located on the network.
- *Intrusion* – a monitored environment alerts an organization about unauthorized activities and allows security managers to respond appropriately

The creation of any successful wireless security policy may include input from end users, the network operations team, the financial team, the management team, and possibly an independent auditor. These groups will combine to decide what items will be covered in the policy, how the policy will be enforced, how the policy will be implemented, and how user friendly the policy should be. A security policy that does not address at least these three areas of implementation will not succeed in its role of protecting the network.

Wireless LAN security policy is never the whole picture; rather, it is one piece of a much larger overall organizational policy that covers security, administration, and other areas. Many organizations implement wireless LANs without first implementing the policy to control the environment. Such an oversight, whether out of ignorance or arrogance, is a mistake with costly future ramifications.

 General templates on corporate security policy can be found at: http://www.sans.org/newlook/resources/policies/policies.htm. Included in this book is a wireless LAN security policy template in Appendix A.

Risk Assessment

Risk assessment is the process of examining each scenario in which an organization can experience financial loss due to negative impact events and ranking predicted losses by level of severity. The next step is to make decisions on cost-effective responses to eliminate or mitigate the risks associated with each scenario. Due to an overwhelming number of security concerns and the recent addition of government regulations concerning security, many organizations are now hiring for or creating the position of Chief Security Officer (CSO) to oversee security related issues, such as the ones listed below.

Risk assessment involves four themes that require analysis prior to creating a security policy. These areas are:

- *Asset protection* – What organizational assets must be protected from an attack? What are the costs and legal ramifications if these assets are compromised?
- *Threat prevention* – What is the organization trying to prevent by securing the network? What kinds of attack, theft, or breach of security are likely?
- *Legal liabilities* – What is an organization legally responsible for if the network is compromised or used to negatively impact another organization? What legal protection does a company have? Can the organization lose privileges (such as Internet services) due to abuse by intruders (e.g., spam)?

- *Costs* – What are the costs associated with securing the wireless network? Are security costs worth the investment, considering the risks, in implementing a wireless LAN? If the network is compromised, what could the potential costs be? How does the potential cost of infiltration and compromise weigh against the costs associated with securing the network?

There are many large organizations that perform risk assessment in today's IT industry. In some cases internal personnel may adequately perform risk assessment, but there is often a high value in having these assessments performed by qualified independent auditors.

Asset Protection

It is not useful to secure a wireless LAN if the data is not worth protecting, but such cases are rare in an enterprise deployment of wireless infrastructure. Some firms haphazardly state that they do not care if the data is available to an intruder because they have nothing to protect. In almost every case there is sensitive data to protect – even if the organization's administrator or manager does not know it. For example, if all of the intellectual property data the organization owns is public information, there may still be personal identity information such as resumes, credit cards, or financial information that should be protected. In many cases, the main obstacle in getting an organization to accept the responsibility of securing the wireless network is an economic one.

In most cases, it takes only minimal effort to enlighten an organization's manager as to potential security threats. For example, consider a real estate firm with an unsecured wireless LAN in place. At first glance, one might consider the data housed within the network as public information, but upon closer inspection, one would find that the firm's customer database would be valuable to its competition. This same firm might access a secured Internet-hosted database such as the Multiple Listing Service (MLS). In order to gain access to this home-for-sale database, the firm must have qualified employees and then must purchase a subscription. Logins to this site could easily be monitored through the unsecured wireless LAN. It is always important to dig deeper than the "first glance" in order to find security holes presented by wireless LANs.

Sensitive Data

Sensitive can mean different things to different companies when the term is applied to a company's intellectual property. Some companies have trade secrets or formulas that would result in financial ruin if they were ever exposed or stolen by competitors. Other companies, such as banking institutions, must protect their customer's data or they could face lawsuits from the customers. Organizations must determine at all levels which items are important to protect. The security professional must work with top-level management to ensure that the appropriate data is being protected and what degree of protection is required. It is possible that the data is so sensitive that a wireless LAN installation would present too high of a security risk and should not be installed at all. Some of the types of information that may need to be secured include:

- intellectual property
- trade secrets
- identity information
- credit card information
- health information
- customer databases

Keep in mind that even if a network has no wireless LAN installed, the organization should still address wireless LAN security in its policy. A hacker can easily *give* a wired network wireless connectivity by placing a rogue access point on the network.

Network Services

Malicious hackers may be looking to undermine the availability of a company's network. Imagine the damage that could be done if an intruder gained access to a retailer's sales database and either disabled the database or corrupted the data. Such actions would surely cause damage to the company's productivity and impact sales. Network services such as the following are critical to most organizations:

- e-mail services
- file services
- database services
- directory services
- Internet connectivity
- web-based applications
- virus and intrusion detection services
- custom application services

There are many other types of services, depending on the organization, that are running on a network at any given time – many of which could cause an unnecessary waste of time and resources if taken off line.

Threat Prevention

Besides assets, there are many other threats to an organization that should be addressed when using wireless LANs. When analyzing a threat, it is important to consider the probability that the particular vulnerability will be exploited. For example, if credit card processing is not a significant part of a business and has been sufficiently secured, the probability of an intruder obtaining credit card information may be quite low. In this case, more attention may be required for those areas where exposure is greatest and the probability is higher for an attack. A detailed analysis might uncover:

- The probability of a virus infecting the network through the wireless LAN is 70%
- The probability of a DoS attack against an access point on the wireless segment is 30%
- The probability of a mobile node having sensitive data that becomes compromised is 80%

Identifying vulnerabilities and assessing their likelihood of compromise will give the organization a method of determining how to proceed with wireless LAN security solutions, how much money to spend, and where to spend the money. The types of attacks that can be experienced and prevented because of a wireless LAN installation are discussed in the following pages.

Denial of Service (DoS)

It is simple to mount an RF jamming attack against a wireless LAN. One need only purchase a high-power, narrowband transmitter that transmits in the band you wish to jam and attach an antenna to this transmitter. "Jammers" fitting this description can easily be made portable through use of a few small cables and a battery. There is only one defense against an RF jamming attack: physical security. Keep the hacker as far from the facility housing your wireless LAN as possible through use of physical barriers and guards where appropriate. Erect tall chain-link fences that will effectively block the RF jamming signal. Using a hospital as an example, it is easy to see that the above measures are not always possible. There are almost always people roaming hospital halls that have not been authorized or authenticated in any way. Any of these people could be carrying an RF jamming device.

Denial of service attacks may also come in the form of packet flooding. Such an attack may be intentional through use of a packet generator or unintentional as seen when an employee decides to pull MP3 files from the Internet over the wireless network. In either of these scenarios, the access point would experience extremely high volume. SNMP traps can be configured on many enterprise class access points to notify the management system of such a high load so that the appropriate personnel may investigate the reason for the interruption in service. Wireless Intrusion Detection Systems, in most cases, would catch both the RF jamming attack and the data flooding attack if reference baselines have been properly measured and implemented.

Equipment Damage or Theft

Wireless infrastructure equipment is subject to theft, damage, or even replacement with more inexpensive gear if the pieces of equipment are not properly physically secured. For this reason, lockable mounting cases should be used wherever possible and wherever appropriate. Consider a public place such as a hospital where there may exist dozens of access points spread throughout remote parts of the facility. If these units are not placed out of sight or in locations where they cannot be found and easily removed, thieves can easily unplug these units and walk away with them unnoticed. Security cases are typically made of steel and have external antenna connectors so that they do not block the RF signal.

Asset protection should be qualified by value of each item type and its exposure level. Qualifying in this manner helps prioritize the focus of the security policy. Consider the following list of assets and their associated values:

- wireless bridge - $800
- access point - $600
- amplifier - $500
- workgroup bridge - $400
- antenna - $200
- PC card - $100

In a breakdown like this, you would first think that the most expensive items require the most security, but when you consider the exposure level, it changes things somewhat. Consider the fact that PC cards are far more numerous than access points in most cases, and they are far more likely to be damaged or stolen than an access point. There might be situations where the exposure level of an access point is similar to that of a PC card. It is not uncommon to see access points placed – unsecured – on top of a bookshelf in a classroom.

Unauthorized Access

Many wireless LAN administrators forget that there is more than one way to manage (access and configure) an access point. Modes of management may include HTTP, HTTPS, SNMP, TELNET, serial port, and custom applications. Once a hacker has gained access to a network infrastructure device such as an access point, there is no end to the damage that the intruder can accomplish. The first point of business for a hacker is typically making other entry points (security holes) into the network, otherwise known as "opening the front door". With wireless, opening the front door can be accomplished through use of management tools native to the access points themselves. Some access points have a feature that allows firmware and configuration files to be pushed from a single access point to many others with a single click of the mouse. This feature is great for updating the wireless network infrastructure as part of a management process, but is just as simple and powerful for hackers to use it to permanently damage a wireless network.

Consider a scenario in which unauthorized access to the network infrastructure is accomplished because the administrator did not change the default login settings on an access point. The hacker decides to *toy* with the network a bit just for fun. The hacker changes the name of the access point to "*You_have_been_hacked*" and instructs the access point to push the configuration file to all other access points in the network, which takes less than a minute. Shortly thereafter, a security guard sees the hacker and chases him off. Feeling spurned, the hacker returns later for a few more interesting games. This time, the hacker Telnets into the PoE switch, readies a command that will disable power on all ports, and proceeds to connect back into the unsecured access point through a browser. He tells the access point to push its firmware to all other access points, and just after initiating the firmware push, he instructs the PoE switch to cut power to all access points. Such action would likely cause the organization to have to disconnect and send each access point back to the manufacturer for repair because of permanent firmware damage, completely disabling the network for days or even weeks.

How much would it cost your organization to do without its wireless LAN for a few days or a few weeks? How much money would it cost to have all access points removed from their mounting points and shipped to the manufacturer? How much would it cost to have the access points reinstalled after their return from the manufacturer? These questions and many more like them must be considered when deciding how secure to make the wireless LAN. This is surely a worst-case scenario, but it is simple for a hacker to accomplish and should be weighed accordingly.

One way to reduce unauthorized access is to disable it through technical mechanisms during non-use hours. If there's no wireless LAN available to attack during off hours, administrators could rest easy during non-business hours knowing their wireless access is secure. It would be beneficial to monitor wireless LAN frequencies when authorized access points and bridges are disabled during non-use hours. This would give the administrator insight into attacks, rogues, or interference.

Credit Card Fraud

Any company that has an online storefront where financial information is gathered from customers and stored on company servers must be concerned about the protection of that data. Any time a hacker exposes the credit card information from a company's network and the media finds out, the reputation of that company becomes tarnished. Public trust in the company to protect the information they collect deteriorates, causing customers to question whether they should or should not do business with the company again.

When malicious hackers are working towards making a financial gain with a hacking attempt, credit card numbers are often one of the top targets. Most companies secure their customer's credit card data from Internet-sourced attacks, but many do not secure their network from the hacker down the street or in their parking lot or even in the office across the hall. It is a simple matter to get network access from the parking lot of many large corporations over a wireless LAN. This type of attack yields far better results than would an Internet-sourced attack due to the speed of the wireless LAN alone. Consider that most small businesses might have a T-1 (1.544 Mbps) to the Internet, whereas an inexpensive wireless LAN offers 11 Mbps of rated bandwidth to the parking lot. When credit card information is being passed over the wireless LAN unencrypted, hackers can simply eavesdrop and gather all of the information they need to commit credit card fraud or to tarnish the reputation of a company.

Identity Theft

Hackers with intent to make financial gains from their hacking attempts may target the type of information that will allow them to assume another person's identity. Identity theft occurs when someone obtains another person's personal information without the victim's knowledge in order to commit fraud or theft. Identity theft is the fastest growing white-collar crime in the United States today.

Once some pieces of personal information are obtained, a thief can attempt to open credit card accounts or bank accounts in the unsuspecting person's name. When the account balances are not paid, the delinquent accounts are then reported on the victim's credit reports and creditors will come to the unsuspecting person seeking payment for purchases they did not make or even know about.

Organizations that store their customers' personal records, account information, or their own employees' personnel files on a computer network can be susceptible to such an attack. Wireless networks simplify these attack scenarios, usually circumventing the physical security barriers that were in place with wired networks.

Corporate Secrets

A company's private information can come in many forms, such as:

- Financial reports
- Email between executives about company status
- Project schedules
- Source code for software
- Formulas for products
- Competitive information
- Human Resource information
- Design specifications for existing and future products
- Top-secret or confidential reports and documents
- Customer databases

There can be a multitude of locations on a computer network where each piece of information may be stored permanently or temporarily. There are also many ways a hacker can attempt to gain access to a network to obtain this information. As part of the risk assessment process, an organization should detail what information is critical to the company and would cause financial distress if the information were disclosed.

Personal Information Exposure

Exposure of personal information by an organization with unsecured networks can be disastrous for both the organization and the individual whose information is exposed. Consider a scenario in which a hacker gains access to a security monitoring service's computer network through an unsecured access point. By obtaining addresses and alarm codes, the hacker would be able to plan robberies against secured homes without much difficulty. When it was determined through an investigation that all of the robberies were tied together through the same monitoring service, the monitoring company would be liable because they did not properly secure their wireless LAN.

Malicious Data Insertion

Malicious data insertion can come in many forms. Viruses, invalid data, and illegal or unethical content can all lead to potential disasters for an organization. Viruses that are inserted into a network can lead to any number of problems. Highly publicized email viruses over the past few years have results in unwanted spam, computers becoming unusable, user information being stolen, etc. When an attacker inserts a virus into a network, trying to determine all the damage that has occurred and trying to remove the virus becomes a time consuming task. Viruses may also lead to network downtime and lost productivity or data because computers and network segments must be taken offline to isolate and remove the problem. Consider how easily a hacker can place a virus onto a wireless client in a peer-to-peer attack or onto a network server through a rogue access point. By renaming the virus file to something that will entice a network user to execute or open it, the hacker entices the user to unknowingly spread the virus.

Malicious data can also take the form of invalid data being inserted into databases or on web servers. Websites are a company's face to the world, and are often targeted for vandalism. By changing the contents of an organization's home page, the public is given the impression that their data may not be secure within the organization if the website cannot be secured. For databases, an incorrect price added to an e-commerce site can be a financial disaster for sales. The removal of a decimal point can suddenly turn a $1000.00 product into a $10.00 product. Consider an unsecured wireless LAN at a government building housing a SQL database server. If the SQL server is not secured (the default administrator password is blank), inserting false legal information or changing legal records is quite simple over the wireless segment.

Another malicious data insertion scenario would be when one employee has a personal vendetta against another. Using an unsecured, untraceable medium such as a wireless LAN, the disgruntled employee can easily set the screensaver or Windows background of another employee's computer to something unethical or offensive such as pornography. When another employee notices this and reports the violation of company policy to the Human Resources department, the target individual may lose his or her job with the company.

Legal Liabilities

Organizations that maintain or are entrusted to handle data for other organizations are often legally bound by contracts to protect that data. As an example, financial institutions handle particularly sensitive personal, credit, and investment data for thousands of people. Attackers exposing or stealing this data open these organizations to lawsuits as well as loss of customer loyalty.

As another scenario, consider a hacker who modifies product design drawings or notes prior to a new product going to production. Errors like this could cost a company millions of dollars in production costs alone, but when these costs are added to the litigation that would eventually ensue if the product were medically related, for example, the outcome could become staggering. Something as simple and inexpensive as unsecured wireless access could be the downfall of a corporation.

Third Party Attacks

Consider a scenario in which broadband Internet services have only recently become available in a neighborhood or in a business district. Before the introduction of broadband, neighborhoods had to suffice with dial-up service, and businesses had to pay excessive connectivity fees for business class Internet service. The new, low cost business class service is a welcomed change, allowing individuals and businesses to be more productive. It may even allow many individuals to start their own home-based business where they could not do so before.

Now consider that these homes and businesses install wireless LANs for the mobility and increased productivity that make wireless LANs such great products for today's SOHO businesses. Assume that a spammer (SPAM is unsolicited bulk email, and a SPAMMER is a person who sends such unsolicited bulk email) decides to use the broadband access over the wireless network to send 200,000 emails. By using your network, he does not have to pay for a connection that will be cut off by the Internet Service Provider for abuse. Instead, *your* connection gets disconnected for abuse after several complaints are received from spam recipients. The spammer may decide to use any or all of the broadband wireless access available in the area until each has been disconnected for abuse. The lack of security on a wireless network (even at home!) can cause loss of access privileges, legal liability, and other problems. Some states have laws against sending spam, and recipients may choose to prosecute the offenders since it can be proven that their connection was used to send such unsolicited email.

Illegal Data Insertion

Intellectual property theft is a constant in today's information technology driven world. Consider how easily stolen content could be placed onto a network through a wireless connection. Software piracy has reached new heights and unscrupulous individuals even use unsecured corporate networks for storage of their stolen software. Suppose a disgruntled employee notified the Business Software Alliance (BSA) just after placing illegally obtained copyrighted software onto their ex-employer's network over the wireless LAN. No one could prove where the software came from, but the company would be liable nonetheless. Such a violation could cost the company tens of thousands of dollars in fines for software piracy.

Costs

When planning for security, it is important to realize that there are many parts to the financial commitment that will need to be made. To implement a secure wireless network and to ensure that it continues to remain secure can have many associated costs. Each of the following should be addressed as part of a security cost analysis prior to moving forward with a wireless LAN installation.

- People
- Training
- Equipment
- Time

Failure to properly address these areas concerning wireless LAN security can impact other areas of the network that may have been relying on a secure and timely implementation.

People

The people involved in implementing secure wireless solutions may be employees or contractors. In either case, the number of people involved in the project can be considerable depending on the size and depth of the solution. Organizations may be required to hire trained wireless LAN administrators or train their existing staff adequately, and consultants may be hired to assist in the more difficult parts of the design and implementation. Consultants are usually expensive – especially those that know the technology well and have much experience – but may well save as much money as they cost. It is typically best to do most of the work in house, saving the most difficult parts for the consultants. It is important to involve a consultant in the beginning so that designs meet business goals and proper solutions are chosen. It should be an important issue that internal administrators learn as much as possible from the consultants while the consultant performs the necessary tasks so that a smooth hand-off can be accomplished.

Training

There are many different types of training to be accomplished as part of a wireless LAN initiative. Administrators, end users, physical security personnel, network security personnel, change management, and departmental management must all be trained for their role in dealing with wireless LAN's particular security issues.

Installation & Configuration

It is common to see individuals in the wireless LAN arena with experience configuring one particular vendor's equipment. This is true because the companies that these individuals have worked for are usually Value Added Resellers (VARs) for one particular manufacturer or another. Working as a site surveyor, installer, or security consultant in this manner is great experience, but being limited to a single vendor's equipment has its disadvantages. Unless the individual is trained on the particular equipment that will be used for their particular implementation, proper security configuration is unlikely, or at least more difficult and time consuming. Also, if a user has been trained on a particular vendor's equipment, yet does not understand the technology behind the particular brand, many issues related to wireless security will be missed.

While there are many books, such as this one, that deal with wireless LAN security, there is no substitute for hands-on training that would be received in a classroom, lab, or real world environment. Spending time getting familiar with configuration interfaces and settings of particular vendors' equipment is vitally important.

Network Operations Training

Once the installation is complete, monitoring, maintenance, auditing, and upgrading must be performed as part of the ongoing support of the wireless LAN. The departments that support the network may go by different names from company to company, but they all have one goal: the security, reliability, and uptime of the company's network and its users. It is critical that the people who are responsible for the security of the wireless LAN have the proper training to thwart attackers and protect company assets.

The training requirements of the network operations department will usually consist of hands on experience with the products being used. When large purchases are made directly from manufacturers, many vendors offer free product training. It is beneficial to take advantage of vendor supplied training where available.

As part of organizational policy, it should be determined how much training internal staff will receive on the technologies in use versus how much money will be spent on outside auditors and consultants. Consultants, as independent experts, should almost always be used to verify or validate designs and security implementations because the risks are too great not to have a second opinion from a qualified professional.

End-User Training

No security solution is useful if the end users won't or are unable to use it properly. Most wireless LAN security solutions require at least some software to be installed on client machines. These solutions usually require users to start an application to establish a secure network link to the network. Such a requirement can pose a problem to many users who have not been properly trained on the software or do not understand the importance of using the software. These users then pose a significant security risk to the organization. When end users do not establish a secure wireless connection to the network, all sorts of information becomes susceptible to being monitored by an unseen hacker. User logins to network services are the most commonly sought after trophies by hackers. FTP, Email, Telnet, HTTP, Directory Services, and countless others are among commonly stolen login information over unsecured wireless networks.

The cost of and time involved in training end users to use wireless LAN security solutions may be quite significant. If the organization has hundreds of users, then the cost of having each one attend a special 2-4 hour class on how and why to use the solution chosen by the organization might be quite high. Security is so critical with wireless networks that organizations should consider having each user acknowledge that they understand the risks associated with use of the wireless LAN and that they will comply with organizational policy regarding its use. Periodic spot checks and small group accountability tied to financial incentives are usually the most effective manner of enforcing compliance with corporate policy regarding wireless LAN solution use. When choosing a solution, an organization should keep in mind the user friendliness of the solution such that even the least technically astute individual at the organization can use the solution.

Equipment

The equipment used to secure a wireless LAN will vary depending on the size of the network, the number of wireless LAN users, the level and type of security needed, mobility requirements, the environment, user friendliness, existing network design, existing network security solutions in place, vendor partnerships, and budget.

Wireless LAN security equipment may come in the form of server or appliance hardware, client hardware, client and server software, and administration, management, and auditing tools. Each solution exists at a particular layer of the OSI model, which means that many solutions can be paired or "layered." Deciding which solution types will be used and how they interoperate with other solutions is the responsibility of the wireless security professional.

In order to illustrate how varied costs can be in deciding on a wireless LAN security solution, consider a small office environment as an example. Suppose this office had 20 wireless users, and, due to the traffic load per user, the company has decided to have 3 access points co-located in a relatively small office. In the most economic scenario, a static WEP key could be used on each access point and client PC card so that no other solutions would be necessary. This presents security, scalability, and management overhead problems (that will be discussed later), but there are no additional costs and a reasonable level of security is in place. Even SOHO class access points and PC cards would support this scenario. Supposing that this organization chose to go with a user-based authentication scheme, they would have to purchase enterprise class access points that support leading edge technologies, which would raise costs of the access points alone by 200%. PC cards would also have to be replaced with PC cards supporting these same technologies natively and/or software would have to be purchased to give the same result on the client side. This upgrade would raise the cost of the client side of the solution by approximately 100%. Next, a user authentication service would have to be installed which could cost more than all three access points and 20 PC cards combined. Software and appliance authentication solutions such as Kerberos, RADIUS, and others that support leading edge wireless authentication technologies are expensive. It is easy to see how security solutions can vary widely in costs. Opting for a happy medium in the scenario above might include purchase of access points that have integrated RADIUS and/or VPN server services.

The cost of solutions, the security they provide, return on investment (ROI), and the security necessary to meet business goals for an organization must be weighed in order to come up with an appropriate security solution. Costs can get out of control quickly when dealing with leading edge solutions. Consider a scenario in which an 802.1x / EAP solution is deployed as a data-link wireless LAN security solution. Then, an IPSec VPN solution is deployed at the network layer as an extra precaution against intrusion. Next, an SSH2 client/server solution (application layer) is deployed as a final security measure for the wireless LAN. Each of these solutions uses RADIUS, which then passes authentication requests to an Active Directory domain controller. This scenario would work just fine, but the costs would be astronomical, the administrative burden would be unbearable in all but the smallest implementations, and the client solution would be so user *un*friendly that few end users would be able to use it.

Time

Time is one of the greatest expenses with any wireless network installation. Few people realize the number of tasks that can consume time during a proper installation, and fewer people realize the time consumed for proper security. When planning the time and scheduling of a secure wireless LAN, some of the tasks that should be planned include:

- Infrastructure equipment staging and testing
- Infrastructure equipment installation
- User solution rollout
- Operational test of the security solution
- End user and help desk training
- End user support (helpdesk)
- Operational staff training
- Physical security training for security guards
- Integration of the solution into existing network management solutions
- Creation of maintenance procedures and schedules
- Wireless LAN Security Policy creation
- Security auditing and intrusion analysis
- Baseline testing and documentation
- Intrusion Detection & Security monitoring

This is far from a comprehensive list. These tasks must be coordinated and performed in the proper order (the list above does not denote any particular order). The order in which these tasks are performed is directly related to you're an organization's particular implementation. For small wireless LANs, these tasks may only take days. For large implementations, these tasks may take months even with a full complement of qualified staff tending to the tasks.

Impact Analysis

Consultants or administrators must ask, "If a malicious hacker were to gain access to the most precious asset of a company, what would the damage be to the company." As part of a risk assessment procedure, threats to business assets should be identified. The impact that such threats could have, if the threat resulted in a genuine incident, should be measured in direct and indirect financial terms. Such analysis should quantify the value of the business assets being protected to decide on the appropriate level of safeguards.

An impact analysis is intended to help understand the degree of potential loss (and other undesirable effects) that could occur. Such analysis should cover not only direct financial loss, but many other issues such as loss of customer confidence, reputation damage, regulatory effects, etc. Much of measuring what the impact to an organization will be upon exposure or exploitation of private information will be based on the scenario, the intent of the hacker, how the situation is handled by security administrators and managers, and the value of the organizational assets obtained by the hacker.

Public Access Networks

Many times, risk auditors may focus on the fact that valuable corporate assets are (or should be) only located on the corporate network behind appropriate security measures. Because of this perspective, the risk assessment and impact analysis may only address half the picture. When wireless networks are implemented, some of the most valuable information resides on exposed hosts through public access networks.

Public access wireless networks (Hot Spots), found in airports and coffee shops, require a whole new manner of thinking about security for mobile nodes. Consider a corporate executive in an airport hotspot checking their email over the unsecured wireless network. Any eavesdropper can obtain all usernames and passwords used by this individual for HTTP, POP, SMTP, FTP, TELNET, SQL, Instant Messengers, and others. Additionally, all traffic types, destinations, emails, and countless other types of information can be obtained through use of a simple protocol analyzer. After obtaining this information, the hacker has full access to the other person's accounts, wherever and whatever they may be. Keep in mind that this information may also provide a valid login to other portions of the corporate network. How many times do administrators use the same password for almost everything on the network?

Consider the fact that a hacker could take the corporate executive's email login information home, put them on his own computer, instruct the email client software to always leave a copy of the email on the server, and then have it check for new email every 1-2 minutes around the clock. The hacker would be able to get the email of the executive before the executive does, and the executive would never know that this situation exists. How many people are reading your email right now because you made the mistake of using an unsecured wireless LAN without proper security measures in place?

The wireless security policy should encompass situations where users may find themselves using wireless access outside the office. Peer-to-peer attacks are common with wireless LANs, and security solutions adequate to prevent these types of attacks should be mandated in policy. Each client protection solution should be thoroughly evaluated by the technology staff for intrusion prevention. In many cases having sensitive client-side data cannot be avoided but strict policy on not using corporate laptops on public access networks is certainly reasonable to create and adhere to.

Legal Implications

Sometimes the impact of an intruder is more far-reaching than might be expected. Instead of equating information theft or malicious information insertion with a dollar amount, consider equating it to legal liabilities. Consider what could happen to a corporate executive if a hacker placed false information in the right place on the network so that when other people find this information, those people would believe that the executive was guilty of serious offenses such as fraud or insider trading. There are new laws in place and under consideration that impose stiff penalties for executives of large, publicly held corporations who are convicted of ethical misconduct.

Consider a situation where a hacker has obtained an employee's email login information and created emails that looked as though they came from the unsuspecting target of the hack. These emails could be used for harassment, breaking business deals, or even committing illegal or fraudulent acts. There would be no way to prove that the emails did not come from the unsuspecting person.

Security Auditing

Wireless security audits identify flaws in wireless networks before the networks become exposed to a malicious threat. Organizations should conduct periodic security reviews (audits) to make sure that changes to the wireless network do not create new security holes. For low risk networks, a yearly audit may suffice, but for larger networks or networks that handle highly sensitive data (e.g. financial, legal, medical, etc.), a review each quarter, if not more often, may be necessary.

Independent Testing

It is advantageous for organizations to enlist the assistance of consultants to validate security solutions both in the design phase and after installation. Outside assistance provides a fresh perspective on potential risks. One mistake often made by companies hiring security consultants is that they are too quick to have the consultant come out for an audit. The rule of thumb here is to do all that you know how to do first, and *then* have the consultant come out to audit. Many companies will install a completely unsecured solution, and then request that an auditor document potential security holes. This approach wastes money because all the auditor can tell you is, "There are no security mechanisms in place to evaluate." The point of hiring a consultant in this capacity is to locate unseen or previously undocumented security holes and to suggest how to repair them. Internal security policy should mandate that external contract auditors be kept to a necessary minimum and used only to aid in security design and to locate security weaknesses in existing security solutions. There are also times when the security solution that is in place must be upgraded. This situation may lead to a wireless network redesign, and consultants should be used where necessary.

Sources of Information

There are instances in which hackers or independent wireless consultants looking for work will find a vulnerable wireless installation and exploit the weaknesses in some minor way. Their intent is often not malicious, and their exploits may go unnoticed. Occasionally, these people will notify an organization of the security hole in efforts to prove the network security is weak and subsequently to derive some income by performing wireless security consulting for the organization that owns the wireless LAN. It is beneficial, in either case, to listen to what these individuals have to say, and thank them for their time and efforts. The information they provide is often valuable in helping an organization secure their network further, and, in the case of a hacker providing the information, the cost is often free for the advice. What is not advisable, and would go against what most people recommend, is to report the minor incident to authorities (in the case of a malicious attack, the incident should be reported). Attempting to prosecute someone for the free advice they have provided may only provoke them into instigating further attacks that may then prove harmful.

In the case of hackers, there will always be some people that attempt to break into a network just to prove they can. If they freely notify an organization how they did it and no damage is discovered, in some cases it is more beneficial to acknowledge their help and fix the problem. This of course is entirely up to the organization, or any state of federal laws to which the organization is subject, as to how they should handle this type of situation.

Summary

This chapter discusses topics associated with building and implementing the General Policy portion of wireless network security policy. The General Policy consists of Getting Started, Risk Assessment, Impact Analysis, and Security Auditing. In the Getting Started section, the importance of resources, privacy, and intrusion issues are considered. Risk Assessment covers areas such as asset protection, threat prevention, legal liabilities, and costs. Impact analysis helps organizations understand the degree of potential and associated loss that could be involved with a network intrusion. The Security Auditing section recommends organizations periodically engage in security reviews involving independent consultants.

Key Terms

Before taking the exam, you should be familiar with the following terms:

Denial of Service (DoS)

impact analysis

risk assessment

Review Questions

1. Wireless LAN security policy can be categorized into which two of the following?

   A. Functional Policy

   B. Physical Policy

   C. Global Policy

   D. General Policy

   E. Solutions Policy

2. Why is end user training on the wireless LAN security solution that the organization chooses important?

   A. The wireless LAN security policy mandates training for end users

   B. End users are likely to place rogue wireless devices on the network if they are not properly trained on the security solution

   C. End users will often find themselves connecting to unsecured wireless networks such as public hotspots

   D. End users will not likely use security solutions they do not understand

3. Which of the following is a critical factor in the success of a wireless LAN security policy?

   A. Auditing

   B. Authentication

   C. Sponsorship

   D. Budget

   E. Planning

4. Asset protection, threat prevention, legal liabilities, and costs are areas associated with which of the following?

    A. Third party attacks

    B. Risk assessment

    C. Impact analysis

    D. Security auditing

5. A high-power, narrowband transmitter with a high-gain antenna can be used to perform what type of wireless LAN attack?

    A. Unauthorized access

    B. RF theft of service

    C. Denial of Service

    D. Malicious data insertion

6. A situation in which a hacker changes the access point configuration information would be considered which of the following types of attacks?

    A. Unauthorized access

    B. RF Jamming

    C. Equipment theft

    D. Man-in-the-middle

7. Which of the following are items that should be addressed as part of a security solution cost analysis?

    A. Equipment to be purchased

    B. Training of network staff

    C. Building floor plan

    D. General Security Policy

    E. Employee time spent on implementation

8. Why is a facility's physical security is important when implementing a secure wireless LAN solution?

    A. Wireless LAN equipment can be stolen or replaced

    B. Intruders could do a risk assessment of the network

    C. Physical security prevents Internet-based wireless attacks

    D. Rogue wireless equipment can be placed on the network

9. What is the term for the process of understanding the risks and potential losses associated with a network intrusion?

    A. Intrusion Study

    B. Hacker Impact Exam

    C. Intruder Investigation

    D. Impact Analysis

10. Organizations should perform which of the following tasks periodically to make assure that changes to the network do not create security holes?

    A. Security Audits

    B. Risk Searches

    C. Impact Studies

    D. Intrusion Tests

Answers to Review Questions

1. A, D
2. C, D
3. C
4. B
5. C
6. A
7. A, B, E
8. A, D
9. D
10. A

Functional Policy: Guidelines & Baselines

CWSP Exam Objectives Covered:

❖ Explain the purpose and goals of the following wireless LAN security policies:

- Password policy

- User training

- On-going review (auditing)

- Acceptable use & abuse policy

- Consistent implementation procedure

- Centralized implementation and management guidelines and procedures

❖ Explain necessary items to include in the creation and maintenance of a wireless LAN security checklist

❖ Describe and recognize the importance of asset management and inventory procedures for wireless LANs

❖ Explain the importance of including wireless LANs in existing change management programs

In This Chapter

Policy Essentials

General Guidelines

Baseline Practices

Policy Essentials

At a minimum, every security policy should have sections that cover the following topics:

- Password policies
- Networking staff and end user training requirements
- Acceptable use
- Consistent implementation / staging procedures
- Readily available implementation and management procedures
- Regular audits and penetration tests by independent professionals

Each of the topics will be described in detail in the following sections.

Password Polices

Passwords are the most widely used method of identifying and authenticating users as they access a computer system; however, the number of ways a password can be compromised seems endless:

- Someone can eavesdrop on a public network (Hot Spot) to obtain the username/password of another person as they attempt to access the network
- An attacker can mount a dictionary attack against a network's authentication server
- Users may loan their passwords to other users
- Users may leave their password out in the open for others to find (the sticky note approach)
- Users may choose passwords that are easy to guess, such as their name, birth date, or just use the default password ('password' for example)

Guidelines

Network protection is only as strong as the weakest link in the security chain, so practicing good password procedures is a key defense in protecting valuable information resources. The objective for choosing a password is to make the password as difficult as possible for a hacker to guess or even stumble upon. The only alternative left for an attacker to use should be a dictionary attack of known words or a brute force attack where all combinations of letters, numbers, and punctuation are attempted. A search of this sort, even conducted on a machine that could try one million passwords per second (most machines can try less than one hundred per second), would require over one hundred years to complete, IF the password is properly created and "strong". Dictionary attacks can be thwarted by setting an account disable function that limits the number of unsuccessful login attempts. This setting creates administrative overhead in some cases, but the security factor usually outweighs the added burden of users contacting the network administration department.

Consider a more rigorous password policy for systems with extremely sensitive information. Administrators should periodically attempt network intrusion through security holes created due to violations of password policy at the organization. (*Hint*: Don't forget to look under the keyboard for a sticky note or in the top desk drawer for a printed list)

In many small office environments, it is common to have a group of close acquaintances or friends. These types of environments give way to lax security practices. For example, as part of a password audit, an administrator might ask Fred (Jane's close friend) for Jane's password because he needs to get something off of her computer while she's out sick. What would the result be in your organization?

Choosing a strong password

What to do:

- Use a password that is mixed case, has punctuation, and uses alpha and numeric digits
- Use something that can be remembered without being written down
- Force periodic (e.g. monthly) password changes through network security mechanisms
- Lockout accounts after 5 unsuccessful login attempts

- Make sure all passwords are at least 8 characters in length

What NOT to do:

- Use a user name, first name, or last name
- Use a pet's name, child's name, or spouse's name
- Use number combinations such as telephone numbers, social security, birth dates, or home address numbers
- Use a common word found in the dictionary
- Allow passwords to be reused

Some market-leading security solutions pass the username in clear text over the wireless link. The password is either encrypted before being sent or only a hash derived from the password is sent. In either case, the problem remains that one piece (the username) of the two-piece puzzle (username/password) is easily captured by a wireless packet analyzer. If the password is not a strong one, the chance of a successful attack against the security solution is high.

Training

There are two main classes of wireless LAN users that must be sufficiently trained to support their role in an organization: network staff and end users. Network staff will also be end users in most cases, but they play a much more involved role in wireless LAN security. For this reason, network staff must receive much more training in order to fulfill their organizational role. End-user training should not be overlooked, and is an ongoing process.

Networking Staff

Network personnel responsible for wireless LAN security need to understand many subject areas including intrusion techniques, wireless security policy, and current security solutions, in addition to having a solid grasp on basic wireless LAN functionality and technology. If an IT professional does not understand the basics of how a wireless LAN functions, that person cannot, and should not, be expected to understand how to *secure* a wireless LAN.

Since today's wireless LAN market is rapidly changing, these individuals will likely find themselves deeply involved in wireless LAN technology whether they originally intended to be or not. Wireless LANs, with their multifaceted array of technologies and standards, can consume almost all of an IT professional's time. There are administrative, security, integration, and design issues at every turn. Just keeping pace with the market and new standards is a challenge, but when required to defend against every new attack, the task can be almost overwhelming. It can be devastating to an organization that deploys an enterprise class wireless LAN if every type of wireless attack is not addressed and defended. After completion of adequate training, network staff should agree *in writing* to strictly follow organizational policy on wireless LAN use and to aid in helping end users do the same.

End Users

End users, especially those working in a non-technical role, must have adequate training in order to properly implement security controls on their computers. End users are notorious for not using proper client-side security controls because the process may be inconvenient or unfamiliar. In order to overcome this hurdle, a reasonable amount of end user training on how to use the wireless LAN security solution chosen by the organization is needed. The end user should learn, as part of the training, that it only takes one person not following organizational policy to create a large security hole that can be exploited by an attacker. After completion of the training, end users should agree in writing to strictly follow organizational policy on wireless LANs and remind other end users to do the same.

End user security training is often overlooked in the measure of Total Cost of Ownership (TCO) of a wireless LAN. Consider the fact that every user of a wireless LAN must have a wireless client device (PCMCIA, PCI, USB, etc.), the necessary security solution (hardware or software or both), and must be trained to use these tools and report possible security breaches.

Usage

Since wireless LANs are a half-duplex medium, they present a throughput challenge. Wireless LANs provide enough bandwidth to even a large group of users for such tasks as checking email, chatting on instant messengers, general network file sharing, and browsing web pages. Sometimes end users do not consider that bandwidth intensive applications such as FTP, peer-to-peer file sharing, and streaming video should only be performed over the wired LAN, especially when there are many wireless stations on each access point in a given environment. This unintentional denial of service attack can cause the wireless LAN to perform badly for all users, effectively negating the reason the wireless LAN was installed. Additionally, when users following wireless LAN policy are denied network services, they are unable to reap the productivity gains that are part of the efficiencies of a wireless LAN. This type of unintentional attack costs organizations time and money.

To prevent such unintentional denial of service occurrences, there should be a section in the wireless LAN security policy regarding acceptable use of the wireless LAN. This section should define what scenarios constitute proper use as well as abuse. Wireless LAN management software can monitor throughput on any given access point – sometimes even per user. This type of tool will provide a network administrator a means of checking current use against known baseline activity in order to locate offenders (another reason for proper baseline documentation). Offenders that have completed organizational training and understand what constitutes acceptable use might be subject to losing their wireless LAN connectivity privileges. The reality of this is that end users are rarely aware of the throughput issues their network activities cause, so some leniency and additional training might be necessary for 'power users'.

Implementation and Staging

Having a consistent implementation procedure is a key function in maintaining wireless LAN security – especially in the face of high employee turnover. It is common for a network administrator to place a wireless LAN infrastructure device onto the network without having first staged and configured the device to meet the organization's security policy. Such disregard for security is, in effect, like placing a rogue access point or bridge on the network. To battle this problem, guidelines on how and when to stage and install each type of infrastructure and client device should be part of the functional security policy.

Procedures

In many companies, new employees are required to read the company policy and later sign that they have read and agree to follow it. Many times, due to the size of the policy book, new hires simply sign the agreement paperwork and that is the last they see of the policy manual. Sometimes they may get to keep their own copy of the manual, but when there is sensitive information in the policy manual, such distribution is rare. Instead, the Human Resources department or departmental managers keep the policy manual behind lock and key, completely inaccessible to the very employees who are required to abide by such policy. It is important that network administrators have the information provided by the company security policy readily available so that they may verify procedural steps while performing their daily tasks. Many times, companies pay astronomical amounts of money to have a very thorough security policy written, and then the policy is not kept up to date and not used by employees. The purpose of the policy manual is to serve as a set of guidelines and procedures for employees to follow on a daily basis. If the policy manual is not accessible to the employees, what good is it? For these reasons, many companies have intranet websites dedicated to presenting the security policy and update it as needed.

Audits

In order to find security holes that are left because of incomplete security solutions, improperly configured solutions, violations of password policy, or wireless network abuse, internal and external audits are a necessary part of wireless network security. Internal audits, performed by network security staff, will usually find most policy violations, but holes in security solutions usually require employing an independent wireless security professional. It is important to perform these audits regularly – as part of a schedule – so that security is kept up-to-date. It should be a common practice to perform unannounced audits both by internal and external staff. This assures that administrators and users are performing their security duties properly.

General Guidelines

Wireless network segments should always be treated as unsecured means of data transit. When passing data over any wireless segment, the following rules should be applied:

- Encrypt email
- Use HTTPS for web logins where possible
- Use SSH2 instead of telnet where possible
- Use Secure FTP (SSH2 or SSL) for file transfers
- Verify the latest operating system updates or service packs are installed

Something to keep in mind is that even though a network infrastructure may be secured, there are times that hackers can do things to thwart this security, such as placing a rogue access point through which to connect to the network, or reconfiguring legitimate access points for optional security. For this reason, it is always a good idea to have end users use secure applications as a fail safe for a secure networking environment.

Security Checklist

As a part of creating policy regarding consistent wireless LAN security implementation procedures, it is advisable to make security checklists for use by network administrators. This type of checklist would include all of the items to verify in configuration and installation of particular wireless LAN devices. These items might include the following details:

- Access point and bridge configuration settings
- Client-side software installation and settings
- Physical security when mounting access points and bridges
- End user security solution training

When the network administrator has verified that these items have been performed and documented properly, the wireless device or client may be added to the network. Not having a checklist introduces guesswork as part of normal procedures, possibly leaving security holes on a daily basis.

Available Network Resources

Many administrators make the mistake of assuming that all network services must be available to the wireless LAN segment just because the wireless segment is a part of the network where authorized users connect. It is not always advisable – or necessary – to allow wireless users full access to the network in the same manner as the wired network stations. The reason for this consideration is that, since wireless LANs present such an added security risk, that added risk may be significantly reduced by eliminating the availability of certain services to the wireless segment.

Due to limited bandwidth on the wireless LAN, only particular services have adequate performance to warrant use over the wireless LAN. Limiting network resources may not be a problem in all environments for this reason.

Asset Management

Many large organizations have implemented rigid hardware and software inventory control mechanisms. Since enterprise class wireless LAN hardware can be quite expensive and since much of it is very small and lightweight, this equipment can be easily stolen if not firmly secured. For this reason, as part of physical security policy, it is necessary to record all wireless LAN hardware for periodic inventory. Employees should be required to sign for the hardware they receive, showing that they are responsible for its care while the equipment is in the employee's possession.

Many employees may want to opt for using their own laptop computers in lieu of corporate laptops since they do not want the added responsibility, but such allowances are generally not good security practice. Only corporate information should be stored on corporate laptops and wireless security solutions deemed appropriate by corporate policy should be used on these corporate laptops at all times. These laptop computers should not be allowed onto public access networks (Hot Spots) without appropriate security solutions in place.

Periodic Inventory

In small organizations, it may be feasible to implement a periodic inventory schedule where all users of corporate wireless client devices verify that they have physical possession of the unit. Additionally, it is a good practice to periodically check infrastructure devices to make sure they are both present and are the correct unit (e.g. the actual unit that was installed, and not a cheap unit substituted by the thief that stole the real unit). Attackers sometimes replace expensive access points with inexpensive ones, and without proper intrusion detection measures in place, administrators might not notice. In large organizations, this type of inventory might be impossible so other inventory control measures might have to be implemented.

Change Management

Wireless LANs should be a part of the existing corporate change management procedures. There are two things to consider about change management with wireless LANs. First, the security policy itself should be periodically evaluated for relevance and modified when necessary. Second, once a secure wireless LAN infrastructure is in place, any changes to it (for troubleshooting or growth purposes) should be documented and approved by proper corporate authorities. The primary purpose behind notifying staff of impending change is so the changes themselves may be evaluated for security purposes. It is almost always much less time consuming to implement a change on-the-fly, but doing so usually introduces unforeseen security holes. It might be days or weeks before such security holes are found, giving hackers more than ample time to intrude.

Spot-checks & Accountability

Network staff and end users must be accountable for properly implementing wireless LAN security mechanisms at all times. Some of the most effective methods for ensuring such accountability may include:

- Thoroughly training end-users
- Spot checking for internal policy adherence
- Tying adherence and enforcement of policy to departmental compensation

Having internal network security staff spot check end users and other network staff on the proper use of wireless LAN security solutions is one of the most effective, low-cost methods of ensuring adherence to corporate security policy. Tying small group (such as departmental) compensation (such as quarterly bonuses) to security policy adherence is an easy way to get employees to spot-check one another other on a daily basis. Consider that one employee with a lax attitude toward security could cost another employee a quarterly bonus. Such incentives can have a dramatic effect on peer pressure to understand, implement, and enforce corporate security policies.

Baseline Practices

Baseline practices should be considered the minimum security "to do" list. This is to say that, from a technical standpoint, "If you do these things, you will eliminate 95% of all wireless LAN security holes." This list may grow over time due to changes in technology, but is considered a thorough list at the time of this writing.

SSIDs

The default SSID should be changed on all access points. The service set identifier (SSID) is meant to differentiate networks from one another. Access points are all set to a default SSID when they are first purchased. For example, all Linksys access points are set to the network name of *linksys,* and all Cisco access points have a default SSID of *tsunami.* These default SSIDs are widely documented on the Internet and are well known by any hacker. When access points are first installed, the SSID should be changed to something cryptic and not something that could be used to determine the company to whom the access point belongs. Changing the SSID to something meaningful such as a company name, or which department the access point belongs to can provide an intruder valuable information, as illustrated in Figure 7.1 below. For example, if your company is named ABC Financial Corp., and you set the SSID as the same in your access points, any intruder will know there could be financial information on the network the access point is attached to. The SSID should be created with the same rules as creating a strong password.

By default, an access point broadcasts the SSID several times per second in beacons. By listening for these beacons, intruders are provided the opportunity to gather the SSIDs of any access point within range. "Closing the system" by not broadcasting SSIDs in beacons prevents intruders from passively locating the network. *Closed system* features are not part of the 802.11 series of standards and thus not supported on all access points. When SSIDs are not broadcast, operating systems like Windows XP do not automatically discover the SSID and configure the computer's NIC. This configuration causes a potential intruder to put forth a little more effort to gain access to the network – something an intruder may not be willing to do. Unless your organization is protecting something that a hacker *knows* is valuable, most hackers will attack the "low hanging fruit" first, meaning that any networks that are broadcasting an SSID will be the first targets for intrusion.

FIGURE 7.1   Listening for SSIDs

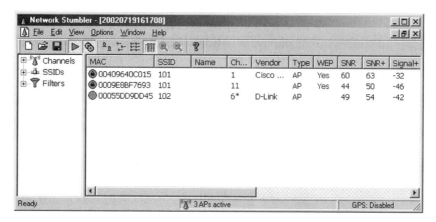

Even when SSID broadcasting is disabled, the SSID can be discovered using utilities that perform active scanning (sending probe request frames) or wireless packet analyzers (which hear all frames types). Sometimes disabling SSID broadcasting may go against business goals, such as with public wireless networks. These networks must be open to allow customers to easily access network resources (usually Internet access). The protection SSIDs provide is only minimal, but when SSIDs are not properly configured, they can present a large security hole.

MAC filters

MAC filters should not be relied upon to prevent unauthorized access to the wireless LAN. MAC address filtering is another method by which the IEEE 802.11 task group attempted to secure wireless networks. The media access control (MAC) address of a network interface card (NIC) is a 12 digit hexadecimal value that is supposed to be unique to every network card in the world (there have been some cases of duplicate MAC addresses). In theory, because every card has its own unique address, it is possible to control network access using these unique addresses. In the real world, and as explained earlier in the Intrusion unit of this book, it is both simple and common for a hacker, a common user, or even an employee of an organization to spoof (emulate) the MAC address of another NIC. This method is commonly used with residential gateways to circumvent the Internet Service Provider's MAC filter, which disallows multiple computers on a single physical connection. In a residential gateway, simply typing the MAC address into a web-based form via the built-in web server can change the MAC address that the ISP sees. In a wireless network, the same function is accomplished by making a change to the Windows registry. By default, the Windows registry has no entry for the MAC address of each known NIC. This entry is called "NetworkAddress", and when added to the registry for a particular NIC, changes the value of the MAC address (as known by Windows) to whatever arbitrary 12 digit hexadecimal value the user deems necessary. Figure 7.2 below shows a screenshot of a MAC address listing in a Windows registry.

FIGURE 7.2 MAC Spoofing Using the Windows Registry

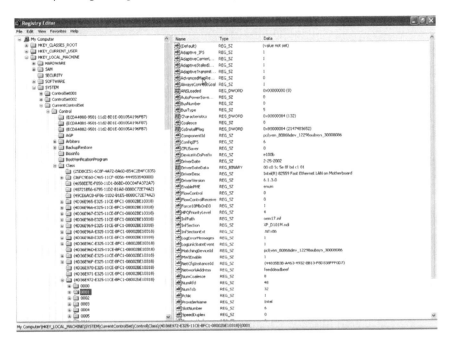

When there is a *NetworkAddress* entry in the registry, its value is used when sending frames over the network. When there is no *NetworkAddress* entry in the registry, Windows uses the MAC address programmed into the ROM on the NIC. There are easy-to-use software utilities on the market for making this change so that a user does not have to find the proper registry key. A sample screenshot from a MAC spoofing software utility is shown in Figure 7.3. A reboot is required after setting a new MAC address, whether in the registry directly or through a software utility.

FIGURE 7.3   Sample MAC Spoofing Software Utility

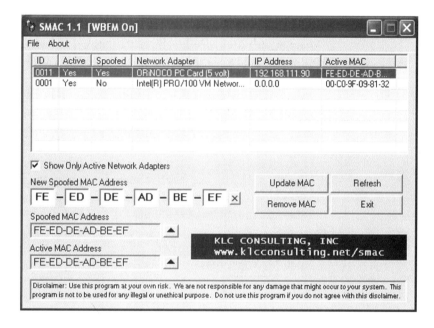

A common scenario is for an intruder to go to the target's location during business hours and capture a series of wireless frames, which hold all of the information needed in order to circumvent MAC filters. After capturing these wireless frames using a wireless protocol analyzer (WildPackets AiroPeek or Network Associates Sniffer Pro Wireless, for example), the intruder can go home and sort out information found in the packet trace. After figuring out which units are the access points and which are the clients by reviewing the BSSIDs (the MAC address of an access point) found in the packet trace, the intruder could then find SSIDs and MAC addresses used by clients. IP subnet information will also be recorded for the purpose of making a useful network connection once associated to the target access point. After recording this data, the intruder would return to the site at a time when security is minimal and no authorized users are on the premises.

In addition to how easily a MAC address can be spoofed, MAC address authentication (filtering) has high administrative costs due to a lack of scalability. Administrators must record and maintain records of all wireless devices' MAC addresses that are permitted to access the network. The records must be kept either on all access points collectively, in a RADIUS server, or in an LDAP compliant or compatible database to which the RADIUS server sends requests for authentication. Any time a device is added, lost, or stolen, the wireless network administrator must update the database of allowed devices.

Tying MAC addresses to user authentication is a scalable and reasonable use of MAC filtering, but when an IT staffer is required to maintain the database manually in all access points, such a practice presents an unbearable administrative burden. For a small company or SOHO environment, MAC filtering may be an appropriate addition to a wireless security solution, but it is not an end-all solution. Because the tools necessary to spoof a MAC address are easily attainable, other security solutions should be considered.

The question is often raised, "What will happen if two stations have the same MAC address on the network?" On a network using hubs, this is not a problem for the network infrastructure, but operating systems and applications relying on unique MAC addresses may have problems. Since most corporate environments use switches for the added throughput, segmentation, and features, it is important to address the effect on switches. The answer in a switched environment depends on what the manufacturer chose to do in their switching software. Some manufacturers even vary among product lines as to how they handle duplicate MAC addresses.

There are two basic ways duplicate MAC addresses can be handled in a switched environment: allow or disallow. When a switch allows duplicate MAC addresses, it will forward traffic destined to that MAC address to both ports (if they are on different ports) where each MAC address resides. In this way, the switch is acting like a hub for that MAC address. When a switch disallows duplicate MAC addresses, it replaces its physical port entry in the switching table when the MAC is seen as being located on a different port than it previously knew about. In a wireless environment, it is important that switches disallow duplicate MAC address entries. To do otherwise would mean that as wireless users roam, eventually the switch would be broadcasting all packets to almost all ports connected to access points.

Using Static WEP

Static WEP may be appropriate for SOHO environments, but not for enterprise wireless LAN implementations. The goal of WEP was to provide an equivalent level of security as that which is normally found in a wired LAN. When static WEP is used, strong keys should be created that are *unrelated* to the following:

- Organization's name, address, or phone number
- Wireless LAN's SSID
- Access points' or bridges' model number(s) or manufacturer's name
- Manufacturer default WEP keys

WEP keys are not quite as easily compromised as the media reports. Given the quantity of data needed to crack a WEP key, WEP is suitable for SOHO environments when strong keys are used. SOHO environments typically do not need scalability, and the traffic that is typically passed over the wireless LAN is quite small when compared to enterprise environments. When implementing a static WEP-based security solution, the largest key size available that is supported by the hardware should be used unless it presents an interoperability problem between multiple vendors' equipment.

Default Configuration Settings

The default configuration settings on all access points should be changed. To help build a useful network as quickly and as easily as possible, the manufacturer pre-configures all access points to certain default settings. As a result, the default configurations minimize security feature use. The Wi-Fi Protected Access (WPA) interoperability certification, created by the Wi-Fi Alliance and discussed in more detail in the Solutions unit, will address shipping wireless infrastructure equipment with no security features (encryption, network authentication, management login, etc.) enabled. WPA will require the person who is configuring the access point to step through a simple procedure of setting up security as part of the initial configuration.

Installing an access point or bridge in default configuration can lead to many problems, and an administrator must think specifically about infrastructure reconfiguration attacks. An infrastructure reconfiguration attack is a situation in which attackers obtain management access to wireless infrastructure devices such as access points and bridges. In so doing, hackers are able to take down the network, change security measures or poke holes in security mechanisms to allow unauthorized network access, or even prevent authorized use of the wireless network.

When an adept hacker finds a rogue access point, the first network resource they will attempt to gain control over is the wireless network infrastructure itself. Consider that an attacker can go through a rogue access point first to get an IP address, and second to locate authorized access points on the network. The next step is to use Telnet, HTTP, SSH, or SNMP to remotely control or manage the wireless infrastructure devices. This action can have the effect of converting all authorized access points into rogues. To prevent this type of attack, the default username and password (if there is one) should be changed on all infrastructure devices before the device is installed.

Firmware Upgrades

Firmware upgrades can provide new security functionality and compatibility, but often they contain bug fixes or security patches as well. Periodic firmware upgrades can often prevent attackers from exploiting a well-known security hole in older firmware. There is always a chance that a firmware upgrade could introduce a new security problem, but at least most brand new security holes are not readily documented for hackers to find. Subscribing to vendor newsletters is a good way to keep up to date on what patches are available. Patches always come with release notes documenting bugs fixed as well as features added. With enterprise wireless LAN equipment vendors, new firmware releases may be frequent. Frequent firmware upgrades may be too time-consuming for administrators responsible for large installations. Checking the firmware release notes helps administrators reduce unnecessary wastes of time.

Firmware should be upgraded as necessary for the following devices:

- Access Points
- Wireless Bridges
- Client Devices
- Client or Workgroup Bridges
- Enterprise Wireless Gateways
- Enterprise Encryption Gateways

Firmware upgrades are suggested as soon as possible in order to gain any of the following security features:

- TKIP (or similar key rotation protocol) support
- Kerberos support
- 802.1x/EAP (-TLS, -TTLS, -LEAP, -PEAP) support
- WPA compliance
- Advanced Encryption Standard (AES) support
- Virtual Private Network (VPN) support
- Rogue access point detection
- RADIUS or LDAP support
- Role-based access control

When performing a firmware upgrade, it is a good practice to test the end-to-end functionality of the firmware (either in a lab environment or in a non-critical production area) prior to rolling it out enterprise wide.

Rogue Equipment

Anytime rogue wireless equipment is present in a network, the incident should be considered a serious security breach. In many cases, employees who want immediate wireless connectivity at their organization install rogue access points. Also, portable laptops may incorporate a wireless LAN client with utilities that employees feel compelled to use. When these employees realize that access points are very inexpensive, they can purchase and install their own onto the company network without understanding the security risks or knowing that they need permission for such installations, although this should be well documented in the corporate security policy. Certainly network administrators could lock down switches to only support a specific MAC address on each port, but a savvy network user that understands MAC spoofing could easily circumvent such a security measure.

Even the strongest wireless security solutions are rendered useless when a single rogue is added to the network. Rogues can be installed by company employees who want wireless access, or by skilled attackers who want to gain access to the network without being seen. In the case of an attacker, he or she must first gain access to the premises through some type of social engineering or lack of physical security. Upon doing so, the intruder can then locate a live Cat5 port on a switch or hub that the access point can be connected to, preferably close to a window so the signal can be received by a client from outside the building.

Eliminating Rogues

Eliminating rogue wireless equipment is a multi-step process, parts of which are ongoing to ensure the security of the network. The process includes:

- Setting Corporate Policy Regarding Rogue Equipment
- Network Administrator Training
- Help Desk & End User Training
- Intrusion Detection Systems & Audits

Rogue Equipment Policy

Would your organization allow someone – end user or IT professional – to install his or her own DHCP server on the wired network? Such an example is the equivalent to allowing a SOHO wireless access point to be installed onto the wired segment of any corporate network. Rogue equipment installations of any kind should be clearly prohibited in the corporate wireless security policy, and offenders of such policy should be disciplined according to company policy for putting corporate assets at risk. A less-considered topic in this area is rogue ad hoc networks. Corporate computer users should not use wireless ad hoc configurations due to the peer attack risk.

A mistake once a rogue access point is discovered is to destroy or reset the rogue access point. One should certainly control the possible damage done or being done by the access point, but the logs within the access point may provide excellent evidence of what damage has already been done. The first thing to do when finding a rogue access point is to unplug its wired Ethernet port from the network. Secondly, logs should be saved, and screen captures of association tables and traffic measuring parameters made if possible.

Network Administrator Training

Proper training of the people who are responsible for the wireless network is essential. It is important to note that, just because an organization does not have a wireless LAN, or even if they have no plans to implement a wireless LAN, it is still important for network security administrators to understand wireless LAN technology and security risks. When an attacker wants access to a network that has no wireless connectivity, it may be his first choice of attack method to place a rogue device onto the LAN. At today's low prices for wireless hardware, and the ability of anyone to buy inexpensive, non-mainstream solutions such as 900 MHz and FHSS radio equipment on Internet auction sites, network administrators must be alert to all of the techniques of a wireless attacker.

Help Desk & End User Training

Help Desk personnel should be trained both in wireless LAN technology, security risks, and security solutions. Being able to recognize when a user is connected to a rogue device or assisting end users with properly configuring wireless security solutions is a key part of help desk activities. End users should attend a user-level class (whether classroom-based or computer-based) on how to properly implement the wireless LAN security solution that has been chosen by the organization. Part of this training should encompass recognizing rogue connections, understanding why not to add rogue devices to the network, and consequences both to the organization and to the individual if network security policy is not followed.

Intrusion Detection Systems & Audits

Wireless network management includes tasks such as monitoring and auditing the network for rogue wireless devices. If an intrusion detection system (IDS, discussed later in this section) is not used, an administrator will need a wireless analyzer capable of locating any rogue devices as he walks the premises of the entire organization on a regular basis – daily or weekly. There are many such specialty hardware devices and software packages produced for this and other purposes on the market today. Wireless packet analyzers are best suited for this type of manual procedure.

Before beginning a manual network scan, an organization must have an up-to-date listing of which access points and bridges *should* be on the network and the MAC addresses and SSIDs of these devices. After the scan, a comparison can be done to compare what is actually found in the search against what should have been found. When performing this type of scan, all physical locations of the company must be searched, not just those that are *supposed* to have wireless access. Rogues are most likely to be added by employees in those areas that do not have wireless access already. Also, because intruders will be likely to plant rogue devices near windows so that the signal can reach the parking lot or other remote location, the surrounding (outside) areas of the facility should be scanned regularly.

One thing most inexperienced administrators miss is scanning for rogue devices in all frequency bands that wireless LAN equipment uses. Most administrators would search for Wi-Fi compliant devices in the 2.4-2.5 GHz band, when a skilled hacker would use a 900 MHz system or 5 GHz system. Another hacker approach is to use FHSS systems as rogues instead of DSSS systems. An IDS would be useful in detecting and alerting administrators as to any new and unauthorized MAC addresses (access points have MAC addresses) on the network, so frequency and spread spectrum technology use would be irrelevant as long as the IDS is able to catch the rogue device.

Outdoor Bridge Security

Outdoor wireless LAN bridge links may often span miles. This use of wireless to connect remote locations can allow an intruder the opportunity to remain undiscovered while hacking into the network through one or both of the bridges. Bridges may act as both a bridge and an access point simultaneously, so an intruder may only need a directional antenna and a client device to make a wireless connection to the bridge. Bridges should be secured the same way as access points – no default settings and strong authentication and encryption. If possible, client connectivity at the bridge should be disabled. Some wireless bridges do not allow this functionality to be disabled, so it may go against corporate security policy to even use such equipment. Check with the bridge manufacturer if it is not clear whether this functionality can be disabled. Use of 802.1x/EAP or Kerberos authentication may also be an option of keeping unauthorized clients off of bridge links. Clear text transmissions should not be allowed to pass between wireless bridges at any time. Passwords, SNMP strings, and other valuable network security credentials could easily be compromised.

In addition to being susceptible to eavesdropping and unauthorized client connectivity, a wireless bridge installation can be compromised through rogue bridges. Rogue bridges can be placed onto a network at a range of several miles in some cases, depending on the strength of the antennas being used. In doing so, the attacker changes the network from point-to-point to point-to-multipoint while remaining completely unnoticed.

RF Cell Sizing

Accurate cell sizing of the RF output generated by an access point or bridge can aid in preventing war drivers from being able to locate your wireless network. Figure 7.4 illustrates a wireless network containing an access point emitting the maximum power available in the unit. As this diagram illustrates, the cell overflows far beyond the physical security parameters put in place by the organization. Any war driver passing by would easily detect the signal and locate the network.

Note that not all access points or bridges offer the administrator the ability to control output power. Such functionality may be one of the criteria in deciding what brand of equipment to use.

FIGURE 7.4   Oversized WLAN cell

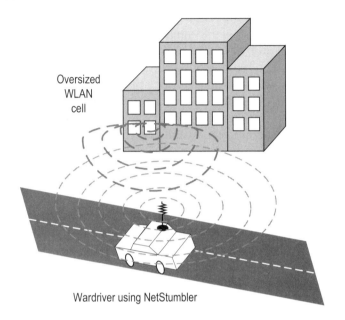

Wardriver using NetStumbler

The output power of a cell should be limited to only the coverage area that is required as defined by the site survey. Emitting more power to cover unnecessary areas only provides a war driver a target for attack. Limiting the output power of a cell does not guarantee that a network will not be located. Figure 7.5 shows the same cell with the power now reduced, but the war driver is now using a more directional antenna to locate wireless networks.

FIGURE 7.5   Correctly sized WLAN cell that is still vulnerable

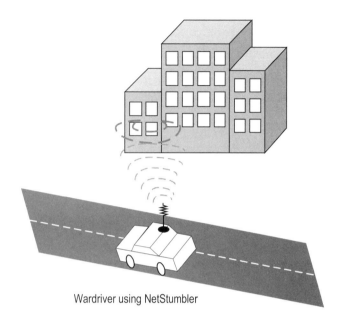

Wardriver using NetStumbler

Because administrators will not know what type of antennas a war driver may be using or how powerful they are, no assumptions should be made about security based on the size of the cell. Within a facility, part of the site survey should include the most appropriate antennas that should be used to get the necessary coverage while still considering the security risks.

Once the wireless cells have been properly configured for power output, administrators should attempt a footprint analysis to determine how easily the network can be targeted from outside the facility. This analysis involves using omni and directional antennas while walking around the facility to determine what distance a war driver would need to be from the facility in order to locate the network. In an office complex where buildings are close together or the building in which the organization resides is open to public access, the distance for someone to pick up the signal is usually minimal.

SNMP Community Strings

SNMP community strings should be changed or disabled. Most enterprise class wireless LAN vendors ship wireless LAN infrastructure devices such as access points and bridges with Simple Network Management Protocol (SNMP) enabled. Default read and write passwords are clearly documented in the users manual. Many administrators make the mistake of securing Telnet and HTTP management interfaces, but leave SNMP settings in the default configuration. This lack of configuration opens the door to attackers using SNMP management software to control these devices in just the same way as using the HTTP or Telnet interfaces. It is even possible to reconfigure the management login information for HTTP and Telnet interfaces using SNMP. SNMP management software is very inexpensive and quite powerful in controlling wireless network devices. It is important to disable SNMP access if it will not be used. If SNMP will be used, set the read and write community strings to complex, non-default values that are unrelated to the network's SSID, WEP key, or organizational information. Also, disable SNMP access from outside the corporate environment by using access control lists or firewall filtering capabilities.

Discovery Protocols

When discovery protocols are not in use, they should be disabled. There are a few proprietary network discovery protocols on the market today. One of the more well known discovery protocols is the Cisco Discovery Protocol (CDP). Cisco Discovery Protocol (CDP) is primarily used to obtain protocol addresses of neighboring devices and to discover the platform of those devices. CDP can also be used to show information about the interfaces your router uses. CDP is media-independent and protocol-independent, and runs at layer 2 on all Cisco-manufactured equipment including routers, bridges, access servers, and switches.

How CDP Works

Use of SNMP with the CDP Management Information Base (MIB) allows network management applications to learn the device type and the SNMP agent address of neighboring devices, and to send SNMP queries to those devices. Cisco Discovery Protocol uses the CISCO-CDP-MIB. CDP runs on all media that support Subnetwork Access Protocol (SNAP), including local-area network (LAN), Frame Relay, and Asynchronous Transfer Mode (ATM) physical media. CDP runs over the data link layer only; therefore, two systems that support different network-layer protocols can learn about one another. Each device configured for CDP sends periodic messages, known as advertisements, to a multicast address. Each device advertises at least one address at which it can receive SNMP messages. The advertisements also contain time-to-live, or holdtime, information, which indicates the length of time that a receiving device should hold CDP information before discarding it. Each device also listens to the periodic CDP messages sent by others in order to learn about neighboring devices and determine when their interfaces to the media go up or down.

Whether using Cisco or another vendor, it is important to disable discovery protocols if they are not in use by the network management system or specifically used for troubleshooting by the network administrator. The reason for this security step is that an intruder that has gained access to an access point may be able to map parts of the network and find vulnerabilities in firmware running on infrastructure devices by querying the access point's CDP information.

Remote Configuration

In the most stringent of high security environments, it may be necessary to disable all configuration interfaces on access points and bridges except the serial console port (if possible). When HTTP, Telnet, or SNMP interfaces are used for remote network management, it is important to consider the possibility that those passwords or community strings may be accidentally passed across an unsecured wireless bridge link. Securing these links allows administrators to perform normal network management functions without worry that authentication information could be compromised. If manufacturer feature sets allow for it, configure access points and bridges so that they *cannot* be configured over the wireless network segment. Make it a point where possible never to log into access points or bridges over an unsecured link or using an unsecured protocol.

Client Security

Using client security solutions can reduce peer-to-peer attacks. Peer-to-peer attacks over wireless LANs are common due to unsecured operating systems. Securing wireless clients from attack is just as important as securing the network infrastructure. Many times, it is while connected to a public access network without proper protective measures in place that wireless LAN users are hacked. Client computers often have valuable corporate information on them, such as passwords, documents, spreadsheets, and reports. If the computer belongs to an administrator, that machine will most likely have account information, logins, and network diagrams. Because of the value of the data that is often transported in portable computers, wireless security policy should limit any sensitive data on client machines that could damage the organization to which it belongs and public access connectivity should likewise be limited if not completely prohibited. One particular security weakness that is commonly exploited by hackers is file and folder sharing on workstations. Shared folders should be limited or even prohibited on wireless client stations.

There are many tools that can be used to protect wireless clients while connected to the wireless network. Some VPN technologies, such as IPSec, when properly implemented, provide protection from peer-to-peer attacks. On the other hand, there are VPN technologies commonly used with wireless LANs that allow unauthenticated peer connections even when the VPN connection is enabled. Personal firewall software installed on wireless client computers can effectively thwart peer-to-peer attacks, but can also introduce added administrative overhead and cost.

In cases where the infrastructure to which the client is attached is secure, such as when using 802.1x/EAP solutions, peer-to-peer attacks are usually limited to authorized users attacking authorized users. This scenario still represents a serious problem considering that 80% of all network attacks come from authorized users. There are some implementations of 802.1x/EAP and VPN technologies that disallow peer-to-peer connectivity while an authorized connection that normally allows such connectivity is in place.

Some VPN users remotely accessing a corporate network utilize VPN software directly from their desktop computer. Other times, the VPN client is a hardware device such as a router. In cases where multiple computers reside behind a hardware VPN device, there may often be access points for mobile access. This configuration allows mobile clients collectively to use the same VPN tunnel into the corporate network. This situation presents a gaping security hole when the wireless network is not secured because unauthorized users may use the same VPN tunnel to access the corporate networks as the authorized users use. This scenario is illustrated in Figure 7.6 below

FIGURE 7.6   Unsecured wireless network behind a remote VPN device

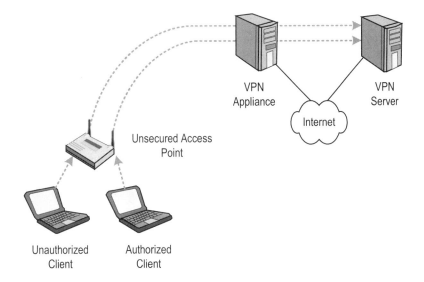

IP Services

One of the first steps in securing IP services in a network is to heighten general awareness of the possibility of rogue IP services such as DHCP servers. Most end users and help desk personnel do not consider this type of attack a real threat, and most would not understand the technical details of such an attack. Using data-link security mechanisms such as 802.1x/EAP solutions (discussed in unit 3) assures that the wireless user is authenticated prior to receiving an IP address from a DHCP server. Earmarking IP ranges for wireless LAN segments is another way to speed location of hackers and to ease network management.

Switches vs. Hubs

Switches should be used to connect to the wired segment, instead of hubs. Connecting access points and bridges to switches allows support for security and network management tools such as VLANs. Many of the leading enterprise class access points now support 802.1q VLAN tagging on the wired port. SSIDs are tied to VLANs as a means of logically separating groups of wireless users. Wireless VLANs allow for segmented network design and secure management over a particular VLAN to which only administrators have access. Switches, as opposed to hubs, allow access points and bridges to have full duplex connectivity to the network, relieving a possible throughput bottleneck.

Hubs present a security issue because hubs broadcast each frame entering any port to every other port, whereas switches do not. Using hubs allows hackers to connect to any access point and hear all traffic being sent across the hub and all other access points connected to it.

Staging and Testing

Staging and testing should occur *prior* to deployment. One common mistake made when deploying wireless networks is to treat security as an afterthought instead of integrating it into the initial configuration before deployment into a production environment. When this mistake is made, the opportunity exists for an attacker to gain access to the network and configure back door security holes that can be used for entry at a later time. This same mistake also allows the attacker to reconfigure access points, perhaps changing or adding a new username/password for their own use. To avoid this scenario, wireless infrastructure devices should be staged and configured in an isolated environment for a secure deployment before they are installed on the network. Network administrators should use approved security configuration checklists to assure that no security holes are created due to lack of following configuration procedures.

Equipment Installation

Equipment should be installed out of sight and reach. Organizations that have access points and other wireless equipment widely deployed often provide no type of theft prevention for their equipment. Access points and antennas, both of which need to be in common areas for the greatest benefit, are especially vulnerable to theft. For example, many hospitals have access points mounted directly to the ceiling in plain view. It would take little effort for a thief to move a chair under an access point and quickly remove the access point. The perpetrator might even go unnoticed if he were to wear the appropriate maintenance or security attire. To prevent theft of wireless network equipment, devices should be:

- Mounted out of reach
- Bolted down or secured in locked steel boxes
- Kept out of plain view

Taking these precautions decreases the possibility that the devices will be stolen, replaced with a cheaper model, or reconfigured through the console port.

Summary

This chapter discussed topics associated with the guidelines and baselines of the functional policy portion of wireless network security policy. Policy essentials cover password policies, training, usage, implementation and staging, procedures, and audits. General guidelines discusses the security checklist, available network resources, asset management, change management, and spot-checks and accountability. Baseline practices consist of several strategic areas that must be considered when implementing wireless LANs, such a basic SSID changes, MAC filtering inadequacies, WEP versus EAP/802.1x solutions, detecting rogue equipment, and wireless bridge security.

Key Terms

Before taking the exam, you should be familiar with the following terms:

brute force attack

discovery protocols

Intrusion Detection Systems

MAC Spoofing

rogue device

SNMP community strings

strong password

VLAN

Wi-Fi Protected Access (WPA)

Review Questions

1. Installing wireless hardware with default configurations can cause security vulnerabilities. What are the three most common points of attack caused by using default configurations?

   A. WEP not enabled

   B. SSID provided by the manufacturer

   C. SSID using the company name or street address

   D. Default password on the access point

   E. Default IP address on the access point

   F. Default MAC address on the access point

2. What are some problems with using MAC address filtering on access points?

   A. Requires on-going manual configuration to add and remove users.

   B. Any client can associate to access points regardless of their MAC address if they have the correct SSID

   C. MAC addresses are broadcasted in the clear which could lead to someone discovering and spoofing a valid MAC address.

   D. Users must remember their MAC address to access the WLAN.

   E. Use of a valid stolen client adapter defeats MAC filters.

3. Physical security of wireless infrastructure devices might include which of the following measures?

   A. Install outdoor wireless bridges in lockable NEMA enclosures

   B. Use the "closed system" feature in all access points

   C. Allow only antennas to protrude through ceiling tiles instead of the entire access point

   D. Use lockable RF cables and connectors

4. Some manufacturers remove the SSID from beacons and do not send the SSID as part of a probe response frame. This is called the "closed system" feature in most implementations. Why is it important to use this feature?

    A. Clients cannot see beacons that do not include the SSID

    B. SSIDs give away important network information used by hackers

    C. Wireless packet analyzers can't analyze beacons and probe response frames that do not have SSIDs

    D. A war driver using NetStumbler would not be able to see access points present on your WLAN when using this feature

    E. Access points do not respond to probe requests frames without SSID information present

5. Which of the following might an administrator seeking to prevent war driving by checking RF cell size around a facility use?

    A. A handheld PC with a wireless PCMCIA card

    B. A spectrum analyzer

    C. A directional antenna

    D. Password recovery software

6. What is the distance that an eavesdropper can hear an RF data signal?

    A. The distance depends on the sensitivity of the receiving radio

    B. The distance depends on the type of antenna used by the eavesdropper

    C. The distance is always less than 300 feet with Wi-Fi equipment

    D. The distance depends on the 2.4 GHz DSSS channels in use

    E. The distance depends on the power output of the access point

7. When configuring an access point, which of the following items will increase the security across an enterprise wireless LAN?

    A. Denying clients using broadcast SSIDs association

    B. Using the same channel on all access points

    C. Setting access point logins to use strong passwords

    D. Using RTS/CTS on all access points

8. Many organizations install access points with SSIDs and WEP keys configured for the company name, phone numbers, or similar company-related information. Why is this not a good security practice?

    A. Firewalls cannot keep out attackers who know the SSID of a network

    B. It makes any VPN solution implemented by the organization vulnerable to attack

    C. Company-related text strings can be easily guessed

    D. It gives away information about the owner/location of the network

9. What is the primary reason to configure WLAN equipment in a staging environment before attempting to use it in a production environment?

    A. Access point power output may violate FCC regulations for your area

    B. Access point security features should be enabled before connecting the access point to the production network to avoid intrusion

    C. Access points could perform hijacking attacks on unsuspecting users

    D. Access points need valid IP addresses assigned in order to access the wired network

10. Which of the following are SNMP related security issues that should be addressed before deployment of access points and wireless bridges?

    A. Default SNMP read and write strings are published in the manufacturer's manual and available to everyone

    B. SNMP encryption should be enabled on all wireless infrastructure devices

    C. SNMPv3 should always be used where possible for backwards compatibility and security

    D. When configuring SNMP strings, you should follow the same guidelines for strong passwords that you do for network access

Answers to Review Questions

1. A, B, D
2. A, C, E
3. A
4. D
5. A, C
6. A, B, E
7. A,C
8. C, D
9. B
10. A, D

Functional Policy: Design & Implementation

CWSP Exam Objectives Covered:

❖ Given a set of business requirements, design a scalable and secure wireless LAN solution considering the following security tactics:

- Wireless LAN segmentation

- Wireless DMZ configuration

- Use of NAT/PAT

- NAT/PAT impact on secure tunneling mechanisms

- Redundancy

- Wireless LAN equipment staging & deployment

- Wireless LAN cell sizing and shaping

- Scalability

- Appropriate use of different antenna types

- Operational verification

❖ Secure equipment configuration and placement

❖ Describe appropriate installation locations for wireless LAN hardware in order to avoid physical theft and tampering, considering the following:

- Security implications of remote placement of devices

- Physical security for remote infrastructure devices

❖ Secure remote connections to wireless LAN infrastructure devices

- ❖ Security solution interoperability and layering
  - ▪ Explain the benefits of interoperable wireless LAN security solutions
  - ▪ Design and implement co-existing wireless LAN security solutions

Interoperability

Network administrators should take into account Interoperability between wireless LAN security solutions before making purchases. For example, if the decision has been made to implement an 802.1x/EAP-based solution, 802.1x is a standard, but many EAP types are proprietary. Suppose an organization initially chooses to implement access points that support 802.1x/EAP-TLS, but later decided to switch to an 802.1x/PEAP solution to reduce network management tasks related to client certificates. If the access points chosen during the initial installation do not support PEAP, then this transition would be overly expensive and would render the initial investment in access points worthless. In addition to interoperability, the administrator must also take into account the level of resources that will be required to maintain the security solution and various upgrade or change paths.

PPTP

Point-to-point Tunneling Protocol (PPTP), which is discussed in detail in the Solutions unit, is widely used in small and medium-sized wireless networks for its authentication and encryption VPN features. Additionally, PPTP is integrated in many windows platforms and available in third party appliances and free Linux implementations. PPTP is a layer 3 VPN protocol that can be used over the top of any layer 2 security solution such as WEP, TKIP, 802.1x/EAP, or a layer 2 VPN technology. This is to say that both a layer 2 security solution and PPTP as a layer 3 security solution can be used simultaneously to create a stronger security solution because they are interoperable.

IPSec

IPSec is a layer 3 VPN technology that has grown in popularity because of its strength in authentication and data privacy. IPSec supports many encryption protocols such as DES, 3DES, and AES. IPSec can be used in the same way as PPTP except that IPSec has fewer security holes than PPTP and supports much stronger encryption. Understanding at what layer of the OSI model each security solution resides gives the administrator the ability to make educated interoperability decisions. In the next section we will discuss the pros and cons of layering security solutions.

Layering

Using multiple layers of security solutions, such as using 802.1x/EAP solutions with IPSec VPN solutions, can provide very high levels of security, but may also introduce a significant amount of complexity to the implementation and administration of the network. There are four components that should be addressed when layering is considered:

- OSI Layer of each solution considered
- Costs versus benefits
- Management resources required
- Throughput & Latency

OSI Layers

Each solution type will be discussed in greater detail in the Solutions section, but for this section, it is important to understand which layer of the OSI model each solution type uses. Some examples of security solutions (encryption & authentication) used with wireless compared with the OSI layers at which they reside are shown below.

Layer 2 (Data-Link Layer)

- WEP (and all variations such as TKIP)
- 802.1x/EAP (and all variations)
- Enterprise Encryption Gateways
- Layer 2 Tunneling Protocol (L2TP)

Layer 3 (Network Layer)

- Point-to-Point Tunneling Protocol (PPTP)
- IP Security (IPSec)

Layer 7 (Application Layer)

- Secure Shell (SSH)
- Secure Shell Version 2 (SSH2)
- Novell Directory Services (NDS or eDirectory)
- Microsoft Active Directory (AD)

Costs

The first cost consideration that must take place is that of comparing the cost of the solution(s) against the asset(s) that the organization is trying to protect. Obviously, if an organization is protecting a billion dollar per year intellectual property asset, that organization could easily justify investing significantly more than an organization that is simply trying to prevent war drivers from gaining access to the Internet through their wireless LAN.

While implementing a multi-layer solution, the cost of any given combination of solutions may be double or more from using a single solution. Costs come in the form of dollars and time spent implementing and managing multiple solutions. Costs of individual solutions are an important factor considering project budgets. Each layer of the security solution that is being considered should first be analyzed by itself to determine what costs will be involved in the purchase of any needed hardware or software.

Combining solutions often results in using two different types of security products from two different vendors, which does not lend itself to the opportunity for volume price discounts, or purchasing combined solutions at a discount. More often than not, different deals will be required with each vendor for their particular part of the layering solution. There are vendors on the market that can provide layer 2 and layer 3 solutions, but rarely do those vendors also have application layer implementations. It would be wise to consider requesting an RFP from an integrator that provides products and services from multiple manufacturers.

Management

While the cost of purchasing multiple solutions may be significant, the cost of administering them may be overwhelming. Consider an organization that chooses to implement 802.1x/EAP-TLS for which client and server certificates are necessary for security. If this organization chooses to implement IPSec client software and server appliances as a network layer solution, the user training expense alone could be enormous, because every end user in the organization must be properly trained. As secure as these solutions may be when paired together, they will be rendered useless the first time a user decides that they are too difficult to use and disregards organizational policy concerning wireless LAN security. Additionally, these same users may be inclined to place and use a rogue wireless access device rather than deal with the frustration of using the required security solutions. Thus, the additional consideration of user-friendliness arises, and must be taken into account when evaluating any solution.

There are costs associated with employees who thoroughly understand complex security solutions such as 802.1x/EAP-TLS and IPSec (from the example above). These employees are rare and usually expensive for an organization to employ. It is also very likely that the number of security administrators deployed by an organization will have to be significantly increased if the organization is very large.

Throughput & Latency

Consider the overhead issues already associated with wired networks in which each layer of the OSI, starting at the Application Layer (layer 7), has its data encapsulated by the next lowest layer. Now consider the overhead introduced by wireless media due to interference, signal blockage, bad signal quality, and the fact that wireless is a half duplex medium using CSMA/CA. CSMA/CA alone introduces approximately 50% overhead due to its backoff algorithms. Retransmissions due to errors in transmission in an RF environment are frequent and further decrease throughput. When these factors are added to the overhead of strong encryption and authentication at Layer 2, strong encryption and authentication at Layer 3, and Layer 7 authentication (which is also typically encrypted) for directory services or applications such as SSH2, it reaches a point where there is so much network overhead that very little actual data traverses the network despite the fact that a tremendous amount of traffic is being sent across the network.

Summary

While layered solutions can help an organization create an extremely secure network, the costs may outweigh the benefits. With added help desk calls to support client-side solutions, administration of server-side devices by network security administrators, added expense of purchasing multiple solutions, on-going maintenance and upgrade of multiple solutions, and decreased throughput in a limited throughput environment, an organization must consider more than just the fact that the wireless segment will be very secure. If the network is not usable for its intended purpose, the point of securing the network is moot.

This is not to say that layered solutions should be avoided, but during the design phase of a security solution, all of the costs must be factored in.

Segmentation & VLANs

Functional wireless network security policy should dictate that all wireless segments of the network be separated from the network backbone by appropriate network traffic control and security devices (a.k.a., segmentation devices) such as:

- Firewalls
- Enterprise Wireless Gateways
- Enterprise Encryption Gateways
- Routers
- Layer 3 Switch (Switch Router)
- VPN Concentrator
- SSH2 Server

Further, if physical separation of the wireless network is not possible, then wired VLANs may be used. Using virtual LANs to separate network segments is standard practice in medium and large installations. All access points may be located on one VLAN along with the "unprotected" interface of the segmentation device, while the network backbone, on which all of the servers reside, is located on another VLAN, along with the "protected" interface of the segmentation device. Figure 8.1 below illustrates such a network design.

FIGURE 8.1   Segmented Design using Wired VLANs

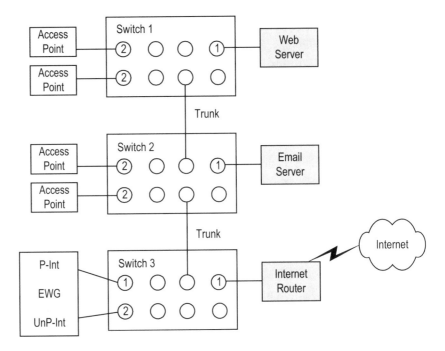

Throughput, authentication, encryption, and traffic control requirements dictate what solution is appropriate, but the design model would not vary significantly regardless of the type of solution chosen.

Wireless VLANs

Wireless VLANs are a relatively new function for wireless LANs, recently added to some enterprise class access points for the purpose of extending VLAN functionality to the mobile client device. 802.1q VLAN tagging is the only non-proprietary implementation available so most devices use it.

While the full criteria for each wireless VLAN deployment is likely to be unique, some standard criteria exist for most rollouts including:

- Common applications used by all wireless LAN end users. The wireless LAN administrator should define:
  o Wired network resources commonly accessed by WLAN users
  o Quality of service (QoS) level required by each application
- Common devices used to access the wireless LAN. The wireless LAN administrator should define:
  o Security mechanisms (WEP, 802.1x/EAP, VPN, etc.) supported by each device type
  o Wired network resources commonly accessed by WLAN device groups
  o QoS level needed by each device group

After the wireless VLAN deployment criteria have been defined, the deployment strategy must be determined. Two standard deployment strategies are:

Segmentation by user groups: Segmentation of the WLAN user community and enforcement of specific access-security policies per user group. For example, three wired and wireless VLANs in an enterprise environment could be created for full-time employee, part-time employee and guest access.

Segmentation by device types: Segmentation of the WLAN to allow different devices with different access-security "levels" to access the WLAN. For example, it is not recommended to allow handheld computers that support only 40/128-bit static-WEP to co-exist with other WLAN client devices using 802.1X with dynamic WEP in the same VLAN. In this scenario, devices should be grouped and isolated with different "levels" of access security into separate VLANs.

Implementation criteria such as those listed above are then defined to include:

- Use of policy filters to map wired policies to the wireless side

- Use of 802.1x to control user access to VLANs using either RADIUS-based VLAN assignment or RADIUS-based SSID access control
- Use of separate VLANs to implement different Classes of Service (CoS)

As a market leader in both wired and wireless infrastructure and a pioneer of wireless VLAN technology, Cisco Systems recommends the following best practices for the wired infrastructure when 802.1q VLAN tagging is extended to access points and bridges. These best practices are dependent on the features supported by the wired infrastructure to which the wireless devices are connected.

- Limit broadcast and multicast traffic to the access point and bridge by enabling VLAN filtering and Internet Group Management Protocol (IGMP) snooping on the switch ports. On the 802.1q trunks to the access point and bridge, filter to allow only active VLANs in the ESS. Enabling IGMP snooping prevents the switch from flooding all switch ports with Layer 3 multicast traffic.
- Map wireless security policies to the wired infrastructure with ACLs and other mechanisms.
- The access point does not support Virtual Terminal Protocol (VTP) or Generic Attribute Registration Protocol VLAN Registration Protocol (GVRP) protocols for dynamic management of VLANs because the access point acts as a "stub" node. The wireless LAN administrator must use the wired infrastructure to maintain and manage the wired VLANs.
- Enforce network security policies via Layer 3 ACLs on the "guest" and management VLANs.
  - o The wireless LAN administrator could implement ACLs on the wired infrastructure to force all "guest" VLAN traffic to the Internet gateway.
  - o The wireless LAN administrator should restrict user access to the native/default VLAN of the access points and bridges with the use of Layer 3 ACLs and policies on the wired infrastructure.

Example: Traffic to access points and bridges via the native/default VLAN is only allowed to and from the management VLAN where all the management servers (CiscoWorks, HP OpenView, Tivoli, etc.) including the RADIUS server reside.

With wireless VLANs, each SSID is mapped to a default VLAN-ID on the wired side of the access point. The WLAN administrator may wish to impose RADIUS-based VLAN access control using 802.1X or MAC address authentication mechanisms. For example, if the wireless LAN is configured such that all VLANs use 802.1x/EAP and similar encryption mechanisms for WLAN user access, then a user can *hop* from one VLAN to another by simply changing their SSID and successfully authenticating to the access point (using 802.1x/EAP). This may not be preferred if the WLAN user is supposed to be confined to a particular VLAN. There are two different ways to implement RADIUS-based VLAN access control features:

RADIUS-based SSID access control: Upon successful 802.1x/EAP or MAC address authentication, the RADIUS server passes back the allowed SSID list for the WLAN user to the access point or bridge. If the user used an SSID on the allowed SSID list, then the user is allowed to associate to the WLAN. Otherwise, the user is disassociated from the access point or bridge.

RADIUS-based VLAN assignment: Upon successful 802.1x/EAP or MAC address authentication, the RADIUS server assigns the user to a predetermined VLAN-ID on the wired side. The SSID used for WLAN access doesn't matter because the user is always assigned to this predetermined VLAN-ID.

In order to have RADIUS return the appropriate attributes to the access point, the RADIUS server must implement the access point vendor's Vendor Specific Attributes (VSA) that defines the allowed SSIDs or static VLAN assignment. As you can see from the information explained above, wireless VLAN functionality gives the access point somewhat similar functions to wireless middleware (EWGs) while maintaining infrastructure security at the network edge (the access point).

Authentication & Encryption

Authentication and encryption are both integral parts of any wireless LAN security solution because they cover the security holes of (1) who can access the network and (2) how the data transmitted via RF signal is protected from intruders. The choice of what type of authentication and encryption to use for the deployment of a secure WLAN will include the consideration of:

- Existing implementations
- Data sensitivity
- Scalability
- Availability
- Budget

Existing Implementations

Organizations that have authentication and encryption mechanisms in place prior to adding a wireless LAN into their network design can often use these existing technologies and extend them to include the new wireless segments of the network. For example, a network that supports remote dialup users using VPN technology and a RADIUS server could use the same VPN and RADIUS implementation for wireless nodes. Also, networks that already use PKI for security may find that an 802.1x/EAP-TLS solution based on certificates is appropriate. Re-use or extended use of directory services, RADIUS, Kerberos, TACACS+, or other authentication tools can save money on hardware/software purchases, end user and network staff training, and implementation man-hours.

Data Sensitivity

Wireless LAN use has spawned a heightened sense of the need for network security in general. Since it is a given that wireless LANs present an unacceptable level of data security without stronger mechanisms in place, many organizations are upgrading their network's authentication and encryption mechanisms as part of the implementation of wireless LAN technology. Network mechanisms that used to be taken for granted, such as security of passwords over a wired network, are no longer considered to have an acceptable level of security. For this reason, many organizations are moving toward more stringent levels of security such as with Kerberos v5 using a directory service back end. These types of implementations are certainly more complex to administer, but they present very high levels of security for local and remote wired clients as well as wireless clients.

Quite often organizations will completely secure the wireless media, such as with an 802.1x/EAP solution, but do nothing to secure the wired network to which the wireless segment ultimately provides access. For example, information traversing the wireless link between client and access point may be encrypted with WEP, but RADIUS requests traversing the wired link between the access point and RADIUS server may not be (and usually are not) encrypted. If the access point is connected to a hub instead of a switch, these RADIUS authentication packets will arrive at every access point's wired interface and be broadcast to all wireless users (depending on the manufacturer of the access point). This type of configuration would allow hackers to obtain user logins with a packet analyzer. For this reason, it makes sense to implement secure authentication mechanisms even on the wired segment, and also to always use switches instead of hubs for connecting access points to the wired segment of an enterprise network.

Scalability & Availability

Some authentication mechanisms are not scalable at all, such as WEP or VPN implementations using a small VPN server with native authentication. In contrast, other implementations may be highly scalable and redundant such as a scaled-down wireless-centric RADIUS server that handles encryption locally and proxies authentication to a redundant pair of large, centralized RADIUS servers. Such a design is shown in Figure 8.2.

FIGURE 8.2   Scalable RADIUS Implementation

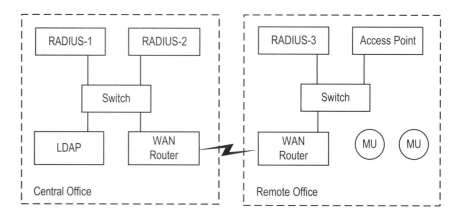

In the example above, one can see how a mobile unit (MU) sends authentication information to the local RADIUS database, which proxies the information over the WAN link to the clustered RADIUS servers that reference the LDAP database for user information. Once RADIUS-3 receives a positive response from RADIUS-1 or RADIUS-2, it will build and maintain an encrypted tunnel across all access points while the user roams the network. Another scalable design would be as shown below in Figure 8.3, in which the local RADIUS servers use the already-scalable directory service configuration.

FIGURE 8.3   Scalable

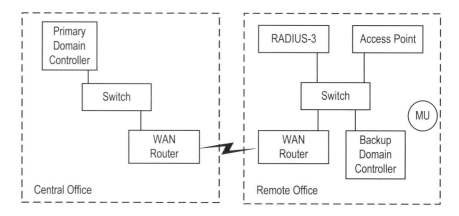

In Figure 8.3, the access points send authentication requests to RADIUS-3, which points to the Backup Domain Controller (BDC) locally. The PDC passes authentication information down to the BDC periodically, or, as with Novell's NDS, the local server may pass authentication requests upstream depending on how the directory is partitioned. With low-cost, wireless-centric RADIUS implementations such as in this design, a substantial savings in product purchases may be realized over scenarios using full-featured RADIUS that leave most features unused.

Authentication systems for large implementations should be highly redundant if centralized or sufficiently distributed, depending on which is more appropriate for the design. Figure 8.2 above shows a design that incorporates an authentication solution configured for hot-failover or clustering at the central site. Figure 8.3 depicts a two-piece authentication solution (RADIUS + Directory Service), which is distributed, and thus reduces the impact of a failure.

No matter which authentication or encryption solution your organization chooses for wireless LAN security, network policy should dictate that it should be able to handle the current workload easily and workloads likely to be realized over the next 3-5 years.

Summary

The Design and Implementation section of the Functional Policy covers interoperability, layering, segmentation and VLANs, and authentication and encryption. Interoperability is the capability of different mechanisms or network processes from differing vendors to be able to communicate. Layering solutions is a method of utilizing solutions from different layers of the OSI model and can be advantageous in wireless networking. Segmentation is a method of implementing solutions that divide the network into smaller, more manageable pieces by using controlled layer 2 and layer 3 boundaries. Authentication and encryption help alleviate security risks involved in implementing wireless solutions, assist in determining who can access the network, and determine whether the data is encrypted while it traverses the wireless segment.

Key Terms

Before taking the exam, you should be familiar with the following terms:

authentication

interoperability

IPSec

Point-to-point Tunneling Protocol (PPTP)

segmentation

solution layering

wireless VLANs

Review Questions

1. Which of the following statements best describes PPTP?

    A. PPTP is a layer 2 VPN protocol that can be used instead of any layer 2 security solution such as WEP, TKIP, or 802.1x/EAP.

    B. PPTP is a layer 3 VPN protocol that can be used over the top of any layer 2 security solution such as WEP, TKIP, 802.1x/EAP.

    C. PPTP is a layer 7 encryption protocol that can be used over the top of most layer 3 VPN technologies such as IPSec.

    D. PPTP is a layer 2 VPN protocol that can be used under any IP-based layer 3 VPN technology such as SSH2

2. Which of the following encryption algorithms are supported by IPSec?

    A. MD5

    B. DES

    C. 3DES

    D. AES

    E. RC4

    F. RC5

3. Name the four components that should be addressed when one is considering implementation of a layered wireless security solution.

    A. _____

    B. _____

    C. _____

    D. _____

4. At which layer of the OSI model do the wireless encryption and authentication protocols WEP and EAP operate?

    A. Layer 2

    B. Layer 3

    C. Layer 7 only

    D. Layers 4 - 7

5. At which layer of the OSI model does the VPN protocol SSH2 operate?

    A. Layer 2

    B. Layer 3

    C. Layer 5

    D. Layer 7

6. Two common deployment strategies for deployment of wireless VLANs are:

    A. Segmentation by wired or wireless user type

    B. Segmentation by operating system types

    C. Segmentation by user groups

    D. Segmentation by device types

7.   Why should functional wireless network security policy dictate that all wireless segments of the network be separated from the network backbone by appropriate network traffic control and security devices?

A.   To prevent high-bandwidth users like software developers and graphic designers from using all of the limited bandwidth of a wireless LAN

B.   Because wireless LANs should always be considered an unsecured network medium with larger bandwidth than most Internet connections

C.   To ensure that AAA functionality on RADIUS servers can positively separate and identify different user groups by the segment of the network on which they reside

D.   To protect the backbone network segment from unauthorized access from the wireless segment of the network

8.   If physical separation of the wireless network from the wired backbone network using physically independent switches is not possible, then what is another option?

A.   SSID segmentation

B.   RADIUS MAC Filters

C.   Wired VLANs

D.   Access Control Lists

9.   What is the only non-proprietary implementation available for wireless VLANs?

A.   802.11r VLAN tagging

B.   802.1q VLAN tagging

C.   802.1i VLAN tagging

D.   802.11d VLAN tagging

10. Why are authentication and encryption considered to be vital pieces of any wireless LAN security solution?

A. Authentication and encryption cover the security holes of (1) who can configure the network and (2) how the data transmitted via RF signal is modulated

B. Authentication and encryption cover the security holes of (1) who can configure the access points and (2) how the client devices' RF signals are detected

C. Authentication and encryption cover the security holes of (1) what devices can associate to a bridge and (2) how the data transmitted between bridges is encapsulated

D. Authentication and encryption cover the security holes of (1) who can access the wired network and (2) how the data transmitted via RF signal is protected from eavesdroppers.

Answers to Review Questions

1. B

2. B, C, D

3. Multiple answers:

   A. OSI Layer of each solution considered

   B. Costs versus benefits

   C. Management resources required

   D. Throughput & Latency

4. A

5. D

6. C, D

7. A, B, D

8. C

9. B

10. D

Functional Policy: Monitoring & Response

CWSP Exam Objectives Covered:

❖ Security management:

- Explain the necessary criteria for regular wireless LAN security reporting and documentation

- Implement and conduct timely and consistent reporting procedures

- Implement & maintain wireless LAN security checklist

❖ Explain how to identify and prevent social engineering

- Educate staff and security personnel

- Implementation and enforcement of corporate policy policy regarding social engineering

- Security marketing and propaganda campaigns to heighten awareness

Physical Security

In some instances, only physical security will suffice as a preventative measure against network attacks. Physical security begins with allowing only authorized personnel into and out of the organization's premises. Most office complexes now have some type of security that may include guards who monitor building entry/exit, card swiping, tailgating, etc. More secure buildings require visitors to sign in and be authorized by the receiving company, and be escorted as they make their way around the building. Receptionists can also provide another line of defense against would-be attackers. Visitors who show up without appointments, or technicians who show up to repair or upgrade systems, should all be escorted throughout the facility only *after* someone else in the company has authorized that person access to the facility. In addition to posting guards, physical security also includes locking doors, cabinets, and drawers.

Rogue Access Points & Ad Hoc Networks

A rogue access point can be placed on the wired network either unintentionally by an uneducated employee, or intentionally by an attacker that has gained physical access to the premises. An employee might install a rogue access point to have wireless LAN access in his or her work area. To prevent employees from unknowingly creating such a huge breach in network security, education about the risks of doing so should be a requirement.

An attacker, who has illegally accessed the building to install an unauthorized access point, clearly intends to take some malicious action toward an organization. Keeping these individuals out of the facility in the first place is the best approach to eliminating the problem. Such prevention may require locking more doors and further restricting access to sensitive areas. Placing security guards in these areas can also deter unwanted activity. Many times, increasing security against external intruders is mostly a matter of training internal staff to report suspicious activity and to question everything and everyone that is suspicious around them.

Part of the security policy must include documentation on how rogues (including access points and ad hoc networks) will be found, how often the area will be scanned for rogues, and what to do when rogues are found. When an attacker installs a rogue device or network (such as in an ad hoc network that has a wired/wireless workstation) on the network backbone, the damage can be much more serious than if the intruder installed the rogue on a network segment already separated from the backbone by security devices. For this reason, searches should especially be focused on network backbone segments.

An automated solution, such as a wireless intrusion detection system (IDS), may be necessary to reduce time spent searching for rogues. A wireless IDS will trigger alarms when rogue MAC addresses or foreign SSIDs are detected on the wired or wireless segments. If only one wireless LAN hardware vendor is used, monitoring for other vendor's equipment (based on MAC address) is one easy way to locate rogue equipment. Keep in mind that administrators should search for rogues that use various wireless technologies and frequencies. Using software and hardware that detect rogues on LAN frequencies that employ common spread spectrum technologies may be an expensive and time consuming task if a hacker is careful to avoid these same technologies and frequencies. For example, the attacker may choose to use 900 MHz DSSS, 802.11a OFDM, or Bluetooth equipment while avoiding the use of Wi-Fi 2.4 GHz DSSS gear that is being monitored.

RF Jamming & Data Flooding

RF Jamming

If there is one type of attack against a wireless LAN that is more difficult to prevent, detect, or block, it would be an RF jamming attack. It is said that, "The best thing about license free wireless LANs is that they are license free, and the worst thing about license free wireless LANs is that they are license free." This double-speak means that you, as a wireless LAN administrator, do not have to pay FCC licensing fees to use wireless LAN equipment. However, it also means that there is no recourse against anyone else using the same frequencies within the confines of FCC rules in the same physical space. This situation is further aggravated by attackers that disregard FCC rules by operating high-power, narrowband transmitters in unlicensed frequency bands (ISM, UNII, etc.) near low-power, spread spectrum wireless LANs.

What can be done to prevent such an attack? Consider that intentional jamming is an attack that can, and does, take wireless LANs off line, completely stopping production environments in many cases. This network outage may cost an organization a substantial amount of money, which may persuade them to take legal action against an attacker – IF they could find this attacker. To take legal action against an individual in a case like this, the organization would have to show that the attacker intentionally meant to cause disruption to an organization's processes.

Another approach is to put up high fences that block RF transmissions (especially those in bands used by wireless LANs) around an organization's facility. A great amount of land located around a facility with a secure perimeter may also suffice because jamming signals would dissipate greatly before reaching the facility. The same approach would work inside a facility using wire mesh substances like chicken wire or other RF shielding in the walls. These prevention mechanisms are often impractical due to high costs, leaving most organizations completely exposed to an RF jamming attack. In places such as office buildings or companies that are located next to roads or in the vicinity of public places, there is nothing that can be done to prevent someone from jamming the wireless LAN. The only foolproof method of avoiding an RF jamming attack is not to have a wireless LAN that uses unlicensed frequency bands. However, it is rarely the case that the risk of such an attack outweighs the benefits of having a wireless LAN.

Consider a scenario in which RF jamming in a manufacturing plant can cause serious production problems. Plants that do high volumes of production frequently use machinery that is synchronized or dependent on real-time transactions. If a computer is providing data to a machine over a wireless LAN link for making a product, and this link is interrupted, it may cause the entire plant to shut down in order to resynchronize machines. This interruption could cost hundreds of thousands of dollars. Another situation that is more common is when wireless product vendors hold seminars around the country for advertising purposes. Consider when an attacker brings a jamming device to this type of seminar and causes demonstrations to malfunction due to unexpected and extreme interference. These attacks can injure the reputation and credibility of the manufacturer in front of potential customers, thus costing the vendor untold amounts of money due to lost sales.

RF jamming attacks, in many cases, may cause users and administrators to lose confidence in the wireless LAN. The performance and reliability of the wireless LAN becomes questioned. This loss of confidence can have far reaching effects, such as, slower sales in the wireless LAN market.

Data Flooding

Data flooding attacks may be intentional or unintentional, and are not unique to wireless networks. In unintentional attacks, users are violating acceptable use of the wireless LAN and treating the wireless segment like it is a high-bandwidth, non-shared medium. This situation can be corrected with proper training, restricted network access, or even disciplinary action. In intentional data flooding attacks, an attacker uses a piece of software capable of generating fake data packets of any given size at any desired rate (up to the maximum possible over the wireless link). The attacker will specify the MAC address of another node (mobile node, access point, or even wired node) and generate bogus data for the purpose of keeping authorized users from having a useful connection through the wireless media. This type of attack has basically the same effect as the RF jamming attack, but requires that the attacker be physically closer to the access point in order to make a meaningful layer 2 connection before sending packets across the network.

Social Engineering

An organization's employees are often the weakest link in any security solution. Accordingly, more attention should be given to raising employee awareness and training employees to recognize and prevent social engineering and hacking. Lack of training often leads to employee laziness or lack of concern, which further leads to mistakes in dealing with social engineering attacks. There are many good books available on social engineering tactics used by expert intruders. It is suggested that organizations have their employees read these books or attend a specialized course on social engineering prevention. Since wireless LAN security technologies have advanced and proliferated at a staggering pace, many hackers take advantage of employees' lack of education by using social engineering tactics.

Awareness

Hackers rely on employees being forgetful, apathetic, or lazy to obtain the information they need. The immediate recognition of attempts at social engineering should be added to employee orientation, even for temporary workers/consultants. Social engineering attacks come in many forms including the ones listed below.

Dumpster diving – Searching through the trash from an organization to locate useful information such as memos, company manuals, phone lists, organizational charts, and security codes or keys.

Phone calls – By far the most common threat, attackers try to locate willing and helpful people from whom to obtain information. Information might include usernames, passwords, WEP keys, and network information. Primary targets of phone call social engineering attacks are help desk personnel and contractors because of their primary responsibility to help others within the organization.

Email – Most companies now rely on email as a primary form of communication. Reply-to and Sent-from email headers can easily be forged making the email request look legitimate. Security information sent via email should be encrypted.

IM – Instant messaging is used in enterprises for quick inter-departmental communication. Many organizations use a standard naming convention for Instant Messaging names. If a social engineer gathers a phone directory and information on the standard naming convention for IM, then the attacker can masquerade as a legitimate employee and request information from authorized sources.

Heightening social engineering awareness within an organization can be accomplished through posting on community bulletin boards, broadcast emails, reiterating it in all company meetings, etc. Having constant reminders keeps employees on their toes against these kinds of attacks.

Prevention

Customer support centers and help desks were created to provide help, and in doing so they usually forget or ignore advice on preventing social engineering because they are trying to do their jobs. Some of the procedures support and administrative personnel should adhere to is:

- Positively identify the person that is calling or requesting help
- Use established, secure channels for passing security information (such as encrypted email)
- Report suspicious activity or phone calls
- Establish procedures that eliminate password exchanges. An administrator should never ask a user for his password, nor even be able to view any password on the system.
- Shred company documents before throwing them in the trash

A well-educated employee is the best defense against social engineering attempts. Employees must become familiar with what types of attacks may occur, what to look for, and how to respond to incidents. An organization's security policy should dictate proper response procedures for perceived social engineering threats. If an employee realizes that he is being targeted but has no means of reporting the incident, the security policy is not helpful. Part of the reporting procedure should be to document what information the attacker was able to retrieve prior to the attack being identified. This documentation should be followed by alerting other employees of the attack so that everyone else will be on heightened awareness. Incidents need to be investigated with the employees that report the incidents; otherwise, the employees may feel the reporting procedure serves no purpose and may not follow procedure the next time.

Audits

One way in which organizations can reduce the threat of social engineering is to have their defenses tested for weaknesses. Penetration tests by security professionals should include social engineering attacks against organizational staff. Depending on the organization, the test could cover only the basics of wireless LAN security such as asking for passwords, WEP keys, and network security solutions currently deployed. The test can also be more comprehensive in order to determine as much information as possible for a thorough report. Many organizations hesitate to perform this type of audit because it can make employees uncomfortable and even angry if the attack succeeds. It is important to handle results of these audits tactfully.

Reporting

Reports that are generated as part of security monitoring procedures can provide valuable information on how the network is being utilized as well as where attacks are occurring. However, the reports are only of value when they are consistently reviewed in a timely manner. Security reports that sit on the desk of an administrator are useless if they permit an attacker to access the network freely until someone notices.

A proper reporting policy will include information on who (what organizational position) is accountable for generating the reports and who is responsible for reading the reports. Training should also be required for the reviewers. Top-level administrators do not need to spend their time reviewing every daily or hourly report that is generated by a system as part of a security monitoring procedure. These tasks can easily be delegated to junior or mid-level network operations personnel as part of their job tasks as long as these individuals have been properly trained in how to interpret and analyze the reports.

System logs and the logs created by intrusion detection systems contain information that can be used by operations personnel to detect anomalies and attacks on a network. Traffic baselining of data flow through the wireless network also provides insight into which users or devices are utilizing the WLAN the most. If one particular access point is being utilized 100% and transmitting hundreds of megabytes of data, yet no employee has been working around that access point, chances are an intrusion has taken place. At best, reports provide insight into how the attack occurred, and where the weak points are in the network. Intrusion systems can alleviate some of the manual searches for attacks by identifying attack patterns (called signatures) and reporting based on pre-set thresholds determined by administrative staff. The downside of reports is that the information contained within them is about what *has* happened to the network, not what *is* happening presently. If reports are generated each morning and they indicate an attack occurred the previous day or night, nothing can be done about information that has already been compromised.

Response Procedures

When attacks are discovered on a wireless network, a proper response can prevent the attack from occurring again. Likewise, if attacks are not handled properly or not addressed with consistency, the WLAN can remain open to further attacks. A security policy should define the steps to take after an intrusion has been recognized. Recommended steps should include the following:

1. *Positive identification* – Reports can indicate both attacks as well as false positives – anomalies in the network that can be attributed to abnormal usage by legitimate users. Administrators must be properly trained to distinguish between an attack and what looks like an attack but is not.

2. *Confirmed attack* - Upon determining if an attack has taken place, damage must be assessed and confirmed, and the appropriate manager(s) should be notified. This notification list may include the director of network operations or quite often senior executives in the organization. The level of severity will usually determine who is notified first.

3. *Immediate action* – If an attack is severe, the wireless segment under attack may have to be taken off line. In the case of a DoS attack on the main network backbone that is originating from the wireless segment, disconnecting the wireless segment from the main network would suffice. The documented wireless LAN Security Policy should dictate appropriate procedures for each type of attack scenario.

4. *Documentation* – All attack findings should be thoroughly documented in a standard form generated by the organization and added to the security policy. This documentation will later be used for a full report to be given to executive management and legal counsel.

5. *Reporting* - If malicious activity and/or data theft has taken place, the appropriate authorities should be notified to record the incident in case any arrests need to be made at a future time. Corporate legal counsel, police, and even IT forensics experts may be needed in this situation.

Summary

Wireless LAN functional security policy should include, but not be limited to, the topics discussed in this chapter. Each organization needs to evaluate and design policies, procedures, and training tailored the unique conditions found in their environment. Physical security is always an important component of a good policy. Stopping unauthorized persons from having physical access to company assets and resources is a good first line defense. If a hacker cannot gain physical access to your facility, he cannot place a rogue access point on your network. Preventing rogue access points and ad hoc networks is both challenging and a critical security function.

Even though some jamming and data flooding cannot be stopped, adequate knowledge of jamming and flooding techniques, devices, and measuring instruments can help determine whether or not the jamming is a result of an attack or interference from another company's system.

Social engineering is a simple and effective method used by hackers to gain enough information to deploy his or her attack on the network. Many employees are not properly educated in detecting and preventing these attacks. Every employee should be made aware of the tactics a hacker can use to gain valuable and sensitive company information. Functional security policy should include the steps to be taken to make employees and support personnel aware of social engineering practices, how to respond to attacks, and how management handles reports on such attacks. Audits should be considered to identify where further training is needed and to measure the effectiveness of current policies.

Key Terms

Before taking the exam, you should be familiar with the following terms:

Ad Hoc networks

confirmed attack

data flooding

positive identification

RF jamming

social engineering

Review Questions

1. Physical security can thwart which of the following attack scenarios?

    A. Placement of rogue wireless LAN equipment onto the network by external attackers

    B. Phone calls by an attacker to obtain sensitive network security information

    C. A repair technician showing up to repair a server that isn't broken

    D. Theft of wireless LAN equipment

2. Rogue access points may use which of the following technologies?

    A. Bluetooth

    B. GSM

    C. 802.11b

    D. Infrared

3. RF Jamming attacks can cause:

    A. Authorized users to roam abnormally

    B. Organizations to switch from Wi-Fi to Bluetooth

    C. Denial of Service attacks against authorized users

    D. Users to lose confidence in the stability of the wireless network

4. Data Flooding attacks are accomplished using:

    A. A packet generator

    B. A Bluetooth transmitter in a Wi-Fi environment

    C. An RF narrowband transmitter and a high-gain antenna

    D. Metal reflector panels and a spread spectrum transmitter

5. Social Engineering attacks often involve:

    A. The latest hacking software

    B. An in-depth knowledge of networking

    C. Phone calls to the help desk

    D. In-depth organizational research such as dumpster diving

6. Social Engineering attacks against a wireless network may occur using:

    A. Instant Messengers

    B. Access point configuration changes

    C. Wireless packet analyzers

    D. Inexpensive rogue access points

7. Help Desk and Administrative personnel should adhere to which of the following to avoid unnecessary risks due to social engineering?

    A. Ignore suspicious phone calls

    B. Never help users that request information related to network security

    C. Shred all company documents before reading them

    D. Positively identify a person requesting proprietary information

8. Network security audits that include social engineering tactics should be performed periodically because:

    A. Users get lazy in staying in compliance with security policy without consistent reminders

    B. Administrators need regular discipline by executive management in order to remain sharp

    C. Changes in the network and employee positions can open new security holes

    D. Security consultants get better at identifying security issues with time

9. Accurate and timely reporting of wireless LAN attacks, _____.

    A. Allows security policy makers to write policy appropriately

    B. Allows organizations to implement adequate security measures to stop current attacks

    C. Allows end users to implement layered security solutions when necessary

    D. Builds end user confidence in wireless LAN use

10. After an attack has been positively identified, a proper response includes:

    A. Security solutions should be changed

    B. False positives should be identified

    C. Presumed attackers should have legal charges pressed against them

    D. Documenting attacks

Answers to Review Questions

1. A, C, D
2. A, C
3. A, C, D
4. A
5. C, D
6. A
7. D
8. A, C
9. B
10. D

Encryption

CWSP Exam Objectives Covered:

❖ Differentiate between the following encryption schemes in terms of efficiency and security

- RC4
- RC5
- DES/3DES
- AES (FIPS 197)

Many types of encryption are used with and over wireless LANs for data privacy and authentication protocols. This lesson covers the most prevalent encryption algorithms, explains their strengths and weaknesses, and describes their most common uses. This lesson is not meant to be an authoritative reference on the operation and limitations of encryption protocols, but rather a quick reference as to what the encryption mechanisms are and how and when they are used with wireless LANs.

RC4

Ron Rivest of RSA Security developed RC4 as a variable length stream cipher that was fast and efficient. RC4 is perhaps the most commonly used stream cipher in existence today. RC4 is used in WEP, TKIP, MPPE, SSL, TLS, and many other security protocols.

A stream cipher is a type of symmetric encryption algorithm. Stream ciphers can be designed to be exceptionally fast - much faster than any block cipher. While block ciphers operate on large blocks of data, stream ciphers typically operate on smaller units of plaintext, usually bits. The encryption of any particular plaintext with a block cipher will result in the same ciphertext when the same key is used. With a stream cipher, the transformation of these smaller plaintext units will vary, depending on when they are encountered during the encryption process.
A stream cipher generates what is called a *keystream*. A keystream is a sequence of bits used as a key. Encryption using a keystream is accomplished by combining the keystream with the plaintext, usually with the bitwise XOR operation. The generation of the keystream can be independent of the plaintext and ciphertext, yielding what is termed a *synchronous* stream cipher, or it can depend on the data and its encryption, in which case the stream cipher is said to be *self-synchronizing*. Most stream cipher designs are for synchronous stream ciphers.

The RC4 algorithm is capable of key lengths of up to 256 bits, and is typically implemented in 64 bits, 128 bits, and 256 bits. RC4 is considered moderately secure by today's cryptography standards. It is commonly known that WEP has been broken and that WEP uses RC4. However, it is not commonly understood that it is WEP that is weak and not the RC4 stream cipher itself. For this reason, TKIP, which fixes the problems with WEP, still uses the RC4 stream cipher.

RC5

Ron Rivest of RSA Security developed RC5 in 1994 and it is currently the fastest and most well-known block cipher. RC5 was developed for use in software, and is extremely efficient on processors such as the Intel Pentium series of processors.

RC5 is a parameterized algorithm with a variable block size, a variable key size, and a variable number of rounds. Allowable choices for the block size are 32 bits (for experimentation and evaluation purposes only), 64 bits (for use a drop-in replacement for DES), and 128 bits. The number of rounds can range from 0 to 255, while the key can range from 0 bits to 2040 bits in size. Such built-in variability provides flexibility at all levels of security and efficiency.

There are three routines in RC5: key expansion, encryption, and decryption. In the key-expansion routine, the user-provided secret key is expanded to fill a key table whose size depends on the number of rounds. The key table is then used in both encryption and decryption. The encryption routine consists of three primitive operations: integer addition, bitwise XOR, and variable rotation. The exceptional simplicity of RC5 makes it easy to implement and analyze.

RC5 is used in applications such as Citrix SecureICA (a technology that provides the foundation for turning any client device - thin or fat - into a very thin client). Both thin clients and strong, efficient encryption are particularly useful with wireless LANs due to their limited available bandwidth and ease of access available to hackers.

On July 14, 2002, Distributed.Net broke a 64-bit RC5 key after 1757 days of computation. Almost 59 billion keys were tested before finding the correct key at a peak rate of more than 270 million keys per second. An effort is currently underway, having started on December 3, 2002, to break a 72-bit RC5 key.

Data Encryption Standard (DES)

In 1972, the National Institute of Standards and Technology (called the National Bureau of Standards at the time) decided that a strong cryptographic algorithm was needed to protect non-classified information. The algorithm was required to be inexpensive, widely available, and very secure. NIST envisioned something that would be available to the general public and could be used in a wide variety of applications. NIST asked for public proposals for such an algorithm, and in 1974, IBM submitted the Lucifer algorithm. Lucifer appeared to meet most of NIST's design requirements, so NIST enlisted the help of the National Security Agency to evaluate its strength. At the time, many people distrusted the NSA due to their extremely secretive activities, so there was initially a degree of skepticism regarding the analysis of Lucifer. One of the greatest worries was that the key length, originally 128 bits, was reduced to just 56 bits, weakening it significantly. The NSA was also accused of changing the algorithm to plant a "back door" in it that would allow agents to decrypt any information without having to know the encryption key, but these fears proved unjustified and no such back door has ever been found.

The modified Lucifer algorithm was adopted by NIST as a federal standard on November 23, 1976 and its name was changed to the Data Encryption Standard (DES). The algorithm specification was published in January 1977, and with the official backing of the government, it became a widely employed algorithm in a short amount of time. Over time, various shortcut attacks were found that could significantly reduce the amount of time needed to find a DES key by brute force, and as computers became progressively faster, it was recognized that a 56-bit key was simply not large enough for high security applications. As a result of these flaws, NIST abandoned their official endorsement of DES in 1997 and began work on a replacement, to be called the Advanced Encryption Standard (AES). Despite the growing concerns about its vulnerability, DES is still widely used by financial services and other industries worldwide to protect sensitive online applications.

To highlight the need for stronger security than a 56-bit key can offer, RSA Data Security has been sponsoring a series of DES cracking contests since early 1997. In 1998, the Electronic Frontier Foundation won the RSA DES Challenge contest by breaking DES in less than 3 days. EFF used a specially developed computer called the DES Cracker, which was developed for under $250,000. The encryption chip that powered the DES Cracker was capable of processing 88 billion keys per second. More recently, in early 1999, Distributed.Net used the DES Cracker and a worldwide network of nearly 100,000 PCs to win the RSA DES Challenge in a record breaking 22 hours and 15 minutes. The DES Cracker and PCs combined were testing 245 billion keys per second when the correct key was found. In addition, it has been shown that, for a cost of one million dollars, a dedicated hardware device can be built that can search all possible DES keys in about 3.5 hours. This example serves to illustrate that any organization with enough resources can break DES with very little effort.

DES encrypts and decrypts data in 64-bit blocks, using a 64-bit key (although the effective key strength is only 56 bits). Often, DES is explained as having 64-bit keys, but every 8th bit is used for parity, making the effective strength only 56 bits. The least significant (right-most) bit in each byte is a parity bit, and should be set so that there are always an odd number of 1's in every byte. These parity bits are ignored, so only the seven most significant bits of each byte are used, resulting in a key length of 56 bits.

DES takes a 64-bit block of plaintext as input and outputs a 64-bit block of ciphertext. Since DES always operates on blocks of equal size and uses both permutations and substitutions in the algorithm, DES is both a block cipher and a product cipher. DES has 16 rounds, meaning the main algorithm is repeated 16 times to produce the ciphertext. It has been found that the number of rounds is exponentially proportional to the amount of time required to find a key using a brute-force attack, so as the number of rounds increases, the security of the algorithm increases exponentially.

Triple DES (3DES)

The Data Encryption Standard (DES) was developed by an IBM team around 1974 and adopted as a national standard in 1977. Triple DES (3DES) is a minor variation of this standard. 3DES is three times slower than regular DES but can be far more secure if used properly. 3DES enjoys much wider use than DES because DES can be broken with today's rapidly advancing technology. 3DES was the answer to many of the shortcomings of DES. Since 3DES is based on the DES algorithm, it is very easy to modify existing software to use 3DES. 3DES also has the advantage of proven reliability and a longer key length that eliminates many of the shortcut attacks that can be used to reduce the amount of time it takes to break DES. However, even this more powerful version of DES may not be strong enough to protect data for very much longer. The DES algorithm itself has become obsolete and is in need of replacement. The National Institute of Standards and Technology (NIST) is currently testing Advanced Encryption Standard (AES) solutions as a replacement for 3DES for the United States Federal Information Processing Standard (FIPS).

3DES takes three 64-bit keys, for an overall key length of 192 bits. The procedure for encryption is exactly the same as regular DES, but it is repeated three times (hence the name "Triple DES"). The data is encrypted with the first key, decrypted with the second key, and encrypted again with the third key as shown in Figure 10.1.

FIGURE 10.1   3DES Encryption Process

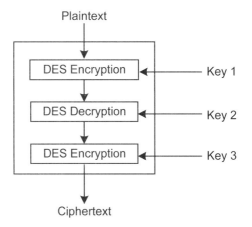

3DES is three times slower than DES, but is much more secure if implemented properly. The procedure for decrypting data is the same as the procedure for encryption, except it is executed in reverse. Like DES, data is encrypted and decrypted in 64-bit chunks. Unfortunately, there are some weak keys that one should be aware of: if all three keys, the first and second keys, or the second and third keys are the same, then the encryption procedure is essentially the same as standard DES. This situation should be avoided because it is the same as using a really slow version of regular DES. Care should be taken to ensure that all three keys are different. Although three 64-bit keys are used, 3DES has an effective strength of only 168 bits because each of the three keys contains 8 parity bits that are not used during the encryption process.

 The United States Government does not allow exporting of 3DES technology.

Advanced Encryption Standard

In 1997, the National Institute of Standards and Technology (NIST) initiated a process to select a symmetric-key encryption algorithm to be used to protect sensitive (unclassified) Federal information in furtherance of NIST's statutory responsibilities. In 1998, NIST announced the acceptance of fifteen candidate algorithms and requested the assistance of the cryptographic research community in analyzing the candidates. This analysis included an initial examination of the security and efficiency characteristics for each algorithm. NIST reviewed the results of this preliminary research and selected MARS, RC6, Rijndael, Serpent, and Twofish as finalists. Having reviewed further public analysis of the finalists, NIST has decided to propose Rijndael (pronounced "Rhine-Dahl") as the algorithm for use in Advanced Encryption Standard (AES). NIST announced selection of AES as part of FIPS 197.

AES is intended to be several orders of magnitude more secure than DES, but only slightly slower. AES is proposed to be adequate to serve as the main worldwide block cipher for the next 20-30 years, and is stronger than 3DES and considerably faster. Many security systems will likely use both 3DES and AES for at least the next 3-5 years as part of a transition period. After that, AES will eclipse 3DES as the default algorithm on most systems if it lives up to its expectations. After the transition period, 3DES will likely be supported only for backwards compatibility reasons. The useful lifetime of 3DES is far from over, even with AES already implemented in several vendors' products, and for the next few years 3DES is an excellent and reliable choice for the security needs of highly sensitive information.

Compared to today's most commonly used wireless LAN encryption algorithm – RC4 – AES is a CPU-intensive algorithm. When AES is used as part of wireless LAN infrastructure devices such as wireless bridges or access points, it will be necessary to use either an encryption co-processor or a very strong main CPU in the devices. Since modern personal computer processors have reached near-supercomputer performance, it is possible for modern computers (including notebook and tablet computers) to process AES encryption without a dedicated co-processor. At the same time, existing WLAN adapters cannot be retrofitted with AES, so new access points and wireless cards will be needed to use AES. New AES-capable devices are expected to support older security technologies for backwards compatibility and interoperability.

Part of the IEEE's 802.11i draft includes definitions for the use of AES for encryption. AES is considered more robust than TKIP and would replace WEP and RC4. AES is capable of 128-, 192-, and 256-bit keys, and is considered uncrackable by leading cryptographers. A comprehensive collection of detailed information is available on AES at the following URL: http://csrc.nist.gov/encryption/aes/.

 The United States Government does not allow exporting of AES technology.

Summary

This chapter discusses many encryption types. RSA's RC4 is used in many security protocols including WEP and SSL. WEP is inherently weak but the weakness is not due to RC4 encryption. TKIP and other similar key rotation schemes correct the problems with WEP while retaining the RC4 stream cipher. RC5, the most well-known block cipher, is a parameterized algorithm with a variable block size, a variable key size, and a variable number of rounds. RC5 utilizes three routines: key expansion, encryption, and decryption. RC5 is used in Citrix's SecureICA thin client technology. DES, an encryption algorithm with 56-bit keys, became the US government's encryption standard in 1977 but will be replaced by AES. DES, while strong at the time, has been found to be unsecured to brute-force attacks. 3DES, an encryption algorithm with 3 successive 56-bit keys, makes DES a stronger solution but is much slower than DES. 3DES will also be replaced by AES. AES utilizes the Rijndael encryption algorithm and specifies a maximum of 256-bit keys. AES is considered uncrackable.

Key Terms

Before taking the exam, you should be familiar with the following terms:

Advanced Encryption Standard (AES)

Data Encryption Standard (DES)

keystream

MPPE

RC4

Rijndael encryption algorithm

SSL

stream cipher

TKIP

TLS

Triple DES (3DES)

WEP

Review Questions

1. RC4 is available in which of the following bit lengths?

    A. 56

    B. 64

    C. 128

    D. 192

    E. 256

2. RC5 is a _____ cipher?

    A. stream

    B. block

    C. chunk

    D. circular

    E. rotating

3. With the DES encryption algorithm, every 8th bit is a parity bit resulting in a _____ -bit key strength.

    A. 56

    B. 64

    C. 104

    D. 128

4. Triple DES is a block cipher that processes data in _____ -bit chunks.

    A. 56

    B. 64

    C. 168

    D. 192

5. AES is specified for use by US Government agencies for protecting sensitive (unclassified) information in what FIPS standard?

A. 167

B. 204

C. 142

D. 197

Answers to Review Questions

1. B, C, E
2. B
3. A
4. B
5. D

Data-Link Security Solutions

CWSP Exam Objectives Covered:

❖ Static and Dynamic WEP & TKIP

- ▪ Explain the functionality, strengths, and weaknesses of WEP and TKIP

- ▪ Explain appropriate scenarios and applications of static and dynamic WEP and TKIP

- ▪ Install and configure static and dynamic WEP & TKIP

- ▪ Illustrate feasibility of WEP exploitation

- ▪ Manage scalable WEP & TKIP solutions

❖ 802.1x and EAP

- ▪ Explain the functionality of 802.1x & EAP\

- ▪ Explain dynamic key generation and rotation for solution scalability

- ▪ Explain the strengths, weaknesses, and appropriate applications of 802.1x & EAP

- ▪ Install and configure 802.1x & EAP, including

  - ▪ LEAP

  - ▪ EAP-TLS

  - ▪ EAP-TTLS

  - ▪ EAP-MD5

  - ▪ PEAP

  - ▪ Manage scalable 802.1x and EAP solutions

802.11 MAC Basics

One of the basic points of 802.11 security is that management and control frames are sent in clear text and unauthenticated. This fact is the basis for many types of attack scenarios. Figure 11.1 shows the authentication and association frame exchange for an IEEE 802.11 compliant wireless LAN. The discussion in this section will cover the methods that manufacturers and organizations are using to enhance both authentication and encryption in wireless LANs.

FIGURE 11.1 Authentication and Association Exchange

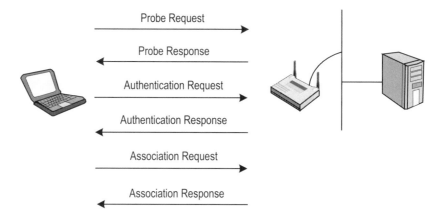

Some attacks mounted against today's wireless LANs simply cannot be prevented. Many of these vulnerabilities will be addressed by the 802.11i standard due for release in late 2003. For some types of attacks, particular vendors have instituted proprietary solutions. For example, in disassociation attacks, the attacker sends disassociation frames to access points with spoofed MAC addresses telling the access point to drop the connection to other nodes. 802.1x/EAP or TKIP using keyed Message Integrity Checks (MICs) prevent this type of forgery and tampering of packets. This prevention is accomplished using an algorithm that allows the receiver (the access point) to verify a known sender has sent a packet (not spoofed) and that the packet has not been altered in transit. Each of these technologies is addressed in the following sections.

Categories of Authentication & Encryption

With current layer 2 wireless LAN security solutions, there are three main categories of authentication and encryption – static WEP, dynamic WEP, and proprietary protocols. There are variations on each type, and each variation has its own usefulness. Each type's uses, strengths, and working processes are discussed in the following sections. We begin the following sections with static WEP, which is a security solution based on unchanging shared keys that are preconfigured on all nodes by the network administrator. TKIP is a type of dynamic WEP solution where WEP keys are rotated on a changeable interval, but a static WEP key is still used as keying material. TKIP is still a hardware-based shared key solution, but repairs the weaknesses found in WEP. Following TKIP, 802.1x/EAP solutions (another form of dynamic WEP) are discussed. 802.1x/EAP solutions base authentication on user criteria such as passwords or certificates. Proprietary protocols are discussed last due to their limited market share and lack of standardization. Proprietary protocols and solutions often provide security superior to published standards for multiple reasons. These reasons include leading edge encryption and authentication and the fact that there is no available information on how the protocols work.

Static WEP

The biggest threat to the security of a wireless LAN is not using any security at all. Even the 802.11 standard's WEP can be used where data privacy is a concern. WEP continues to be a deterrent against the vast majority of attacks that occur on wireless networks; however, WEP was not intended to be a complete security solution. WEP protects the wireless link with simple authentication and data encryption, but not the wired link. The wired network should employ additional security measures as part of a complete wireless LAN security solution.

WEP was intended to provide a level of security on the wireless network roughly equivalent to the security of a wired network. Through use of simple authentication and encryption, the 802.11 standard designers it believed that this goal could be accomplished. Authentication was to be used to keep unauthorized users from accessing the network, while the encryption would prevent eavesdroppers from gathering data passed across the network in clear text format. These protocols would be used to keep out all but the most determined hackers. Determined hackers can attack a wired network just as effectively as a wireless network with enough thought and effort.

Usage

It has been widely publicized that WEP has been broken. In fact, many companies have based their marketing around publicizing how "weak" WEP is. It is a well-known fact among wireless industry professionals that it takes between several hours and several days to collect enough "interesting" packets, even on a fully loaded wireless network, to crack WEP using one of the common WEP cracking tools such as WEPcrack or Airsnort. Given the large amount of time it would require to mount an attack against a person's home wireless network or a SOHO environment, it is likely the value of stolen data is not worth the effort to steal it. The probability of a hacker sitting around for many hours or days in an effort to accumulate enough data to crack the WEP key is not realistic unless the hacker has inside information about the value of what is stored on the network. For example, a flower shop that has a WLAN and uses WEP likely does not have to worry about someone trying to crack their WEP key when there are so many other unsecured wireless networks housing and transmitting more valuable information.

Cracking WEP

The media has oversimplified the amount of work it takes to crack WEP and find a usable WEP key. Cracking WEP requires three things:

- Large number of captured packets
- Long periods of time to capture those packets
- Fast machine to process the information contained in the packets to derive the WEP key

Research on cracking WEP has placed the upper limit on performing a crack in the order of 1-2 days. On a highly saturated network, WEP cracking programs can potentially collect enough packets to guess the key in three or four hours. If the network has very low quantities of traffic, it can take days to get enough data. Since the attack is based on probability, the actual number of packets required to guess a given key varies from key to key, sometimes significantly. Packet monitoring does not have to be all done in one session, though. Five hours one day and five the next works out to be about the same as ten hours in a row.

TKIP

Temporal Key Integrity Protocol (TKIP) is a set of modifications to the existing WEP algorithm. In response to the security issues with WEP, the IEEE 802.11i task group created TKIP as a measure to provide security to legacy equipment.

WEP Weaknesses Addressed

The TKIP algorithms address the following weaknesses found in WEP

- Forgery
- Weak-key attacks
- Collision attacks
- Replay attacks

Forgery

Although WEP supports per-packet key mixing and message integrity, WEP does not support per-packet authentication. Forgery attacks are performed by capturing encrypted packets, changing some of the data within them, and then resending the packets. TKIP uses an improved message-integrity check (MIC) called "Michael" to thwart attempts to tamper with packets en route. The MIC is sent with the data packet to the receiver as shown in Figure 11.2, who can then use a verification routine to verify if the message has experienced tampering. The use of MICs adds significant network overhead, thus decreasing throughput.

FIGURE 11.2 Message Integrity Check (MIC) and Sequencing

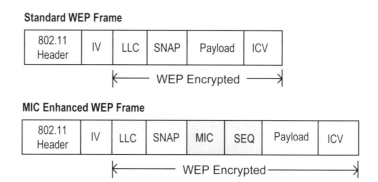

Weak Key Attacks

WEP constructs a per-packet RC4 key by concatenating an RC4 base key and the packet Initialization Vector (IV). Weak key attacks look at a series of packets with different IVs to determine the RC4 base key. TKIP uses key-mixing to derive short-lived encryption keys. The TKIP process begins with a 128-bit "temporal key" shared among clients and access points. The temporal key is combined with the client's MAC address and a relatively large 48-bit initialization vector is added to produce the key that will encrypt the data. This procedure ensures that each station uses different key streams to encrypt their data. TKIP's dynamic scheme is designed to remedy WEP's static key problem by changing the temporal key every 10,000 packets.

Collision Attacks

A collision attack refers to a situation in which a key is repeated using the same IV, allowing the data to be recovered. TKIP expands the amount of bits used for the IV from 24 to 48 so as to increase the possible number of IVs that can be used. Packets received with numbers that are not higher than previous packets are discarded and duplicate keys are not possible.

Replay attacks

Replay attacks occur when an attacker is eavesdropping and recording transmitted data. At a later time, the data is then retransmitted, replaying the old data as shown in Figure 11.3.

FIGURE 11.3   Replay Attack

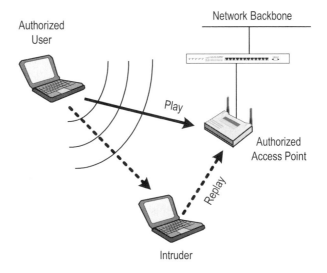

Because a MIC cannot be used to detect a replay attack, TKIP addresses replay attacks by using a sequencing number for generated packets. When TKIP keys are regenerated, both sender and receiver reset the sequence back to zero and start over. For each packet sent, the sequence is incremented by 1. If any packets arrive out of sequence, the receiver discards them.

Availability

For those products that are currently Wi-Fi certified, most can be upgraded to support TKIP, assuming the vendor has made a firmware upgrade available. Those devices that cannot be upgraded to use TKIP will still interoperate with new TKIP supporting components, except that they will use WEP for security instead of TKIP.

According to the IEEE, TKIP is not a long-term solution for the problems associated with WEP. TKIP provides minimal security on devices that use it (although it is better than WEP) and degrades the performance of the network. TKIP will serve as an interim solution until devices implementing the more advanced AES encryption are made available in the market. AES will replace WEP and will use the Rijndael algorithm instead of RC4. Because faster hardware is needed to process AES encryption, older hardware cannot be upgraded to support AES. The introduction of AES into wireless LAN hardware will result in the need to replace existing hardware to gain the security advantages of AES. Devices that use the AES algorithm will likely be backward compatible with older devices, but will continue to use the older and weaker security functionality to communicate.

Usage

If the only security on a WLAN is WEP, firmware upgrades that support TKIP should be applied to the hardware in use if available. TKIP is the middle-road alternative between those networks that use no security or WEP, and those that use more full-featured security solutions such as 802.1x/EAP, VPNs, etc. Where costs associated with advanced wireless security solutions are prohibitive, TKIP provides an adequate security patch that addresses the security weaknesses of WEP.

802.1x / EAP

802.1x with use of Extensible Authentication Protocol (EAP) implements what is generally referred to as "dynamic WEP." EAP is a flexible layer 2 authentication protocol used as a replacement to PAP and CHAP under PPP. There are several different EAP protocol types used with wireless LANs today, many of which will be discussed in the following sections.

The dynamic WEP solution provides for unique and changing encryption keys (re-keying). With dynamic WEP, a network can be configured such that an intruder will never be able to collect enough data to crack the encryption keys. This preventative measure is first accomplished through per-user per-session encryption keys. Each time a user logs into the network, a new key is created for that session. No other user will have that same session key, and the key lengths are such that re-use of keys would be impossible to predict. The second part of the solution is configuration of how often the keys are updated *during* the user's session. By periodically renewing the keys - every 15 minutes for example – the user's key is constantly changing, thereby preventing the capture of enough data using the same key for an attacker to do any meaningful decryption of the WEP key.

Consider a high traffic environment where it might be possible to collect enough data to crack the WEP key in 4 hours, which would require between one and five million encrypted packets. If the encryption keys used with dynamic WEP were set to expire every 15 minutes, an intruder would never have enough data to mount an attack. Because key renewal adds little overhead to the network, performing the rekeying as often as 15 minutes has a negligible impact on network performance.

An additional security solution implemented by some vendors, but not specifically addressed by the 802.11i working group, is broadcast key rotation (BKR). Since broadcast keys are typically implemented in a static fashion, they present a major security risk. By periodically (a user-defined interval) rotating the broadcast WEP key, this problem is eliminated. In order to implement BKR, there is generally a time-interval setting in the access point, and the user has the option of enabling or disabling this function.

Usage

802.1x/EAP is appropriate for medium to large enterprise environments because this solution makes data encryption and user authentication easier to administer. WEP keys are no longer entered on access points or into wireless client utility software manually and user authentication is added.

Basing authentication on individualized user credentials such as usernames and passwords, certificates, smartcards, and other like methods is more secure than basing network security as a whole on a single pass phrase such as is done with WEP. Use of 802.1x and EAP allow flexibility in how user authentication and connectivity is accomplished.

Some vendors enable TKIP as part of their dynamic WEP solution. In this type of solution, TKIP optionally replaces WEP, creating an even stronger solution, albeit a bit redundant in some areas.

802.1x Standard

802.1x is an IEEE standard that provides an authentication framework for 802-based LANs. 802.1x is not purely a wireless standard – it applies to almost all of the IEEE 802 technologies. 802.1x users are identified by individualized user credentials rather than hardware identifiers such as MAC addresses. 802.1x provides port-based access control so that, before the switch or access point (depending on whether a wired or wireless connection is used) will establish a connection (layer 2 link), the user credentials must be verified, as shown in Figure 11.4.

Port based access control provides a mean of authenticating and authorizing devices attached to a LAN port that has point-to-point connection characteristics when used with an authentication mechanism such as EAP. When authorization fails, access to the port is prevented. This mechanism makes use of the physical access characteristics of IEEE 802.3 LAN infrastructures, but for 802.11 WLANs, the port is virtual between a client and an access point.

The 802.1x standard was originally used in wired networks and has since been adapted for wireless networks. 802.1x is a flexible security framework that enables the plug-in of new authentication or key-management methods without changing hardware such as wireless cards or access points. The wireless cards and access points act as pass-through devices, allowing the security conversation to occur between the client software and the authentication server software.

FIGURE 11.4   How 802.1x Works

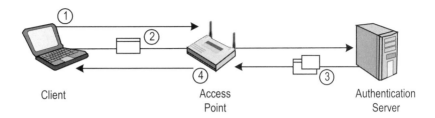

Client   Access   Authentication
                                    Point   Server

1. A client sends a "start" message to an access point, which requests the identity of the client
2. The client replies with a response packet containing an identity, and the access point forwards the packet to an authentication server
3. The authentication server sends an "accept" packet to the access point
4. The access point places the client port in an authorized state, and traffic is allowed to proceed.

There are three terms defined by the IEEE standard that describe the devices used in 802.1x:

Supplicant – the supplicant is a client that is being authenticated (by the authenticator). The supplicant may be connected to the authenticator at one end of a point-to-point link of the wired segment, or one end of the wireless segment when using 802.11.

Authenticator – the authenticator is an access layer device that requires supplicants to be authenticated in order to pass traffic through it. In 802.1x, the authenticator is usually an access point or bridge, which acts as a pass-through for the authentication request.

Authentication server – the authentication server is the device doing the authentication of the supplicant. The credentials from the supplicant are verified, and, if the identity of the supplicant is valid, authorization is granted and the authenticator is notified. The authentication server is typically a RADIUS server in wireless 802.1x/EAP implementations.

These devices are shown in Figure 11.5. The supplicant and the authentication server leverage the main CPU resources for cryptographic calculations, while the authenticator acts as a pass-through. This configuration makes 802.1x ideal for wireless access points, which are typically built with small processors and have little memory and processing power.

FIGURE 11.5   802.1x Components

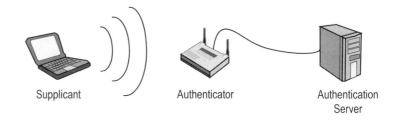

Supplicant   Authenticator   Authentication
                                                               Server

The 802.1x standard addresses only access control and authentication framework and does not address data privacy, so that the problems with WEP still exist in 802.1x. The secure connection that is implemented by EAP eliminates the problems introduced by static WEP keys through dynamic key generation upon authentication. Laptops or wireless cards that are lost no longer present a problem because they are not required to hold useful information when used as part of an 802.1x/EAP solution.

802.1x Advantages

802.1x has many advantages including:

- Maturity & Interoperability
- User-based identification
- Dynamic key management
- Flexible authentication

Maturity & Interoperability

The industry's choice to use 802.1x in wireless networks was partially based upon its time-proven use in wired networks. 802.1x supports use of EAP and RADIUS, both of which are mature protocols that provide leading edge flexibility and options for authentication. 802.1x, various EAP types, and RADIUS are open standards providing for maximum interoperability in centralized user identification and key management.

User-based Identification

With 802.1x/EAP-based wireless security solutions, identification is no longer based on a particular wireless network device connecting to the network, but rather an actual user. Basing this authentication on a scalable database such as RADIUS or other databases that RADIUS directly supports (Active Directory, NDS, LDAP, SQL, Windows NT, etc.) allows for hundreds or thousands of authenticated users. Centralized authentication and management save administration time and money and allow organizations to know who is using the network and how they are using it.

Dynamic Key Management

802.1x/EAP solutions overcome many of the deficiencies of static WEP keys. Per-user per-session keys eliminate attacks based on obtaining the WEP key. Automated key management systems allow keys to be reissued without an administrator's intervention.

Flexible Authentication

802.1x/EAP solutions allow for increased flexibility in responding to security vulnerabilities because changing authentication methods is simplified. There are several supported authentication solutions to choose from, each with different features and benefits that can meet the customer's needs. Changing the authentication mechanism does not require any hardware to be replaced, so the latest and best authentication methods can be implemented at lower costs. Hardware costs and complexity are decreased because authentication does not require special hardware.

EAP

Understanding EAP first requires understanding Point-to-Point Protocol (PPP). Although most commonly used for dial-up connections to the Internet, PPP is also used to establish a connection over a point-to-point link. Upon establishment of the link, PPP provides for an optional authentication before proceeding to the network-layer protocol phase. Originally EAP was designed to provide an extensible (flexible) method for a PPP server to authenticate its clients. The EAP protocol has been adapted for use in wireless networks to provide a method of conducting an authentication conversation between a wireless user and an authentication server (typically a RADIUS server) through an access point.

EAP Process

EAP and 802.1x are intimately woven together so that 802.1x provides port-based access control and EAP provides the authentication method itself. The step-by-step process to gain authentication can be described below.

1. The client sends an EAP-start message to the access point.
2. The access point detects the client and enables the port to an unauthorized state. This event initiates a series of message exchanges in an effort to authenticate the client.
3. The access point replies with an EAP-request identity message to determine the identity of the client.
4. The client sends an EAP-response packet to the authenticator. The response packet contains the client's identity information. This EAP-response is forwarded to the authentication server.
5. The authentication server attempts to verify the client's identity. This verification process could be done through some type of PKI validation (if certificates are used), a database lookup using LDAP, or a number of different authentication methods.
6. The authentication server replies with an "accept" or "reject" message to the access point.

7. The access point replies to the client with an EAP-success or
    EAP-reject message. If the authentication is successful, the
    access point will transition the port to an authorized state
    allowing the client to forward additional traffic to the network
    (called association in a wireless network).

The generic authentication flow of an 802.1x/EAP solution with mutual
authentication (both the client and the server are authenticated by each
other) is shown in Figure 11.6. There are many areas where this process
can be specialized to fit particular implementations of EAP, which is the
reason there are so many kinds of EAP in the market now.

FIGURE 11.6   802.1x / EAP Process Flow Ladder

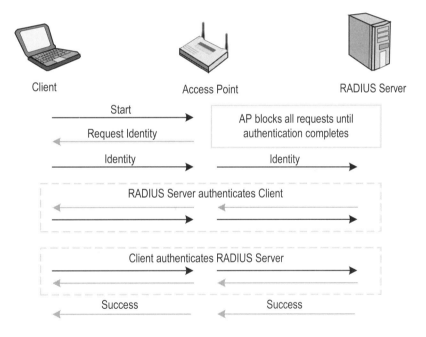

Use of 802.1x began with wired clients, with switches as authenticators,
and either TACACS+ or RADIUS authentication servers. Figure 11.7
shows the authentication flow of 802.1x over an 802.3 network.

FIGURE 11.7   802.1x / EAP over 802.3 Process Flow Ladder

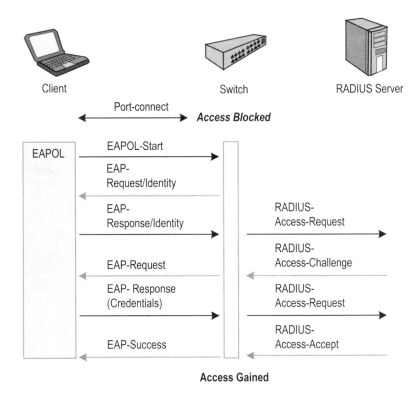

In a wireless system using 802.1x, the access point filters (blocks) all non-802.1x traffic from the client prior to authentication. The access point accepts only EAP packets until authentication succeeds, at which time the access point removes the filter and allows the supplicant to access the upstream network, as shown in Figure 11.8.

FIGURE 11.8   *802.1x / EAP over 802.11 Process Flow Ladder*

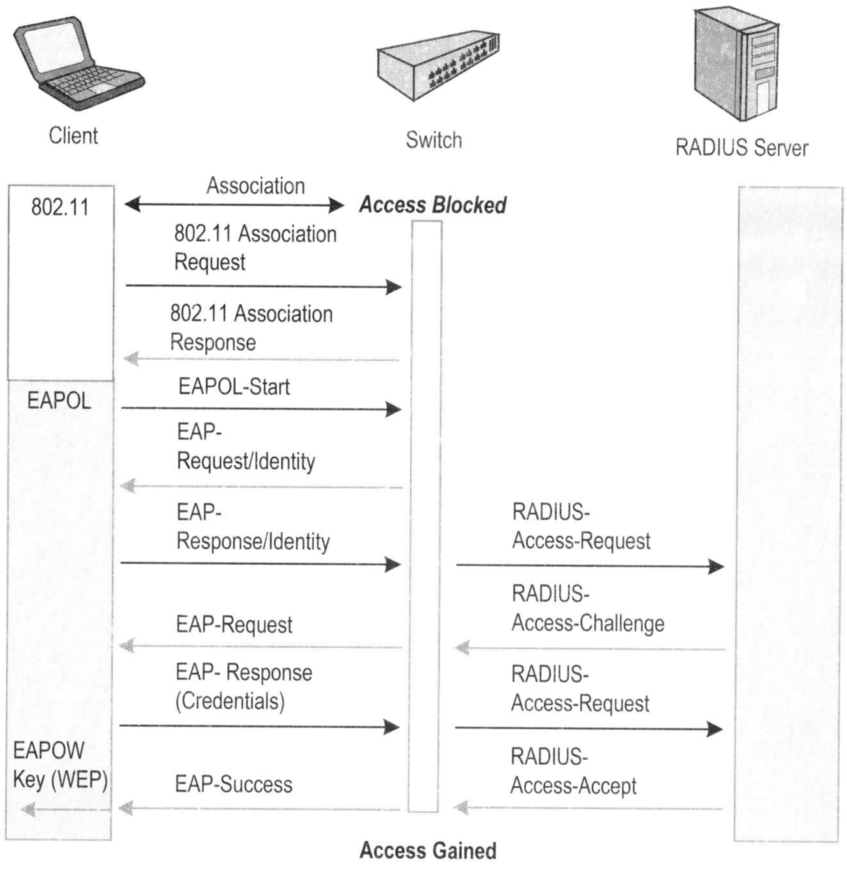

EAP Framework

PAP and CHAP are password-based authentication methods, but EAP can support two- and three-factor authentication (passwords, certificates, biometrics, etc). EAP allows new development of authentication methods without requiring the installation of new code on network access servers (NAS), such as access points. Therefore, the NAS does not need to be aware of the specific EAP type, and just passes through the request. There are exceptions to the rule, mainly because some access points do not support all EAP types. Figure 11.9 illustrates how different forms of EAP fit into the communication framework.

FIGURE 11.9 Where EAP fits

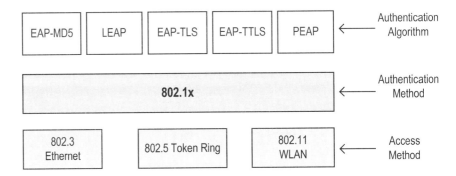

One goal in the creation of EAP was to prevent proprietary authentication solutions from being implemented, which would have had a negative effect on the interoperability and compatibility between systems. The software that provides the general EAP framework (which will support most any EAP type) resides on the authentication server and within the operating system or application software on the client devices. Windows XP natively supports EAP.

EAP Authentication Types

There are many available EAP types. Some are complicated to deploy, some are more secure than others, and some are not considered secure. Understanding the difference between the types of EAP that can be deployed in a wireless LAN environment is important in relation to security, costs, and timely deployments. The EAP types discussed in this text are:

- EAP-MD5
- EAP-TLS
- LEAP
- EAP-TTLS
- PEAP

EAP-MD5

EAP-MD5 was the first authentication type created by RFC2284 for 802.1x. EAP-MD5 is considered mandatory by the RFC and is simple to implement. EAP-MD5 uses the same challenge handshake protocol as PPP-based CHAP, but the challenges and responses are sent as EAP messages, as shown in Figure 11.10.

FIGURE 11.10 EAP-MD5 Process Flow Ladder

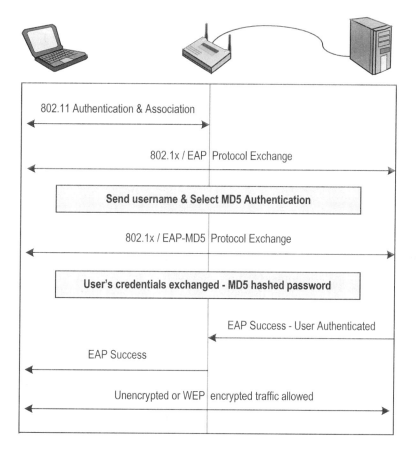

EAP-MD5 is rarely used because it has three security issues when used in a wireless LAN:

- One-way authentication
- Challenge passwords
- No per-session WEP keys

One-way Authentication

MD5 authenticates only the supplicant, and does nothing to authenticate the authentication server. This characteristic is a major problem with wireless LANs since an impersonator could be added as a rogue RADIUS server to obtain the login credentials of a legitimate user.

Challenge Passwords

MD5 is a password-based protocol that has the authentication server challenge the supplicant with a random string of text. The supplicant then hashes the challenge with its password and sends the response back to the server. The server validates the response based on its knowledge of the password. This protocol allows an eavesdropper to obtain both the challenge and the encrypted response, at which time a dictionary attack using the same algorithm can be performed to obtain the user's password.

No per-session WEP keys

MD5 does not use per-session WEP keys. Therefore, immediately after authentication, communication between the client and the access point is either not encrypted or is encrypted with a static WEP key. This characteristic of MD5 allows eavesdropping to occur on the data communication over the wireless LAN or presents vulnerability in the fact that static WEP can be broken.

 Because of its lack of security in a wireless environment, some vendors have chosen not to allow MD5 as an authentication method.

EAP-TLS

EAP-Transport Level Security (EAP-TLS) authentication was developed by Microsoft and standardized by the Internet Engineering Task Force (IETF), and is based on the Secure Socket Layer (SSL) protocol used for secure web traffic. EAP-TLS uses both server-side and client-side certificates for user identification and is generally more appropriate for organizations that have already deployed a Public Key Infrastructure (PKI). If a PKI is not already in place, the starting point for a new infrastructure would involve installing, configuring, and managing (or paying a third party for use of) a certificate authority (CA), a registration authority, a directory, and a certificate management system, all of which can be time consuming and expensive. Managing both server-side and client-side certificates across a large enterprise can be an overwhelming task for organizations with limited resources.

Digital certificates are data structures distributed by a certificate authority that join a public key to a user. A digital certificate is generally made up of the following pieces of information and, in many instances, complies with the X.509 standard:

- Certificate version
- Serial number
- Certificate issuer
- User Name
- User's public key
- Validity period
- Optional extensions
- Signature algorithm
- Signature

The digital signature is derived by combining the certificate version, serial number, issuer, user, user's public key, and validity period and running the values through a keyed hash function. The certificate authority keys the hash with its own private key.

Some organizations have decided that other authentication systems, such as token-based authentication, align more closely with their business models and security policies. In addition, not all RADIUS servers that support EAP also support the TLS authentication method.

EAP-TLS provides for mutual authentication between supplicant and authentication server, negotiation of the encryption method, and secured private key exchange. Until the recent introduction of Protected EAP (PEAP), EAP-TLS was the only EAP method used in Windows XP. Windows XP's service pack 1 introduced Microsoft's first support for PEAP.

There are very few differences between SSLv3 (which is supported by all current versions of Web browsers) and TLS. Most people think of SSL (or TLS) largely in terms of the result: an encrypted session between the browser and the web server. But as part of setting up the session, SSL starts with an authentication phase, and that is what is being used in any EAP-TLS operation.

TLS authentication within EAP is very simple. Each part of the session establishment dialog between the supplicant and the authentication server is placed inside of an EAP-TLS packet. When the TLS authentication dialog succeeds, the authenticator is informed and access to the network is granted. The following sets of steps outline the authentication processes for both TLS and EAP-TLS for comparison.

TLS Authentication

The TLS process begins with the handshake process:

1. The SSL client connects to a server and makes an authentication request
2. The server sends its digital certificate to the client
3. The client verifies the certificate's validity and digital signature
4. The server requests client-side authentication
5. The client sends its digital certificate to the server
6. The server verifies the certificate's validity and digital signature
7. The encryption and message integrity schemes are negotiated
8. Application data is sent over the encrypted tunnel via the record protocol

EAP-TLS Authentication

The EAP-TLS authentication process is as follows:

1. The client sends an EAP Start message to the access point

2. The access point replies with an EAP Request Identity message
3. The client sends its network access identifier (NAI), which is its username, to the access point in an EAP Response message
4. The access point forwards the NAI, encapsulated in a RADIUS Access Request message, to the RADIUS server
5. The RADIUS server responds to the client with its digital certificate
6. The client validates the RADIUS server's digital certificate
7. The client replies to the RADIUS server with its digital certificate
8. The RADIUS server validates the client's credentials against the client digital certificate
9. The client and RADIUS server derive encryption keys
10. The RADIUS server sends the access point a RADIUS ACCEPT message, including the client's WEP key, indicating successful authentication
11. The access point sends the client an EAP Success message
12. The access point sends the broadcast key and key length to the client, encrypted with the client's WEP key.

An illustration of the EAP-TLS process is shown in Figure 11.11.

FIGURE 11.11 EAP-TLS Process Flow Ladder

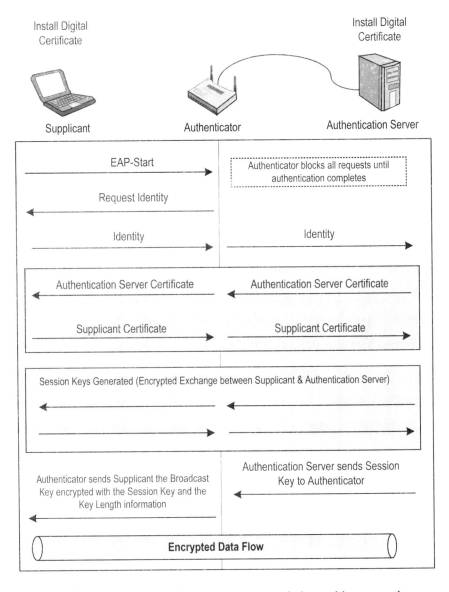

Although TLS is used to configure an encrypted channel between the authentication server and the supplicant, this channel is not used because the supplicant wants to talk to the authenticator, not the authentication server. Instead, a piece of the keying material, created during the TLS session establishment for that channel, is sent to the authenticator. Then, the supplicant (which already knows the TLS-established secret key) and the authenticator use that key for WEP encryption.

In EAP-TLS, certificates are used to authenticate the authentication server to the supplicant, and, optionally, to authenticate the supplicant to the authentication server. The authentication server starts the process by sending its digital certificate to the supplicant. The most common authentication used today on the web with SSL is one-way authentication. With one-way authentication, a server sends its certificate to a browser to prove its identity. However, with TLS-EAP, administrators should be more interested in mutual authentication to protect the network against man-in-the-middle attacks.

The advantages of EAP-TLS make it a preferred authentication method. Both wireless clients and access points are strongly authenticated using digital certificates. As a side effect, a per-session WEP key is set up, and the client can be re-authenticated and re-keyed as often as needed without inconveniencing the end user. EAP-TLS has been scrutinized extensively without being broken or revealing any significant security flaws in the protocol itself, but some implementations have suffered problems with software bugs.

It is important to note that the username is passed from client to server in a TLS exchange before certificates are exchanged, so usernames can easily be observed by passive packet analysis.

 For remote access connections using Windows 2000, if smart cards are being used, the EAP-TLS authentication method must be used.

EAP-Cisco Wireless (LEAP)

Cisco supports 802.1x/EAP based authentication through their proprietary Lightweight Extensible Authentication Protocol (LEAP), which was developed to support networks with a variety of operating systems that may not natively support EAP. At a time when authentication standards used in wireless environments were still evolving rapidly, LEAP offered a convenient way to ensure mutual authentication between a client and a RADIUS server. LEAP provides user-based, centralized authentication as well as per-user per-session WEP keys. LEAP is primarily (but not exclusively) used in Cisco's Aironet products, and all three pieces of the 802.1x design (supplicant, authenticator, & authentication server) must support LEAP. The LEAP process is shown in Figure 11.12.

FIGURE 11.12 LEAP Process

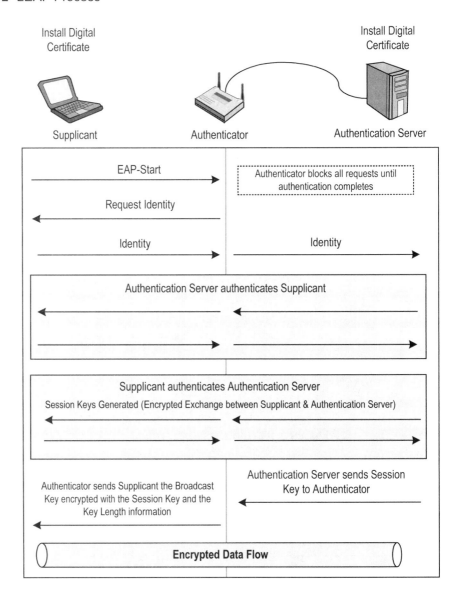

Because LEAP uses only password authentication, its security level can be considered moderate or strong based on the strength of the passwords used. Due to the relatively simple deployment involved with LEAP and the popularity of the Cisco Aironet product line, LEAP has become the most popular form of EAP in use today and is supported by almost all RADIUS vendors. Cisco has LEAP client software that runs on almost all popular operating systems and hardware platforms. Cisco has begun moving toward the new Protected EAP standard, which will be covered later in this section.

EAP-TTLS (Tunneled Transport Layer Security)

EAP-TTLS is an extension to the functionality of the EAP-TLS authentication protocol. EAP-TTLS was co-developed by Funk Software and Certicom for the purpose of building a secure and more easily managed version of EAP. EAP-TTLS requires only an authentication server certificate and removes the EAP-TLS requirement of the supplicant-side certificate, thereby greatly easing deployment overhead.

TTLS uses the TLS channel to exchange "attribute-value pairs" (AVPs), much like RADIUS. (In fact, the AVP encoding format is very similar to RADIUS.) The general encoding of information allows a TTLS server to validate AVPs against any type of authentication mechanism. TTLS implementations today support all methods defined by EAP, as well as several older methods. TTLS can easily be extended to work with new protocols by defining new attributes to support new protocols.

During the initial authentication phase of EAP-TTLS, the authentication server is authenticated using its digital certificate and an encrypted tunnel is established between the supplicant and the authentication server. This tunnel is used to pass the supplicant's authentication credentials (digital certificate, passwords, etc.) to the authentication server using the administrator's authentication algorithm of choice. Some key security features and flexibilities afforded by EAP-TTLS are:

- Almost any kind of supplicant authentication credentials (passwords, certificates, tokens, etc.) can be used inside the encrypted tunnel

- Requirement of only having a server-side certificate eliminates much of the overhead associated with client-side certificate deployment
- Many types of authentication algorithms may be used inside the encrypted tunnel – MS-CHAPv2, MS-CHAP, CHAP, PAP, EAP-MD5, and others are supported.
- Strong protection against eavesdroppers seeking to perform dictionary attacks
- Mutual authentication, fast reconnections while roaming, and automatic re-keying of encryption keys

Enterprise users that want the security of TLS but have legacy authentication methods or token-based authentication methods should consider TTLS as a viable EAP method. The EAP-TTLS process is shown in Figure 11.13.

FIGURE 11.13 EAP-TTLS Process

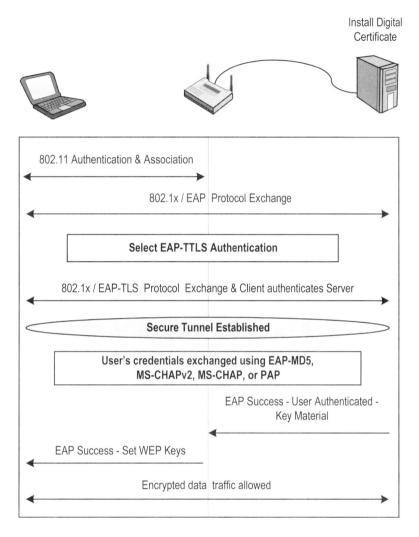

Install Digital
Certificate

802.11 Authentication & Association

802.1x / EAP Protocol Exchange

Select EAP-TTLS Authentication

802.1x / EAP-TLS Protocol Exchange & Client authenticates Server

Secure Tunnel Established

**User's credentials exchanged using EAP-MD5,
MS-CHAPv2, MS-CHAP, or PAP**

EAP Success - User Authenticated -
Key Material

EAP Success - Set WEP Keys

Encrypted data traffic allowed

Products using EAP-TTLS are becoming more common in the market.
The RADIUS server and the supplicant software must support this type of
EAP authentication for the solution to work.

One question commonly asked about TTLS is, "How does the client know
that the server's certificate is valid?" The answer is commonly
accomplished through deployment of a copy of the server's certificate as

part of the supplicant software package. In this way, the supplicant can compare the certificate it was given during installation with the one given to it by the server when it authenticates to the wireless network.

Protected EAP

Just months after EAP was deployed, a number of weaknesses began to appear. These weaknesses include:

Unprotected user information during the EAP negotiation - When using EAP, the initial identity request/response is sent in the clear, so an attacker capturing and analyzing packets could obtain user identities for use in later attacks.

No support for fast reconnections when roaming – EAP authentication on a wireless network can be slow, and when a client is roaming this slow authentication can be a problem when trying to associate with a new access point while network traffic is flowing.

No support for fragmentation and reassembly – EAP does not include packet management, so individual vendors were required to handle packet fragments and reassembly.

To remedy these problems, multiple EAP types were developed. Each type (discussed below) is based on EAP-TLS and is considered suitably strong for wireless networks. Each type corrects the above deficiencies for wireless LAN implementations and has similarities with the other types since they were all derived from the same version. The table in Figure 11.14 compares the available TLS-based EAP types.

FIGURE 11.14 EAP Type Comparison Table

	EAP-TLS (RFC 2716)	EAP-TTLS (IETF Draft)	PEAP (IETF Draft)
Software			
Client Implementations	Cisco, Funk, Meetinghouse, Microsoft, Open1x	Funk, Meetinghouse	Microsoft
Supported Client Platforms	Linux, Mac OSX, Windows 95/98/Me/NT/2k/XP	Linux, Mac OSX, Windows 95/98/Me/NT/2k/XP	Windows XP
Authentication Server Implementation	Cisco, Funk, HP, FreeRADIUS, Meetinghouse, Microsoft	Funk, Meetinghouse	Cisco
Authentication Methods	Client Certificates	CHAP, PAP, MS-CHAP, MS-CHAPv2, EAP	Any EAP method
Protocol Operations			
Basic Protocol Structure	Establish TLS session and validate certificates on both client and server	Two phases: (1) Establish TLS between client and TTLS server (2) Exchange attribute-value pairs between client and server	Two parts: (1) Establish TLS between client and PEAP server (2) Run EAP exchange over TLS tunnel
Fast Session Reconnect	No	Yes	Yes
WEP Integration	Server can supply WEP key with external protocol (e.g. RADIUS extension)		
PKI & Certificate Processing			
Server Certificate	Required	Required	Required
Client Certificate	Required	Optional	Optional
Cert Verification	Through certificate chain or OCSP TLS extension (current Internet draft)		
Effect of Private Key Compromise	Re-issue all server and client certificates	Re-issue certificates for servers (and clients if using client certificates in first TLS exchange)	
Client and User Authentication			
Authentication Direction	Mutual: Uses digital certificates both ways	Mutual: Certificate for server authentication, and tunneled method for client	Mutual: Certificate for server, and protected EAP method for client
Protection of User Identity Exchange	No	Yes; protected by TLS	Yes; protected by TLS

Protected EAP (PEAP) addresses these deficiencies by wrapping EAP in a TLS tunnel. PEAP was developed by Microsoft, Cisco, and RSA Security, and is now an IETF draft. PEAP was designed to protect EAP communication between clients and authenticators. PEAP provides support for identity protection by using TLS to create an encrypted tunnel from the authentication server to the supplicant after verifying the identity of the authentication server. PEAP extends a TLS connection, and once the encrypted tunnel is established, a second EAP authorization process occurs inside the tunnel. The client is authenticated in the second EAP authentication running inside the TLS connection using any implemented EAP authorization type (tokens, passwords, certificates, etc.). PEAP has built-in support for packet fragmentation and reassembly, as well as fast reconnects.

PEAP is administered through a RADIUS server. The administrator must configure PEAP as an EAP type for a given connection policy. On the client-side, PEAP must be supported by the client software and in some cases the firmware also. The PEAP process is shown in Figure 11.15.

FIGURE 11.15 PEAP Process

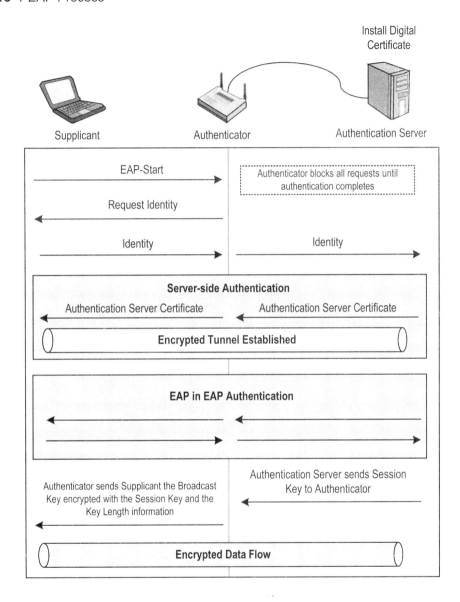

PEAP Authentication

PEAP authentication begins in the same way as EAP-TLS:

1. The client sends an EAP Start message to the access point
2. The access point replies with an EAP Request Identity message
3. The client sends its network access identifier (NAI), which is its username, to the access point in an EAP Response message
4. The access point forwards the NAI to the RADIUS server encapsulated in a RADIUS Access Request message
5. The RADIUS server responds to the client with its digital certificate
6. The client validates the RADIUS server's digital certificate

From this point on, the authentication process diverges from EAP-TLS:

7. The client and server negotiate and create an encrypted tunnel
8. This tunnel provides a secure data path for client authentication
9. Using the TLS Record protocol, a new EAP authentication is initiated by the RADIUS server
10. The exchange includes the transactions specific to the EAP type used for client authentication
11. The RADIUS server sends the access point a RADIUS ACCEPT message, including the client's WEP key, indicating successful authentication

Comparison

Both EAP-TTLS and PEAP were developed in response to market need, but both remove the large hurdle of a PKI required for using EAP-TLS. Client certificates are far from the ideal way to authenticate clients for a variety of reasons, the most predominant of which is management overhead. Many of the older methods of user authentication such as MS-CHAPv2 are basically as secure as certificate-based authentication, but come without the added management overhead required to implement certificates. Both EAP-TTLS and PEAP were designed to use older authentication methods while maintaining the strong cryptographic foundation of TLS.

The structure of TTLS and PEAP are quite similar. Both are two-stage protocols that establish security in stage one and then exchange authentication in stage two. Stage one of both protocols establishes a TLS tunnel and authenticates the authentication server to the client with a certificate. (TTLS and PEAP still use certificates to authenticate the wireless network to the user, but only server-side certificates are required, so it is much more manageable.) Once the secure tunnel has been established, client authentication credentials are exchanged in the second stage.

Availability

PEAP uses the TLS tunnel to protect a second EAP exchange. Authentication must be performed using a protocol that is defined for use with EAP. In practice, the restriction to EAP methods is not a severe drawback because any "important" authentication protocol would be defined for use with EAP in short order so that PEAP could use it. A far greater concern is client software support. Microsoft and Cisco both support PEAP. Client software is built into Microsoft's operating systems and third party add-on software is now available.

TTLS has beaten PEAP to the marketplace, and there are currently more implementations available for TTLS. RADIUS support for TTLS is currently broader than for PEAP, though with Cisco and Microsoft backing PEAP, it should not be long before support for PEAP is included in most versions of RADIUS. Cisco's Aironet Client Utility (ACU) and Windows XP with Service Pack 1 both have support for PEAP. With Microsoft putting native support for PEAP into Windows operating systems such as Windows XP and Windows.NET and Cisco developing cross-platform clients, PEAP implementations and applications should continue to grow in wireless networking.

There are currently two types of PEAP supported by Microsoft: PEAP-EAP-MS-CHAPv2 and PEAP-EAP-TLS. With PEAP-EAP-TLS, server and client side certificates are required, and this is considered the strongest possible level of security. With PEAP-EAP-MS-CHAPv2, password or certificate authentication can be used on the client side. As part of the PEAP process, MS-CHAPv2 supports certificate authentication whereas apart from PEAP, it supports only password authentication. As stand alone authentication protocols, MS-CHAPv1 supports only one-way authentication whereas MS-CHAPv2 supports mutual authentication between client and server using hashed shared secrets (passwords).

EAP Considerations

With the many different features and functionality offered by each EAP implementation, selecting the appropriate one for an installation requires careful consideration. The factors to include when deciding are:

- Mutual Authentication
- Dynamic Key Generation, Rotation, and Distribution
- Costs and Management Overhead
- Industry Acceptance, Standardization, and Support
- Availability and Implementation

Mutual Authentication

EAP methods supporting mutual authentication are recommended for wireless LANs. By having the client authenticate the server as well as the server authenticate the client, attacks from intermediate rogue devices and rogue servers can be prevented. Mutual authentication also ensures that a client is connecting to the correct network. EAP-MD5, which supports only client authentication, is susceptible to man-in-the-middle attacks as shown in Figure 11.16. In this illustration, the attacker receives a copy of the client's request and returns a success message.

FIGURE 11.16 Man-in-the-Middle Attack

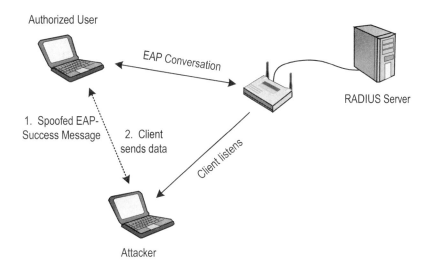

Dynamic Key Generation, Rotation, and Distribution

Keys that are generated per-user for each login session are typically referred to as "dynamic" keys. Each time a user logs into the wireless network, the EAP authentication process creates a new WEP key for the duration of the session or until the end of the preconfigured re-keying period. Because WEP keys are not reused, cracking them is nearly impossible. As keys are regenerated, they are redistributed to the wireless clients from the authentication server.

Broadcast key rotation is also a key consideration. Broadcast keys are not per-user per-session based, so implementing a feature such as broadcast key rotation can eliminate a large security hole.

Costs and Management Overhead

When considering which EAP implementation meets the needs of an organization, you should consider how much on-going maintenance, management, and project startup overhead is required. Costs in both manpower and money should be considered. For example, if hundreds or thousands of wireless users were going to be deployed on the network, management would be considerable if EAP-TLS were used without a previously installed PKI. In this case, client certificates must be installed on each machine, and when a machine is lost or stolen, a certificate must be revoked. Using EAP-TTLS, on the other hand, would only require each workstation to have client software installed, and the authentication occurs through usernames and passwords – eliminating the client certificate problem. Loss or theft of a machine would not pose as great of a security concern provided the username and password were not saved on the machine.

Other costs may come in the form of additional hardware and software, such as software licenses for server applications and per-machine licenses for client software that needs to be purchased. Some RADIUS software packages are more expensive than others, and some 802.1x/EAP client software packages are free while others are not. Purchasing a certificate server software package instead of purchasing hundreds of certificates through a certificate authority may be another consideration.

Industry Acceptance, Standardization, and Support

Proprietary solutions can have the effect of locking organizations into one vendor's hardware or software, and companies are then at the mercy of their vendor for support and upgrades. LEAP (Cisco), PEAP (Microsoft, Cisco, and RSA), EAP/TLS (Microsoft), and Symbol's implementation of Kerberos are each examples of proprietary solutions. Each of these solutions, because each is backed by one or more major vendors in the industry, has the potential to become an industry standard. Once a feature set or particular type of implementation reaches that stage, many more – or even all – hardware and software manufacturers tend to support it.

In the leading edge of layer 2 security, EAP-TTLS and PEAP both have noted industry acceptance due to the major organizational weight behind both. There is no clear leader at this time, because the quality and security levels are so similar, but the key to their future lies within the industry acceptance, support, and marketing. Both have IETF drafts in place, and will both become ratified standards in time.

Availability and Implementation

Two important questions to ask before an EAP purchase are, "What solutions are on the market now that the budget is allocated?" and "How difficult is this solution to implement?" There is always a better solution in the near future, especially when the market is moving as fast as the wireless LAN market is. At some point though, the administrator has to make the decision to buy something. That decision brings with it many questions. No single product suits every need, so careful scrutiny is warranted in order to save time and money. It is suggested that prospective vendors review the organization's network needs, suggest possible solutions, and explain how one solution may fit the organization's needs better than another. This decision process further points out the need for the network administrator to be well versed in most available wireless LAN security solutions.

There are many parts to a solution, and any given network may already have some of these parts in place. For example, many organizations have RADIUS in place already, but the RADIUS software package in use may not support the latest EAP standards. Perhaps only an upgrade to the next version is required to support the wireless LAN, but it is possible that an entirely new package will be required. This one piece of the puzzle may have long-reaching ramifications within a large organization. What if the organization uses a Linux-based RADIUS package, has Linux-trained administrators, and yet the only RADIUS package available to support the EAP standard chosen runs on Windows only? What if the organization is Windows-centric and the appropriate RADIUS package is available but is far more expensive than one that is implemented on Linux? Would that mean hiring a Linux administrator just for the wireless network? There are endless questions that must be asked in situations like this. These types of questions should be considered before moving forward and addressed prior to making a decision. The chart in Figure 11.17 provides a quick reference to what the major EAP types offer.

FIGURE 11.17 EAP Quick Reference Chart

	EAP-MD5	LEAP (Cisco)	EAP-TLS (MS)	PEAP (MS/Cisco)	EAP-TTLS (Funk)
Security Solution	Standards-based	Proprietary (supported by many vendors)	Standards-based	Standards-based	Standards-based
Certificates – Client	N/A	N/A	Yes	No	No
Certificates – Server	N/A	N/A	Yes	Yes	Yes
Client Password Authentication	Yes	Yes	N/A	Yes	Yes
Credential Security	Weak	Moderate (depends on password strength)	Strong	Strong	Strong
Dynamic Key Exchange	No	Yes	Yes	Yes	Yes
Mutual Authentication	No	Yes	Yes	Yes	Yes
Support for legacy Authentication Methods	N/A	N/A	N/A	No	Yes

Selection of an appropriate authentication method is a key decision in securing a wireless LAN deployment. The authentication method drives the choice of authentication server, which in turn drives the choice of client software. Fortunately, selecting an authentication method is a reasonably straightforward endeavor. Unless an existing PKI is already deployed, bypass EAP-TLS to avoid the client certificate administration overhead. Though there is not a large technical difference between the TTLS and PEAP protocols, TTLS has a few advantages. In addition to a degree of flexibility at the protocol level, TTLS products are more readily available and support a much wider variety of client operating systems. Once PEAP support becomes more widely used in the market, it will be a difficult decision as to which is the better choice.

Proprietary Protocols

Proprietary protocols are sometimes used with wireless for many reasons. Some of these reasons are:

- Added security through per packet authentication
- Added security through use of leading-edge encryption algorithms not yet supported by standards
- Added security due to the entire communications process between client and server being strongly encrypted
- Compression to increase throughput over the half-duplex medium

Enterprise Encryption Gateways (EEGs) use proprietary protocols in order to achieve stronger security and increased throughput over the wireless LAN segment. Though there are obvious advantages to these leading-edge features, the main disadvantage here is being proprietary. In today's market place, vendor interoperability is extremely important, and having such leading features makes the target market for such a vendor very specific. In a case like this, the most likely target market candidate would be a government organization.

Use of proprietary protocols gives EEGs the ability to implement features not yet available on the market in any other types of products. Additionally, stronger encryption algorithms can be used as a competitive advantage in the market place.

Summary

This chapter covered the three basic categories of authentication and encryption in wireless LANs: static WEP, dynamic WEP, and proprietary protocols. A brief overview was given on WEP's usage and its inherent insecurity. TKIP and a Message Integrity Check were discussed as a solution to WEP's weaknesses. The different types of Extensible Authentication Protocols were reviewed in detail. Each EAP process flow was shown to allow a better understanding of how each protocol performs authentication. Advantages of dynamic key management and their implementation methods were compared along with the EAP types including EAP-MD5, EAP-TLS, LEAP, EAP-TTLS, and PEAP. Considerations for questions network administrators should ask before selecting enterprise wireless solutions were presented. Finally, proprietary protocols and their benefits in wireless solutions were reviewed.

Key Terms

Before taking the exam, you should be familiar with the following terms:

authentication server

authenticator

broadcast key rotation (BKR)

EAP-Cisco Wireless (LEAP)

EAP-Transport Level Security (EAP-TLS)

EAP-TTLS (Tunneled Transport Layer Security)

Extensible Authentication Protocol (EAP)

Initialization Vector (IV)

Message Integrity Check (MIC)

mutual authentication

network access identifier (NAI)

Point-to-Point Protocol (PPP)

Protected EAP (PEAP)

Public Key Infrastructure (PKI)

RADIUS

supplicant

Temporal Key Integrity Protocol (TKIP)

Review Questions

1. _____ frames may be authenticated on a wireless LAN.

   A. Management

   B. Data

   C. Control

   D. Response

2. Which of the following is used to prevent tampering of packets in transit between the source and destination hosts?

   A. RADIUS

   B. Message Integrity Check

   C. 802.1x

   D. Initialization Vector

3. TKIP addresses which of the following weaknesses in WEP?

   A. Direct multicast attacks

   B. Man-on-the-side attacks

   C. Weak-key attacks

   D. Replay attacks

4. 802.1x / EAP solutions allows strong _____ and _____ due to RADIUS support and rotating keys.

   A. authentication

   B. authorization

   C. mobility

   D. encryption

5. The 802.1x standard defines _____

    A. Authentication

    B. Packet filtering

    C. Subnet roaming

    D. Port-based access control

6. Which of the following EAP types are based on an implementation derived from EAP-TLS?

    A. LEAP

    B. PEAP

    C. EAP-MD5

    D. EAP-TTLS

    E. EAP-SIM

7. _____ can prevent rogue access points from hijacking legitimate users on the wireless network.

    A. Mutual authentication

    B. PKI

    C. Proprietary protocols

    D. Supplicant filtering

8. Which version(s) of EAP require certificates?

    A. LEAP

    B. EAP-MD5

    C. EAP-TLS

    D. EAP-TTLS

    E. PEAP

9. Which of the following are pieces of an 802.1x system?

   A. Encryption algorithm

   B. Supplicant

   C. Authenticator

   D. Supplicator

   E. Authentication Server

10. Which versions of EAP build and use encrypted tunnels between the client and RADIUS before authentication happens?

    A. EAP-TLS

    B. LEAP

    C. EAP-TTLS

    D. PEAP

    E. EAP-MD5

11. EAP-TLS is most easily implemented when a _____ is already in place.

    A. GPRS

    B. PKI

    C. AES

    D. SQL

12. Which version of EAP does not support mutual authentication?

    A. EAP-TTLS

    B. LEAP

    C. EAP-MD5

    D. EAP-TLS

13. Which version of EAP supports use of MS-CHAPv2 for authentication inside of an encrypted tunnel?

    A. LEAP

    B. EAP-MD5

    C. PEAP

    D. EAP-TTLS

14. In an 802.1x-based network, the client is considered which of the following?

    A. Authentication Catalyst

    B. Mobile Roamer

    C. Supplicant

    D. Authenticator

    E. Authentication Server

Answers to Review Questions

1. B
2. B
3. C, D
4. A, D
5. D
6. B, D
7. A
8. C, D, E
9. B, C, E
10. C, D
11. B
12. C
13. C, D
14. C

802.11i & Wi-Fi Protected Access

CWSP Exam Objectives Covered:

❖ 802.11i and Wi-Fi Protected Access (WPA)

802.11i

The IEEE 802.11i standard, which addresses wireless LAN security, is still in draft format as of this writing. This new standard specifies use of Temporal Key Integrity Protocol (TKIP) and 802.1x/EAP with mutual authentication as possible security solutions. Multiple methods of using AES are also specified as part of 802.11i, and any wireless LAN equipment complying with this standard will likely require a hardware upgrade due to the cryptographic overhead inherent with AES.

The following list contains some of the currently available information from within the 802.11i draft.

- The CCM protocol (CCMP), based on AES-CCMP, is the mandatory encryption algorithm and it is currently under consideration by NIST.
- An ad hoc solution including per-station broadcast keys and pair-wise unicast keys will be available. Each station will act as a supplicant and authentication server.
- 802.11i TKIP = Simple Secure Networking (SSN) TKIP = WPA TKIP

Wi-Fi Protected Access (WPA)

Wi-Fi Protected Access was co-developed by the Wi-Fi Alliance and the IEEE 802.11 Task Group I as an interim security solution while the 802.11i Task Group addresses the details involved with securing wireless LANs. WPA (in its initial rollout) is the implementation and standardization of TKIP and 802.1x/EAP technologies as a subset of the forthcoming IEEE 802.11i standard. The second version of WPA, due out at the end of 2003, will be a standard that complies with most, if not all, of the 802.11i standard. Having multiple and growing versions of WPA will undoubtedly cause some confusion among end-users and hardship on wireless network administrators. The Wi-Fi Alliance has begun WPA compliance testing as part of the Wi-Fi certification process, but compliance will not be mandatory until the fourth quarter of 2003.

WPA is designed to run on existing hardware as a security upgrade firmware patch. Firmware upgrades are already being rolled out according to the Wi-Fi Alliance. The goals of WPA are strong data encryption through TKIP and mutual authentication through 802.1x/EAP solutions. In its initial version, WPA will *not* include the following 802.11i items:

- Secure IBSS
- Secure fast handoff
- Secure de-authentication and disassociation
- Advanced Encryption Standard

One consideration regarding use of TKIP solutions prior to Wi-Fi certification testing is the possible lack of interoperability between vendors. Just as with WEP, incompatibilities due to differing implementations will cause problems for organizations that wish to implement multi-vendor solutions.

Pre-Shared Key

In a home or Small Office/Home Office (SOHO) environment, in which there are no central authentication servers and no EAP framework, WPA runs in a special home mode. This mode, also called Pre-Shared Key (PSK), allows the use of manually entered keys or passwords and is designed to be easy for the home user to configure. All the home user needs to do is enter a password (also called a "master key" or "pass phrase") in their access point or home wireless gateway as plaintext (no hex) and each PC associated to the Wi-Fi wireless network. WPA takes over automatically from that point. First, the password allows only devices with a matching password to join the network, keeping out eavesdroppers and other unauthorized users. Second, the password automatically starts the TKIP encryption process.

Mixed Mode Deployment

In a large network with many clients, Wi-Fi access points may be upgraded before all of the Wi-Fi clients. Some access points may operate in a "mixed mode", which supports clients running both Wi-Fi protected access and clients running original WEP security. While useful for transition, the net effect of supporting both types of client devices is that security will operate at the less secure level (WEP) that is common to all the devices. Therefore, organizations will benefit by accelerating the move to WPA or other security solutions for all Wi-Fi clients and access points.

Deployment

As part of the Wi-Fi product certification, the Wi-Fi Alliance will initially allow vendors to ship units with WPA disabled, but easily enabled and configured. When WPA is included as a mandatory part of Wi-Fi certification testing, devices must ship with WPA security enabled by default. At that time, a user will have to configure a master key or authentication server as part of the initial installation and configuration.

Limitations

TKIP is built around WEP, and TKIP and WEP have not, nor can either one be expected to, receive recognition by security compliance authorities. Government deployments require that encryption technologies be certified to comply with the FIPS 140 standard published by NIST, while hospitals and medical facilities must comply with security guidelines outlined by HIPAA legislation. The financial industry must comply with regulations regarding the protection of customer records. In all of these cases, data encryption must be provided through the use of 3DES or AES technology, which is most typically implemented using IPSec based VPN technology.

Summary

This chapter discusses the IEEE 802.11i draft and its importance in securing existing and future wireless networks. WPA is a new set of tools defined by the IEEE and implemented by the Wi-Fi Alliance to secure wireless networks. WPA compliance will be necessary in order for vendors to receive or maintain product certification from the Wi-Fi Alliance. There will be multiple modes of WPA operation to allow for varying environments. PSK will accommodate small office/home office networks that have no central authentication server, EAP framework, or VPN solutions. Mixed Mode Deployment will compensate for environments that may have several types of authentication and encryption solutions in place by smoothing the transition between legacy and leading edge security standards. United States government restrictions on security require higher levels of encryption than those offered in WEP and TKIP solutions. These restrictions push wireless manufacturers toward standardization on security solutions that implement 3DES or AES.

Key Terms

Before taking the exam, you should be familiar with the following terms:

CCM protocol (CCMP)

pre-shared key

Simple Secure Networking (SSN)

Wi-Fi Protected Access (WPA)

Review Questions

1. What encryption technology has the IEEE 802.11i Task Group chosen as its next generation encryption technology.

    A. PSK

    B. RC6

    C. AES

    D. 3DES

2. The Wi-Fi Alliance is adding wireless LAN security to its interoperability testing. Which two of the following are included in the Wi-Fi Alliance's WPA standard?

    A. 802.1x / EAP

    B. WEP-256

    C. TKIP

    D. WVPN

    E. WTLS

3. What is the most significant drawback of implementing AES as part of a wireless LAN security solution?

    A. All hardware and software in the wireless LAN solution must be replaced

    B. Very expensive VPN servers must be purchased

    C. Mathematical calculations must be performed by the IT staff before entering keys into devices

    D. Existing WLAN infrastructure devices must be replaced

4.   WPA supports a special home mode for SOHO implementations. What does this home mode use as a security mechanism?

A.   RADIUS

B.   Pre-shared Keys

C.   Encrypted Tunnels

D.   Mutual Authentication

5.   The Wi-Fi Alliance plans to adjust the implementation of WPA to match which of the following standards when it is released?

A.   IEEE 802.11i

B.   IEEE 802.11g

C.   IEEE 802.11f

D.   IEEE 802.11e

6.   The Wi-Fi Alliance has chosen to use _____ as part of its initial implementation of WPA to ensure strong authentication and data integrity.

A.   AES

B.   802.1x / EAP

C.   TKIP

D.   3DES

E.   WVP

Answers to Review Questions

1. C
2. A, C
3. D
4. B
5. A
6. B, C

Wireless VPN Technology

CWSP Exam Objectives Covered:

❖ Virtual Private networks

- Implement, configure, and manage the following VPN solutions in a wireless LAN environment:

  - PPTP

  - IPSec

  - L2TP

- Explain the importance and benefits of session persistence in a wireless VPN environment

- Explain the differences, strengths, and limitations of each of the following as a wireless VPN solution

  - Routers

  - VPN Concentrators

  - Firewalls

- Describe benefits of mobile VPN solutions

❖ Software Solutions

- Implement software solutions for the following

- SSH2 Tunneling

- Securing wireless thin clients

- Port redirection

- Transport Layer Security (TLS)

Virtual Private Networks

This chapter covers VPN technology as it relates to how and when it is used in a wireless environment. The details of the inter-workings of each VPN technology discussed are beyond the scope of this text.

Virtual private networks (VPN) provide a method for a combination of computer and networks to securely communicate together over public or unsecured network connections. The Internet is often used as a public medium for transporting data between private networks. VPNs use authentication to ensure that only authorized users can access the network and encryption to ensure that third parties cannot read data in transit.

Before VPNs, the only way to safely connect multiple sites within or between organizations was through expensive, dedicated leased lines that linked the various local area networks (LANs). This type of solution was limited to very large corporations because of the high expense and time required to install dedicated lines. By using an inexpensive public medium for transmission, VPNs can be used to create a secure connection at a fraction of the cost of a leased line. The combination of the Internet and VPN technologies has resulted in wide industry acceptance of VPNs as an alternative to leased lines for use in preventing unauthorized access and data privacy. VPNs typically employ a form of encapsulation (tunneling) where one protocol is carried inside of another from one end-point to another within the VPN. Since the Internet is the prime example of an unsecured and public network, it will be used as the example throughout this chapter. Any time that the Internet is mentioned, you may assume that the same principle applies with any public access or unsecured network.

VPN connections have the following properties:

encapsulation – private data is encapsulated with a header that allows the data to traverse the transit internetwork

user authentication – the VPN server can authenticate the client to verify that the client has permission to access the network. If mutual authentication is used, the client will also verify the VPN server's identity.

data integrity – cryptographic checksums can be included so that the receiver can verify the data originated at the sender and was not tampered with in the process of transmission

data encryption – data is encrypted by the sender and decrypted by the receiver using a key. The size of the key and which encryption algorithm used determines how easily an attacker may decrypt the data. The type of encryption used is an important factor in the latency of the transmission because stronger encryption algorithms require more time by the VPN server and client device to encrypt and decrypt.

Wireless VPNs

The use of VPN technology over a wireless medium is often referred to as a *wireless VPN*. Using wireless VPNs allows mobile users to securely access a corporate network from remote locations (such as a wireless hot spot) or from a segmented part of the local area network such as behind an enterprise wireless gateway or firewall device. The goal of a wireless VPN is to ensure data privacy over an unsecured network segment. An attacker can easily analyze wireless data connections. Analyzing unsecured wireless data could provide the attacker with passwords or sensitive data.

VPN Process

The components that make up a VPN consist primarily of resources already in place, enhanced by VPN hardware products, software packages, or both. These additional components implement the VPN security protocols. Most organizations use VPN protocols sparingly, and only implement them in cases where the messages are traversing the Internet. The VPN's security mechanisms are applied between a pair of endpoints, each of which connects via the Internet to one or more computers. A device that initiates a connection to a VPN server (also called a VPN concentrator) is a VPN client. A VPN client can be an individual computer obtaining remote access (Figure 13.1) or a router that obtains a peer-to-peer (also called a router-to-router) VPN connection (Figure 13.2).

FIGURE 13.1 Client/Server VPN Configuration

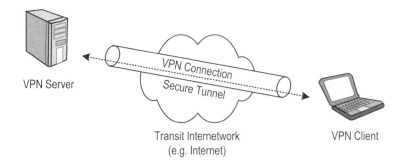

FIGURE 13.2 Peer-to-Peer VPN Configuration

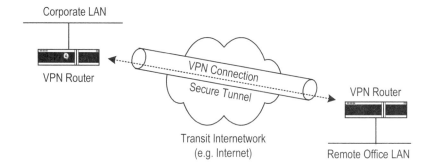

When a VPN is configured between two or more locations, the connection between the locations is referred to as a "tunnel". Encapsulating one protocol inside another creates the "tunnel." Authentication at the peer or VPN server device is accomplished through the use of credentials provided by the client or peer device. Passwords, smart cards, certificates, biometrics, and other methods are commonly deployed for VPN authentication.

The type of VPN technology used is selected and configured when the VPN is installed. During tunnel setup, the devices on each side of the tunnel agree on the details of authentication and encryption, and a VPN is then created between the two end points based on the tunneling protocol used. The tunneling protocols are communication standards used to build and manage the tunnels and to encapsulate private data. Some standard protocols, described later in this section, include PPTP (Point-to-Point

Tunneling Protocol), L2TP (Layer 2 Tunneling Protocol), and IPSec (Internet Protocol Security). The data is encrypted on one end, transmitted, and decrypted on the other end. When one side terminates the connection, the VPN ends.

VPN Considerations

VPN technology is an important part of an overall security design and is often implemented in one form or another regardless of the network's design. However, with wireless networking, VPNs do not always fulfill every design requirement. For maximum security, both layer 2 and layer 3 of the OSI model should be secured in any wireless environment. Of course, this level of security may often present high costs, reduced throughput, high network overhead, and high administrative overhead, but the cost of the solution should be directly related to the value of the data that is being protected by that solution.

Acceptance

VPNs enjoyed broad industry acceptance well before they were used as a wireless LAN security solution. Security administrators have understood the concepts behind VPN technologies for a number of years – well before the recent proliferation of wireless LANs. Due to the higher costs and sometimes difficult implementation of VPNs, 802.1x solutions have taken somewhat of a front-seat in the wireless security market. Some manufacturers produce both VPN and 802.1x/EAP solutions and are quick to say that 802.1x/EAP solutions are better suited to wireless as a single solution. These manufacturers do not suggest incorporating layer 2 solutions with layer 3 solutions because of high costs, high encryption overhead, and redundant authentication. For these reasons, 802.1x/EAP solutions have been gaining in popularity in some markets.

Advantages

Advantages of using VPNs in wireless environments include:

- Very secure encryption is available
- Connections are point-to-point, increasing security

- Well established standards are readily available from many vendors
- Many security administrators already understand VPN technology
- Most VPN servers work with established authentication methods like RADIUS
- Class-of-Service (CoS) mechanisms like RBAC can be deployed
- VPNs reduce broadcast domains in comparison with 802.1x/EAP solutions
- Authentication can be performed through a web browser, allowing almost any type of user access to the network

Disadvantages

Some disadvantages of VPN technology in wireless environments include:

- Expensive in almost any size network
- Hot failover designs are very expensive
- Advanced routing is difficult
- Lack of interoperability between vendors of VPN technology
- Lack of operating system support across multiple platforms
- Clients and servers can be difficult to configure, deploy, and maintain
- High encryption/decryption overhead (reduced throughput)
- Based on layer 3 technology so subnet roaming will break

Security Issues

Since wireless networks operate at layer 2 of the OSI model, layer 3 VPNs have an inherent security hole when used in wireless networks. This weakness is that the access points and/or wireless bridges are left open to attack. This problem is most apparent when using enterprise wireless gateways (EWGs) or VPN server appliances as a wireless LAN solution. While the advantages to using an EWG may outweigh its security holes, this problem can be a serious one if not dealt with properly. For this reason, the current 802.1x solutions have shared in the market success of wireless VPNs and increased use of layered security solutions.

One danger that is often encountered by those who deploy wireless in combination with VPN technology is unintentional sharing of the VPN connection. Consider a situation where a doctor wants to telecommute securely from home, and the network administrator installs a VPN client device at his residence. This allows the doctor to use any of his computers to access the hospital network securely. The doctor decides that a wireless LAN in his home would be a great convenience and installs a SOHO class access point for Internet, print, and file sharing. This doctor's neighbor can now associate to the doctor's access point and is allocated an IP address from the doctor's home network. Now the neighbor has secure access into the hospital just as though he were the doctor. When the neighbor decides to plunder through the hospital network, the hospital's intrusion detection system starts sending alarms to the network administrator who immediately traces the activity to the doctor's connection. Then the doctor has to go visit the hospital CIO about why he has been looking through files that do not concern him. Such a simple scenario is often overlooked both in deciding on a particular solution and in educating the users on such a solution.

Administration

It is common to see wireless VPNs administered from a remote NOC or IT data center. It is also common to have unsecured wired networks between these points of management and the VPN devices. For these reasons, it is typical to see VPN servers managed over a VPN tunnel. Many vendors in the wireless middleware market space securely manage hotspots and campus environments in this manner. Often, distributed VPN servers terminating tunnels to wireless clients will wrap all user data in another upstream tunnel to deliver the data securely to a centralized VPN server that connects to the Internet and/or a corporate network. This method of management is used in many wireless hot spot networks as shown in figure 13.3 below.

FIGURE 13.3   Multiple VPN Tunnel Hops over Local and Wide Area Networks

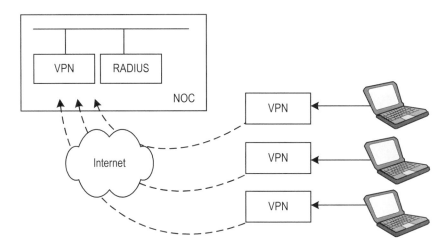

Scalability

As a wireless network expands to hundreds or thousands of users, a wireless VPN solution that can scale and meet the growing demand of users is essential. The best solutions will grow with an organization without constant replacement and end user re-training. When choosing a solution, be aware of:

- Prices of new components – both hardware and software
- Standards support and the maturity of those standards
- Proprietary solutions
- Vendor interoperability
- How new devices fit within the existing network, security, and management architectures

Subnet Roaming

Another major hindrance to the use of wireless VPN security solutions, if not corrected with proper feature sets, is subnet roaming. Wireless users roam, which is one of the primary reasons for installing a wireless network. When a user roams across routers, the computer typically obtains a new IP address from the new subnet using DHCP. This process of roaming and changing IP addresses will break VPNs and any kind of data flow in process. For this reason, MobileIP has been successfully introduced as part of a VPN solution. MobileIP VPNs will be discussed in a later section. Some vendors use routing protocols and bridged interfaces (wireless and wired are bridged together) to solve subnet roaming while using a VPN solution. This combination works well, but can be complicated to configure and manage in large environments.

Role-based Access Control

A significant advantage that VPNs exhibit over 802.1x solutions is that of Role-based Access Control, or RBAC. The ability to assign guest user, authorized user, administrator user and other types of privileges (such as server access or high bandwidth levels) based on a user's role in the network has many advantages. For example, if a guest wireless network user wanted to pull MP3 files from an FTP server on a network with large WAN pipes, that user alone could saturate the wireless network quickly – denying access to authorized users. RBAC can prevent such an unintentional denial of service. Another advantage would be reducing administrative overhead such as when a contractor, guest, or other type of user uses the Internet through your wireless network. The company may have no interest in encrypting this user's data, and by assigning the guest user to a particular role, no user registration or other confusing tasks are necessary, and no support calls are generated. Being able to individualize account features and put users into roles has significant value in some vertical markets.

VLANs

VPNs will cause the wireless security design to differ greatly from that of an 802.1x/EAP solution. For example, with 802.1x/EAP, it may be necessary to deploy a network-wide VLAN (or multiple VLANs) just for use with wireless. This method is the accepted standard and widely used today, but requires significant administrative overhead for deployment. VPNs servers are essentially encrypting routers with authentication support. For this reason, segmentation will happen at layer 3 in your network rather than layer 2 as with 802.1x/EAP solutions. This solution is equally overhead heavy, and requires skilled and experienced IT professionals to implement.

VPN Types

There are many VPN uses, including remote access, extranets, branch offices, SOHO, and wireless. Though a VPN has many uses, there are only two types of connections made with a VPN – remote access connections and router-to-router connections.

 A thorough discussion of each VPN type is beyond the scope of this book, and only an overview of VPN technology used with wireless LANs will be discussed.

Remote Access Connections

A remote access VPN is created when a client initiates a connection to a VPN server, as shown in Figure 13.4. The VPN server can provide upstream network access to the client, or just to those network resources that the VPN has available locally. Packets transmitted through the tunnel originate from the client and are sent to the server or vise versa since the remote access VPN is a point-to-point connection. Some VPNs can be configured for mutual authentication of client and server for added security, though in many cases (such as dial-up RAS) authentication is not mutual, and only the server authenticates the client.

When VPN technology is used in a wireless environment, the client "dials" the VPN server (as in the case of PPTP) or sends "interesting traffic" to the server (as in the case of IPSec). In either case, the client must have VPN software loaded – whether a computer or a router is used as the client. Again, this VPN connection over the wireless medium leaves the access point open to attack. Access points are layer 2 devices that can be managed at layer 3. Since they are layer 2 devices, they do not care what kind of traffic is traversing the wireless medium. They will simply forward all traffic from the wireless side to the wired side without regard for security.

Some manufacturers have implemented the VPN server directly inside the access point, making the access point more of a wireless router than just an access point. This feature, plus secured management features such as HTTPS, provides a very secure solution. This type of solution also presents a problem: slow processing. Access points are generally

inexpensive devices that lack powerful CPUs. The overhead of VPN
setup and teardown added to management features, access point features,
routing functions (VPN servers are inherently routers), and high
encryption overhead tend to degrade the performance of these units fairly
quickly.

Another feature seen in this solution is secure VPN redirection, which
occurs when an access point is configured to allow incoming VPN traffic
to be sent only to a single VPN server host. In this scenario, only one
VPN server is being used, but each wireless router is redirecting the VPN
traffic to a specified IP address.

The most common implementation of VPNs in wireless LAN
environment comes in the form of Enterprise Wireless Gateways, or
EWGs. EWGs usually have firewall features, Role-Based Access Control
(RBAC), VPN features, throughput management, remote management,
and many other interesting features.

FIGURE 13.4   Remote Access VPN

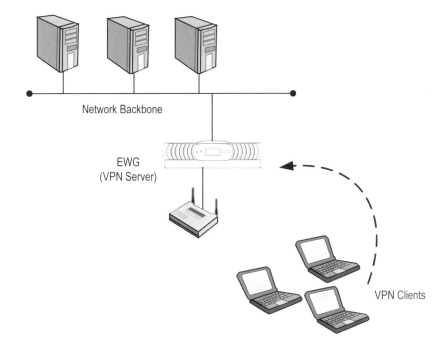

Peer-to-Peer Connections

Peer-to-Peer (router-to-router) VPN connections connect two private networks. The networks can be in buildings next to each other, as on a school campus, or they can exist miles apart, in different states, or even in different countries. Packets sent from either router across the VPN connection typically do not originate at the routers, but at some client that is connected to the network behind the router.

Peer-to-Peer connections are often seen when VPNs are implemented across wireless bridge links as shown in Figure 13.5. This scenario has the advantages of authentication of remote sites at the hub site (in a point-to-multipoint environment), strong encryption using established standards, and scalability. Disadvantages include leaving bridges open to attack and the added routing management and IP subnetting overhead.

FIGURE 13.5 Peer-to-Peer VPN over Bridge Links

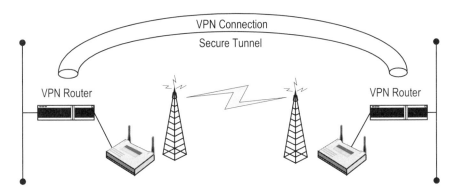

Another common scenario for peer-to-peer VPNs is when EWGs or VPN Servers connect to each other across wired networks, often across unsecured layer 3 boundaries such as when roaming between hotspots or between corporate offices. This scenario is shown in Figure 13.6. Secure connections between the VPN servers or gateways are necessary anytime the data traverses an unsecured or uncontrolled network segment between the units. Users often roam across unsecured layer 3 boundaries, necessitating this kind of back-end security. The scenario has also given rise to new VPN technologies such as MobileIP IPSec VPNs, which will be discussed later in this lesson.

FIGURE 13.6   Peer-to-Peer VPN between EWGs

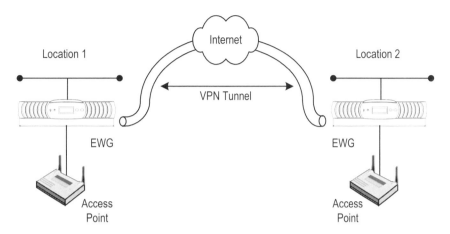

VPN Protocols

There are many types of VPN protocols used in conjunction with wireless LANs such as PPTP, L2TP, IPSec, and SSH2. All of these protocols rely on tunneling of some form and usually employ encryption. Encryption levels deployed with each of these VPN types vary greatly, and the method in which the encryption is implemented also varies. Each of these VPN protocols is discussed below.

Acceleration & Latency

Encryption and decryption are performed either in hardware or software. Hardware encryption/decryption accelerators will decrease latency and increase throughput, whereas software-based encryption/decryption typically has the opposite effect. High latency in a network can rule out use of some types of applications and some uses of the network itself such as voice or video.

Some access points include accelerators (sometimes called offload processors) for speeding the encryption/decryption of WEP, and likewise, many VPN servers have additional processors that do the same. If the VPN server is implemented in a PC server, the accelerator may come in the form of a PCI card and accompanying software. If implemented in a

VPN appliance such as an EWG, the accelerator is often another chip on the motherboard.

Many of the newest EWGs come with Gigabit Ethernet interfaces. Most of the time, these units cannot push more than 100 Mbps of heavily encrypted (e.g. IPSec using 3DES or AES) traffic and only have Gigabit interfaces for use when encryption is not desired. Even when encryption is not used, it is common to see EWG units push no more than 300 Mbps.

PPTP

Point-to-Point-Tunneling Protocol (PPTP) is a simple VPN technology that supports multiple encapsulated protocols, authentication, and encryption and is based on the Point-to-Point Protocol (PPP). PPTP enables users to access remote or wireless networks securely and easily. PPTP uses a client/server architecture, and is characterized as a low cost and easily implemented solution. Microsoft developed PPTP and most of Microsoft's desktop and server operating systems support PPTP natively.

PPTP supports Microsoft Point-to-Point Encryption (MPPE) using the RC4 algorithm with a 128-bit key. Most VPN servers supporting PPTP do both local authentication and/or external authentication using RADIUS. PPTP support has been implemented in the Linux server software called POPTOP and is fully compatible with Microsoft PPTP client software. Since the only pieces of information needed to form a PPTP connection are the destination IP address, encryption parameters, and username/password pair, using PPTP over wireless networks is very popular.

PPTP works by forming a tunnel between the client and server as shown in Figure 13.7. PPTP is most often implemented as an IP-in-IP tunnel where the client/server connection has an IP subnet, and the tunnel itself has a different subnet. DHCP can be used for both subnets inside and outside the tunnel, eliminating much administrative overhead. Tunnel IP addresses are usually handed out by the PPTP VPN server.

Many protocols can be encapsulated inside of IP for use with PPTP, but with wireless networks, IP-in-IP is by far the most common. The PPTP client connects with the server by "dialing" the server over the IP network. The server then authenticates the user, establishes tunnel addresses, and begins passing traffic to and from the client.

FIGURE 13.7   PPTP Network

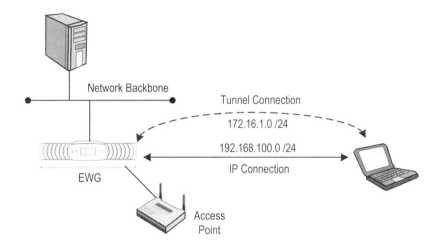

The authentication methods used by PPTP are typically PAP, MS-CHAP or MS-CHAPv2. Due to stringent and scalable security requirements placed on wireless LAN implementations by most organizations, MS-CHAPv2 authentication against a RADIUS or LDAP compliant database with MPPE encryption is most often used. Using the 128-bit Microsoft Point-to-Point Encryption (MPPE) will be adequate protection for most SOHO networks or networks with no extremely valuable data or systems to protect. Encrypting data with 128-bit MPPE inside a tunnel provides enough protection to stop the casual or unskilled war driver while keeping administrative and network overhead low and keeping costs down.

L2TP

L2TP is one of the key building blocks for virtual private networks in the dial access space and is supported by Cisco and other internetworking industry leaders. L2TP combines the best of Cisco's Layer 2 Forwarding (L2F) protocol and Microsoft's Point-to-Point Tunneling Protocol (PPTP).

L2TP is commonly used in the telco/ISP space for large implementations of PPP call terminations. There are two distinct parts to the L2TP network – the L2TP Access Concentrator (LAC) and the L2TP Network Server (LNS). The LAC terminates the client's physical connection (such as with a dial-up connection to the Internet), and the upstream LNS terminates the PPP session. A typical L2TP connection scenario is shown in Figure 13.8. Using this model, LACs can route PPP sessions to various service providers or locations, making this solution highly scalable. L2TP does not define any encryption standard and thus is often combined with IPSec for security. IPSec is used for mutual authentication using shared keys or certificates and strong encryption.

FIGURE 13.8 L2TP over IPSec

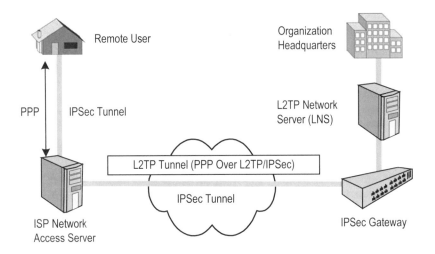

L2TP is rarely used with wireless networks at this point, but it is likely to gain in popularity as wireless networks grow in size and L2TP support is included in EWGs. As Wireless ISPs (WISPs) gain market share, telecommuters and hotspot users will likely find using L2TP/IPSec over wireless an appropriate and adequate security solution. Both Microsoft Windows 2000 and Windows XP support L2TP/IPSec VPN technology.

Similarities to PPTP

L2TP/IPSec and PPTP are similar in the following ways:

- Both provide a logical transport mechanism to send PPP frames.

- Both provide tunneling and encapsulation so that PPP frames based on any protocol can be sent across an IP network.

- Both rely on the PPP connection process to perform user authentication, typically using a user name and password, and protocol configuration.

Differences from PPTP

L2TP/IPSec and PPTP are different in the following ways:

- With PPTP, data encryption begins after the PPP connection process (and, therefore, PPP authentication) is completed, so the user authentication process is not encrypted. With L2TP/IPSec, data encryption begins before the PPP connection process, so that the user authentication process is encrypted.

- PPTP connections use MPPE, which uses the Rivest-Shamir-Aldeman (RSA) RC-4 encryption algorithm and 40, 56, or 128-bit encryption keys. L2TP/IPSec connections use the Data Encryption Standard (DES) algorithm, which uses either a 56-bit key for DES or three 56-bit keys for Triple DES (3DES). The Microsoft L2TP/IPSec VPN client supports only DES encryption.

- PPTP connections require only user-level authentication through a PPP-based authentication protocol. L2TP/IPSec connections require two levels of authentication. To create the IPSec security associations (SAs) to protect the L2TP-encapsulated data, an L2TP/IPSec client must perform a computer-level authentication with a certificate or a pre-shared key. After the IPSec SAs are successfully created, the L2TP portion of the connection performs the same user-level authentication as PPTP.

Advantages of Using L2TP

The following are the advantages of using L2TP/IPSec:

- IPSec provides per-packet data origin authentication (proof that the data was sent by the authorized user), data integrity (proof that the data was not modified in transit), replay protection (prevention from resending a stream of captured packets), and data confidentiality (prevention from interpreting captured packets without the encryption key). By contrast, PPTP provides only per-packet data confidentiality.

- L2TP/IPSec connections require stronger authentication by requiring two levels of authentication: a computer-level authentication using certificates or pre-shared keys for the IPSec session and a user-level authentication using a PPP authentication protocol for the L2TP tunnel.

- PPP frames exchanged during user-level authentication are never sent in an unencrypted form because the PPP connection process for L2TP/IPSec occurs after the IPSec SAs are established. The PPP authentication exchange for some types of PPP authentication protocols, if captured as plaintext, can be used to perform offline dictionary attacks and determine user passwords. By encrypting the PPP authentication exchange, offline dictionary attacks are only possible after the encrypted packets have been successfully decrypted.

Historically, one of the problems with L2TP/IPSec is that IPSec peers cannot be placed behind a network address translator (NAT) because Internet Key Exchange (IKE), the protocol used to negotiate SAs, and IPSec-protected traffic is not NAT-translatable. However, a new set of Internet standards describe IPSec NAT traversal, in which IKE messages and processing are modified and IPSec-protected packets are encapsulated as User Datagram Protocol (UDP) messages. This process allows L2TP/IPSec connections to be created for client and server computers that support IPSec NAT traversal and are located behind one or multiple NATs.

Until the release of Microsoft L2TP/IPSec VPN client, L2TP/IPSec could only be used with Windows XP and Windows 2000 VPN clients because only those clients support the L2TP protocol and IPSec. With the release of Microsoft L2TP/IPSec VPN client, computers running Windows 98 (all versions), Windows Millennium Edition, and Windows NT Workstation 4.0 can also create L2TP/IPSec remote access connections.

IPSec/IKE

IPSec/IKE actually refers to a collection of IETF standards (RFCs 2401 to 241X) that include specifics on key management protocols (such as Internet Key Exchange - IKE), as well as the encrypted packet formats/protocols (IP Security - IPSec). IPSec/IKE supports a wide variety of encryption algorithms (DES, 3DES, AES, RC4) as well as data integrity mechanisms (MD5, SHA-1). IPSec Data integrity comes in two types: 128-bit strength *Message Digest 5* (MD5)-HMAC or 160-bit strength *secure hash algorithm* (SHA)-HMAC. Because the bit strength of SHA is greater, it is considered more secure. It is recommended to use SHA because the increased security outweighs the slight processor increase in overhead (in fact, SHA is sometimes faster than MD5 in certain hardware implementations).

The standard also names support for pre-shared secrets and X.509 digital certificates for authenticating VPN peers. IPSec is a network layer VPN technology, meaning that IPSec operates independent of the application(s) that may use it. IPSec encapsulates the original IP data packet with its own packet, thus hiding all application protocol information (when using Tunnel Mode IPSec). Once an IPSec tunnel is negotiated via IKE, one-to-many connections of various types (web, email, file transfer, VoIP) can flow over it, with each connection destined for different servers behind the VPN gateway.

Security Features

IPSec provides a number of security features that prevent:

eavesdropping – by encrypting headers and data, only the receiver can understand the data that is transmitted.

data modification - guarantees that packets transmitted are not intercepted and altered in any way. IPSec uses cryptography-based keys available only to the sending and receiving computers. A checksum is included with each packet, and any alteration by an attacker would alter the checksum.

forgery – the keying of data and the encryption of identities prevents an attacker from inserting packets into the transmission.

reply attacks – traffic is sequenced so data cannot be retrieved by an attacker, and then resent at a later time.

man-in-the-middle attacks – mutual authentication and shared keys prevent an intruder from claiming to be a valid client or server. *denial-of-service* – the packet filtering features of IPSec can be setup to block communications that do not come from a valid IP range, are not using an authorized protocol, or are not from a specific port.

IPSec is widely used in wireless environments mainly because of IPSec support in EWGs, Mobile IP solution support, VPN appliance support, and VPN server software packages. U.S. government mandates for strong authentication and encryption help promote IPSec as the leading VPN security solution. High cost and high administrative overhead due to configuration and troubleshooting complexities are typically the shortcomings of wireless VPNs using IPSec.

IPSec Protocols

There are two main protocols used with IPSec – Authentication Header and Encapsulating Security Payload. Each will be discussed briefly in this section.

Authentication Header

Authentication Header (AH) provides authentication and integrity to the datagrams passed between two systems. This authentication and integrity are achieved by applying a keyed one-way hash function to the datagram to create a message digest. If any part of the datagram is changed during transit, the receiver will detect the change when it performs the same one-way hash function on the datagram and compares the value of the message digest that the sender has supplied. The fact that the one-way hash also involves the use of a secret shared between the two systems means that authenticity can be guaranteed. AH may also enforce anti-replay protection by requiring that a receiving host set the replay bit in the header to indicate that the packet has been seen. Without it, an attacker may be able to resend the same packet many times.

The AH function is applied to the entire datagram except for any mutable IP header fields that change in transit, such as Time To Live (TTL) fields that are modified by the routers along the transmission path. Do not confuse "hash" with "encrypt." The hashing function is simply taking a snapshot of what is there and recording it for later use in authentication as shown in figure 13.9 below. AH works as follows:

- The IP header and data payload is hashed for integrity
- The hash is used to build a new AH header, which is appended to the original packet
- The new packet is transmitted to the IPSec peer router
- The peer router hashes the IP header and data payload, extracts the transmitted hash from the AH header, and compares the two hashes. The hashes must match exactly. If even one bit is changed in the transmitted packet, the hash output on the received packet will change and the AH header will not match.

FIGURE 13.9   AH Mode

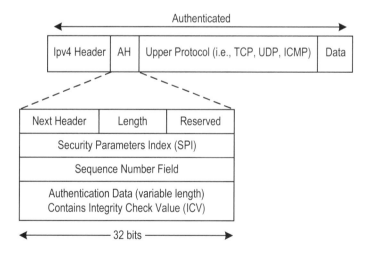

Encapsulating Security Payload

Encapsulating Security Payload (ESP) is a security protocol used to provide confidentiality (encryption), data origin authentication, integrity, optional anti-replay service, and limited traffic-flow confidentiality by defeating traffic-flow analysis. ESP provides confidentiality by performing encryption at the IP layer as shown in figure 13.10 below. It supports a variety of symmetric encryption algorithms. The default algorithm for IPSec is 56-bit DES. This cipher must be implemented to guarantee interoperability among IPSec products.

FIGURE 13.10 ESP Mode

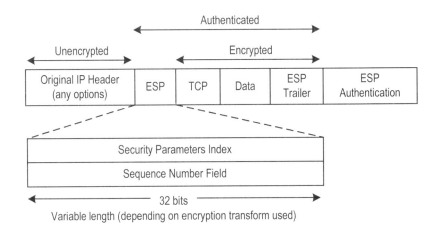

Modes

IPSec has support for two modes: Transport and Tunnel. Transport mode encrypts only the data portion (payload) of each packet, but leaves the header unencrypted. The more secure Tunnel mode encrypts both the header and the payload. Since in Transport mode, only the data portion of the packet is encrypted, the address of the originating machine behind the VPN gateway is transmitted in the clear and is available to anyone watching the traffic on the public (unsecured) network. Using Tunnel mode, the entire packet is encapsulated by the IPSec gateway and a new header is put on the packet. The internal header, with its sensitive addresses, is encrypted along with the data. Only the publicly available gateway address is openly available to the public.

Transport mode is rarely used for enterprise VPNs, because information about the internal structure of the network can be obtained by eavesdropping. Obtaining these addresses gives the opportunity for an attacker to perform a spoofing attack in order to gain network access.

Transport mode is used between end-stations or between an end-station and a gateway, if the gateway is being treated as a host. An example of a gateway being treated as a host would be an encrypted Telnet session from a workstation to a router, in which the router is the actual destination.

Tunnel mode is most commonly used between gateways, or at an end-station to a gateway, the gateway acting as a proxy for the hosts behind it.

There's an old saying among those IT professionals familiar with IPSec: "Transport on the LAN and Tunnel on the WAN." This statement is a shortcut to remembering which of the two is secure and how. Figures 13.11 and 13.12 below illustrate how using AH and ESP protocols with Transport and Tunnel modes works at the packet level.

FIGURE 13.11 Comparison of AH with Transport and Tunnel modes

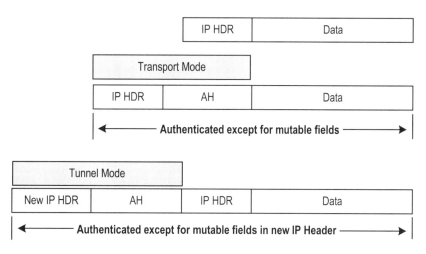

FIGURE 13.12 Comparison of ESP with Transport and Tunnel modes

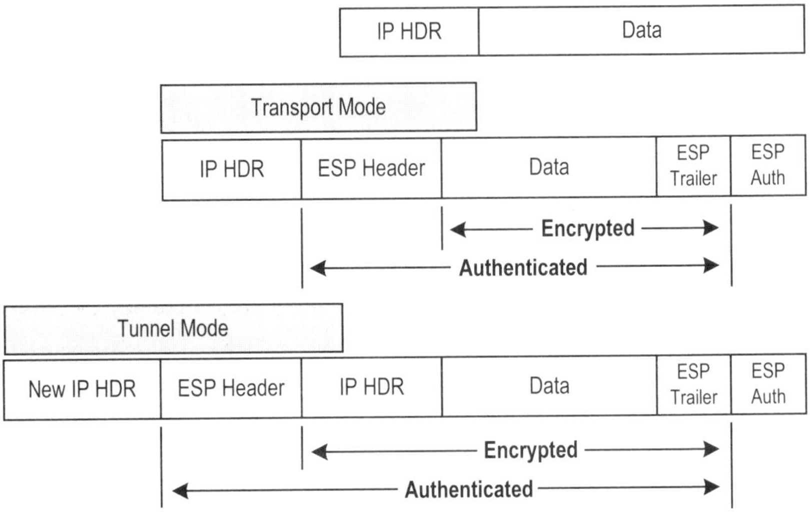

Choosing a Protocol

Deciding whether to use AH or ESP in a given situation may seem complex, yet can be simplified to a few rules. When you want to make sure that data from an authenticated source gets transferred with integrity and doesn't need confidentiality, use the AH protocol. If you need to keep data private (confidentiality), then you must use ESP. ESP will encrypt the upper-layer protocols in transport mode and the entire original IP datagram in tunnel mode so that neither is readable from the wireless medium.

Remote Access Differences

Use of IPSec/IKE in a remote access (like wireless) scenario is unlike using PPTP in that no dial-up session is established. Rather, the connection is simply an IP connection that uses special encapsulation or headers between two end-points. Configuration of IPSec on the client machine is most often done through client software (whether native or third party). Client configuration consists of setting authentication and encryption rules (also called a policy) to follow when the client machine is connecting to another IPSec host or gateway. When traffic is sent to the remote destination, the connection is authenticated and encrypted, and then traffic proceeds across the connection. This process is transparent to the user once the client software/policy is configured.

Policies

Part of IPSec administration is the configuring of policies on client and server devices. These policies address what connection parameters (authentication and encryption) will be used for a particular connection. Policy items may include most, if not all, of the following:

- Whether to secure a single connection or all connections
- Connection type and ID (such as a secure gateway tunnel and IP address)
- Mode (Transport or Tunnel)
- ID Type (such as Digital Certificate or Pre-Shared Key)
- Negotiation Mode (Main or Aggressive)
- Perfect Forward Secrecy (enabled/disabled)
- PFS Key Group (Diffie-Hellman type)
- Replay Detection (enabled/disabled)
- Phase I proposal (encryption algorithm, hash algorithm, SA life, key group)
- Phase II proposal (SA life, compression, ESP/AH)

IPSec VPNs Pros and Cons

Pros

- All IP types and services are supported
- Failover without dropping sessions is available from multiple vendors
- High performance is available
- Dynamic re-keying, strong algorithms, and long key lengths make encryption very strong
- Same technology base works in client-to-site, site-to-site, and client-to-client

- Supports strong authentication technologies and directory integration
- VPN server/gateway is typically co-resident, and therefore integrated, with firewall functions for access control, content screening, and other security controls
- IPSec client solution manufacturers are starting to bundle personal firewall, and other security functions (e.g. anti-virus and intrusion detection) with IPSec client products
- Once a key exchange is complete, many connections can utilize the established tunnel

Cons

- Typically requires a client software installation; not all required client operating systems may be supported
- Connectivity can be adversely affected by firewalls between the client and gateway (if the firewall policy doesn't allow IKE or IPSec)
- Connectivity can be adversely affected by Network Address Translation (NAT) or Proxy devices between the client and gateway
- Requires client configuration before the tunnel is established
- Interoperability IPSec clients and IPSec servers/gateways is weak, mainly due to configuration issues
- Once a client has a tunnel (effectively a "PVC") into an organization, this can be a target of hackers (i.e. the remote access client can effectively be turned into a router which provides a path into the organization), unless mitigated by personal firewalls and/or access controls at the VPN gateway)

The IPSec standards support IP unicast traffic only. Another tunneling protocol must be used if multiple protocols or IP multicast tunneling is needed. PPTP or L2TP should be used when support for tunneling packets other than IP unicast types.

A solid understanding of the advantages and disadvantages of certificate use in IPSec authentication versus that of pre-shared keys is important when making decisions on which to deploy.

Using Digital Certificates

Advantages

Advantages to using digital certificates for authentication include:

- Users no longer have to maintain a set of passwords for entities that need to be authenticated when using certificates. For L2TP/IPSec connections, the entity being authenticated using the certificate is a computer. Passwords still need to be maintained for the user authentication portion of the L2TP/IPSec connection.
- CAs issue certificates only to trusted entities.
- Because the issuer signs each certificate, new certificates are difficult to create and existing certificates are difficult to duplicate (without obtaining a copy), making it difficult for a malicious user to impersonate a certificate holder.

Disadvantages

The main disadvantage to using digital certificates for authentication is that you must deploy a PKI to issue certificates to users.

Pre-Shared Key Authentication

Advantages

The advantage to pre-shared key authentication is that it does not require investment in a PKI, which is necessary for using certificates for L2TP/IPSec authentication. Pre-shared keys are easy to configure on a remote access client.

Disadvantages

The following are disadvantages to using pre-shared key authentication:

- A computer running Windows 2000 Server can configure only one pre-shared key for all L2TP/IPSec connections that require a pre-shared key for authentication. Therefore, all users using Microsoft L2TP/IPSec VPN client that connect to the Windows

2000 VPN server using pre-shared key authentication must configure the same pre-shared key.

- The pre-shared key can be either typed or pasted into the Microsoft IPSec VPN Configuration Utility. If the pre-shared key is typed, there exists the probability of configuration error by the user.

- If the pre-shared key on a VPN server is changed, a client using a pre-shared key will be unable to connect to that server until the pre-shared key on the client is changed.

- A pre-shared key is a sequence of characters whose secrecy depends on the method of distribution and its strength. For example, if pre-shared keys are distributed to users through email (not recommended), then anyone receiving, intercepting, or reading the email has access to the pre-shared key. A strong pre-shared key contains a random sequence of upper and lower case letters, numbers, and punctuation. A short, easy-to-guess pre-shared key is susceptible to an online dictionary attack. If the pre-shared key is compromised, an attacker can successfully authenticate the IPSec portion of the connection. However, they must still present a valid set of credentials for the PPP portion of the connection. In contrast, it is very difficult to compromise a certificate.

- Unlike certificates, the origin, history, and valid lifetime of a pre-shared key cannot be determined.

For these reasons, the use of pre-shared keys to authenticate L2TP/IPSec connections is considered a relatively weak authentication method. If you want a long term, strong authentication method, you should use a PKI and certificates.

Pre-Shared Key Considerations

The pre-shared key for L2TP/IPSec VPN client can be any string of any combination of keyboard characters from 8 to 255 characters long. When you choose a pre-shared key, consider the fact that users may have to type the pre-shared key manually. A key that is long and complex enough to provide adequate security might be difficult for the majority of users to type accurately. If the pre-shared key configured for the L2TP/IPSec

VPN client is not exactly the same as the pre-shared key configured on the VPN server, IPSec authentication will fail.

The Microsoft IPSec VPN Configuration Utility allows you to paste a character string for the pre-shared key. If the pre-shared key is pasted from text that you send to your users, the pre-shared key can be long and complex provided it is correctly pasted into the Microsoft IPSec VPN Configuration Utility dialog box.

SSH2

SSH is an open standard that is guided by the IETF. SSH2 (Secure Shell v2) is a protocol implemented in an application that provides a cryptographically secure TCP/IP tunnel between two computers with authentication. Encryption occurs at a special SSH transport layer, and authentication is implemented within the application. SSH2 works based on a client/server model where the client must initiate the request for a secure connection, thus SSH2 implementations require special client and server software to communicate. Most applications allow the client to be authenticated using its public key or the client's username and password or both methods in series for added security.

SSH2 provides three main capabilities, which provide for many secure solutions:

- Secure command shell
- Secure file transfer
- Port forwarding

SSH2 mitigates the following types of attacks that are common to wireless networks.

- Eavesdropping
- Man-in-the-middle attacks
- Insertion and Replay attacks

Secure Command Shell

Command shells such as those available in Linux, Unix, Windows, or the familiar DOS prompt provide the ability to execute programs and other commands, usually with character output. A command-shell or remote logon allows the user to edit files, view the contents of directories, and access custom database applications. Systems and network administrators can remotely start batch jobs, start, view or stop services and processes, create user accounts, change permissions to files and directories and more.

Managing WLAN infrastructure devices such as access points, wireless bridges, and wireless workgroup bridges via telnet is an unnecessary security risk. Many of the enterprise wireless LAN hardware manufacturers are enabling SSH2 features in their infrastructure devices. In order to interface with these units using SSH2, the management station must have an SSH2 software package loaded. Additionally, many administrators tend to manage wired infrastructure devices using telnet and they do so across unsecured wireless links. By using SSH2 to manage these devices, there is no significant security risk if there are any unsecured wireless links between the management station and the device being configured.

Port Forwarding

Port forwarding is a powerful tool that can provide security to TCP/IP applications including e-mail, sales and customer contact databases, and in-house applications. Port forwarding, sometimes referred to as tunneling, allows data from normally unsecured TCP/IP applications to be secured. After port forwarding has been configured, Secure Shell reroutes traffic from a program (usually a client) and sends it through the encrypted tunnel. The traffic is then delivered to a program on the other side (usually a server). Multiple applications can transmit data over a single multiplexed channel, eliminating the need to open additional vulnerable ports on a firewall or router. For some applications, a secure remote command shell isn't sufficient and graphical remote control is necessary. Secure Shell's port forwarding capabilities can be used to create an encrypted tunnel over which an application can be run.

SSH2 uses IP port 22 to route encrypted traffic from client to server and vice versa. There are two types of port forwarding commonly used with wireless LANs: local and remote. With local port forwarding a SSH2 client is configured to listen for traffic destined to specific ports and to redirect this traffic into the SSH2 tunnel on port 22 while the data is still on the local machine. When the traffic is de-tunneled at the SSH2 server, the server simply forwards the traffic to its original destination as illustrated in figure 13.3 below.

With remote port forwarding, the client establishes a secure tunnel using SSH2 with the server, and sends requests to the server to have it perform all remote functions. For example, if the host was directed to retrieve email from a POP3 server, it would request that the SSH2 server send a POP3 request using the client's user credentials to the appropriate server on its behalf. When the server receives the mail, the mail is forwarded to the client through the SSH2 tunnel. The same is true of any request made in this manner. Both of these scenarios are easily configured and scalable. The most difficult task is usually configuring the client side of the connection, but recently released software packages make this configuration a snap.

FIGURE 13.13 SSH2 over a wireless LAN

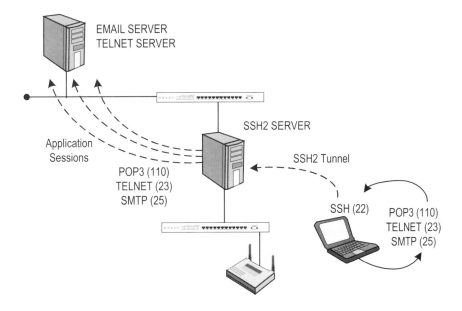

Secure File Transfer

Secure File Transfer Protocol (SFTP) is a subsystem of the Secure Shell protocol. In essence, SFTP is a separate protocol layered over the Secure Shell protocol to handle file transfers. SFTP has several advantages over non-secure FTP. First, SFTP encrypts both the username/password and the data being transferred. Second, SFTP uses the same port as the Secure Shell server, eliminating the need to open another port on the firewall or router. Using SFTP also avoids the network address translation (NAT) issues that can often be a problem with regular FTP.

SFTP is not typically used simultaneously with local or remote port redirection since the same port is used. Non-secure FTP usernames and passwords sent over unsecured wireless links are easy targets for application layer analyzers such as WinSniffer or ettercap. Using secure protocols such as SSH2 (or any subset thereof) is a good alternative to securing wireless links provided the wireless LAN does not allow unsecured connectivity to any valuable network resources.

Public Key Authentication

Public key authentication is one of the most secure methods used to authenticate Secure Shell. Public key authentication uses a pair of computer-generated keys, one public key and one private key. Each key is usually between 1024 and 2048 bits in length, and appears like the sample below. Even though you can see the contents of the key, it is useless unless you have the corresponding private key:

```
---- BEGIN SSH2 PUBLIC KEY ----
Subject:
Comment: my public key
AAAAB3NzaC1kc3MAAACBAKoxPsYlv8Nu+fncH2ouLiqkuUNGIJo8iZ
aHdpDABAvCvLZnjFPUN+SGPtzP9XtW++2q8khlapMUVJS0OyFWgl0R
OZwZDApr2olQK+vNsUC6ZwuUDRPVfYaqFCHrjzNBHqgmZV9qBtngYD
19fGcpaq1xvHgKJFtPeQOPaG3Gt64FAAAAFQCJfkGZe3alvQDU8L1A
VebTUFi8OwAAAIBk9ZqNG1XQizw4ValQXREczlIN946Te/1pKUZpau
3WiiDAxTFlK8FdE2714pSV3NVkWC4xlQ3x7wa6AUXIhPdLKtiUhTxt
ctm1epPQS+RZKrRIXjwKL71EO7UY+b8EOAC2jBNIRtYRy0Kxsp/NQ0
YYzJPfn7bqhZvWC7uiC+D+ZwAAAIEAmx0ZYo5jENA0IinXGpc6pYH1
8ywZ8CCI2QtPeSGP4OxxOusNdPskqBTe5wHjsZSiQr1gb7TCmH8Tr5
0Zx+EJ/XGBU4XoWBJDifP/6Bwryejo3wwjh9d4gchaoZNvIXuHTCYL
NPFoRKPx3cBXHJZ27khllsjzta53BxLppfk6TtQ=
---- END SSH2 PUBLIC KEY ----
```

Public-private keys are typically generated using a key generation utility. Both keys in the pair are generated at the same time and, while the two are related, a private key cannot be computed from a corresponding public key. In addition to authentication, keys can also be used to sign data. To access an account on a Secure Shell server, a copy of the client's public key must be uploaded to the server. When the client connects to the server, it proves that it has the secret, or private counterpart to the public key on that server, and access is granted. The private key never leaves the client machine, and therefore cannot be stolen or guessed like a password can. Usually the private key has an associated passphrase, so even if the private key is stolen, the attacker must still guess the passphrase in order to gain access. Public key authentication does not trust any information from a client or allow any access until the client can prove it has the "secret" private key.

Data Encryption

When a client establishes a connection with a Secure Shell server, the client and server must agree which cipher will be used to encrypt and decrypt data. The server generally presents a list of the ciphers it supports, and the client then selects the first cipher in its list that matches one in the server's list. Both the client and the server randomly generate session keys during establishment of a connection. Both the client and host use the same session key to encrypt and decrypt data although a different key is used for the send and receive channels. Session keys are generated after host authentication is successfully performed but before user authentication so that usernames and passwords can be sent encrypted. These keys may be replaced at regular intervals (e.g., every one to two hours) during the session and are destroyed at its conclusion.

Data Integrity

Data integrity guarantees that data sent from one end of a transaction arrives unaltered at the other end. Even with Secure Shell encryption, the data being sent over the network could still be vulnerable to someone inserting unwanted data into the data stream. SSH2 uses Message Authentication Code (MAC) algorithms to greatly improve upon the original Secure Shell's (SSH1) simple 32-bit CRC data integrity checking method.

Other Benefits

Compression, another feature of the Secure Shell protocol, is performed prior to encryption and can significantly reduce the computational cost of encrypting data. Compression can also noticeably improve the efficiency of a connection and is especially beneficial in file transfers. Secure Shell provides helpful output or log messages. These messages can be turned on or off or configured to give varying levels of detail. Log messages can prove very helpful when troubleshooting a problem. For example, if a client were unable to connect to a given server, this log output would be the first place to look to determine the source of the problem.

Mobile IP

Mobile IP is a protocol that is used to solve the problem of mobile clients roaming across subnet boundaries as shown in figure 13.14. When users receive an IP address via DHCP from one segment, then roam across a router by associating with an access point on another network segment, the layer 3 connection is broken. It is impractical to have DHCP servers on every network segment, and even if this were possible, when a mobile client roams to a network outside the control of the network administrator, such as at another company, DHCP might not be available.

Mobile IP is specified in RFC2002 and is an increasingly common wireless LAN solution. No security is specified in RFC2002 so Mobile IP is often combined with IPSec to form Mobile IP VPN solutions. This type of solution allows for maximum flexibility and security while roaming.

FIGURE 13.14 Subnet roaming problem

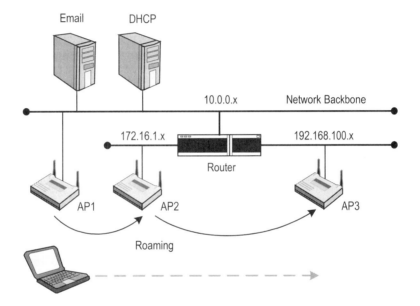

Mobile IP is made up of two primary components: a Home Agent (HA) and a Foreign Agent (FA), and is illustrated in figure 13.15 below. The HA is a server or router sitting on what is known as the "home" network. It has a static IP address and serves as a VPN tunnel server to mobile clients. Client machines must have Mobile IP software installed (usually vendor-specific) in order to participate in the Mobile IP VPN. When the client attaches to the home network, it registers with the HA that it is "home." This registration lets the HA know not to participate in communications between the client and other hosts. When the client roams to a "foreign" network (any network other than the home network), the client registers (notifies) the HA of its new address on the foreign network. This address is known as a "care-of" address. The client forms a VPN tunnel between itself and the HA for data security. The HA then acts on behalf of the client on the home network, answering any traffic destined to the client's home IP address (which is static) and forwarding this traffic to the client at its care-of address.

While on the foreign network, the client may DHCP an IP address and notify the HA of this new care-of address or it may broadcast for an FA. Foreign Agents are placed on networks where Mobile IP clients may roam for the purpose of assisting clients in making IP and VPN connections back to the HA when there is no DHCP server. It is generally preferred for the client to have the ability to DHCP an address and the client routes traffic to the HA by itself. When no DHCP server is present, the FA can act as a liaison between the client and the HA. The FA is preconfigured with HA connectivity information, and acts as the care-of address for the client. A proprietary layer 2 protocol is sometimes used between the client software and the FA to carry information received by the FA on behalf of the client.

FIGURE 13.15 Mobile IP solution

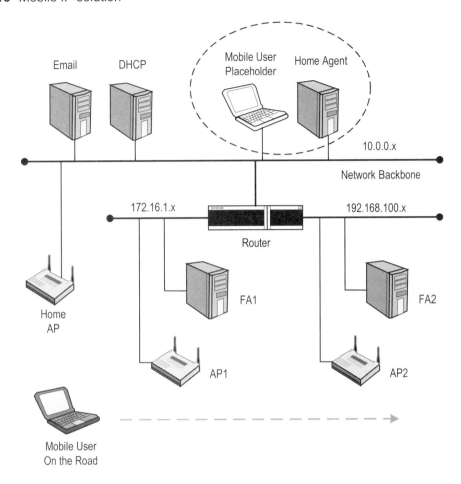

Mobile IP Process

Mobile IP encapsulates an IP datagram within another IP datagram. This encapsulation allows a mobile system to have two different addresses. The first address is the mobile node's home address. The second address is the mobile node's care-of address that changes at each new point of attachment. To solve the roaming problem, Mobile IP specifies that a tunnel be created from the home agent to the current location for the mobile node. The steps that allow a mobile node to roam without losing connectivity are:

1. The mobile node roams onto a foreign network and requests an IP address from a DHCP server. If no IP address is received, the client locates the Foreign Agent through broadcasting. The mobile node notifies the Foreign Agent of its presence on the network.

2. The Foreign Agent registers the mobile node's new care-of address with the mobile node's Home Agent.

3. The Home Agent accepts packets destined to the mobile node on behalf of the mobile node. The home agent impersonates the mobile node in order to accept the data.

4. The Home Agent redirects packets from the home network to the care-of address by creating a new IP header with a destination address of the care-of address. The new header encapsulates the original packet so that the mobile node's home address has no effect on the routing until it arrives at the care-of address.

5. The Foreign Agent unwraps the packet and forwards it to the destination mobile node

6. Whenever the mobile node moves, it registers a new care-of address with its Home Agent

Security

The Mobile IP specification addresses only redirection attacks, and leaves all other security issues open for resolution by employing additional security layering in addition to Mobile IP. A redirection attack occurs when an attacker tells a Home Agent that the mobile node has a new care-of address. The attacker is attempting to get the Home Agent to send all packets destined to the mobile node to the attacker's machine. The specification requires that a mobile-home authentication extension be present in all registration requests and registration replies to eliminate problems of remote redirects.

There are some noted issues with using Mobile IP and firewalls. Enterprise firewalls are usually configured to block packets entering via the Internet that are destined to machines behind the firewall. This configuration can present difficulties to mobile nodes attempting to communicate with other computers in their home network.

The opposite is sometimes true as well. When a mobile node is on a foreign network and sending traffic to the HA outbound through a firewall, the firewall may not let the return traffic back in, and hence the conversation is broken. To fix this situation, some manufacturers wrap the entire conversation in HTTP when firewalls are involved in this manner.

Summary

There are many types of VPNs available on the market, and due to strong and scalable authentication and encryption as well as proven reliability and market acceptance, VPNs are a good solution for wireless LAN security. Since most VPNs exist at layers 3-7, they can, in some cases, be combined with layer 2 security solutions yielding a very strong security solution.

Key Terms

Before taking the exam, you should be familiar with the following terms:

Authentication Header (AH)

Class of Service (CoS)

data integrity

data encryption

Encapsulating Security Payload (ESP)

encapsulation

foreign agent (FA)

home agent (HA)

Internet Key Exchange (IKE)

IPSec (Internet Protocol Security)

L2TP (Layer 2 Tunneling Protocol)

message authentication code (MAC)

Microsoft Point-to-Point Encryption (MPPE)

Mobile IP (RFC2002)

port forwarding

PPTP (Point-to-Point Tunneling Protocol)

Role-based Access Control (RBAC)

secure shell v2 (SSH2)

transport mode

tunnel mode

VPN tunnel

Review Questions

1. VPN security solutions have the following properties:

   A. data flow reversal

   B. data integrity

   C. data displacement

   D. data encryption

   E. data reordering

2. The goal of a VPN is to _____.

   A. ensure data privacy over an unsecured connection

   B. verify that the data sender's policy is secure

   C. ensure data flow is consistent over a secured connection

   D. create a secure point-to-multipoint link

3. VPNs generally take on one of two formats. Choose these two formats from the list below.

   A. peer-to-peer

   B. point-to-multipoint

   C. client/server

   D. hub and spoke

4. Choose the VPN protocols typically used with wireless LANs from the list below.

    A. IPSec

    B. L3F

    C. PPTP

    D. IETF

    E. 802.11i

    F. WPA

    G. WPAN

5. An advantage to using VPN technology with wireless LANs is:

    A. Low encryption overhead

    B. Low cost in almost any configuration

    C. Simple to implement hot-failover mechanisms

    D. Class-of-Service mechanisms like RBAC can be deployed

6. Role Based Access Control allows a wireless network administrator to _____.

    A. Control bandwidth usage per user

    B. Control access to network resources

    C. Control authentication of control frames

    D. Monitor and log user activity on the network

7. If VLANs are used to separate wireless LAN traffic from the network backbone, what type of device must sit between the backbone VLAN and the wireless VLAN in order to pass traffic between the two?

    A. EEG

    B. switch

    C. router

    D. hub

8. Which two of the following best describe SSH2 as a type of VPN technology?

   A. Application Layer

   B. Symmetric Key

   C. Data Link Layer

   D. Public / Private Key

9. An L2TP VPN is comprised of which two pieces?

   A. LAC

   B. LMO

   C. LNS

   D. LTS

   E. LLR

10. Microsoft's Point-to-Point Tunneling Protocol (PPTP) supports what type of encryption?

   A. RC6

   B. MPPE

   C. IPSec

   D. L2F

   E. AES

11. L2TP was a culmination of two VPN protocols. Choose these two VPN protocols from the list below.

   A. EAP

   B. MS-CHAPv2

   C. PPTP

   D. L2F

   E. IPSec

   F. Blowfish

   G. Mars

12. IPSec uses two main protocols. Choose these two protocols from the list below:

    A. Encapsulating Security Payload

    B. Aggressive Listing

    C. Authentication Header

    D. Forwarding Secrecy

13. IPSec uses two modes. Choose these two modes from the list below.

    A. tunnel

    B. encapsulation

    C. insertion

    D. transport

14. When using IPSec with AH, _____.

    A. The header is encrypted, but the payload is not

    B. The header is authenticated and the payload is encrypted

    C. The header and the payload are authenticated and encrypted

    D. The header is authenticated and the payload is unencrypted

15. When using IPSec with ESP, _____.

    A. The header and payload are authenticated, but not encrypted

    B. The data payload is encrypted in transport and tunnel modes

    C. The CRC is removed from all packets

    D. The header is encrypted, but the payload is not

16. SSH2 has three main capabilities. Choose these three capabilities from the list below.

    A. Secure command shell

    B. Layer 3 VPN support

    C. Secure file transfer

    D. 802.1x / EAP support

    E. Port forwarding

    F. Symmetric encryption

17. Use of MobileIP as part of a wireless VPN solution allows _____.

    A. Use of varying layer 3 protocols between client and server

    B. Physical layer application spoofing based on port

    C. Roaming between subnets

    D. Presentation layer connections between host and gateway

18. Two advantages of using the SSH2 protocol as a wireless VPN solution are:

    A. Compression

    B. Point-to-multipoint connections

    C. Split tunneling

    D. Reverse data shadowing

    E. Data integrity

19. SSH2 uses Internet Protocol port number ____.

    A. 21

    B. 22

    C. 23

    D. 25

20. Two primary components of a MobileIP solution are the _____ and the _____.

    A.   Local Agent

    B.   Home Agent

    C.   Secure Agent

    D.   Secret Agent

    E.   Foreign Agent

    F.   Internal Agent

Answers to Review Questions

1. B, D
2. A
3. A, C
4. A, C
5. D
6. A, B
7. C
8. A, D
9. A, C
10. B
11. C, D
12. A, C
13. A, D
14. D
15. B
16. A, C, E
17. C
18. A, E
19. B
20. B, E

Segmentation Devices

CWSP Exam Objectives Covered:

❖ Enterprise Wireless Gateways

- Understand the functionality of enterprise wireless gateways

- Recognize strengths, weaknesses, and appropriate applications for an enterprise wireless gateway

- Describe common security features, tools, and configuration techniques among enterprise wireless gateway products

- Install and configure an enterprise wireless gateway, including profiles and VPNs

- Manage and recognize scalability limitations of an enterprise wireless gateway

❖ Firewalls and Routers

- Given a wireless LAN topology, explain where firewalls can be added for security

- Describe the wireless security benefits of routers

- Explain the benefits of implementing access control lists

- Given a wireless LAN design, demonstrate how to implement a wireless DMZ

- Explain the benefits of network segmentation in a wireless network

- Implement segmentation of wireless LAN segments on a network

Considerations

Because wireless LANs present the unique problem of having no physical barrier, networks using wireless LANs have to be designed with security in mind. One of the most prevalent design characteristics today is segmentation of the wireless network. Segmentation means placing the wireless access points on a network segment that is separated from the backbone network by some type of security device. We will discuss the types of security devices commonly used in today's wireless LAN networks and the strengths and weaknesses of each. There are many facets of choosing the proper segmentation device, and even more design issues introduced by these devices.

Redundancy

Because segmentation introduces a single point of failure for the entire wireless LAN or, at a minimum, a segment of the wireless LAN, redundancy should be considered when designing a wireless network. Redundancy can take many forms in a wireless LAN, such as hot/cold failover access points, access point co-location, and even use of multiple frequency bands as with 802.11a and 802.11b. There is also a need to address redundancy in network segmentation. Suppose that all of a network's access points were on the same VLAN separated from the main VLAN by a router. If that router failed, the entire wireless LAN segment would be unable to connect to the network backbone. This situation represents a complete outage on the wireless network, and usually constitutes a flawed network design.

There are many ways to design and build a redundant network. Traditionally, backup router protocols such as VRRP or HSRP have been used, but in today's wireless networks, routers are not the only segmentation devices used. For this reason, manufacturers of Enterprise Wireless Gateways (EWGs), firewalls, and other device types have been forced to adopt some type of backup mechanism, sometimes making their own proprietary protocol.

Network Address Translation

Network Address Translation (NAT) is most often used to conserve public IP space by translating private IP ranges into public ones. With wireless networks, NAT is most often used in a very common format called Network Address Port Translation (NAPT). NAPT, also called Port Address Translation (PAT) or NAT overloading, presents unique challenges in VPN and 802.1x/EAP networks. A router performing NAPT allows a network administrator to configure the network for many computers inside the router with private IP addresses and to use only one public IP address provided by the Internet Service Provider on the outside interface of the router. The router maintains a dynamic table of inside-to-outside translations allowing many private IP users to access the Internet through a single public IP address.

First, many VPN protocols do not support NAT or NAPT. Second, even if the protocols do support NAT/NAPT, the router in use may not. However, NAPT, if used correctly, can be a good solution for use with segmented wireless LANs because NAPT can conserve backbone IP space. By using private IP ranges in the wireless LAN segments, backbone IP space can be conserved.

As an example of a situation where NAPT might cause a configuration issue, consider use of an EWG connected to a network backbone performing NAPT on all traffic traversing between the WLAN and the LAN backbone. The first consideration would be management of access points from a management workstation on the wired LAN. Because port mapping is typically the only way to go backwards through a NAPT router (using virtual servers), only one access point could be managed. Since such a scenario isn't feasible, the best remaining solution is to have the EWG do 1:1 static NAT mappings in which the EWG assigns backbone IP addresses to the access points and answers on behalf of each access point. When the EWG answers on behalf of the access point, it forwards traffic between the protected segment (the backbone) and the unprotected segment (the wireless LAN segment). This type of segmentation design requires that the EWG have 1:1 static NAT mapping capability as shown in figure 14.1

FIGURE 14.1 1:1 Static NAT mapping for access point management using an EWG

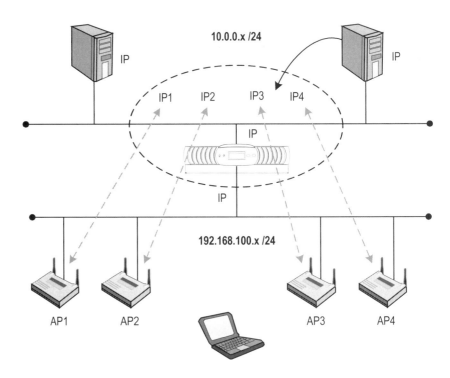

Another situation that might arise when using NAPT is when 802.1x port-based access control is used on access points located on the unprotected segment of the EWG. The RADIUS server will be located on the backbone (protected) segment, which means that 802.1x/EAP traffic must pass through the EWG and be IP addresses translated onto the backbone segment using NAT. When the access point sends traffic to the RADIUS server, the RADIUS server will see the traffic as coming from each statically NAT'd address on the backbone segment. The static NAT table entry will take precedence over NAPT because the static NAT entry will be in the NAT table before any NAPT translation is ever attempted. During configuration of the RADIUS server, each NAS entry must be configured with the IP address that resides on the backbone segment (which the EWG will then translate onto the wireless segment). The EWG handles the return translation and session information in these cases as shown in figure 14.2. In this type of design, the RADIUS server recognizes the wireless users as a single IP address (the EWG's backbone

IP address), and each access point individually according to how static 1:1 NAT is configured.

This situation requires one additional configuration as well. The access points must be configured to have a gateway address. Because the access point is not on the same network segment as the RADIUS server, RADIUS requests must be routed by the EWG to the RADIUS server.

FIGURE 14.2   Using NAPT with 802.1x/EAP through an EWG to a RADIUS server

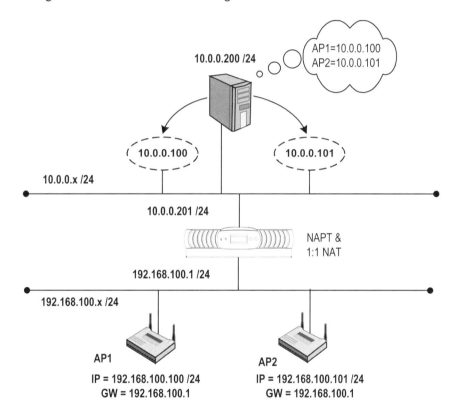

Subnet Roaming

Where layer 3 devices such as routers, layer 3 switches, VPN concentrators, firewalls, or EWGs are used with wireless LANs, clients that roam across access points located behind different layer 3 devices present connectivity problems. Many of the devices discussed in this section are network layer devices and suffer from these shortfalls. Mobile IP solutions were created to solve the problem of subnet roaming.

Routers

Routers are intelligent devices, but routers are also slow. The strongest level of security supported by a router is a firewall feature set that is equivalent to a strong set of access control lists (ACLs). Though this type of security can be effective if used properly, it is almost always very slow because of how the access lists are used. Access points can each push approximately 5 Mbps of wireless traffic. As an economical solution, a router used as a segmentation device would need to handle the traffic from approximately 15-20 access points (75-100 Mbps of throughput). Routers that can handle this amount of traffic are very expensive, so routers do not always make the best segmentation devices. Moderately priced routers generally have slow interfaces (physical ports) because their CPU cannot push a large amount of traffic anyway. Some router software, such as Cisco's IOS, supports Mobile IP and may be used in conjunction with Mobile IP software packages.

Most routers allow no authentication, but rather, by using ACLs, assure that clients match a pre-determined set of criteria. This is very weak security, and should be avoided in wireless LAN designs, in which authentication is extremely important.

Layer 3 Switches

Layer 3 switches have many names: route switches, switch routers, Layer 3 switches, network layer switches, and others. Layer 3 switches are simply routers that can perform switching functions. This switching functionality is performed by adding virtual interfaces (interfaces that exist only logically). The Layer 3 switch routes network traffic between virtual interfaces and switches traffic between physical interfaces assigned underneath the virtual interfaces. Physical interfaces can be made to be routed interfaces as well. See Figure 14.3 for a graphical representation of this functionality.

In Figure 14.3, VE1 is an acronym for Virtual Ethernet Interface #1. Any number of physical switched interfaces can be assigned to a logical routed interface. The "R" in the picture designates a routed interface, which will be assigned an IP address just as a router's interface would have. The "S" in the picture designates a switched interface. Nodes attached to switched interfaces are switched to other interfaces falling under the same VE, but are routed to nodes attached to any other ports.

FIGURE 14.3   Layer 3 Switch Logical and Physical Interface Representation

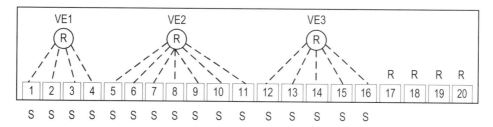

Layer 3 switches are very fast and somewhat expensive. Layer 3 switches typically have fast, distributed CPUs (per port or per block of ports). Security is still performed through use of access control lists on routed interfaces, though processing of these lists is greatly enhanced. Some manufacturers claim that processing access lists does not slow their throughput at all. When used as a segmentation device in a wireless LAN design, Layer 3 switches are much faster and more versatile than routers, but have the same security limitations in that they do not provide any means of authentication. Few Layer 3 switches support Mobile IP.

VPN Concentrators

VPN servers, better known as VPN concentrators, are made by many manufacturers and have a reputation as the "king" of secure remote access. Typical VPN concentrators support RADIUS or TACACS+ authentication, multiple types of VPN technologies and protocols, and can scale from supporting only a few users to many thousands of users. From small to very large, VPN concentrators are known for being expensive, getting significantly more expensive as the number of simultaneously supported VPN tunnels increases.

The purposes of VPN concentrators are, first, to block layer 3 traffic from entering the backbone segment of the network without proper authentication; and, second, to build an encrypted point-to-point connection between the client and the concentrator so that malicious eavesdropping will yield no results.

Both the client and server end of the VPN tunnel must use the same VPN protocol, and settings on each end must match. VPNs are recognized for strong authentication and encryption, but with strong encryption comes high overhead. High overhead always means decreased throughput. The security level with VPNs depends on the protocol used. Some VPN protocols are more mature and more supported in the market place than others. Interoperability between concentrators and client software should always be taken into consideration during the network design phase.

When VPN concentrators are used as a WLAN segmentation device, keep in mind that the access points are left unprotected, as with any layer 3 security device. VPN concentrators are never purpose-built for wireless environments, hence the introduction of the EWG, which has VPN concentrator functions in a gateway specifically designed for wireless. Enterprise wireless gateways arrived on the market shortly after the weaknesses of wireless LANs were realized.

Firewalls

Firewalls have varied in their use over the years. First, firewalls were used to filter between networks such as an intranet and the Internet. Firewalls performed this particular function well. As high bandwidth links became affordable, firewalls were enhanced to keep up with throughput demands.

Then came Demilitarized Zones (DMZs). Suddenly firewalls were being used to route and filter between many segments as multi-port NICs were introduced. Stateful inspection and other detailed tasks performed by firewalls were added to keep out intruders. Due to the plethora of features and the granularity with which firewalls could filter, existing routers choked on all the traffic and network throughput slowed.

Just as with the mainframe and the PC, the arguments between purpose-driven firewalls and all-purpose firewalls ensued. One group maintains that a firewall is the best device for all filtering situations, and the other assures its customers that firewalls should be task oriented, purposefully designed units. The *all-purpose* group added VPN concentrator functionality followed by RADIUS support, and now wireless LAN security support. These firewalls have an almost impossible task of filtering unlike types of traffic at incredible speeds from a variety of audiences. The *purpose-built* group segmented firewalls into several different types including Internet firewalls, wireless LAN firewalls, and other types, depending on their use.

Typical Internet firewalls have to deal with between 1.5 Mbps and 10 Mbps of Internet traffic. At this rate, stateful inspection and any other types of low-level packet filtering and review may be performed adequately. With access points pushing 5 Mbps each, and because common enterprise wireless LAN designs consist of 100 or more access points in a network, the amount of filtering that can be accomplished by an Internet firewall may be minimal without forming a bottleneck in the network.

Authentication and encryption must also be addressed. Authentication requires either RADIUS support or a local database of users. A firewall may incorporate these features in the form of an integrated VPN concentrator, but, in so doing, the firewall takes on multiple types of functions and types of traffic. Authentication, routing, tunnel building, and data encryption are added to the filtering function.

When used in conjunction with other solutions, firewalls offer great security. Consider an example in which a firewall is used to segment the wireless segment and clients must use an SSH2 client to connect to an SSH2 server located on the backbone behind the firewall. In such a design, the firewall would block all traffic except SSH2 tunnel traffic destined to the IP address of the SSH2 server as shown in figure 14.4 below. The overhead of encryption, routing, authentication, firewalling, and others would be shared between the SSH2 server and the firewall, resulting in greater throughput between the wireless LAN and the backbone segment of the network.

FIGURE 14.4   SSH2 Tunnel through a firewall

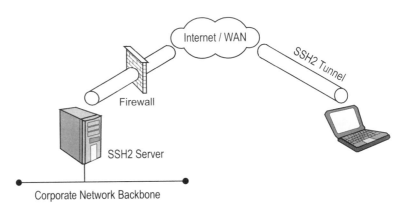

Firewalls have one distinct advantage in the wireless market place: firewalls are already in place before the wireless LAN is designed or installed. For this reason, many organizations have used firewalls for wireless LAN segmentation. Many of these organizations came to realize that a firewall might not be the best standalone solution as their wireless LAN environment rapidly grows. In such a situation, a firewall certainly has its place and may be part of an overall wireless LAN security design.

Enterprise Encryption Gateways

The Enterprise Encryption Gateway (EEG) is a newcomer to the wireless LAN security arena. The EEG is unlike any other type of device on the market and deserves recognition while discussing segmentation devices. EEGs serve as a gateway device because they segment wireless networks from a network's backbone, but the similarities with other types of devices end there. Figure 14.5 below depicts two EEGs, each supporting multiple access points. An authentication server such as RADIUS or an Access Control Server (ACS) and a management station are also shown. The access points and EEGs are managed from the unencrypted segment of the network.

FIGURE 14.5   Enterprise Encryption Gateways

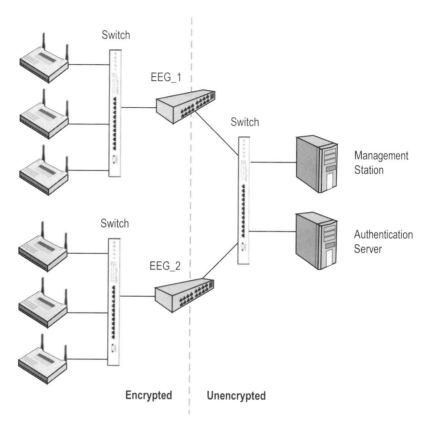

EEGs are layer 2 encryption devices that take Ethernet frames, originating from or destined to the wireless LAN segment, and place them in proprietary frame formats that traverse both the wireless and wired segments. This scenario is basically a layer 2 VPN design, in which each link is an encrypted point-to-point tunnel between the client and the gateway. Once the traffic arrives at the gateway, the layer 3-7 information is removed from the proprietary frame and placed in a standard Ethernet frame for delivery upstream to the destination station.

EEGs are assigned an IP address for management purposes only and do not perform routing. Using the proprietary frame format, gateways and clients can compress the data payload for increased throughput. Throughput gains are directly related to the amount of payload compression, which varies based on what type of data is being compressed. Strong encryption such as 3DES or AES adds significant overhead and latency thereby reducing throughput. Encryption and decryption on a dedicated off-load processor and use of compression can each make a noticeable difference in throughput.

Access point management is part of the configuration of an EEG. The IP and MAC address of each access point behind a gateway are configured in the gateway. Additionally, layer 4 port filtering might be used to limit the types of management that can be performed (such as telnet, http, https, etc.). When a request allowed by the filter is sent to an access point (or bridge) located on the encrypted side of an EEG, the EEG sends the traffic to the wireless infrastructure device unencrypted so that the device may properly read the traffic.

Enterprise Encryption Gateways offer support for RADIUS authentication or authentication via a proprietary Access Control Server. Additionally, the ACS may then redirect authentication requests to a RADIUS server for seamless integration with an existing environment. The ACS will have vendor-specific security and other management features that are not found in RADIUS, and is a valuable addition to the wireless network.

Enterprise Wireless Gateways

Enterprise Wireless Gateways (EWGs) are the culmination of several different pieces of networking hardware and software. Since routers, layer 3 switches, firewalls, and VPN concentrators all have their weak points, cost too much to deploy all at the same time, and are far too complex to install and administer simultaneously, a new type of device was created: the Enterprise Wireless Gateway. The EWG has features common to all of these devices types plus more. The additional features have to do specifically with wireless networks. The principal weakness among EWGs is lack of protection for the access point. The access points themselves are left vulnerable and must be separately protected from intruders.

Network Positioning

EWGs are positioned between the wireless network segment and the network backbone as a gateway through which wireless LAN clients can access the network core (or backbone) as seen in Figure 14.6. If VLANs are used to separate wireless LANs from backbone networks, then the EWG will reside between VLANs. EWGs act as a router, having one interface on the wireless (unprotected) side and one interface on the wired (protected) side. Each interface has its own IP address, and NAT can be performed in both directions (each direction having a different purpose). Interfaces are always Fast Ethernet or Gigabit Ethernet, which is necessary due to the volume of wireless traffic on most enterprise networks. Higher end units have stronger CPUs, more memory, and faster interfaces since all three of these factors together determine throughput through the EWG.

FIGURE 14.6 Enterprise Wireless Gateway placement in the network

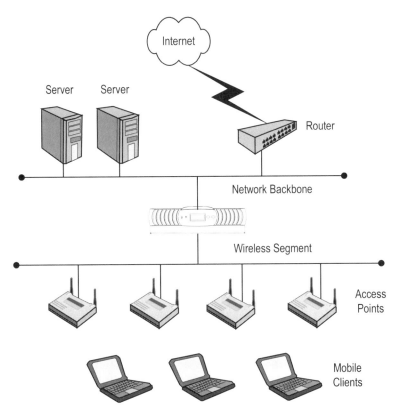

Firewall Functionality

Many EWGs have integrated firewall features; however, it is rare that an EWG would have a set of features comparable to an enterprise firewall software package because of costs and the amount of traffic that will traverse the EWG in comparison to that of the enterprise firewall. One must also consider that the more complex the analysis of inbound and outbound traffic becomes, the slower the firewall's ability to process traffic will be. When complex firewall filtering is done on an EWG, the number of simultaneously supported access points goes down, and, along with it, the number of simultaneously supported wireless clients. Most administrators find the firewall features found in an EWG to be user friendly to some degree, but of course that comfort level will depend on the individual's knowledge of firewall technology.

VPN Concentrator Functionality

The main security feature of most EWGs is the VPN concentrator function. The most common VPN types, such as PPTP, L2TP, and IPSec, are usually supported. Since IPSec is becoming the industry standard, full-scale versions of IPSec VPN implementations with diverse feature sets are usually integrated. RADIUS support, optional local user databases, LDAP support, and more authentication methods are common.

Options more specific to wireless networks, such as rate limiting, are often integrated with VPN technologies like PPTP. In this way, users connecting to the EWG through a VPN tunnel can be rate limited. Some vendors implement proprietary solutions such as distributed VPN edge devices with a centralized VPN controller and concentrator. These VPN edge devices sit directly behind access points so that the VPN is pushed all the way down to the wireless LAN edge. One advantage of this design is the elimination of peer-to-peer wireless attacks and eavesdropping. A second advantage is off-loading of encryption processing from the central VPN server so that more VPN tunnels can be supported simultaneously.

Wireless-Oriented Features

Some features found in EWGs are geared specifically to wireless. Features such as rate limiting, role-based access control (RBAC), and proprietary methods of subnet roaming are common to wireless gateway devices. These new innovations are primarily due to the unique mobile nature of wireless clients and the lack of user authentication and authorization found in current wireless LAN standards.

Rate Limiting

801.11b access points offer a maximum throughput of approximately 5 Mbps because 802.11 wireless LANs use a half-duplex medium. This available throughput is then shared between simultaneous users on each access point. It is often desirable to limit the available bandwidth a single node can consume. EWGs sometimes provide bandwidth control (rate limiting) on a per-role or per-user basis. Classifying service in this manner allows administrators to control the network environment in such a way as to provide a better user experience for all users of the network. Rate limiting features may defeat denial of service attacks (whether intentional or unintentional) that occur when a user consumes all of the available bandwidth.

For example, consider a wireless network that permits both management personnel and engineering personnel wireless connectivity. It is likely that engineers would push and pull very large documents across the wireless network, watch a substantial amount of streaming training videos over the wireless network, and other network-intensive tasks. Only 3 or 4 such sessions could saturate an access point, easily denying service for other key personnel. In this situation, in which there may be 20 to 30 people who require wireless access in a given area, some type of class of service (CoS) such as rate limiting would be a valuable feature.

Subnet Roaming

A common inconvenience to mobile users occurs when their network sessions are broken as they roam across subnet boundaries. Session and network layer address persistence, through the use of subnet roaming solutions, solves this problem; however, vendor support for such a feature is often proprietary. Some EWG manufacturers produce client/server or master/slave solutions in which one box manages many others as part of the solution. In this scenario, there are distinctly two kinds of units: one doing the controlling and another being controlled. Other EWGs are standalone and self-sufficient. In order to perform subnet roaming, peer EWGs must talk to each other or one unit must be configured as a master to some of the others. Designs vary, but in any case, most EWG manufacturers provide for subnet roaming solutions in one form or another.

 The forthcoming 802.11f standard addresses seamless mobility through the Inter Access Point Protocol (IAPP), and IETF RFC2002 addresses the MobileIP protocol in particular.

RBAC

Role Based Access Control is a feature that is becoming more common in EWGs. RBAC works by creating "roles" based on job description or network use requirements in which any user assigned to a role will inherit the properties of that role. For example, all network administrators may be assigned to the "Administrator" role, and that role has full bandwidth capabilities and may access the Internet and the corporate intranet. Another role called "Guest" may be created that only has 100 kbps of bandwidth over the wireless network and can only access the Internet. This feature set aids in both bandwidth control and network security.

Performance

Performance is a key consideration when comparing EWGs. There are now many companies in this market space providing many different types of EWGs. Each EWG type has its own specific advantages. Each EWG manufacturer carves out a niche in the wireless LAN security market by finding a weakness in one or more other products in their industry.

Interfaces and management vary greatly between units because the EWG industry segment has not yet had time to standardize on particular interfaces and management styles. Most vendors in this market space are targeting large enterprise corporations and are creating units that scale to accommodate very large workloads.

Some of the performance factors to keep in mind when purchasing EWGs are:

Number of simultaneous users – How many users can each unit support? If the total wireless user base for an organization is in the thousands, many units may be needed to support these users.

Unencrypted throughput – What is the maximum amount of unencrypted data that can be passed through the unit at any given time? If the machine is supporting the maximum number of users and all users are active, can the EWG keep up with the load or will the EWG become the bottleneck on the network? The "unencrypted" throughput is the number most vendors are likely to tell a customer because that number is more impressive; however, the primary purpose of the EWG is for authentication and encryption.

Encrypted throughput – Most EWGs will be used with encryption enabled, so the encrypted data throughput during peak usage should be considered during the design phase of the network. This encrypted data throughput number is usually significantly lower than the unencrypted throughput, depending on the encryption used, and always far less than the speed of the interfaces both upstream and downstream. Just because an EWG has very fast interfaces does not mean it can push as much traffic as the interfaces can pass.

Scalability

Network growth, standards support, and capabilities (features) should all be contemplated when considering the scalability of an EWG. As networks grow, more clients, more access points, and more bandwidth are all issues that can cause your EWG to become a bottleneck. In many cases, the interfaces are fast enough, but CPUs are unable to keep up with the increased workload. Supporting 802.11b devices works well for today, but now that other wireless technologies are becoming more readily available, such as 802.11a, 802.11g, Bluetooth, and others, EWGs must be technology independent in order to scale with these new technologies. Additionally, some of these new wireless technologies are much faster than the current and older technologies. For example, replacing 802.11b access points with 802.11a or perhaps co-locating 802.11g with 802.11b would produce a scenario where the EWG could easily become overloaded if it was not designed for such high bandwidths. Through firmware or software upgrades, EWGs should support the latest technologies available on the market, including VPN technology, RADIUS authentication, and advanced encryption technologies. Looking forward, if the EWG vendor will not keep the firmware or software updated, the customer will reach a point of having to replace the EWGs to grow the network.

Hardware or Software?

There are two main types of EWGs present in today's market place. First, and the more prevalent of the two, are EWG appliances. These units are stand-alone boxes that sometimes resemble a rack-mountable PC in a 1U or 2U chassis. They often run versions of Linux or FreeBSD as the operating system, and the EWG software and operating system are combined into one unit. These units are almost always managed by both a console port and through a web interface using HTTP. Other management types such as telnet, HTTPS, and SNMP may also be supported. In order to upgrade these units, a replacement firmware file (usually in binary format such as .bin) must be uploaded to the unit through a management interface.

The second common type of EWG is the software EWG, which is becoming more prevalent in the marketplace. This software can be installed on a typical Intel PC with 2 Ethernet interfaces. Some versions run on top of operating systems like Windows and Linux and others come as a complete operating system / application in the form of a network appliance. There are even other EWG applications that come as multiple part software systems such as a master/slave or client/server package, in which one centralized piece of software controls many client pieces. These types usually run on top of an operating system like Windows or Linux.

Each type of EWG has its own advantages and disadvantages. With hardware EWGs, the costs are usually higher for the solution. With software EWGs, one must consider the cost of the additional computer(s), operating system software (if needed), and other items such as introducing a single point of failure on the network. Management of the two types is roughly the same in terms of time and difficulty. If an organization already has extra computers and operating system licenses, then the software solution might present the best value.

Summary

There are many types of WLAN security solutions. Segmentation is often used to separate the wireless LAN from the wired LAN. NAT and NAPT (or PAT), while helpful in conserving IP addresses, introduce challenges to network administrators. Roaming across subnets in wireless networks also creates problems which will eventually be resolved by new IEEE standards and Mobile IP. A comparison was made between capabilities in routers, layer 3 switches, VPN concentrators, and firewalls. Finally the newest technologies, Enterprise Encryption Gateways, Enterprise Wireless Gateways, and their features were reviewed.

Key Terms

Before taking the exam, you should be familiar with the following terms:

access control list (ACL)

Demilitarized Zone (DMZ)

Enterprise Encryption Gateway (EEG)

Enterprise Wireless Gateway (EWG)

Layer 3 switches

Network Address Translation (NAT)

Port Address Translation (PAT)

rate limiting

subnet roaming

TACACS+

VPN concentrators

Review Questions

1. What is the primary advantage a Layer 3 switch has over a router when used to segment wireless LANs from the corporate backbone?

   A. Stateful Inspection

   B. Access List filtering

   C. Speed

   D. Virus Scanning

2. What is the effect of using Port Address Translation on the segmentation device?

   A. Making all wireless clients look like they have the same IP address to backbone nodes

   B. Aiding in mobility when using MobileIP

   C. Reducing encryption overhead due to authenticated headers

   D. Increasing the flexibility of network management

3. Layer 3 switches may route between what types of interfaces?

   A. Logical interfaces

   B. Switched interfaces

   C. Physical interfaces

   D. Interfaces in a collision domain

4. VPN Concentrators typically support which of the following authentication server types?

   A. 802.1x/EAP

   B. RADIUS

   C. Diffie-Hellman

   D. TACACS+

   E. PAP

5. Enterprise Wireless Gateways are available in two different packages. Choose these two packages from the list below.

    A. Software

    B. Client / Server

    C. Hardware

    D. Peer-to-Peer

    E. Fibre-Channel

    F. iSCSI

6. Enterprise Encryption Gateways encrypt and compress data at which layer of the OSI model?

    A. Layer 2

    B. Layer 3

    C. Layer 4

    D. Layer 7

7. What is a key performance factor that should be taken into consideration when choosing a hardware-based Enterprise Wireless Gateway?

    A. Memory

    B. 802.1x/EAP support

    C. Rack size

    D. Operating system support

    E. Encrypted throughput

Answers to Review Questions

1. C
2. A
3. A, C
4. B, D
5. A, C
6. A
7. E

Additional Security Solutions

CWSP Exam Objectives Covered:

❖ Describe the following types of intrusion detection methods and tools for wireless LANs

- 24x7 centralized, skilled monitoring

- Honey pots

- Professional security audits

- Accurate, timely reporting

- Distributed agent software

- Security spot checking

- Available wireless LAN intrusion detection software and hardware tools

This chapter deals with items relating to wireless LAN security that seem to be in a category of their own. Each item covered in this section has a useful and unique approach to wireless LAN security and warrants coverage in this text. The items found in this chapter are unrelated to each other, or other categories, which is why they are covered as "additional" security solutions.

Intrusion Detection Systems

Intrusion Detection Systems (IDS) have been used for wired networks for years, and are now beginning to appear in the market specifically designed for wireless networks. An IDS inspects inbound and outbound traffic and attempts to identify suspicious activity that could be the result of a hacker trying to break into or compromise a network. An IDS is different than a firewall in that a firewall monitors for intrusions to stop them from occurring, while an IDS evaluates a suspected intrusion once it has taken place and signals an alarm. A firewall also serves to limit access between networks, and typically provides alarms in the form of log files when attacks or anomalies occur within a network. An IDS may also watch for attacks that originate from within a system.

Wired network IDS products are implemented in the network according to the category to which they belong. IDS types are discussed later in this section. Wired network IDS products typically provide minimal security in a wireless environment. DoS attacks can be avoided, but many of the problems that can be exploited by a hacker in a wireless network, such as man-in-the middle attacks, client hi-jacking, jamming, or rogue access points would go unnoticed by a wired network IDS.

Newer, wireless-based IDS products can search a wireless LAN for vulnerabilities, detect and respond to intruders, and help manage a wireless LAN. A wireless IDS has functionality to detect session hijacking, spoofing, identity theft, and DoS attacks before those packets ever reach the wired network. IDS provide continuous, real-time monitoring using automated analysis to reduce "false positives" and isolate real attacks. Some wireless IDS implementations on the market today use sensors that operate near access points and some are even part of the access point firmware as shown in figure 15.1. These sensors monitor all wireless traffic and report information to the central monitoring server. The sensors provide 24x7 real-time monitoring by capturing all traffic from access points and stations and then sending the data back to the central server for analysis.

FIGURE 15.1   Screenshots of Access Point with Integrated Rogue AP Detection

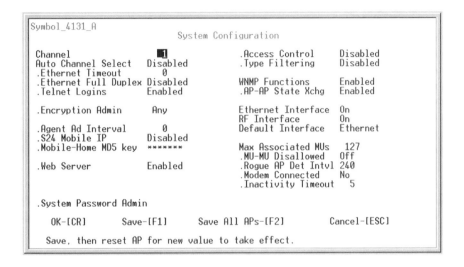

Both wired and wireless IDS are susceptible to false positives. False positives are alarms that are raised due to boundary or policy violations, but are actually legitimate operations within the network. For example, a wireless client may be uploading a very large file to the network server. To an IDS, this spike in throughput may appear as a policy being violated if that data transmission quantity is considered abnormal.

Features

Some features/options of IDS include:

- Network-based vs. Host-based monitoring
- Passive vs. Reactive monitoring
- Misuse detection
- Anomaly detection
- Vulnerability detection
- Performance monitoring

Network-based vs. Host-based

The question always arises, whether the network environment is wired or wireless, "Which type of IDS is best?" The answer to this question depends mostly on your network design, but there are some baseline requirements in a wireless LAN environment that should be taken into account.

Network-based IDS

On a traditional network-based IDS, all packets in the network are analyzed. Gathered data can be analyzed for malicious activity and used to adjust security policies and increase the efficiency of the system. Wireless LANs are a high-speed environment, so, if an organization is using network-based IDS, the IDS must be able to process inputs fast enough when network traffic loads are at their peek.

Network-based wireless intrusion detection systems have the necessary ability to "listen" on the wireless segment through wireless sensors. These wireless sensors must be placed strategically across the network so that all wireless traffic can be monitored, which means placing sensors at, in, or near every access point in order to detect rogue access points or jamming devices. Some network-based IDS place their sensors upstream from the switch to which all of the access points connect. This type of design is less desirable than those with wireless sensors because this sensor placement cannot *hear* what is happening on each wireless segment.

Host-based IDS

In a host-based system, the IDS will examine data on each host computer. Host-based systems require that IDS agents be running on each node in order to report suspicious activity back to the central server. Host-based systems are able to monitor attacks against an individual computer more thoroughly than a network-based system; however, without wireless sensors, detection of rogue access points, RF jamming devices, and other RF DoS equipment is not possible.

Which type of IDS is better? Each has its own purpose, and both may be necessary in a particular environment. Costs, implementation, management overhead, and other factors must be considered before deciding on a solution set for your wireless environment.

Passive vs. Reactive

Real-time monitoring can be used to detect attacks such as identify theft, DoS, and man-in-the-middle attacks as they occur. As these attacks occur, various alarms can be raised, if the IDS is working in passive mode, to allow the appropriate security personnel to take action. Because some networks are not monitored by people all of the time, a 24x7 IDS can be configured to be reactive to certain attacks and eliminate threats. This type of IDS may be configured to restrict access to services, shut down services, disconnect certain connections, etc. All of these settings would be configured through a policy in the IDS. Care must be taken not to negatively impact authorized users any more than is necessary when this type of solution is implemented.

Misuse Detection

To detect misuse or abuse of a network, the IDS analyzes gathered information and monitors business rules for the wireless LAN. Some of the rules might include:

- Limiting access points to only operate on specific channels
- Require all wireless LAN traffic to be encrypted
- Prohibit SSIDs from being broadcasted unmasked
- Limit traffic on the wireless LAN to occur only within certain hours of the day

In this manner, an IDS may act almost like a traditional management system. In some cases the IDS is tied directly into a wireless management software package in order to affect necessary changes.

Anomaly Detection

The anomaly detector portion of an intrusion detection system monitors network segments to compare their current status to the normal baseline and look for anomalies. Any anomalies can then be alerted to the appropriate personnel. Baselines can – and should – be established for typical network load, protocols, and packet size. By monitoring the performance of the network, users consuming more than average bandwidth can be identified.

Vulnerability Detection

Vulnerabilities to wireless LANs, such as rogue access points on the network or the creation of Ad Hoc networks can be detected in real-time. Recall that a peer-to-peer attack is just one way an intruder can attempt to gain access to a network; therefore, locating any ad-hoc networks that are actively transmitting traffic is one way to keep peer-to-peer attacks from occurring. Remember that peer-to-peer attacks can also happen through an access point, particularly an open rogue access point that has hi-jacked an authorized user.

Performance Monitoring

Since wireless LANs share a very finite amount of bandwidth, an important factor for network optimization is to determine who is using the bandwidth and when. Subsequently, the administrator should verify that users are not saturating the network with unnecessary traffic such as streaming audio, video, or peer-to-peer file-sharing applications. If an enterprise wireless gateway with built-in rate limiting functionality is being used, performance monitoring features in the IDS may not be required to locate and control network abusers, but can still be used to report on usage statistics.

One of these statistics reported by IDS performance monitoring might include access point bandwidth load over time. This kind of feature would enable management reports that can be compared to site surveys to determine where and when growth of the network needs to occur to meet user requirements.

Monitoring

An IDS system is only as good as the people that monitor the results and reporting of the IDS. IDS specialists must be well versed in how to properly respond to incidents. An attack can come at any time, so the monitoring must be active 24x7 to be effective. When attacks or anomalies occur, the security policy in place must define primary and secondary contact personnel, how they are to be notified, and what steps to take to respond properly to the incident. For example, some security policies may have the individual respond by attempting to track down the attacker as the attack is occurring (if possible), while another policy may require shutting down the network immediately. Security policy authors should take care to include a section on IDS incident handling.

The reports that are generated from an IDS must be treated with the utmost importance if monitoring is going to be of any value. Detailed and understandable reports that are delivered to the proper person in a timely manner can be the difference in the IDS being an effective tool or an expensive waste of time and money. Responding to incidents poorly or in an untimely manner would allow an attack to proceed in most cases. Intrusion detection systems may or may not include vendor training, but vendor training is always highly recommended due to the complexities of today's products and wireless intrusion detection itself.

Maintenance

After the IDS is installed and running, periodic upgrades to the system (host-based agent updates and network-based software/firmware) and ongoing training for the IDS Specialist will ensure continued success in effective use of the IDS. If remote sensors are used, they should be periodically checked for proper operation. If new wireless LAN segments are added, these new segments must be incorporated into the IDS. The IDS system itself can be augmented through the use of honey pots, to trap potential hackers, and professional security audits, to test for weaknesses in the IDS. Periodic spot-checking of the IDS should be considered mandatory to measure and improve its effectiveness.

Thin Clients

The thin client model is based on a hybrid of the mainframe-terminal model and the client-server model. Clients run an operating system of their own, but all processing is done at the server with only mouse clicks, screen updates, and keystrokes traversing the network. Using thin clients with wireless is a highly efficient and cost-effective approach to networking and sharing applications.

Wireless thin clients can come in the form of thin client software running on a notebook computer, or an actual thin client machine, which is basically a stripped down computer, almost like a terminal. Thin clients connect to servers loaded with host applications – Microsoft Word for example. The thin client does not have Word installed, but instead executes and views the software on a network server through the thin client software.

Thin clients are aimed at cost-conscious IT managers who see the value of simple and inexpensive desktop boxes that leave administration and deployment of software licenses to a central IT team that is no longer required to physically access each desktop. Wireless thin client devices are ideal for situations where an institution desires to deploy a fleet of devices that will be shared among "near mobile employees" who are roaming a campus and accessing clinical or corporate information from their local area network using 802.11 standard wireless networks. Thin clients have a low Total Cost of Ownership (TCO) because they are inexpensive and can be programmed, monitored, and maintained centrally. Thin clients have no moving parts (such as hard drives) and are less expensive than typical laptops. Providing drivers and client utilities for particular wireless network cards as part of the embedded firmware image on the thin client is essential to a successful and simple deployment in many cases. Security solutions provided by wireless LAN vendors (such as Cisco's LEAP) and thin client security solutions (such as Citrix's Secure ICA) are both viable wireless LAN security solutions in this product type.

Bandwidth of most wireless LANs is quite limited in most cases so efficient use of this bandwidth by clients is essential. Thin clients pass screenshots, mouse clicks, and screen updates – each of which take only minimal amounts of bandwidth. By consolidating data, applications, and processing power on servers, thin client environment reduces security risks of data loss due to equipment theft or hacking attacks against unsecured client computers. Since no sensitive data is stored on the client, peer-to-peer attacks yield no useful information. The advantages of thin client software go beyond security, but they present a strong case for both secure and efficient wireless communication.

As with normal wireless clients, thin clients use some type of authentication to gain access to the network. For example, after the user is logged in, SSH2 could be used to authenticate and subsequently tunnel encrypted wireless traffic between the client and server.

Authenticated DHCP Services

Dynamic Host Configuration Protocol (DHCP) provides a framework for passing configuration information to hosts on a TCP/IP network. Dynamic addressing simplifies network administration because the software keeps track of IP addresses rather than requiring an administrator to manage the task. Using DHCP means that a new computer can be added to a network without the hassle of manually assigning it a unique IP address. In a medium where the network is not physically secured, such as a wireless LAN, administrators may wish to constrain the allocation of IP addresses to only authorized network users.

Static IP assignment is especially desirable when network security is critical. Today, many wireless networks grant an IP address to any wireless client that requests one without any authentication credentials required. At the very least, this lack of authentication allows hackers to use an organization's bandwidth to surf the web or to browse network resources. If a hacker joins the network and automatically obtains a valid network address, chances are the hacker will also probe the network to see what other security vulnerabilities exist.

IETF RFC 3118 defines a new DHCP option that adds authentication to DHCP. With authenticated DHCP, a host can verify that a particular DHCP server can be trusted to provide valid configuration information. Additionally, a DHCP server can use the technique described in RFC 3118 to decide whether a request for DHCP information comes from a client that is authorized to use the network.

Among the chief benefits of RFC 3118 is that DHCP clients and servers are able to authenticate one another, so that rogue and possibly malicious DHCP clients and servers cannot mount denial-of-service attacks or gain unauthorized access to an organization's network. An authenticating DHCP client can confirm the identity of the DHCP server it chooses in an unsecured network environment, such as a cable-based Internet service provider (ISP) or a standard corporate Ethernet network. The standard defines a technique that can provide both entity authentication and message authentication.

To implement RFC 3118 authentication, network administrators must deploy RFC 3118-compatible software on all computers attached to the network and upgrade existing DHCP servers to support DHCP authentication. Users must also devise an authentication key scheme and distribute the authentication schemes to all authenticated DHCP clients. After upgraded DHCP clients and servers are in place and the keys have been distributed, the DHCP clients will automatically authenticate themselves. Many of today's directory services can restrict use of both DHCP and DNS based on authentication and some have rogue DHCP server detection features.

DHCP Attacks

DHCP allows a client to easily join a network, and in doing so invites several attacks in a wireless environment to occur:

- Denial of Service (DoS)
- Hijacking
- Theft of service

The purpose of authenticated DHCP is to reduce the possibilities of these attacks occurring.

DoS & Hijacking

One method of DHCP attack in a wireless network is to jam a DSSS channel causing an authorized user to roam to a channel with less interference. By running a rogue software access point on a laptop computer along with DHCP server software (like home gateway software), a hijacker can jam nearby access points, causing authorized users to roam to the hacker's network, which can be just a laptop computer. Windows 2000 and XP clients automatically renew their DHCP lease when their data link layer connection is broken and then re-established. After authorized clients roam and lease an IP address from the rogue DHCP server, these clients can then easily be attacked using intrusion software in peer-to-peer fashion through the access point. When the hacker hijacks the data link connection of the authorized user, the authorized user is no longer able to access their home network. Both a DoS attack and hijacking can occur at layers 2 and 3 of the OSI model.

Theft of Service

Theft of service can occur when an attacker gains access to an open network without permission. Most often, this access is gained with the intent of using network resources (such as Internet access), searching the network for any type of information or corporate secrets, or even reconfiguring portions of the network to allow further access. Using authenticated DHCP, using static IP addresses, or implementing a secure infrastructure, with Kerberos for example, are options to alleviate theft of services.

Traffic Baselining

Baselining is a procedure where the performance of selected network segments is analyzed over a period of time ranging from several hours to several days. Baselining calculates the historical traffic volume and rate derived from data sources, links, or ports. By analyzing the traffic patterns of the network, administrators provide reference points for use when adding new services or users, identifying performance issues, and for security.

Baselining for Reference

Once a new wireless installation is complete, baselining provides a reference point that represents network normalcy. Network normalcy could be defined as traffic quantities and types that are found on the network over a period of time and at particular times of a day or week causing a measurable amount of load on the network infrastructure resources.

Baselining for Performance

The baseline reference information can be used to determine what modifications need to be made for the wireless network to support new users and new applications. Once additional users are added, a new baseline can be recorded and compared with the original baseline results in order to calculate how much additional network bandwidth the added load consumed. If any problems occur within the network, comparing the reference baseline to the current network performance can be used to help identify problem areas.

Baselining for Security

Since a wireless LAN is a limited-bandwidth, half-duplex environment, it is easy to see how a single attacker could easily saturate network bandwidth either through stealing sensitive data over the wireless LAN or through a data flooding attack. Minimum, maximum, or average values from baseline data can be used for setting alarm thresholds in intrusion detection software. When an intruder exceeds network normalcy, alarms are triggered and security administrators are notified. Anomaly detection and statistical analysis are effective ways to respond to DoS attacks. Anomaly-based detection, often found in baselining tools, has the ability to notice attacks that may otherwise go unnoticed in an organization. Most organizations only recognize and respond to those DoS attacks that bring the network to a halt, while using baselines for DoS attack analysis may allow more sensitive recognition and earlier response.

Summary

This chapter offers a look at several additional solutions aimed at wireless networks. Intrusion Detection Systems are used to identify and log suspicious activities in wired and wireless networks. IDS are either network-based or host-based and can utilize passive or active monitoring. IDS also perform misuse detection, anomaly detection and vulnerability detection. Thin clients offer an efficient and cost-effective approach to networking and sharing applications. Authenticated DHCP services are forthcoming and should be considered in network environments. DHCP authentication will prevent malicious DHCP clients from joining the network and reduce potential for DoS, hijacking, and theft of service. Baselining provides reference points that assist in identifying performance and security issues.

Key Terms

Before taking the exam, you should be familiar with the following terms:

Authenticated DHCP

Host-based IDS

Intrusion Detection Systems (IDS)

Network-based IDS

Thin Client

Review Questions

1. Which statement below best describes the difference in operation between a firewall and an intrusion detection system?

   A. A firewall monitors the network for intrusions in order to log them only, while an intrusion detection system evaluates a suspected intrusion before it has taken place and signals an alarm.

   B. A firewall monitors the network for intrusions in order to stop them from occurring, while an intrusion detection system evaluates a suspected intrusion while it is taking place and signals an alarm.

   C. A firewall monitors for intrusions only on certain workstations, while an intrusion detection system evaluates suspected intrusions across an entire wide area network.

   D. A firewall monitors and signals an alarm once an intrusion has taken place, while an intrusion detection system evaluates suspected intrusions in order to stop them from occurring.

2. Which two statements best describe host-based and network-based intrusion detection systems (IDS)?

   A. Network-based IDS analyzes attacks directed against computers

   B. Network-based IDS analyzes traffic patterns for attack signatures

   C. Host-based IDS analyzes wireless segment traffic only

   D. Host-based IDS analyzes attacks directed against workstations and servers

3. How are active versus passive settings configured on most intrusion detection systems (IDS)?

   A. On a firewall behind the IDS

   B. Active settings can only be performed by pairing the IDS with a Syslog server while passive settings can be manually configured by the administrator

   C. Through policy settings in the IDS.

   D. Automatically by the IDS, and require no administrator intervention

4. What types of attack does unsecured DHCP invite in a wireless LAN environment? Choose the best three answers.

   A. Denial of Service (DoS)

   B. Man-in-the-middle

   C. Hijacking

   D. Theft of service

   E. Data flooding

   F. Peer-to-peer

5. Which of the following is/are true of wireless Intrusion Detection Systems?

   A. A wireless IDS must use access points as wireless sensors

   B. A wireless IDS must use PoE for sensors

   C. A wireless IDS removes the need for administrators to manually scan the network for rogue infrastructure devices

   D. Wireless client stations are used as wireless sensors in a wireless IDS

6. Which of the following is a security advantage presented by thin clients in a wireless environment?

   A. Thin clients run applications locally which keeps sensitive data from being passed over the network

   B. Thin clients have native encryption offload processors to reduce encryption/decryption latency

   C. Thin clients use only directional antennas which prevent most hijacking attacks

   D. Thin clients pass only keystrokes, mouse clicks, and screen updates which an be encrypted

7. Why are thin clients safe from wireless peer-to-peer attacks?

   A. A thin client only connects to an access point once per session, so peer-to-peer attacks yield no useful information.

   B. Thin client data transmissions are encrypted by default, so peer-to-peer attacks yield no useful information.

   C. Thin clients are not capable of wireless LAN connectivity, so wireless peer-to-peer attacks yield no useful information.

   D. No sensitive data is stored on the client, so peer-to-peer attacks yield no useful information.

8. Why is the use of DHCP a potential security hole for a wireless LAN implementation?

   A. DHCP requests and replies are encrypted, but not authenticated

   B. Unsecured DHCP will grant an IP address to any wireless client that requests one without any authentication credentials required.

   C. DHCP requests are encrypted, but DHCP replies are in clear text.

   D. DHCP servers are not capable of authentication

9. What two effects does the hacking technique known as "jamming" have on a wireless client?

    A. The client will simply shut down its wireless connection

    B. The wireless client will lose the wireless LAN signal on the frequency that is being jammed

    C. The wireless client will attempt to renew its leased IP address once the data-link connection is broken

    D. The wireless client will seek out another access point on a channel with less interference and the same SSID as the client

    E. The wireless client will automatically roam to the access point with the strongest signal regardless of SSID, and associate to that access point.

10. How can measuring and recording baselines on a wireless LAN contribute to an increased level of network security?

    A. Minimum, maximum, or average values from baseline data can be used for setting alarm thresholds in intrusion detection software.

    B. Anomaly-based detection, often found in baselining tools, has the ability to notice attacks that may otherwise go unnoticed in an organization.

    C. When an intruder exceeds network normalcy, alarms are triggered and security administrators are notified.

    D. Using baselines for DoS attack analysis may allow more sensitive recognition and earlier response.

Answers to Review Questions

1. B
2. B, D
3. C
4. A, C, D
5. C
6. D
7. D
8. B
9. B, D
10. A, B, C, D

Wireless LAN Authentication

CWSP Exam Objectives Covered:

❖ Given a list of wireless LAN configuration and security requirements, select and implement the appropriate type of authentication from among the following

- Kerberos
- EAP / LEAP / PEAP
- WEP / TKIP
- VPN
- Certificates
- 2-factor & 3-factor authentication
- PAP / CHAP / MS-CHAP-v2
- LDAP / Directory Services
- RADIUS / AAA

In This Chapter

Kerberos

Remote Access Dial In User Service (RADIUS)

Lightweight Directory Access Protocol (LDAP)

Multi-factor Authentication

Kerberos

Kerberos is a trusted, third party authentication protocol that was developed under Project Athena at MIT. In Greek mythology, Kerberos (also seen with the Latin spelling "Cerberus") is a three-headed dog that guards the entrance to the Underworld. Now in Version 5, some wireless LAN vendors have implemented Kerberos as a strong data privacy alternative to static WEP. Kerberos provides both user authentication and encryption key management to guard networks from all forms of attacks on data in transit including interruption, interception, modification, and fabrication. Kerberos got its name for it's three-pronged security approach – the client, the server, and the trusted intermediary (the Key Distribution Center).

Kerberos is designed to enable two parties to exchange private information across an otherwise open network. There are multiple components that make up a Kerberos system:

- The Key Distribution Center (KDC)
- The client and server software components
- Kerberos security policies
- "Kerberized" applications

In a typical network environment, server computers run services that users access. Each of these services may access the same or different authentication databases, but a problem lies in the fact that many of these services allow user credentials to be passed across the network in clear text. There are many types of attacks that can take advantage of this type of unsecured design. Kerberos implements centralized authentication combined with encryption and control of all services and client functions on the network. Using symmetric key cryptography, Kerberos authenticates clients to other entities on a network (usually servers) of which a client requires services.

The rationale and architecture behind Kerberos can be illustrated by looking at a university environment as an example. In such an environment, there are thousands of locations for workstations, local networks, and computer clusters. Client locations and computers are not secure, so one cannot assume the cabling is secure. Messages, therefore, are not secure from interception. However, a few specific locations and servers can be secured and can serve as trusted authentication mechanisms for every client and service on that network.

Key Distribution Center (KDC)

The KDC is a single service running on a server providing two functions: the Authentication Service and the Ticket-Granting Service.

Authentication Service (AS)

This service issues ticket-granting tickets (TGTs) for connection to the ticket-granting service. Before a client can ask for a ticket to another computer, it must request a TGT from the authentication service, which checks its identity. The authentication service returns a TGT for the ticket-granting service, and the TGT can be reused until it expires.

Ticket-Granting Service (TGS)

This service issues tickets for connection to services running on server computers. When clients want access to a service located on another computer, they contact the ticket-granting service, present the TGT obtained from the Authentication Service, and ask for a ticket to the computer. This process is shown in Figure 16.1.

FIGURE 16.1 Process of using the TGS

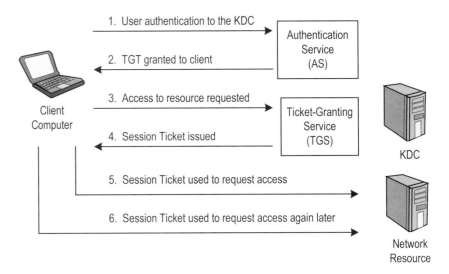

Microsoft Kerberos Implementation

The KDC for a domain is located on a domain controller, as is the Active Directory for the domain. Both services are started automatically by the domain controller's Local Security Authority (LSA) and run as part of the LSA's process. Neither service can be stopped. If the KDC is unavailable to network clients, then the Active Directory is also unavailable and the domain controller is no longer controlling the domain. The Microsoft KDC Service is shown in figure 16.2 below.

Windows 2000 ensures availability of these and other domain services by allowing each domain to have several domain controllers, all peers. Any domain controller can accept authentication requests and ticket-granting requests addressed to the domain's KDC.

FIGURE 16.2   Microsoft KDC Service

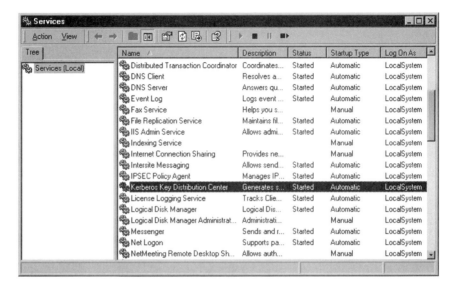

Symbol Kerberos Appliance

Symbol calls their proprietary Kerberos KDC appliance the Spectrum24
Mobility Server. The Spectrum24 Mobility Server authenticates user
names and passwords and supports dynamic key distribution - issuing a
unique key per session per client and a new key at regular time intervals
and on every roam. Because the Spectrum24 Mobility Server is
inexpensive in comparison to a large Kerberos infrastructure, it enables
the deployment of authentication services at wireless LAN sites without
the high costs associated with a centralized solution across a wide area
network. The Spectrum 24 Mobility Server is shown in figure 16.3
below.

FIGURE 16.3 Symbol Spectrum24 Mobility Server Kerberos Appliance

Process

The basic principles of Kerberos operation follow:

1. The KDC knows the secret keys of all clients and servers on the network.
2. The KDC initially exchanges information with the client and server by using these secret keys.
3. Kerberos authenticates a client to a requested service on a server through TGS, and by issuing temporary symmetric session keys for communications between the client and KDC, the server and the KDC, and the client and server.
4. Communication then takes place between the client and the server using those temporary session keys.

The exchange of messages among the client, TGS Server, Authentication Server, and the server that is providing the service requested by the client is examined in more detail in the next section.

Client to TGS Server: Initial Exchange

To initiate a request for service from a server, the user enters an ID and password on the client workstation. The client temporarily generates the client's secret key from the password using a one-way hash function. The one-way hash function performs a mathematical encryption operation on the password that cannot be reversed. The client sends a request for authentication to the TGS server using the client's ID in the clear. Note that no password or secret key is sent. If the client is in the Authentication Server database, the TGS server returns an encrypted client/TGS session key in the secret key of the client, and a Ticket Granting Ticket (TGT) encrypted in the secret key of the TGS server. Thus, neither the client nor any other entity except the TGS server can read the contents of the TGT because only the TGS server knows the TGS server's secret key.

The TGT is comprised of the client ID, the client network address, the starting and ending time the ticket is valid, and the client/TGS session key. The client decrypts the message containing the session key with its secret key and will now use this session key to communicate with the TGS server. Then the client erases its stored secret key to avoid compromising the secret key.

Client to TGS Server: Request for Service

When requesting access to a specific service on the network from the TGS server, the client sends two messages to the TGS server. In one message, the client submits the previously obtained TGT, which is encrypted in the secret key of the TGS server, and the identification of the server(s) from which service is requested. The other message is an authenticator that is encrypted in the assigned session key. The authenticator contains the client ID, a timestamp, and an optional additional session key.

TGS Server to Client: Issuing of Ticket for Service

After receiving a valid TGT and an authenticator from the client requesting a service, the TGS server issues a ticket to the client that is encrypted in the server's secret key, and a client/server session key that is encrypted in the client/TGS session key.

Client to Server Authentication: Exchange & Providing of Service

To receive service from the server(s), the client sends the Ticket and an authenticator to the server. The server decrypts the message with its secret key and checks the contents. The contents contain the client's address, the valid time window, and the client/server session key, which will now be used for communication between the client and server. The server also checks the authenticator and, if that timestamp is valid, it provides the requested service to the client.

Kerberos Vulnerabilities

Kerberos addresses the confidentiality and integrity of information. It does not directly address availability and attacks such as frequency analysis. Furthermore, because all the secret keys are held and authentication is performed on the Kerberos TGS and the authentication servers, these servers are vulnerable to both physical attacks and attacks from malicious code.

Replay attacks can be accomplished on Kerberos if the compromised tickets are used within an allotted time window. Tickets passed between clients and servers in the Kerberos authentication model include timestamp and lifetime information. This allows Kerberos clients and Kerberized servers to limit the duration of their users' authentication. While the specific length of time for which a user's authentication remains valid after his initial ticket issued is implementation dependent, Kerberos systems typically use small enough ticket lifetimes to prevent brute-force and replay attacks. In general, no authentication ticket should have a lifetime longer than the expected time required to crack the encryption of the ticket.

Because a client's password is used in the initiation of the Kerberos request for the service protocol, password guessing can be used to impersonate a client. The keys used in the Kerberos exchange are also vulnerable. A client's secret key is stored temporarily on the client workstation and can be compromised as well as the session keys that are stored at the client's computer and at the servers.

Kerberos is vulnerable to a dictionary attack because there are components of some messages that are encrypted with the user's permanent secret key (the one derived from the user's current password) that can, in combination with components of other messages, be correctly deciphered if a correct guess at the user's password is applied to them.

In Kerberos IV, all encryption is performed using the DES algorithm. While DES was considered unbreakable at the time of the release of Kerberos IV, it is now believed that a sufficiently motivated attacker could, with only modest computing resources, conceivably crack DES encryption in a relatively short period of time. Some researchers have been able to do just that under specific circumstances. Since the integrity of Kerberos authentication depends entirely on the strength of the underlying encryption technology used by the system, this poses a threat to the security of Kerberos IV. In the current release of Kerberos, Kerberos V, support is provided for "plug-in" symmetric encryption algorithms. Kerberos V systems can use, for example, the much more secure 3DES or IDEA encryption algorithms. The overall structure of Kerberos V remains the same as that of Kerberos IV.

Example

Consider a wireless client wanting to check their email on an email server, and this server requires a Kerberos "ticket" prior to processing the request. The process for checking email on a network secured with Kerberos would be:

1. The client associates to the access point, but the access point blocks network access while mutual authentication with the KDC is in progress.

2. After mutual authentication concludes, the client requests and receives a TGT from the Authentication Service

3. The client uses the TGT to get an access point ticket that the client will use to mutually authenticate with the access point.

4. After mutual authentication with the access point, the client is allowed network access. Before network access is granted, the only traffic allowed onto the network from the client is authentication information destined to the KDC.

5. Using the TGT obtained previously, the client requests a ticket for the email server from the TGS. The TGS sends the email service ticket back to the client.

6. The client sends the email service ticket and its credentials to the email server requesting service.

7. The email server will give the client its email if the ticket and credentials are deemed valid. If not, the ticket is rejected and the service does not occur.

All Kerberos authentication traffic is encrypted, but traffic resulting from services such as email, Web, and others are not encrypted between the client and the server hosting the service. Each access point is responsible for encryption key generation, and additional features must be implemented for periodic key rotation while a client is connected to the same access point. Figure 16.4 below illustrates the Kerberos authentication process in a wireless LAN.

FIGURE 16.4 Kerberos Services on a Wireless Network

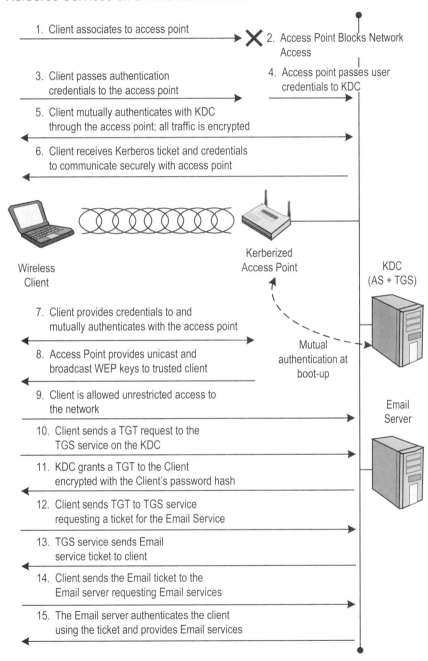

1. Client associates to access point

2. Access Point Blocks Network Access

3. Client passes authentication credentials to the access point

4. Access point passes user credentials to KDC

5. Client mutually authenticates with KDC through the access point; all traffic is encrypted

6. Client receives Kerberos ticket and credentials to communicate securely with access point

Wireless Client

Kerberized Access Point

KDC (AS + TGS)

Mutual authentication at boot-up

7. Client provides credentials to and mutually authenticates with the access point

8. Access Point provides unicast and broadcast WEP keys to trusted client

9. Client is allowed unrestricted access to the network

Email Server

10. Client sends a TGT request to the TGS service on the KDC

11. KDC grants a TGT to the Client encrypted with the Client's password hash

12. Client sends TGT to TGS service requesting a ticket for the Email Service

13. TGS service sends Email service ticket to client

14. Client sends the Email ticket to the Email server requesting Email services

15. The Email server authenticates the client using the ticket and provides Email services

Kerberos Policy & Delegation

The Windows 2000 Kerberos Policy Options are shown in figure 16.5 below. Kerberos ticket policy is implemented by the KDC and usually has some subset of the following configurable policy items:

- Allow postdated tickets
- Allow forwardable tickets (delegation)
- Allow renewable tickets
- Set maximum ticket age
- Set maximum renewal age
- Set maximum proxy ticket age
- Forcibly log off users when tickets expire
- Maximum tolerance for computer clock synchronization

FIGURE 16.5   Windows 2000 Kerberos Policy Options

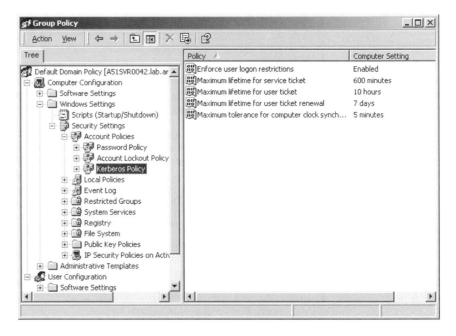

One particular feature of Kerberos policy that warrants a detailed discussion is delegation. Delegation refers to a service's ability to impersonate an authenticated user so that the user doesn't need to authenticate to multiple services. In other words, the user authenticates to one service, and that intermediary service authenticates on the user's behalf to other services. The latter services think they are communicating directly with the user, whereas in reality, an intermediary service sits between them and the user.

Today's Internet-oriented world provides many classic examples of delegation. Consider a client accessing their email via a browser. The web server is delegated the authority of passing the user's credentials to the back-end server – in this case an email server, as shown in figure 16.6.

FIGURE 16.6   Windows 2000 Kerberos Delegation (TGT forwarding)

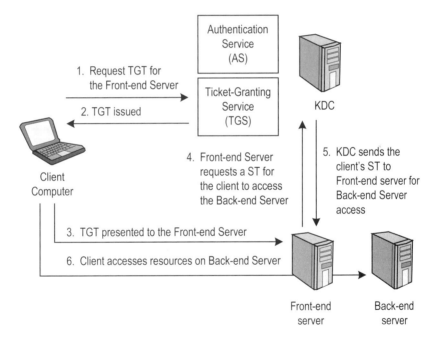

Kerberos can support delegation because of its unique ticketing mechanism. When sending a ticket to a server, the Kerberos client can add information that the server can reuse to request other tickets on the user's behalf from the Kerberos Key Distribution Center (KDC). For example, the web server that accesses the email inbox on behalf of a remote user can use an existing user ticket that the user machine forwarded to the web server to request a new ticket from the KDC. This new ticket gives the web server access to the inbox.

One reason that Kerberos delegation is rarely used in Windows 2000 is that few people really understand it. Another reason is that the Windows 2000 implementation lacks some important security-related configuration options.

In Windows 2000, when a computer is trusted for delegation, it can impersonate a user to any other service on any other computer in the Windows 2000 domain. In other words, when a Windows 2000 administrator trusts a computer for delegation, the delegation is complete; no configuration options can make the delegation more granular. For example, to retrieve user-specific data from a Microsoft SQL Server database server, a Windows 2000 Web application server's computer account must be trusted for delegation. However, the Windows 2000 Web application server isn't limited to retrieving data from the SQL Server database on the user's behalf; it can also contact other servers, such as file servers or other application servers, in the user's name and retrieve other data or execute transactions without the user's knowledge. The exposure could get even worse if the Web application server were used by a dishonest internal Web programmer or compromised by an external intruder.

Windows 2000 delegation lets a Kerberos client forward a user's ticket-granting ticket (TGT) to a service. A Kerberos TGT is a powerful security token - a digital piece of evidence that proves that the Kerberos KDC has validated a user's identity and enables the user to request service tickets. In Windows 2000, a service can use a TGT to obtain a service ticket for the service itself and for other services on the user's behalf.

The S4U2Proxy extension, a new Kerberos protocol extension feature added in Windows 2003 Server, lets a service reuse a user's service ticket to request a new service ticket from the KDC. In other words, there's no more need to forward a user's TGT to the service - as was the case in Windows 2000. The simple fact that the service can present a user's service ticket to a KDC is enough to prove a user's identity to the KDC.

The S4U2Proxy feature has the same security hole as Windows 2000: The intermediary service can access any other service on any authenticated user's behalf. To close the hole, Microsoft has added support for fine-grain delegation configuration into Windows 2003 Server. Now, an administrator can configure which services a machine or service is allowed to access on a user's behalf.

Wireless Specifics

Some vendors have introduced Kerberos-enabled access points where the access point and a key distribution center (KDC) establish reciprocal trust at boot-up. Wireless users associating to the access point mutually authenticate with the KDC and the access point to join the network. By using Kerberos, wireless devices and users are drawn into existing policies and security procedures that many large IT departments have already deployed.

Kerberos also has exceptionally low overhead, making it well suited for wireless-LAN applications; however, Kerberos is complex and requires a certain amount of training and experience to implement. Kerberos' mutual authentication uses a technique that involves a shared secret, which works much like a password. Many authentication techniques (including RADIUS) actually send passwords in the clear, allowing them to be compromised if intercepted by an unauthorized party (such as an eavesdropper using a wireless LAN card operating in "RF monitor mode", which allows all traffic within range to be intercepted). Kerberos solves this problem with encryption. Rather than sending the password, an encrypted key derived from an MD5 hash of the password is communicated and thus the password is never sent in the clear. The Kerberos service running on the client performs this hash function automatically. This technique can be used to authenticate a client, but can also be used for mutual authentication of a server. Once authentication takes place, all future traffic is encrypted allowing even new encryption keys to be communicated without undue fear of compromise.

Typical Kerberos implementation in a wireless environment includes a number of key features and benefits:

- Encryption-key distribution is dynamic, and keys can be changed and securely distributed whenever desired. Key lifetimes can be set from minutes to infinity.

- Keys are generated at the start of every session and are allocated per client. No sharing of keys among clients is allowed. Key generation also works seamlessly with roaming between access points – new keys are generated upon user roaming or when a load-balancing operation is performed.

- Mutual authentication assures that rogue access points cannot capture user data, and encryption prevents a wireless node operating in RF monitor (sometimes called promiscuous) mode from seeing any user data in the clear.

- Kerberos can scale to support very large networks, and the Kerberos server can be located anywhere on the network.

While the details can be complex, the structure of Kerberos is actually quite elegant and designed for general application in a wired or wireless network. Kerberos is particularly well suited to authentication, encryption, and key distribution on a wireless LAN.

Kerberos in a Wireless LAN Example

Symbol Technologies is an example of a wireless vendor that supports Kerberos on the access point. Symbol allows two methods of access point integration with Kerberos – with the KSS and without the KSS. The Kerberos Setup Service (KSS) is an optional application provided by Symbol that runs on the Key Distribution Center (KDC) server. The KSS is used to administer authorized Symbol's Spectrum24 access points in a Kerberos authentication environment.

The KSS has two databases. One database stores valid access point information (AP Setup Account) using each access point's MAC address as the primary identifier. The second database (Kerberos Entry Account) stores Kerberos account information for each access point using the SSID as the primary identifier (all access points with the same SSID are grouped together). When an access point requests information from the KSS, the KSS queries the AP Setup database to validate the access point (using the access point's MAC address). If the access point is valid, the KSS will query its Kerberos Entry Account database for the access point's Kerberos information. The information contained in the Kerberos Entry Account is packaged and forwarded to each access point that requests authentication with the KDC. The access point then uses this information to authenticate with the KDC. This process uses the KSS as a central repository of KDC authentication information for groups of access points so that Kerberos authentication information does not have to be stored locally on the access point.

Each access point must be entered into the AP Setup Account in the KSS – whether manually or automatically. Symbol's KSS has an Open Enrollment mode where the KSS dynamically creates entries in the AP Setup Account for each access point requesting one. The KSS continues to do this until the administrator disables Open Enrollment. After the administrator disables Open Enrollment, foreign access points cannot obtain information from the KSS. Only access points that were successful in gaining access to the KSS during Open Enrollment are given Kerberos authentication information after it is disabled. Open Enrollment is a great tool for quickly staging an entire wireless network for Kerberos operation when using Symbol's KSS. Symbol's KSS configuration screen is shown below in figure 16.7.

FIGURE 16.7   Symbol's AP-4131 access point KSS configuration screen

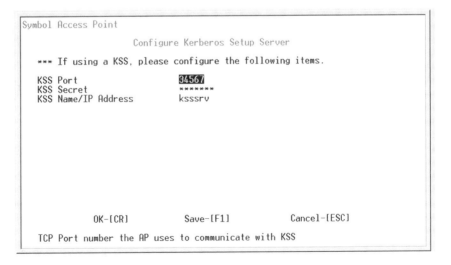

The KSS uses Network Time Protocol (NTP) or the system clock on the Kerberos server to provide clock synchronization (timestamp) between

the KDC and access points as part of the authentication process. Clock synchronization is essential since the expiration time is associated with each request for resources. If the clock skew is exceeded between any of the participating hosts, requests are rejected.

Kerberos support is available for Symbol's AP-4131 access point without the use of the KSS software.

FIGURE 16.8 Sample Kerberos-enabled access point configuration screen

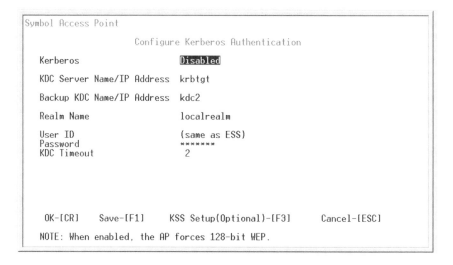

```
Symbol Access Point
                      Configure Kerberos Authentication
     Kerberos                      Disabled

     KDC Server Name/IP Address  krbtgt

     Backup KDC Name/IP Address  kdc2

     Realm Name                  localrealm

     User ID                     (same as ESS)
     Password                    *******
     KDC Timeout                 2




      OK-[CR]    Save-[F1]    KSS Setup(Optional)-[F3]    Cancel-[ESC]

     NOTE: When enabled, the AP forces 128-bit WEP.
```

This configuration requires a minimum of Windows 2000 Server with SP2. To configure Kerberos support, as shown in Figure 16.8 above, without the KSS:

- Enter the access point account information into Active Directory. It is recommended to use one access point account for all access points.
- Configure the access point for use of the Network Time Protocol (NTP) and define an NTP server by IP address.
- Configure each access point for the Active Directory username and password, the IP address of the KDC, and the domain name (also called the *realm*)

Process Details

When the access point boots up, it contacts the KSS to obtain KDC information. The AP sends an Authentication Service Request (AS_REQ) to the KDC. The KDC looks up the username (ESSID in the case of access points), the associated password, and other authentication information including the current time stamp. If the AP has provided the correct information, the KDC responds with an Authentication Service Response (AS_REP). These initial Kerberos messages are used to obtain the client credentials and the session key (the TGT). A client (mobile unit) is required to authenticate with the KDC before the access point allows any RF bridging. The client appears to associate but because it has not been authenticated, the AP does not bridge any non-Kerberos authentication packets to the network. The access point acts as a conduit (the AP will proxy the client requests/replies to and from the KDC) passing AS_REQ, AS_REP, Ticket Granting Service Request (TGS_REQ), and Ticket Granting Service Reply (TGS_REP) between the client and the KDC until authentication is successful.

Once a ticket is issued and the authentication process is completed, the access point continues to bridge data with the client even if the KDC/KSS are unavailable. Once their tickets expire, access points and clients stop passing Kerberos data if the KDC/KSS are still unavailable to issue tickets.

The authentication process for a client is similar to access point authentication. The difference being that the client sends all requests through the access point with one additional step: sending the KDC a TGS_REQ for RF services. The TGS_REQ message is encrypted with the encryption key that the client received during the first part of the authentication process. The ticket the client received in the AS_REP includes the ESSID of the access whose RF services it wishes to access. The access point proxies (forwards) the client request to the KDC. The KDC verifies the request and responds with a TGS_REP sent to the client through the access point (which proxies the reply to the client). The access point proxy does not read the client TGS_REQ but replaces the header information with an IP header (the access point's IP address). Conversely, the access point replaces the TGS_REP header with a Symbol proprietary Wireless Network Management Protocol (WNMP) header and forwards the response to the client. Once the client has verified the message, it prepares an Application Request (AP_REQ) for the access point. This AP_REQ contains the ticket the KDC has sent to the access point. The access point decrypts the ticket. If the ticket is valid, the access point responds with an AP_REP (the access point generates and includes a 128-bit WEP encryption key in the reply) and permits the client to pass data to the network.

Roaming & Re-authentication

When a client authenticates through the KDC, it specifies that it wants access to the access point that it has associated with. When the client completes the full ASREQ/AS-REP, TGT-REQ/TGT-REP, and AP-REQ/AP-REP hand-shake sequence, it possesses a ticket and a session key (WEP encryption key) for use in communicating with that access point. However, since the username and password are the same for all access points, that ticket decrypts and validates with any access point. After a client has associated with the new access point (during roaming), it sends to the new access point the same AP-REQ that it sent to the access point that it first authenticated with. The new access point decrypts the ticket and validates the authenticator in the AP-REQ message. It then sends back an AP-REP with a new session key to the client and normal communication through the new access point can continue.

Future Direction

It is important to point out here that no matter how good a given authentication and encryption technique might be, hackers and crackers are getting smarter all the time. It is impossible to develop an impenetrable security technology, so the goal of any security philosophy is to make it extremely difficult for unauthorized individuals to obtain access to network resources and information. A Kerberos-based approach to wireless does exactly that with an efficient, proven, standards-based implementation that supports user roaming while addressing all of the known security deficiencies in the current 802.11 standard. The 802.11i standard, when approved, is expected to provide for an extensible framework, allowing a variety of techniques, including Kerberos, to be included with a specific security solution implemented at a given site.

For more information on putting Kerberos to work in Windows 2000, be sure to see "MCSE/MCSA Implementing and Administering Security in a Windows 2000 Network: Study Guide and DVD Training System (Exam 70-214)" by Will Schmied, Syngress Publishing 2003 (ISBN: 1931836841).

RADIUS

Remote Access Dial-In User Service (RADIUS) is an authentication and accounting service used by many enterprises and ISPs. When accessing the network, a username and password are entered and passed by the Network Access Server (NAS) to a RADIUS server, which verifies the information is correct and present in its database. RADIUS then authorizes access to the system according to rules configured by the network administrator.

In the wireless LAN, the access point plays the roll of the NAS. One of the most important steps to securing a wireless LAN in a scalable manner is transitioning from hardware authentication (MAC addresses) and shared keys (WEP) to user-based authentication (RADIUS). Figure 16.9 below illustrates a simple wireless LAN configuration using RADIUS with 802.1x authentication.

FIGURE 16.9   How RADIUS works with 802.1x

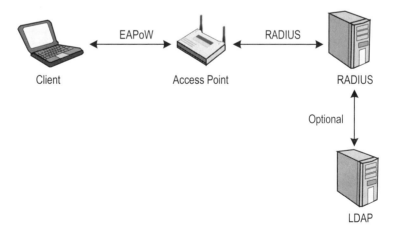

RADIUS may use an internal (native) database of users or may optionally point to an external (usually LDAP compliant or compatible) database such as Active Directory or Novell Directory Services. The 802.1x protocol does not recommend an authentication process, though RADIUS has been overwhelmingly adopted as the preferred authentication process for WLANs using 802.1x based security solutions. Reasons for this preference include:

- Authentication is not based on hardware, which reduces costs and administration overhead when upgrades occur or authentication data is changed.
- Stolen hardware does not necessarily mean that security will be compromised because user authorization is required.
- RADIUS is already in use in many organizations for wired networks, making adoption for the wireless segment easier
- Accounting and auditing are available, allowing enterprises to audit usage and create alarms for intrusion

RADIUS works just as well with VPNs in a wireless environment as it does with 802.1x/EAP based solutions. In fact, the only significant differences are the NAS device type and authentication protocol used. From the RADIUS server's perspective, what kind of NAS device is present is only relevant from a supported protocol standpoint.

RADIUS Options

The RADIUS server that is chosen will be central to the success of a wireless LAN security implementation. Some RADIUS server features include:

- Scalability
- EAP Support
- Clustering and Failover Support
- Accounting
- Legacy Authentication Protocol Support
- Mutual Authentication Support

- Multiple RAS Vendor Support
- Software and Appliance Implementations

Scalability

A wireless LAN that has thousands of users will require a RADIUS server that can meet the demand of the workload. For new deployments, purchasing the bare minimum in terms of hardware and software will only cost more in the long term as the network and user base grows in size. RADIUS servers should be capable of handling the transaction load as determined by a proper site survey. Scalability is often determined by a RADIUS server's ability to pass authentication requests to another authentication service such as another RADIUS server or an LDAP compliant user database. This particular functionality is called Proxy Authentication. Without Proxy Authentication, the RADIUS server's native database is the only one used, and can be a limiting factor.

EAP support

If an administrator decides that a particular type of EAP will meet his or her organization's needs, the RADIUS server should support the type of EAP that will be used. If an existing RADIUS server is already in place for the organization and may not be changed, then the wireless infrastructure devices chosen must support an EAP type matching what the server supports.

Clustering and Failover

Some RADIUS packages support a clustered design, meaning that multiple servers can run as a single computer where each shares in the workload of the application. Typically, for the application (such as RADIUS) to be used in a clustered configuration, the operating systems must support clustering themselves. Depending on the operating system vendor, this may require additional licensing, upgrades to existing software, and more.

Accounting

RADIUS accounting is an additional feature of the RADIUS standard that permits a RADIUS server to track when users start and stop their dial-in connections and to acquire statistics about each session. Using RADIUS accounting, the RADIUS server can maintain:

- A history of all user dial-in sessions, indicating start time, stop time, and various statistics for the session
- A current user list indicating which users are currently connected to which Remote Access Servers (RAS)

The data collected by RADIUS accounting may be easily exported to spreadsheets, databases, or specialized billing software. Another feature that is becoming more common among RADIUS packages is concurrency statistic monitoring. Monitoring concurrent logins per user along with accounting features gives a WISP or HotSpot operator the ability to charge the client extra for such events. In cases in which multiple simultaneous logins are performed, the ISP is assuming that an authorized user has shared his or her login information with a friend. The provider then charges accordingly at an advertised rate.

Legacy Authentication Protocols

Up-to-date RADIUS server software typically supports MS-CHAP, MS-CHAPv2, multiple EAP types, and other types of authentication. It is important to select a RADIUS software package that will support the authentication protocol(s) that are being used by the particular NAS units.

Support for more mature, but often less secure authentication protocols is sometimes desirable when legacy RAS devices are in place. For example, some VPN solutions use PAP and CHAP for authentication. Integrating support for legacy and leading edge authentication protocols simultaneously makes the transition between older and newer systems easier. This is particularly important when moving between wireless VPN systems and 802.1x/EAP based solutions.

Mutual Authentication

Mutual authentication offers users a two-way login validation instead of a one-way authentication, eliminating man-in-the-middle and rogue access point attacks. With one-way authentication, the client sends authentication credentials to the RADIUS server for verification. With two-way authentication, the server also identifies itself to the client as a valid authentication server, usually prior to the client authentication. Mutual authentication support should be considered a requirement when choosing a RADIUS package for use with wireless systems. In some cases mutual authentication also refers to both the client and the access point having to authenticate to the authentication server.

Multiple RAS Vendors

There are many types of RADIUS protocols. Think of a RADIUS protocol as a dialect of a spoken language. If you had a three-way conversation going on in English between a French-speaking person, a Spanish-speaking person, and German-speaking person who all speak some English, all could likely carry on a reasonable conversation, but there would be certain words or phrases that may not be understood. These differences cause problems between a NAS and a RADIUS server, so the administrator must configure the RADIUS server to speak the proper "dialect." RADIUS protocol support is one particular feature to look for when purchasing a RADIUS server package. The administrator should assure that the RADIUS server will work with that organization's NAS in particular.

Various Implementations

RADIUS servers may come in various forms: hardware appliances, software packages, and integrated into wireless infrastructure devices such as access points. Most RADIUS appliances are rack-mountable units in a metal 1U chassis. They have traditionally run FreeBSD or Linux operating systems with open-source RADIUS applications, but are more recently being offered running Windows 2000 Professional. Appliance implementation has the advantage of a software-free roll out for the administrator. RADIUS appliances may provide a centralized solution for controlling wireless LAN users or they may act as a RADIUS authentication proxy device. Appliance solutions are appropriate for large enterprises where distributed proxy RADIUS devices may be necessary to alleviate congested WAN links. RADIUS appliances are also well suited to small- and medium-sized businesses in which a simple RADIUS solution with moderate scalability may be more practical and easier to manage than a highly scalable and redundant implementation. An example of a RADIUS appliance is Funk Software's Steel-Belted RADIUS server appliance shown in figure 16.10.

FIGURE 16.10 RADIUS Appliance Solution

RADIUS servers are available as software that may run on Windows, Linux, or Unix servers. RADIUS software packages range from free to very expensive depending on platform support, feature sets, and scalability. A software RADIUS server package is installed as any other type of software on a machine and then configured with an administrative software tool. The biggest advantages of software-based RADIUS solutions are scalability and redundancy. Funk Software's Steel-Belted RADIUS software is shown in figure 16.11 below.

FIGURE 16.11 General Purpose RADIUS Software Solution

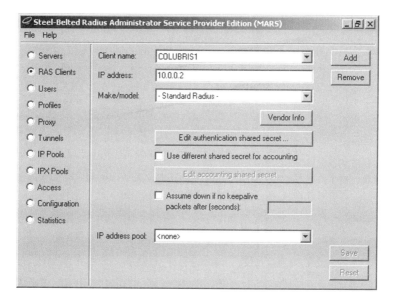

There are specific times when having a small-scale, purpose-built RADIUS implementation would serve as a better solution than a large, centralized RADIUS server. One of these times is in the case of distributed wireless LANs. Consider a situation where a wireless ISP has many wireless Hot Spots. At each of these Hot Spots, users need to authenticate to the network in order to have a secure connection to the wireless LAN. If these Hot Spots were located over a broad geographic area, WAN lines would have to be used to carry authentication requests, encryption keys, and much more information back to the central NOC.

For a more scalable design, it would be advantageous to have inexpensive RADIUS servers located at each site that could perform key rotation/distribution, proxy authentication, and other wireless-specific functions locally. These "scaled-down" RADIUS servers would have to implement 802.1x/EAP in its various formats in order to be effectively used with wireless LANs. Having this type of implementation as a software solution would further decrease costs. Such a design is what Funk Software has done with its Odyssey Server product as shown in figure 16.12 below.

FIGURE 16.12 Purpose-built software RADIUS for Wireless Networking

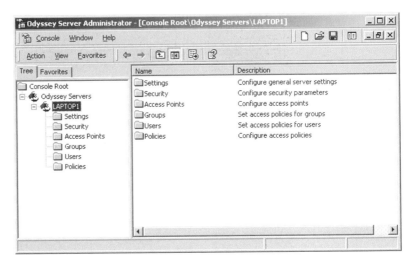

Access points are now available with integrated RADIUS servers. Some use internal user databases for authentication lookup while others can verify user credentials using another vendor's database (proxy authentication). This type of stand-alone solution would be appropriate in SOHO environments where there are a small number of users and the security solution is designed to minimize costs. Intermec's MobileLAN access point with integrated RADIUS is shown in figure 16.13.

FIGURE 16.13 Access Point with Integrated RADIUS

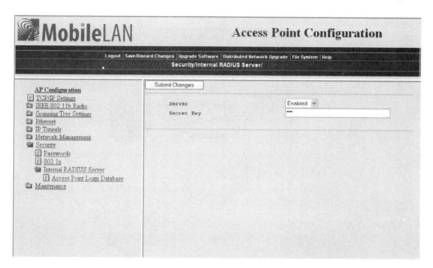

Authentication Design Considerations

This section will cover some typical deployment scenarios for RADIUS authentication solutions. Having an understanding of how and where to deploy RADIUS servers in wireless environments is essential to building cost effective and scalable wireless network designs. The following RADIUS configuration scenarios are described in this section:

Single site deployment

Distributed autonomous sites

Distributed Sites, Centralized Authentication & Security

Distributes Sites & Security, Centralized Authentication

Combination Architectures

1. Single Site Deployment

This, the simplest scenario (Figure 16.14), is characterized as follows:

▪   All WLAN users are located at a single site

▪   A central authentication database handles all user authentication

- One or more RADIUS servers manage WLAN and/or remote access use, authenticating users and setting up secure WLAN connections.

FIGURE 16.14 Single Site Deployment

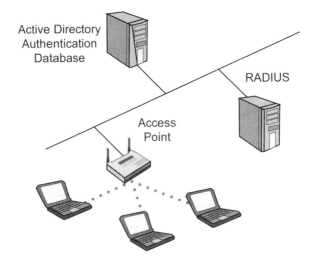

This architecture presents the following benefits:

- You can authenticate your WLAN users against any back-end authentication database your RADIUS server supports. (You will see in the sections below that certain architectures are better suited to certain authentication schemes.)
- To scale, add access points and RADIUS/AAA servers to authenticate users against the central authentication database.

The only considerations are those associated with scaling. If you experience a large spike in your WLAN user population, it may make sense to re-architect your network into one of the distributed scenarios described below.

2. Distributed Autonomous Sites

This scenario, shown in Figure 16.15, is characterized as follows:

- Distributed autonomous sites or networks
- The authentication database is replicated from the central site downstream to each autonomous site or network, so that all user authentication happens locally
- One or more RADIUS servers managing WLAN and/or remote access use are located at each autonomous site or network. Each RADIUS server performs the following tasks:
  - Handles user authentication locally
  - Sets up secure WLAN connections
  - If required, records accounting data
  - Availability of central site network or operating hub is not an issue

FIGURE 16.15 Distributed Autonomous Sites

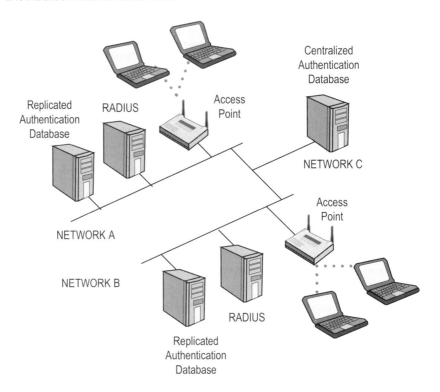

This architecture presents the following benefits:

- Access to your network is governed locally, and is not subject to the reliability of a link back to a central authentication store.
- The distributed RADIUS servers handle the full computational load associated with setting up the secure WLAN connection. You can easily add RADIUS servers to absorb the performance hit associated with adding new WLAN users.

This architecture is appropriate on networks on which are deployed authentication databases that can be easily and reliably replicated, for example Windows or LDAP. It may not be appropriate for authentication systems that are not easily replicated, such as some token systems or SQL databases.

3. Distributed Sites, Centralized Authentication & Security

This scenario, shown in Figure 16.16, is characterized as follows:

- Distributed sites, networks, or clusters of access points
- WLAN access points at each site or on each network authenticate users against an authentication database located at a central site or operating hub.
- One or more RADIUS servers at the central site manage all WLAN and/or remote access use. The central site RADIUS server:
  - Handles user authentication locally
  - Sets up the user's secure connection
  - If required, records accounting data
  - Availability of central site network or operating hub is an issue
  - Link bandwidth usage may be an issue

FIGURE 16.16 Distributed Sites, Centralized Authentication & Security

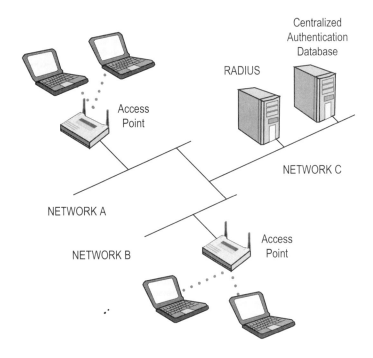

While this scenario carries certain cost benefits – you do not need a RADIUS/AAA server on each satellite site, network, or AP cluster – it presents two issues that bear consideration:

- First, the ability of a WLAN user to connect to the network is dependent on the status of the link between the distributed networks and the central site or operating hub. If that link goes down, users will not be able to connect to the network. Users who are already connected will be disconnected once they are required to re-key for security purposes.
- Second, not only is the RADIUS/AAA server at the central site responsible for authenticating users, it must also perform the cryptographic computations necessary to set up the secure WLAN connection. This may result in a performance bottleneck if you are managing – or plan to manage – a large number of WLAN users. You can alleviate this problem by adding RADIUS servers as your WLAN user population grows.

This scenario is likely to be deployed in environments where it is not practical (or you do not wish) to replicate the authentication database to each distributed network, for example when you're requiring your WLAN users to authenticate via some types of tokens. It is also appropriate for networks that are connected by very fast, highly reliable links.

4. Distributes Sites & Security, Centralized Authentication

This scenario, shown in Figure 16.17, is characterized as follows:

- Distributed sites, networks, or clusters of access points
- The authentication database is located at the central site or network hub
- One or more RADIUS servers managing WLAN and/or remote access use are located at each site, network, or AP cluster. The distributed RADIUS server performs the following tasks:
  - Queries the central site for user authentication
  - Handles setting up the secure connection itself
  - If required, records accounting data locally, or forwards data to the central site
  - Availability of central site network is an issue

FIGURE 16.17 Distributed Sites & Security, Centralized Authentication

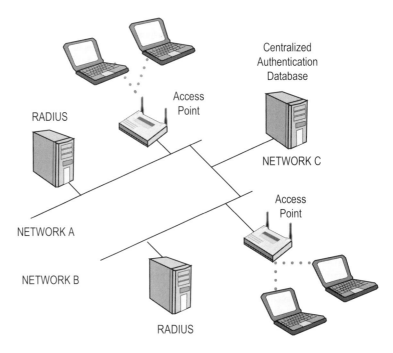

While this scenario presents the same issue as Scenario #3, namely that you're at the mercy of the reliability of the link between the distributed network and the central site or operating hub, it does present an additional benefit. Here, you can distribute the load associated with setting up the secure WLAN connection to the RADIUS servers located on the distributed networks. This may result in better performance, and will use less bandwidth on the link between the distributed and central sites.

As above, this scenario is probably most appropriate in environments where it is not practical (or you do not wish) to replicate the authentication database to each satellite network, for example when you're requiring your WLAN users to authenticate via some tokens. It is also appropriate for networks that are connected by very fast, highly reliable links.

5. Combined Architectures

One of the benefits of 802.1x is its flexibility. It is worth noting that the architectural scenarios presented above can be mixed and matched on your network.

For example, even if you have adopted a more distributed approach to your WLAN deployment (Scenario #2 or #4), some of your distributed networks may be quite small, consisting of only a few WLAN users. If those networks are linked reliably to your central site, you may want forego installing a RADIUS server there, and instead just have your central site RADIUS server handle their authentication and security.

Even if you've deployed a centralized authentication and security scheme (Scenario #3), you may have one or two remote offices that are not reliably linked to your central network. In this case, you will probably need to distribute RADIUS servers to those networks – even if only a few WLAN users are there – so these users can reliably connect.

LDAP

If you have ever worked in a small business, you have no doubt come to realize that a good operations manager can make all the difference in the world. The operations manager can be counted on to know at all times what is happening within the business, where important files are located, who to contact for various business services, and who can take care of a particular task or problem. Although perhaps not completely versed in all the technical details of the business, this person is usually very resourceful, and it is usually well understood that he or she is the one to talk to when you really need results.

From a software point of view, operations management is exactly what the Lightweight Directory Access Protocol (LDAP) does. As a lightweight version of the X.500 Directory Access Protocol, LDAP is the key to creating better enterprise networks. LDAP is a simple protocol that acts as a storehouse of information for applications, but is also important enough to become a central part of modern operating system services. It binds together system information, distributed across multiple computers, with system services and client applications that make it simpler to access user preferences, application configuration data, and security configuration data, and to locate services on the network.

LDAP applications and use

LDAP was designed to contain small records of information in a hierarchical structure. This structure appears much like the directory tree of a file system, with individual nodes containing attributes and connecting to other sub-trees. However, unlike the multi-megabyte files in most user directories, the nodes in an LDAP tree are usually fairly small, as shown in Figure 16.18.

FIGURE 16.18 LDAP Directory Tree in a LDAP Viewer Application

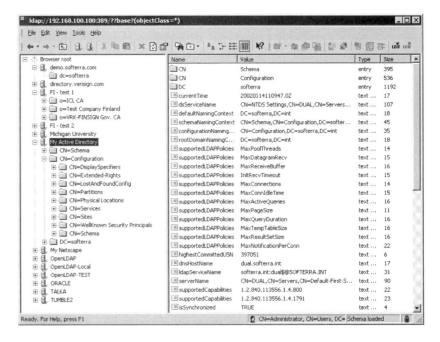

Unlike existing database systems, LDAP is not designed to hold many hundreds of thousands of entries. It might be best to think of LDAP as a hierarchically organized lightweight database. An LDAP server may use a small, embedded database to contain its information for faster access, but this database is nothing like the large commercial databases such as Oracle, Sybase, DB/2, or SQL Server.

To date, there are still only a handful of native LDAP servers, including the following.

- OpenLDAP server (Linux)
- Innosoft's Distributed Directory Server (Linux)
- Netscape Directory Server (Linux)
- Sun Microsystems's Directory Services (Solaris)
- IBM's DS Series LDAP Directory (AIX)
- University of Michigan's SLAPD (various forms of Unix)

There are a number of other directory service systems that also support LDAP queries. These include Novell's eDirectory, Microsoft's Active Directory, and Lotus Domino. These directory services primarily use proprietary APIs, but also provide interfaces for LDAP communications. Microsoft's Active Directory, for example, uses LDAP natively but also "extends" the protocol.

Uses for LDAP

There are several ways to look at LDAP. LDAP is:

A data retrieval protocol - used directly as an application server to retrieve information from a directory. For example, an LDAP server can contain a list of personnel contact information, similar to a white pages phone book.

An application service protocol - used by different applications to retrieve the information these applications require. For example, a user creates a query to be sent to a search engine, the query is matched against an LDAP server, and this points to the place where the actual data is located. Another example of this use would be a DNS server that structures its records internally in an LDAP hierarchy.

An inter-application data exchange interface - used by one application to exchange data with another, or as a gateway between two incompatible applications. For example, a Lotus Notes database can store a record into an LDAP server so that a Microsoft Outlook client can retrieve the record.

In this sense, the LDAP database could also be used as a simple interface for creating vendor-neutral database queries.

A system service protocol - used by an operating system to communicate information between its different resources or components. For example, an LDAP server can contain the access rights of user accounts that are referenced by the login system, the file system, and the application execution environment.

To provide a detailed example of how LDAP is involved in system services, consider the case of user login authentication. The LDAP service can host information about user accounts and preferences for a group of machines. The login authentication service on each system is directed to query the LDAP servers each time a user attempts to log in. The authentication service checks the results of the query to validate the user. If the user is authorized, it then locates and loads his or her home directory and other personal preferences.

Rather than creating complex APIs for each type of information service (e.g., a user authentication service, a network host information service, a network file system locator service, etc.), LDAP provides a handful of common APIs to provide the same service. The applications, of course, have to be written to use these APIs properly. Still, LDAP provides the basic service of locating information. LDAP can thus be used to store information for other system services, such as Kerberos and RADIUS.

LDAP Communications

There are two sides to LDAP: client-to-server communications and server-to-server communications. Basic client-to-server communications allow user applications to contact an LDAP server to create, retrieve, modify, and delete data with the standard LDAP commands. Server-to-server communications define how multiple servers on a network share the contents of an LDAP directory information tree and how they update and replicate information between themselves.

Currently, the client-to-server communications side is well defined. The basic command set of LDAP is enough to provide all that client applications should need. With the addition of the extended command operation in LDAP version 3, there is even room to add more operations, should the need arise. It is also not unreasonable to expect that some vendors will create proprietary extended operations to fit the needs of their environments.

LDAP Architecture

The basic structure of LDAP is a simple tree of information. Starting at a root node, the tree contains a hierarchical view of all its data and provides a tree-based search system for this data (this is one of the most common ways to search data). The actual data contents can vary, depending on how you use the LDAP server. For example, you could have a set of LDAP servers focused solely on servicing login information requests for the thousands of users that are being supported. Another server could contain host address information used by your DNS and DHCP servers. On the other hand, if you do not have a large network, the information could be combined into a single tree.

The tree itself is called the *directory information tree* (DIT). Sub-trees of the DIT contain all the information on that LDAP server. Every node in the tree is known as an entry, or directory service entry (DSE). These entries contain the actual records that describe different real and abstract objects in the computing environment, such as users, computers, preferences, etc. Some entries can be aliases leading to other parts of the directory, if the real contents already exist somewhere else. The root node of the tree doesn't really exist and can't be accessed directly. There is a special entry called the root directory specific entry, or *rootDSE*, that contains a description of the whole tree, its layout, and its contents, but this really isn't the root of the tree itself. Each entry contains a set of properties, or attributes, in which data values are stored. Simply said, each entry is a data structure of variables.

For example, a tree defining the crew of the starship Enterprise could start with a hierarchical description of the ranks of the crew, starting from *Captain* at the top, and going down to *Ensign* at the bottom. At each rank, there would be a single person as well as links to those subordinate to that rank. Each person (entry) would have attributes such as his or her name, serial number, office location, e-mail address, etc. Each attribute would in turn have a specific value (e.g., the name attribute could have the value of *DeAnna Troy* while the e-mail address attribute would have the value of *dtroy@enterprise.federation*). As you can see, the actual data contained can be fairly small. Of course, there could be other attributes, like a 3D representation of the person, which could be a very large piece of data. Typically, however, the LDAP node would simply contain a pointer to the place where the actual contents of such a large value would be located.

To refer to each entry in the DIT uniquely, you must use a distinguished name (DN). Normally, this distinguished name is the very first attribute of the entry. The DN presents the full name of the entry within the entire tree. For example, the DN for DeAnna Troy could be:

uid=troy, ou=counselor, dc=enterprise, dc=federation

Having to specify the DN every single time to access an entry could become cumbersome, especially when you are just looking at a small subset of the tree. If you already know which subset to examine, you need only specify the name relative to this position. All of these subsets are therefore relative distinguished names (RDNs). For example, relative to *enterprise.federation* there can be several names:

ou=first_officer uid=riker

ou=engineering uid=laforge

ou=medical_officer uid=crusher

The Role of LDAP in Wireless LAN Security

Many of today's wireless LAN security devices, such as Enterprise Wireless Gateways, have native LDAP client software. Understanding what LDAP is and how a client device would interface with the LDAP directory is essential in implementing user-based authentication in many of today's wireless LAN infrastructures.

In addition to direct LDAP access via LDAP client software, many of today's wireless solutions use RADIUS for user authentication. Most of today's RADIUS software packages have support for interfacing with LDAP compliant or compatible directories for scalability.

Suppose an organization, like a wireless ISP, has an LDAP user database. Implementing RADIUS as an authentication solution would be an excellent choice considering its wide range of standards support in the wireless marketplace, but if all users from the database must be entered into the native RADIUS database alongside the LDAP database, this solution would be far too cumbersome to justify its existence in the network. Instead, it makes sense that the RADIUS server be able to query the LDAP database for user authentication. This situation is very common among organizations using Microsoft's Active Directory and Novell's eDirectory.

This same scenario directly applies to Kerberos networks. In some instances, such as with Microsoft's Active Directory, Kerberos services are integrated with the Active Directory (LDAP compatible) user database. This kind of solution is somewhat seamless and easier to manage than disparate platforms and services.

Multi-factor Authentication

Multi-factor authentication solutions authenticate a user on more than one credential. There are three different types of authentication criteria that can be combined to create a multi-factor solution:

knowledge – usernames/passwords (something you know)

possessions – token, SecureID, SmartCard (something you have)

biometrics – fingerprints, eye scan, hand scan, implants, keystroke dynamics (something you are)

Two-factor authentication is typical in today's market because anything further would present high administrative overhead and unnecessary complexity. Consider a bank ATM card as an example. The ATM card is a type of smart card and presents security from a possession standpoint. This is coupled with a PIN number (a password) for added security in case the card is lost or stolen. In a scenario like this, it is common for weak passwords (short PIN numbers) to be used. Given today's computer technology, it is wise to implement strong passwords in cases like this. It is easy to see how multi-factor authentication can be over-done. Consider the work and costs involved in implementing strong passwords, smart cards that use digital certificates, and thumb print scanners all on the wireless laptop computer.

There are many types of possession credentials and biometric credentials to be taken into consideration when planning a wireless LAN security solution. For example, with possession credentials there are smart cards, smart tokens, digital certificates, and others. With biometrics, there are many different types of scanning that can be accomplished depending on how much time and money the organization is willing to invest. Some of these scanning types include hand scans, eye scans (retina or iris), fingerprints, facial recognition, voiceprints, and others.

Choosing a Solution

When looking for a multi-factor authentication solution for use with wireless LANs, there are two specific things to consider:

- Management & Integration
- Proven Technology

Management & Integration

Enterprise class two-factor authentication solutions that offer capabilities for centralized and remote management of devices should be considered. The solution must also work with the underlying operating system the devices will be installed upon. Many devices are specific to Windows-based architectures and will not function in a Unix-based environment. Integration with the existing network security infrastructure should be a primary design consideration.

On average, today's enterprise workers have to remember 20 different passwords to access all of their Web-based, client-server, desktop, and legacy applications. It significantly eases administrative overhead when the user needs only to perform a single strong authentication. Once users authenticate, they should be able to swiftly access other protected applications or websites. When a user launches a target application that requires authentication, the authentication solution should automatically enter the necessary credentials into the authentication dialog box just as if the user were submitting the information. This functionality saves users time and enhances their productivity.

Proven Technology

There are many new companies competing to be the leader in the industry of biometrics, a relatively new and fast-changing industry. Although the concept of biometric authentication remains the same, the technology behind storing the data and how to compare and access the data is changing. It is important to consider the vendor reputation, other companies with implementations similar to your proposed implementation, and the results that others have had with a particular solution. Most vendors are eager to share "case studies" and "reference customers" that showcase their products.

Research each particular solution in order to find known security holes that exist with the solution. Even fingerprint scans have been shown to be susceptible to forgery by placing a piece of gum over a scanner, which activates the fingerprint of the person that used the device previously. In a wireless environment, the method in which the solution carries out authentication needs to be considered as well. For example, if part of the authentication is a fingerprint and the fingerprint scan is then transmitted unencrypted to the authentication server, the scanned image can be intercepted by listening to the wireless media with a packet analyzer for the data and reassembling the information with a packet re-assembler such as an application sniffer.

Summary

This chapter discussed several authentication solutions in use in wireless and wired networks. Kerberos provides user authentication and encryption key management. RADIUS is an authentication and accounting service that supports many types of authentication. LDAP is a data retrieval protocol that information storehouses can implement that provides an inter-application exchange interface. LDAP is important in RADIUS implementations because RADIUS servers are commonly configured to query LDAP compliant or compatible databases for user authentication. Multi-factor authentication solutions commonly use two of the three different types of authentication criteria: knowledge, possessions, and biometrics. It is important to choose solutions that will integrate and perform well in your existing infrastructure.

Key Terms

Before taking the exam, you should be familiar with the following terms:

Authentication Service Request (AS_REQ)

Authentication Service Response (AS_REP)

Kerberos

Kerberos Authentication Service (AS)

Kerberos Setup Service (KSS)

Kerberos Ticket-Granting Service (TGS)

Key Distribution Center (KDC)

LDAP

Local Security Authority (LSA)

multi-factor authentication

Network Time Protocol (NTP)

Remote Access Dial-In User Service (RADIUS)

Ticket Granting Ticket (TGT)

Review Questions

1. Which of the items below is not a component that makes up the Kerberos system?

    A. Kerberos License Server

    B. Client and server components

    C. Kerberos Security Policies

    D. KDC

2. What are the two functions performed by the KDC?

    A. Application Service and the Token-Generating Service

    B. Active Directory Integration and a Kerberos Appliance

    C. Authentication Service and the Ticket-Granting Service

    D. Association Service and the Authentication-Tracking Service

3. Kerberos TGS and authentication servers are especially vulnerable t which two of the following?

    A. Wireless packet analyzers

    B. Attacks from malicious code

    C. SMTP snooping

    D. Physical attacks

4. Kerberos ticket policy is implemented by the:

    A. TGS

    B. TAS

    C. TGT

    D. KDC

5. RADIUS is an _____ and _____ service used by many enterprises and ISPs.

    A. Authentication

    B. Encryption

    C. Accounting

    D. Association

6. A RADIUS server's ability to pass authentication requests to another authentication service such as another RADIUS server or an LDAP compliant user database is called:

    A. EAP Authentication

    B. Proxy Authentication

    C. Proxy Mobile IP

    D. Authentication Mobilization

7. LDAP is a:

    A. Data retrieval protocol

    B. An inter-application data exchange interface

    C. An application service protocol

    D. An X.500 compliant database protocol

8. There are two types of LDAP communication in a network. What are they?

    A. Client-to-client

    B. Client-to-server

    C. Server-to-server

    D. Client-to-KDC

9. Multi-factor authentication solutions authenticate users using what types of credentials?

    A. Possessions

    B. Biometrics

    C. Passwords

    D. None of the above

10. What items should be considered when considering authentication solutions for wireless LANs?

    A. Management overhead

    B. Proven technology

    C. Access Point placement

    D. Ease of Integration

    E. RF Interference in the environment

Answers to Review Questions

1. A
2. C
3. B, D
4. D
5. A, C
6. B
7. A, B, C
8. B, C
9. A, B, C
10. A, B, D

Wireless LAN Security Policy

Use the following template to build a comprehensive corporate wireless LAN security policy. Each section and subsection contains a heading and then brief instructions or suggestions for what that section should contain. The final result should be integrated with the existing corporate security policy. Organizations may not need all of the sections listed in this template, but we have included a comprehensive list to choose from. The policy may need revision when new wireless network vulnerabilities and/or solutions arrive in the market place. An electronic version (Adobe PDF) of this template is available when you subscribe to the CWNP e-mail newsletter.

General Policy

This first section, General Policy, is used as an introduction to why the organization is adding a wireless section to their corporate security policy (its purpose) and what role this policy will play in keeping the network safe from intrusion. Even if the organization has no wireless capabilities, a wireless security policy should be in place to address a minimum of rogue equipment discovery.

Introduction

An introductory section on what the General Policy section covers and how it applies to the organization.

Statement of Authority

Define the authority that put this policy in place.

Executive Sponsorship

List the executive sponsors who back this policy and their contact information.

Emergency Response Team

Large organizations usually have an Emergency Response Team to handle corporate security issues for both facility and network emergencies. List ERT network representatives and the team's contact information.

Applicable audience

Define the audience to whom this policy applies, including employees, visitors, and contractors.

Scaled down versions of the Wireless LAN Security Policy may be needed for IT staff, end users, visitors, and contractors as an easy-to-read type of "To Do" and "Not To Do" list.

Violation reporting procedures and enforcement

Part of the security policy must address policy enforcement. When policy is violated, there must be a procedure in place to address what actions the organization will take against the individual that violates policy directives. Define and describe what will be done to reinforce policy directives after a violation and what reports will be written by whom and whom they will be given to.

Risk Assessment

Asset Protection

Sensitive Data

List and discuss the organization's intellectual property, trade secrets, identity information, credit card information, health information, customer databases, and any other information stores that could be jeopardized by wireless network compromise.

Network Services

List and describe email, file, database, directory, custom application services, Internet connectivity, web-based applications, and virus and intrusion detection services that could be compromised by network infiltration.

Threat Prevention

Explain the steps necessary to reduce or prevent wireless network threats, such as:

- Denial of Service (DoS)
- Equipment Damage or Theft
- Unauthorized Network Access
- Credit Card Fraud
- Identity Theft
- Corporate Secret Theft
- Personal Information Exposure
- Malicious Data Insertion

Legal Liabilities

Document legal liabilities that could be incurred in the event of a wireless network compromise and how to react to each type of situation appropriately. These liabilities should also include third party attacks and illegal data insertion.

Note that if exposure to legal liabilities presents a problem that could cost significant amounts of time and money due to an intrusion, then adequate resources should be proactively applied to the security weaknesses.

Costs

Management must consider costs involving people, training, and equipment when implementing wireless LAN security solutions. Keeping quality employees who fully understand the network and its vulnerabilities is especially important. Training is continually required for installation and configuration tasks. Training is imperative to maintaining network operations, end-user capabilities, and security solution upgrades.

This section should give way to Finance & Budget documentation for extensive details, but should outline the importance of appropriate spending to assure security levels are appropriate. List the various expenses that are expected in implementing and maintaining proper wireless network security.

Impact Analysis

An Impact Analysis should be performed so that administrators understand the degree of potential loss involved in a network compromise. The following items, as a minimum, must be considered during the Impact Analysis:

- Financial Loss
- Data Loss
- Loss of Customer Confidence
- Reputation Damage
- Regulatory Effects

Policy should address accessing the network from outside the organization, especially from public access locations (i.e. wireless hot spots).

Security Auditing

Independent Testing

This section is about hiring external consultants to perform independent security testing of wireless network systems. This step is often taken after internal resources and knowledge have been exhausted or to get a fresh perspective on security design and solution selection. The tests allowed to be performed by the consultant should be documented and cleared through internal legal channels. Any anticipated vulnerabilities or limitations of the security solutions chosen should be documented before the auditor begins any testing.

Sources of Information

There are many tools hackers can employ to infiltrate wireless networks. Audits should employ as many of these tools as possible:

- Wireless LAN Discovery
- Password Capture & Decrypt
- Share Enumerators
- Network Management & Control
- Wireless Protocol Analyzers
- Manufacturer Defaults
- Antennas & WLAN Equipment
- OS Fingerprinting & Port Scanning
- Application Layer Analyzers
- Networking Utilities
- Network Discovery Tools
- RF Jamming Tools
- Hijacking Tools
- WEP Decryption Tools
- Operating System Exploit Tools

List and describe the tools that are, have been, or will be used in auditing the wireless segment of the network.

Functional Policy – Guidelines and Baselines

Policy Essentials

Policy Change Control and Review

Contacts and Responsibilities

Include the specific contacts and their responsibilities for policy change control management.

Change Management Procedures

List the specific procedures for making changes to organizational policy.

Change Control Enforcement

Describe the procedures used when enforcing organizational policy change control.

Password Policy

Guidelines

Create guidelines that help users implement strong passwords and help administrators enforce password policy.

Password Implementation

If passwords are used as a security mechanism, set password policies for the following network devices as a minimum.

- Access points
- Wireless client software
- Other wireless infrastructure devices
- Windows platforms
- Linux/Unix platforms
- VPN solutions

- Applications

Networking Staff and End User Employee Training Requirements

Networking Staff

Explain training requirements for the networking staff.

End Users

Explain training requirements for end users.

Non-Employee Wireless Access

Visitors

Explain access restrictions for visitors.

Consultants

Explain access restrictions for consultants.

Acceptable Use Policy

Acceptable Use

Explain acceptable uses of the wireless network.

Unacceptable Use

Explain unacceptable uses of the wireless network.

Violation Enforcement

Define the methods used to enforce the Acceptable Use Policy.

Staging, Implementation, and Management Procedures

Describe the procedures that will be used to maintain consistency when staging, implementing, and managing wireless network devices. These procedures must be readily available and up-to-date when used by support staff to manage the devices. This section may include checklists, interface types used for management, and how the wireless infrastructure will be installed.

Auditing and Compliance

Internal recurring process by support staff

Support staff must perform penetration testing and reporting, vulnerability scanning, and risk assessments on an ongoing basis. Audits should follow the policies established in the Risk Assessment section of the Wireless LAN Security Policy. Define established timelines and processes for recurring internal audits.

External periodic process by independent professionals

Independent professionals should be considered as a valid periodic method of performing penetration testing and reporting, vulnerability scanning, and risk assessments. Define established timelines and processes for recurring external audits.

General Guidelines

Security Checklist

Create a security checklist that addresses the expectations of the security policy. This checklist will be used during product staging, implementation, and management to verify configuration parameters are set correctly. This checklist should comply with the Baseline Practices section below.

Available Network Resources

Define the restrictions that wireless users have compared to wired network users regarding use of existing network resources. It is not always necessary to give wireless users the same level of access to network resources as wired users.

Asset Management

Describe the asset management practices in place and how they affect the wireless network. This may include an intrusion detection and management software package or similar asset management tool.

Periodic Inventory

Show the organization's inventory schedule and the team responsible for the schedule.

Change Management

Make appropriate annotations about how existing change management procedures should include wireless LAN infrastructure devices. This should list the steps to be followed in order to properly implement a change on the wireless network so as to assure adherence with all sections of this policy.

Spot-checks & Accountability

Perform regular spot checks to prevent rogue access points and similar devices and to verify policy compliance. End users and network staff should be held accountable to the corporate policy. Establish timelines and processes for conducting spot checks.

Baseline Practices

Establish baseline practices to help create operating procedures and implementation checklists for wireless LAN equipment and security. These areas need to be considered:

- Access point default SSID modification
- MAC filtering
- Use of static WEP
- Default access point configuration modification
- Firmware upgrades for wireless network equipment
- Rogue equipment

- Outdoor bridge security
- RF cell sizing and AP placement
- SNMP configuration
- Discovery protocol configuration
- Remote access configuration
- Client configuration
- IP services configuration
- AP network connectivity
- Pre-deployment staging and testing
- Equipment installation

Functional Policy – Design and Implementation

Interoperability

Consider solutions that interoperate and document how interoperability affects purchasing decisions. For example, if 128-bit WEP is chosen as a security solution and multiple wireless LAN infrastructure equipment providers are used, then interoperability testing should be performed before an enterprise rollout is attempted and before a large amount of equipment is purchased.

Layering

If solutions that use different layers of the OSI model are used, it is important to document which solution types will be used and to assure that they have been tested together. An example of this is using 802.1x/EAP (layer 2) solutions with IPSec (layer 3). Define policy for implementing layered security solutions.

Segmentation & VLANs

Wireless LANs should be segmented from the wired network backbone by an appropriate security solution. Wired and wireless VLANs offer a method of segmenting users and networks. The importance of segmentation should be explained here, and the type(s) of segmentation solution required to properly secure the network should be listed. Any necessary security and mobility features should be documented here.

Authentication & Encryption

Choose and document authentication and encryption types based on existing implementations, data sensitivity, scalability, availability, and access control.

Existing Implementations

Authentication system integration with existing user databases and authentication systems and support for the latest standards, security features, and protocols is paramount. Existing equipment may not be able to support the latest available encryption, so an evaluation of the level of security provided by these more legacy devices is warranted. Describe and document the current level of encryption on existing systems and devices.

Data Sensitivity

Define and document authentication and encryption solutions that support the required level of security. Keep in mind that authentication systems do not typically provide data payload encryption. In most cases, authentication and data encryption must be handled by separate mechanisms.

Scalability & Availability

Security solutions should be scalable and provide a high degree of availability for users. Wireless networks allow employees to be mobile which means that new ways of using the network will be found. This will translate into increased network usage and dependency on the network. The network's design should lend itself to ease of growth at a reasonable cost. Define and describe the levels of scalability and availability that are required for the wireless network to grow with the organization.

Access Control

Having a wide range of devices types may dictate a degree of flexibility in choosing security solutions. Create corporate security solutions that can handle access control for a variety of wireless network device types, manufacturers, and operating systems. Solutions may include client and server software applications that run on various operating systems, authentication and encryption appliances, and a plethora of infrastructure devices such as access points, workgroup bridges, and wireless bridges. Access may be controlled based on roles, groups, device types, etc. Define and document the different levels of access control to be implemented on the wireless network segment.

Functional Policy – Monitoring and Response

Physical Security

Address unauthorized visitors in the facility's physical security policy. Physical access and security of wireless infrastructure devices is extremely important in preventing hackers from entering the facility to place their own wireless devices onto the network and to keep thieves from stealing equipment or accessing console ports of infrastructure devices. Define and describe the facility's physical security required as a result of implementing the wireless network.

Rogue Access Points & Ad Hoc Networks

Prevent rogue access points and Ad Hoc networks inside the corporate work area. A well-defined wireless security policy can help prevent most rogue access points – whether placed by employees or intruders. Make periodic manual scans or have a wireless IDS in place to detect unauthorized equipment. Define and describe the regularity and processes for preventing and detecting rogue wireless devices.

RF Jamming

RF jamming should be addressed so that network administrators understand how to recognize and appropriately react to unintentional and intentional jamming of any kind – to include spread spectrum and narrowband. Explain how RF jamming is accomplished and explain appropriate preventative or responsive steps.

Data Flooding

Give end users a clear definition of what it means to be a good wireless network user. End users may inadvertently flood the wireless network when downloading large files. Help end users understand what should and should not occur over the wireless LAN. Explain baselining as a task to be performed by the network administrator, and reinforce the importance of maintaining baselines over time and changes to the network. Explain how baselines are to be used as a comparative tool to help identify network attacks. Explain how data flooding is accomplished, and list any preventative steps.

Social Engineering

Ensure employees are aware of the data they are making available to others and what hackers might do with the knowledge they gain from that data. Train end users in the proper handling of social engineering tactics, such as:

- Dumpster diving
- Phone calls
- Email
- Instant messaging
- Onsite Visits

Prevention

Teach employees how to prevent intrusion attempts by verifying identification, using secure communication methods, reporting suspicious activity, establishing procedures, and shredding corporate documents.

Define established procedures for employees to report or respond to various types of attacks.

Audits

Employ external consultants to perform periodic audits and social engineering attempts to test employees and the network security. Define regularity of audits by external consultants.

Reporting

Develop clear procedures for who is responsible for generating reports and who reviews the reports. Timely, accurate, and comprehensible reports are essential in future attack prevention and pinpointing hacker activity. Define and describe the types of reports, details within the reports, and proper archival of all reports for historical reference.

Response Procedures

Define the steps to take after an intrusion has been recognized. Recommended steps should include a minimum of the following:

- Positive identification
- Confirmed attack
- Immediate action
- Documentation
- Reporting

Appendices

Glossary

Include a glossary to define words readers may not understand or those that require further clarification.

Whitepapers

Include any applicable industry whitepapers that may help during implementation, analysis, prevention, or recovery.

Education / Certification

List any classes, self-study materials, and certifications that would be beneficial to employees (end users and IT staff) toward the goal of securing the wireless network.

Computer Fraud & Abuse Act

THE COMPUTER FRAUD AND ABUSE ACT

UNITED STATES CODE

TITLE 18 - CRIMES AND CRIMINAL PROCEDURE
PART I - CRIMES
CHAPTER 47 - FRAUD AND FALSE STATEMENTS
_____

Sec. 1030. Fraud and related activity in connection with
computers

(a) Whoever --

(1) knowingly accesses a computer without authorization or
exceeds authorized access, and by means of such conduct obtains
information that has been determined by the United States
Government pursuant to an Executive order or statute to require
protection against unauthorized disclosure for reasons   of
national defense or foreign relations, or any restricted data, as
defined in paragraph y of section 11 of the Atomic Energy Act of
1954, with the intent or reason to believe that such information
so obtained is to be used to the injury of the United States, or
to the advantage of any foreign nation;

(2) intentionally accesses a computer without authorization or
exceeds   authorized access, and thereby obtains information
contained in a financial record of a financial institution, or of
a card issuer as defined in section 1602(n) of title 15, or
contained in a file of a consumer reporting agency on a consumer,
as such terms are defined in the Fair Credit Reporting Act (15
U.S.C. 1681 et seq.);

(3) intentionally, without authorization to access any computer
of a department or agency of the United States, accesses such a
computer of that department or agency that is exclusively for the
use of the Government of the United States or, in the case of a
computer not exclusively for such use, is used by or for the
Government of the United States and such conduct adversely
affects the use of the Government's operation of such computer;

(4) knowingly and with intent to defraud, accesses a Federal
interest computer without authorization, or exceeds authorized

access, and by means of such conduct furthers the intended fraud and obtains anything of value, unless the object of the fraud and the thing obtained consists only of the use of the computer;

(5) (A) through means of a computer used in interstate commerce or communications, knowingly causes the transmission of a program, information, code, or command to a computer or computer system if--

  (I) the person causing the transmission intends that such transmission will--

    (I) damage, or cause damage to, a computer, computer system, network, information, data, or program; or

    (II) withhold or deny, or cause the withholding or denial, of the use of a computer, computer services, system or network, information, data or program; and

  (ii) the transmission of the harmful component of the program, information, code, or command--

    (I) occurred without the authorization of the persons or entities who own or are responsible for the computer system receiving the program, information, code, or command; and

    (II) (aa) causes loss or damage to one or more other persons of value aggregating $1,000 or more during any 1-year period; or

      (bb) modifies or impairs, or potentially modifies or impairs, the medical examination, medical diagnosis, medical treatment, or medical care of one or more individuals; or

  (B) through means of a computer used in interstate commerce or communication, knowingly causes the transmission of a program, information, code, or command to a computer or computer system--

    (I) with reckless disregard of a substantial and unjustifiable risk that the transmission will--

      (I) damage, or cause damage to, a computer, computer system, network, information, data or program; or

(II)   withhold   or   deny   or   cause   the withholding   or   denial   of   the   use   of   a   computer,   computer services, system, network, information, data or program;   and

(ii) if the transmission of the harmful component of the program, information, code, or command--

(I)   occurred without the authorization   of the   persons   or   entities   who own   or are   responsible   for   the computer   system   receiving   the program,   information,   code,   or command;   and

(II)   (aa) causes loss or damage to   one   or more   other persons   of a value aggregating $1,000 or more   during any 1-year period;   or

(bb) modifies or impairs, or potentially modifies   or impairs, the medical examination, medical diagnosis, medical treatment, or medical care of one or more individuals;

(6) knowingly and with intent to defraud traffics (as defined   in section   1029)   in   any password or similar   information   through which a computer may be accessed without authorization, if--

(A) such trafficking affects interstate or foreign commerce; or

(B)   such computer is used by or for the Government   of   the United States;

shall be punished as provided in subsection (c) of this section.

(b) Whoever attempts to commit an offense under subsection (a) of   this section shall be punished as provided in subsection   (c) of this section.

(c) The punishment for an offense under subsection (a) or (b)   of this section is--

(1)   (A) a fine under this title or imprisonment   for   not more   than   ten   years, or both, in the case of an offense   under subsection   (a)(1) of this section which does not occur   after   a conviction   for   another   offense under such   subsection,   or   an attempt   to commit an offense punishable under this subparagraph;

and

        (B) a fine under this title or imprisonment for not more than twenty years, or both, in the case of an offense under subsection (a)(1) of this section which occurs after a conviction for another offense under such subsection, or an attempt to commit an offense punishable under this subparagraph; and

        (2) (A) a fine under this title or imprisonment for not more than one year, or both, in the case of an offense under subsection (a)(2), (a)(3) or (a)(6) of this section which does not occur after a conviction for another offense under such subsection, or an attempt to commit an offense punishable under this subparagraph; and

        (B) a fine under this title or imprisonment for not more than ten years, or both, in the case of an offense under subsection (a)(2), (a)(3) or (a)(6) of this section which occurs after a conviction for another offense under such subsection, or an attempt to commit an offense punishable under this subparagraph;

        (3) (A) a fine under this title or imprisonment for not more than five years, or both, in the case of an offense under subsection (a)(4) or (a)(5)(A) of this section which does not occur after a conviction for another offense under such subsection, or an attempt to commit an offense punishable under this subparagraph; and

        (B) a fine under this title or imprisonment for not more than ten years, or both, in the case of an offense under subsection (a)(4) or (a)(5) of this section which occurs after a conviction for another offense under such subsection, or an attempt to commit an offense punishable under this subparagraph; and

    (4) a fine under this title or imprisonment for not more than 1 year, or both, in the case of an offense under subsection (a)(5)(B).

(d) The United States Secret Service shall, in addition to any other agency having such authority, have the authority to investigate offenses under this section. Such authority of the United States Secret Service shall be exercised in accordance with an agreement which shall be entered into by the Secretary of the Treasury and the Attorney General.

(e) As used in this section--

(1) the term "computer" means an electronic, magnetic, optical, electrochemical, or other high speed data processing device performing logical, arithmetic, or storage functions, and includes any data storage facility or communications facility directly related to or operating in conjunction with such device, but such term does not include an automated typewriter or typesetter, a portable hand held calculator, or other similar device;

(2) the term "Federal interest computer" means a computer--

(A) exclusively for the use of a financial institution or the United States Government, or, in the case of a computer not exclusively for such use, used by or for a financial institution or the United States Government and the conduct constituting the offense affects the use of the financial institution's operation or the Government's operation of such computer; or

(B) which is one of two or more computers used in committing the offense, not all of which are located in the same State;

(3) the term "State" includes the District of Columbia, the Commonwealth of Puerto Rico, and any other commonwealth, possession or territory of the United States;

(4) the term "financial institution" means--

(A) an institution with deposits insured by the Federal Deposit Insurance Corporation;

(B) the Federal Reserve or a member of the Federal Reserve including any Federal Reserve Bank;

(C) a credit union with accounts insured by the National Credit Union Administration;

(D) a member of the Federal home loan bank system

and any home loan bank;

(E) any institution of the Farm Credit System under the Farm Credit Act of 1971;

(F) a broker-dealer registered with the Securities and Exchange Commission pursuant to section 15 of the Securities Exchange Act of 1934;

(G) the Securities Investor Protection Corporation;

(H) a branch or agency of a foreign bank (as such terms are defined in paragraphs (1) and (3) of section 1(b) of the International Banking Act of 1978); and

(I) an organization operating under section 25 or section 25(a) of the Federal Reserve Act.

(5) the term "financial record" means information derived from any record held by a financial institution pertaining to a customer's relationship with the financial institution;

(6) the term "exceeds authorized access" means to access a computer with authorization and to use such access to obtain or alter information in the computer that the accesser is not entitled so to obtain or alter; and

(7) the term "department of the United States" means the legislative or judicial branch of the Government or one of the executive departments enumerated in section 101 of title 5.

(f) This section does not prohibit any lawfully authorized investigative, protective, or intelligence activity of a law enforcement agency of the United States, a State, or a political subdivision of a State, or of an intelligence agency of the United States.

(g) Any person who suffers damage or loss by reason of a violation of the section, other than a violation of subsection (a)(5)(B), may maintain a civil action against the violator to obtain compensatory damages and injunctive relief or other equitable relief. Damages for violations of any subsection other than subsection (a)(5)(A)(ii)(II)(bb) or (a)(5)(B)(ii)(II)(bb) are limited to economic damages. No action may be brought under this subsection unless such action is begun within 2 years of the

```
date of the act complained of or the date of the discovery of the
damage.
```

Electronic Communications Privacy Act – Chapter 119

ELECTRONIC COMMUNICATIONS PRIVACY ACT

UNITED STATES CODE

TITLE 18. CRIMES AND CRIMINAL PROCEDURE
PART I--CRIMES
CHAPTER 119--WIRE AND ELECTRONIC COMMUNICATIONS INTERCEPTION AND
INTERCEPTION OF ORAL COMMUNICATIONS

_____

Sec. 2511. Interception and disclosure of wire, oral, or
electronic communications prohibited

   (1) Except as otherwise specifically provided in this chapter
any person who -

   (a) intentionally intercepts, endeavors to intercept, or
procures any other person to intercept or endeavor to intercept,
any wire, oral, or electronic communication;

      (b) intentionally uses, endeavors to use, or procures
any other person to use or endeavor to use any electronic,
mechanical, or other device to intercept any oral communication
when -

         (i) such device is affixed to, or otherwise
transmits a signal through, a wire, cable, or other like
connection used in wire communication; or

         (ii) such device transmits communications by
radio, or interferes with the transmission of such communication;
or

         (iii) such person knows, or has reason to know,
that such device or any component thereof has been sent through
the mail or transported in interstate or foreign commerce; or

         (iv) such use or endeavor to use (A) takes place
on the premises of any business or other commercial establishment
the operations of which affect interstate or foreign commerce;
or (B) obtains or is for the purpose of obtaining information
relating to the operations of any business or other commercial

establishment the operations of which affect interstate or foreign commerce; or

(v) such person acts in the District of Columbia, the Commonwealth of Puerto Rico, or any territory or possession of the United States;

(c) intentionally discloses, or endeavors to disclose, to any other person the contents of any wire, oral, or electronic communication, knowing or having reason to know that the information was obtained through the interception of a wire, oral, or electronic communication in violation of this subsection;

(d) intentionally uses, or endeavors to use, the contents of any wire, oral, or electronic communication, knowing or having reason to know that the information was obtained through the interception of a wire, oral, or electronic communication in violation of this subsection; or

(e) (i) intentionally discloses, or endeavors to disclose, to any other person the contents of any wire, oral, or electronic communication, intercepted by means authorized by sections 2511(2)(A)(ii), 2511(b)-(c), 2511(e), 2516, and 2518 of this subchapter, (ii) knowing or having reason to know that the information was obtained through the interception of such a communication in connection with a criminal investigation, (iii) having obtained or received the information in connection with a criminal investigation, and (iv) with intent to improperly obstruct, impede, or interfere with a duly authorized criminal investigation,

shall be punished as provided in subsection (4) or shall be subject to suit as provided in subsection (5).

(2)(a)(i) It shall not be unlawful under this chapter for an operator of a switchboard, or on officer, employee, or agent of a provider of wire or electronic communication service, whose facilities are used in the transmission of a wire or electronic communication, to intercept, disclose, or use that communication in the normal course of his employment while engaged in any activity which is a necessary incident to the rendition of his service or to the protection of the rights or property of the provider of that service, except that a provider of wire communication service to the public shall not utilize service observing or random monitoring except for mechanical or service quality control checks.

(ii) Notwithstanding any other law, providers of wire or electronic communication service, their officers, employees, and agents, landlords, custodians, or other persons, are authorized to provide information, facilities, or technical assistance to persons authorized by law to intercept wire, oral, or electronic communications or to conduct electronic surveillance, as defined in section 101 of the Foreign Intelligence Surveillance Act of 1978, if such provider, its officers, employees, or agents, landlord, custodian, or other specified person, has been provided with--

(A) a court order directing such assistance signed by the authorizing judge, or

(B) a certification in writing by a person specified in section 2518(7) of this title or the Attorney General of the United States that no warrant or court order is required by law, that all statutory requirements have been met, and that the specified assistance is required, setting forth the period of time during which the provision of the information, facilities, or technical assistance is authorized and specifying the information, facilities, or technical assistance required. No provider of wire or electronic communication service, officer, employee, or agent thereof, or landlord, custodian, or other specified person shall disclose the existence of any interception or surveillance or the device used to accomplish the interception or surveillance with respect to which the person has been furnished a court order or certification under this chapter, except as may otherwise be required by legal process and then only after prior notification to the Attorney General or to the principal prosecuting attorney of a State or any political subdivision of a State, as may be appropriate. Any such disclosure, shall render such person liable for the civil damages provided for in section 2520. No cause of action shall lie in any court against any provider of wire or electronic communication service, its officers, employees, or agents, landlord, custodian, or other specified person for providing information, facilities, or assistance in accordance with the terms of a court order or certification under this chapter.

(b) It shall not be unlawful under this chapter for an officer, employee, or agent of the Federal Communications Commission, in the normal course of his employment and in discharge of the monitoring responsibilities exercised by the Commission in the enforcement of chapter 5 of title 47 of the United States Code, to intercept a wire or electronic communication, or oral communication transmitted by radio, or to disclose or use the information thereby obtained.

(c) It shall not be unlawful under this chapter for a person acting under color of law to intercept a wire, oral, or electronic communication, where such person is a party to the communication or one of the parties to the communication has given prior consent to such interception.

(d) It shall not be unlawful under this chapter for a person not acting under color of law to intercept a wire, oral, or electronic communication where such person is a party to the communication or where one of the parties to the communication has given prior consent to such interception unless such communication is intercepted for the purpose of committing any criminal or tortious act in violation of the Constitution or laws of the United States or of any State.

(e) Notwithstanding any other provision of this title or section 705 or 706 of the Communications Act of 1934, it shall not be unlawful for an officer, employee, or agent of the United States in the normal course of his official duty to conduct electronic surveillance, as defined in section 101 of the Foreign Intelligence Surveillance Act of 1978, as authorized by that Act.

(f) Nothing contained in this chapter or chapter 121, or section 705 of the Communications Act of 1934, shall be deemed to affect the acquisition by the United States Government of foreign intelligence information from international or foreign communications, or foreign intelligence activities conducted in accordance with otherwise applicable Federal law involving a foreign electronic communications system, utilizing a means other than electronic surveillance as defined in section 101 of the Foreign Intelligence Surveillance Act of 1978, and procedures in this chapter and the Foreign Intelligence Surveillance Act of 1978 shall be the exclusive means by which electronic surveillance, as defined in section 101 of such Act, and the interception of domestic wire and oral communications may be conducted.

(g) It shall not be unlawful under this chapter or chapter 121 of this title for any person -

(i) to intercept or access an electronic communication made through an electronic communication system that is configured so that such electronic communication is readily accessible to the general public;

(ii) to intercept any radio communication which is transmitted –

(I) by any station for the use of the general public, or that relates to ships, aircraft, vehicles, or persons in distress;

(II) by any governmental, law enforcement, civil defense, private land mobile, or public safety communications system, including police and fire, readily accessible to the general public;

(III) by a station operating on an authorized frequency within the bands allocated to the amateur, citizens band, or general mobile radio services; or

(IV) by any marine or aeronautical communications system;

(iii) to engage in any conduct which –

(I) is prohibited by section 633 of the Communications Act of 1934; or

(II) is excepted from the application of section 705(a) of the Communications Act of 1934 by section 705(b) of that Act;

(iv) to intercept any wire or electronic communication the transmission of which is causing harmful interference to any lawfully operating station or consumer electronic equipment, to the extent necessary to identify the source of such interference; or

(v) for other users of the same frequency to intercept any radio communication made through a system that utilizes frequencies monitored by individuals engaged in the provision or the use of such system, if such communication is not scrambled or encrypted.

(h) It shall not be unlawful under this chapter -

   (i) to use a pen register or a trap and trace device (as those terms are defined for the purposes of chapter 206 (relating to pen registers and trap and trace devices) of this title); or

   (ii) for a provider of electronic communication service to record the fact that a wire or electronic communication was initiated or completed in order to protect such provider, another provider furnishing service toward the completion of the wire or electronic communication, or a user of that service, from fraudulent, unlawful or abusive use of such service.

   (3)(a) Except as provided in paragraph (b) of this subsection, a person or entity providing an electronic communication service to the public shall not intentionally divulge the contents of any communication (other than one to such person or entity, or an agent thereof) while in transmission on that service to any person or entity other than an addressee or intended recipient of such communication or an agent of such addressee or intended recipient.

   (b) A person or entity providing electronic communication service to the public may divulge the contents of any such communication -

   (i) as otherwise authorized in section 2511(2)(a) or 2517 of this title;

   (ii) with the lawful consent of the originator or any addressee or intended recipient of such communication;

   (iii) to a person employed or authorized, or whose facilities are used, to forward such communication to its destination; or

   (iv) which were inadvertently obtained by the service provider and which appear to pertain to the commission of a crime, if such divulgence is made to a law enforcement agency.

   (4)(a) Except as provided in paragraph (b) of this subsection or in subsection (5), whoever violates subsection (1) of this section shall be fined under this title or imprisoned not more than five years, or both.

(b) If the offense is a first offense under paragraph (a) of this subsection and is not for a tortious or illegal purpose or for purposes of direct or indirect commercial advantage or private commercial gain, and the wire or electronic communication with respect to which the offense under paragraph (a) is a radio communication that is not scrambled, encrypted, or transmitted using modulation techniques the essential parameters of which have been withheld from the public with the intention of preserving the privacy of such communication, then -

(i) if the communication is not the radio portion of a cellular telephone communication, a cordless telephone communication that is transmitted between the cordless telephone handset and the base unit, a public land mobile radio service communication or a paging service communication, and the conduct is not that described in subsection (5), the offender shall be fined under this title or imprisoned not more than one year, or both; and

(ii) if the communication is the radio portion of a cellular telephone communication, a cordless telephone communication that is transmitted between the cordless telephone handset and the base unit, a public land mobile radio service communication or a paging service communication, the offender shall be fined under this title.

(c) Conduct otherwise an offense under this subsection that consists of or relates to the interception of a satellite transmission that is not encrypted or scrambled and that is transmitted --

(i) to a broadcasting station for purposes of retransmission to the general public; or

(ii) as an audio subcarrier intended for redistribution to facilities open to the public, but not including data transmissions or telephone calls, is not an offense under this subsection unless the conduct is for the purposes of direct or indirect commercial advantage or private financial gain.

(5)(a)(i) If the communication is --

(A) a private satellite video communication that is not scrambled or encrypted and the conduct in violation of this chapter is the private viewing of that communication and is not for a tortious or illegal purpose or for purposes of direct or indirect commercial advantage or private commercial gain; or

(B) a radio communication that is transmitted on frequencies allocated under subpart D of part 74 of the rules of the Federal Communications Commission that is not scrambled or encrypted and the conduct in violation of this chapter is not for a tortious or illegal purpose or for purposes of direct or indirect commercial advantage or private commercial gain,

then the person who engages in such conduct shall be subject to suit by the Federal Government in a court of competent jurisdiction.

(ii) In an action under this subsection--
(A) if the violation of this chapter is a first offense for the person under paragraph (a) of subsection (4) and such person has not been found liable in a civil action under section 2520 of this title, the Federal Government shall be entitled to appropriate injunctive relief; and

(B) if the violation of this chapter is a second or subsequent offense under paragraph (a) of subsection (4) or such person has been found liable in any prior civil action under section 2520,

the person shall be subject to a mandatory $500 civil fine.

(b) The court may use any means within its authority to enforce an injunction issued under paragraph (ii)(A), and shall impose a civil fine of not less than $500 for each violation of such an injunction.

Electronic Communications Privacy Act – Chapter 121

ELECTRONIC COMMUNICATIONS PRIVACY ACT

UNITED STATES CODE

TITLE 18. CRIMES AND CRIMINAL PROCEDURE
PART I--CRIMES
CHAPTER 121—STORED WIRE AND ELECTRONIC COMMUNICATIONS AND
TRANSACTIONAL RECORDS ACCESS

---

18 U.S.C. §§ 2701-2711

§ 2701. <u>Unlawful Access to Stored Communications</u>

   (a) Offense - Except as provided in subsection (c) of this
section whoever -

      (1) intentionally accesses without authorization a facility
through which an electronic communication service is provided; or

      (2) intentionally exceeds an authorization to access that
facility; and thereby obtains, alters, or prevents authorized
access to a wire or electronic communication while it is in
electronic storage in such system shall be punished as provided in
subsection (b) of this section.

   (b) Punishment - The punishment for an offense under subsection
(a) of this subsection is -

      (1) if the offense is committed for purposes of commercial
advantage, malicious destruction or damage, or private commercial
gain -

         (A) a fine under this title or imprisonment for not more
than one year, or both, in the case of a first offense under this
subparagraph; and

         (B) a fine under this title or imprisonment for not more
than two years, or both, for any subsequent offense under this
subparagraph; and

      (2) a fine under this title or imprisonment for not more than
six months, or both, in any other case.

(c) Exceptions - Subsection (a) of this section does not apply with respect to conduct authorized -

    (1) by the person or entity providing a wire or electronic communications service;

    (2) by a user of that service with respect to a communication of or intended for that user; or

    (3) in section 2703, 2704 or 2518 of this title.

§ 2702. <u>Disclosure of Contents</u>

  (a) Prohibitions - Except as provided in subsection (b) -

    (1) a person or entity providing an electronic communication service to the public shall not knowingly divulge to any person or entity the contents of a communication while in electronic storage by that service; and

    (2) a person or entity providing remote computing service to the public shall not knowingly divulge to any person or entity the contents of any communication which is carried or maintained on that service -

        (A) on behalf of, and received by means of electronic transmission from (or created by means of computer processing of communications received by means of electronic transmission from), a subscriber or customer of such service; and

        (B) solely for the purpose of providing storage or computer processing services to such subscriber or customer, if the provider is not authorized to access the contents of any such communications for purposes of providing any services other than storage or computer processing.

  (b) Exceptions - A person or entity may divulge the contents of a communication -

    (1) to an addressee or intended recipient of such communication or an agent of such addressee or intended recipient;

    (2) as otherwise authorized in section 2517, 2511(2)(a), or 2703 of this title;

(3) with the lawful consent of the originator or an addressee or intended recipient of such communication, or the subscriber in the case of remote computing service;

(4) to a person employed or authorized or whose facilities are used to forward such communication to its destination;

(5) as may be necessarily incident to the rendition of the service or to the protection of the rights or property of the provider of that service; or

(6) to a law enforcement agency -

(A) if such contents -
(i) were inadvertently obtained by the service provider; and
(ii) appear to pertain to the commission of a crime.
(B) if required by section 227 of the Crime Control Act of 1990.

§ 2703. Requirements for Governmental Access

(a) Contents of Electronic Communications in Electronic Storage - A governmental entity may require the disclosure by a provider of electronic communication service of the contents of an electronic communication, that is in electronic storage in an electronic communications system for one hundred and eighty days or less, only pursuant to a warrant issued under the Federal Rules of Criminal Procedure or equivalent State warrant. A governmental entity may require the disclosure by a provider of electronic communications services of the contents of an electronic communication that has been in electronic storage in an electronic communications system for more than one hundred and eighty days by the means available under subsection (b) of this section.

(b) Contents of Electronic Communications in a Remote Computing Service -

(1) A governmental entity may require a provider of remote computing service to disclose the contents of any electronic communication to which this paragraph is made applicable by paragraph (2) of this subsection -

(A) without required notice to the subscriber or customer, if the governmental entity obtains a warrant issued under the Federal Rules of Criminal Procedure or equivalent State warrant;

or

      (B) with prior notice from the governmental entity to the subscriber or customer if the governmental entity -
(i) uses an administrative subpoena authorized by a Federal or State statute or a Federal or State grand jury or trial subpoena; or
(ii) obtains a court order for such disclosure under subsection (d) of this section;
      except that delayed notice may be given pursuant to section 2705 of this title.
   (2) Paragraph (1) is applicable with respect to any electronic communication that is held or maintained on that service -

      (A) on behalf of, and received by means of electronic transmission from (or created by means of computer processing of communications received by means of electronic transmission from), a subscriber or customer of such remote computing service; and

      (B) solely for the purpose of providing storage or computer processing services to such subscriber or customer, if the provider is not authorized to access the contents of any such communications for purpose of providing any services other than storage or computer processing.

  (c) Records Concerning Electronic Communication Service or Remote Computing Service -

    (1)(A) Except as provided in subparagraph (B), a provider of electronic communication service or remote computing service may disclose a record or other information pertaining to a subscriber to or customer of such service (not including the contents of communications covered by subsection (a) or (b) of this section) to any person other than a governmental entity.

      (B) A provider of electronic communication service or remote computing service shall disclose a record or other information pertaining to a subscriber to or customer of such service (not including the contents of communications covered by subsection (a) or (b) of this section) to a governmental entity only when the governmental entity -
(i) obtains a warrant issued under the Federal Rules of Criminal Procedure or equivalent State warrant;
(ii) obtains a court order for such disclosure under subsection

(d) of this section;
(iii) has the consent of the subscriber or customer to such disclosure; or
(iv) submits a formal written request relevant to a law enforcement investigation concerning telemarketing fraud for the name, address, and place of business of a subscriber or customer of such provider, which subscriber or customer is engaged in telemarketing (as such term is defined in section 2325 of this title).
(C) A provider of electronic communication service or remote computing service shall disclose to a governmental entity the name, address, local and long distance telephone toll billing records, telephone number or other subscriber number or identity, and length of service of a subscriber to or customer of such service and the types of services the subscriber or customer utilized, when the governmental entity uses an administrative subpoena authorized by a Federal or State statute or a Federal or State grand jury or trial subpoena or any means available under subparagraph (B).

(2) A governmental entity receiving records or information under this subsection is not required to provide notice to a subscriber or customer.

(d) Requirements for Court Order - A court order for disclosure under subsection (b) or (c) may be issued by any court that is a court of competent jurisdiction described in section 3127(2)(A) and shall issue only if the governmental entity offers specific and articulable facts showing that there are reasonable grounds to believe that the contents of a wire or electronic communication, or the records or other information sought, are relevant and material to an ongoing criminal investigation. In the case of a State governmental authority, such a court order shall not issue if prohibited by the law of such State. A court issuing an order pursuant to this section, on a motion made promptly by the service provider, may quash or modify such order, if the information or records requested are unusually voluminous in nature or compliance with such order otherwise would cause an undue burden on such provider.

(e) No Cause of Action Against a Provider Disclosing Information Under This Chapter - No cause of action shall lie in any court against any provider of wire or electronic communication service, its officers, employees, agents, or other specified persons for providing information, facilities, or assistance in accordance with the terms of a court order, warrant, subpoena, or certification under this chapter.

(f) Requirement To Preserve Evidence -

(1) In general. - A provider of wire or electronic communication services or a remote computing service, upon the request of a governmental entity, shall take all necessary steps to preserve records and other evidence in its possession pending the issuance of a court order or other process.

(2) Period of retention - Records referred to in paragraph (1) shall be retained for a period of 90 days, which shall be extended for an additional 90 day period upon a renewed request by the governmental entity. §2704. Backup Preservation

(a) <u>Backup Preservation</u> -

(1) A governmental entity acting under section 2703(b)(2) may include in its subpoena or court order a requirement that the service provider to whom the request is directed create a backup copy of the contents of the electronic communications sought in order to preserve those communications. Without notifying the subscriber or customer of such subpoena or court order, such service provider shall create such backup copy as soon as practicable consistent with its regular business practices and shall confirm to the governmental entity that such backup copy has been made. Such backup copy shall be created within two business days after receipt by the service provider of the subpoena or court order.

(2) Notice to the subscriber or customer shall be made by the governmental entity within three days after receipt of such confirmation, unless such notice is delayed pursuant to section 2705(a).

(3) The service provider shall not destroy such backup copy until the later of -

(A) the delivery of the information; or

(B) the resolution of any proceedings (including appeals of any proceeding) concerning the government's subpoena or court order.

(4) The service provider shall release such backup copy to the requesting governmental entity no sooner than fourteen days after the governmental entity's notice to the subscriber or customer if such service provider -

(A) has not received notice from the subscriber or customer that the subscriber or customer has challenged the governmental entity's request; and

(B) has not initiated proceedings to challenge the request of the governmental entity. (5) A governmental entity may seek to require the creation of a backup copy under subsection (a)(1) of this section if in its sole discretion such entity determines that there is reason to believe that notification under section 2703 of this title of the existence of the subpoena or court order may result in destruction of or tampering with evidence. This determination is not subject to challenge by the subscriber or customer or service provider.

(b) Customer Challenges -

(1) Within fourteen days after notice by the governmental entity to the subscriber or customer under subsection (a)(2) of this section, such subscriber or customer may file a motion to quash such subpoena or vacate such court order, with copies served upon the governmental entity and with written notice of such challenge to the service provider. A motion to vacate a court order shall be filed in the court which issued such order. A motion to quash a subpoena shall be filed in the appropriate United States district court or State court. Such motion or application shall contain an affidavit or sworn statement -

(A) stating that the application is a customer or subscriber to the service from which the contents of electronic communications maintained for him have been sought; and

(B) stating the applicant's reasons for believing that the records sought are not relevant to a legitimate law enforcement inquiry or that there has not been substantial compliance with the provisions of this chapter in some other respect.

(2) Service shall be made under this section upon a governmental entity by delivering or mailing by registered or certified mail a copy of the papers to the person, office, or department specified in the notice which the customer has received

pursuant to this chapter. For the purposes of this section, the term "delivery" has the meaning given that term in the Federal Rules of Civil Procedure.

(3) If the court finds that the customer has complied with paragraphs (1) and (2) of this subsection, the court shall order the governmental entity to file a sworn response, which may be filed in camera if the governmental entity includes in its response the reasons which make in camera review appropriate. If the court is unable to determine the motion or application on the basis of the parties' initial allegations and response, the court may conduct such additional proceedings as it deems appropriate. All such proceedings shall be completed and the motion or application decided as soon as practicable after the filing of the governmental entity's response.

(4) If the court finds that the applicant is not the subscriber or customer for whom the communications sought by the governmental entity are maintained, or that there is a reason to believe that the law enforcement inquiry is legitimate and that the communications sought are relevant to that inquiry, it shall deny the motion or application and order such process enforced. If the court finds that the applicant is the subscriber or customer for whom the communications sought by the governmental entity are maintained, and that there is not a reason to believe that the communications sought are relevant to a legitimate law enforcement inquiry, or that there has not been substantial compliance with the provisions of this chapter, it shall order the process quashed.

(5) A court order denying a motion or application under this section shall not be deemed a final order and no interlocutory appeal may be taken therefrom by the customer. §2705. Delayed Notice

(a) Delay of Notification –

(1) A governmental entity acting under section 2703(b) of this title may –

(A) where a court order is sought, include in the application a request, which the court shall grant, for an order delaying the notification required under section 2703(b) of this title for a period not to exceed ninety days, if the court determines that there is reason to believe that notification of the existence of the court order may have an adverse result described in paragraph (2) of this subsection; or

(B) where an administrative subpoena authorized by a Federal or State statute or a Federal or State grand jury subpoena is obtained, delay the notification required under section 2703(b) of this title for a period not to exceed ninety days upon the execution of a written certification of a supervisory official that there is reason to believe that notification of the existence of the subpoena may have an adverse result described in paragraph (2) of this subsection.

(2) An adverse result for the purposes of paragraph (1) of this subsection is -

(A) endangering the life or physical safety of an individual;

(B) flight from prosecution;

(C) destruction of or tampering with evidence;

(D) intimidation of potential witnesses; or

(E) otherwise seriously jeopardizing an investigation or unduly delaying a trial.

(3) The governmental entity shall maintain a true copy of certification under paragraph (1)(B).

(4) Extensions of the delay of notification provided in section 2703 of up to ninety days each may be granted by the court upon application, or by certification by a governmental entity, but only in accordance with subsection (b) of this section.

(5) Upon expiration of the period of delay of notification under paragraph (1) or (4) of this subsection, the governmental entity shall serve upon, or deliver by registered or first-class mail to, the customer or subscriber a copy of the process or request together with notice that -

(A) states with reasonable specificity the nature of the law enforcement inquiry; and

(B) informs such customer or subscriber -

(i) that information maintained for such customer or subscriber by the service provider named in such process or request was supplied to or requested by that governmental authority and the date on which the supplying or request took place;
(ii) that notification of such customer or subscriber was delayed;
(iii) what governmental entity or court made the certification or determination pursuant to which that delay was made; and
(iv) which provision of this chapter allowed such delay.

    (6) As used in this subsection, the term "supervisory official" means the investigative agent in charge or assistant investigative agent in charge or an equivalent of an investigating agency's headquarters or regional office, or the chief prosecuting attorney or the first assistant prosecuting attorney or an equivalent of a prosecuting attorney's headquarters or regional office.

  (b) Preclusion of Notice to Subject of Governmental Access - A governmental entity acting under section 2703, when it is not required to notify the subscriber or customer under section 2703(b)(1), or to the extent that it may delay such notice pursuant to subsection (a) of this section, may apply to a court for an order commanding a provider of electronic communications service or remote computing service to whom a warrant, subpoena, or court order is directed, for such period as the court deems appropriate, not to notify any other person of the existence of the warrant, subpoena, or court order. The court shall enter such an order if it determines that there is reason to believe that notification of the existence of the warrant, subpoena, or court order will result in -

    (1) endangering the life or physical safety of an individual;

    (2) flight from prosecution;

    (3) destruction of or tampering with evidence;

    (4) intimidation of potential witnesses; or

    (5) otherwise seriously jeopardizing an investigation or unduly delaying a trial.

§2706. Cost Reimbursement

  (a) Payment - Except as otherwise provided in subsection (c), a governmental entity obtaining the contents of communications, records, or other information under section 2702, 2703, or 2704 of this title shall pay to the person or entity assembling or providing such information a fee for reimbursement for such costs as are reasonably necessary and which have been directly incurred in searching for, assembling, reproducing, or otherwise providing such information. Such reimbursable costs shall include any costs due to necessary disruption of normal operations of any electronic communication service or remote computing service in which such information may be stored.

   (b) Amount - The amount of the fee provided by subsection (a) shall be as mutually agreed by the governmental entity and the person or entity providing the information, or, in the absence of agreement, shall be determined by the court which issued the order for production of such information (or the court before which a criminal prosecution relating to such information would be brought, if no court order was issued for production of the information).

   (c) Exception - The requirement of subsection (a) of this section does not apply with respect to records or other information maintained by a communications common carrier that relate to telephone toll records and telephone listings obtained under section 2703 of this title. The court may, however, order a payment as described in subsection (a) if the court determines the information required is unusually voluminous in nature or otherwise caused an undue burden on the provider.

§ 2707. Civil Action

   (a) Cause of Action - Except as provided in section 2703(e), any provider of electronic communication service, subscriber, or customer aggrieved by any violation of this chapter in which the conduct constituting the violation is engaged in with a knowing or intentional state of mind may, in a civil action, recover from the person or entity which engaged in that violation such relief as may be appropriate.

   (b) Relief - In a civil action under this section, appropriate relief includes -

      (1) such preliminary and other equitable or declaratory relief as may be appropriate;

      (2) damages under subsection (c); and

      (3) a reasonable attorney's fee and other litigation costs

reasonably incurred.

(c) Damages - The court may assess as damages in a civil action under this section the sum of the actual damages suffered by the plaintiff and any profits made by the violator as a result of the violation, but in no case shall a person entitled to recover receive less than the sum of $1,000. If the violation is willful or intentional, the court may assess punitive damages. In the case of a successful action to enforce liability under this section, the court may assess the costs of the action, together with reasonable attorney fees determined by the court.

(d) Disciplinary Actions for Violations - If a court determines that any agency or department of the United States has violated this chapter and the court finds that the circumstances surrounding the violation raise the question whether or not an officer or employee of the agency or department acted willfully or intentionally with respect to the violation, the agency or department concerned shall promptly initiate a proceeding to determine whether or not disciplinary action is warranted against the officer or employee.

(e) Defense - A good faith reliance on -

(1) a court warrant or order, a grand jury subpoena, a legislative authorization, or a statutory authorization;

(2) a request of an investigative or law enforcement officer under section 2518(7) of this title; or

(3) a good faith determination that section 2511(3) of this title permitted the conduct complained of;

is a complete defense to any civil or criminal action brought under this chapter or any other law.

(f) Limitation - A civil action under this section may not be commenced later than two years after the date upon which the claimant first discovered or had a reasonable opportunity to discover the violation.

§ 2708. Exclusivity of Remedies
The remedies and sanctions described in this chapter are the only judicial remedies and sanctions for nonconstitutional violations of this chapter.

§2709. <u>Counterintelligence Access to Telephone Toll and</u>
<u>Transactional Records</u>

   (a) Duty to Provide - A wire or electronic communication service
provider shall comply with a request for subscriber information
and toll billing records information, or electronic communication
transactional records in its custody or possession made by the
Director of the Federal Bureau of Investigation under subsection
(b) of this section.

   (b) Required Certification - The Director of the Federal Bureau
of Investigation, or his designee in a position not lower than
Deputy Assistant Director, may -

      (1) request the name, address, length of service, and local
and long distance toll billing records of a person or entity if
the Director (or his designee in a position not lower than Deputy
Assistant Director) certifies in writing to the wire or electronic
communication service provider to which the request is made that -

         (A) the name address, length of service, and toll billing
records sought are relevant to an authorized foreign
counterintelligence investigation; and

         (B) there are specific and articulable facts giving reason
to believe that the person or entity to whom the information
sought pertains is a foreign power or an agent of a foreign power
as defined in section 101 of the Foreign Intelligence Surveillance
Act of 1978 (50 U.S.C. 1801); and

      (2) request the name, address, and length of service of a
person or entity if the Director (or his designee in a position
not lower than Deputy Assistant Director) certifies in writing to
the wire or electronic communication service provider to which the
request is made that -

         (A) the information sought is relevant to an authorized
foreign counterintelligence investigation; and

         (B) there are specific and articulable facts giving reason
to believe that communication facilities registered in the name of
the person or entity have been used, through the services of such
provider, in communication with -
(i) an individual who is engaging or has engaged international
terrorism as defined in section 101(c) of the Foreign Intelligence

Surveillance Act or clandestine intelligence activities that
involve or may involve a violation of the criminal statutes of the
United States; or
(ii) a foreign power or an agent of a foreign power under
circumstances giving reason to believe that the communication
concerned international terrorism as defined in section 101(c) of
the Foreign Intelligence Surveillance Act or clandestine
intelligence activities that involve or may involve a violation of
the criminal statutes of the United States.
    (c) Prohibition of Certain Disclosure - No wire or electronic
communication service provider, or officer, employee, or agent
thereof, shall disclose to any person that the Federal Bureau of
Investigation has sought or obtained access to information or
records under this section.

    (d) Dissemination by Bureau - The Federal Bureau of
Investigation may disseminate information and records obtained
under this section only as provided in guidelines approved by the
Attorney General for foreign intelligence collection and foreign
counterintelligence investigations conducted by the Federal Bureau
of Investigation, and, with respect to dissemination to an agency
of the United States, only if such information is clearly relevant
to the authorized responsibilities of such agency.

    (e) Requirement That Certain Congressional Bodies Be Informed -
On a semiannual basis the Director of the Federal Bureau of
Investigation shall fully inform the Permanent Select Committee on
Intelligence of the House of Representatives and the Select
Committee on Intelligence of the Senate, and the Committee on the
Judiciary of the House of Representatives and the Committee on the
Judiciary of the Senate, concerning all requests made under
subsection (b) of this section.
§ 2710. Wrongful Disclosure of Video Tape Rental or Sale Records

    (a) Definitions - For purposes of this section -

        (1) the term "consumer" means any renter, purchaser, or
subscriber of goods or services from a video tape service
provider;

        (2) the term "ordinary course of business" means only debt
collection activities, order fulfillment, request processing, and
the transfer of ownership;

        (3) the term "personally identifiable information" includes

information which identifies a person as having requested or obtained specific video materials or services from a video tape service provider; and (4) the term "video tape service provider" means any person, engaged in the business, in or affecting interstate or foreign commerce, of rental, sale, or delivery of prerecorded video cassette tapes or similar audio visual materials, or any person or other entity to whom a disclosure is made under subparagraph (D) or (E) of subsection (b)(2), but only with respect to the information contained in the disclosure.

(b) Video Tape Rental and Sale Records -

(1) A video tape service provider who knowingly discloses, to any person, personally identifiable information concerning any consumer of such provider shall be liable to the aggrieved person for the relief provided in subsection (d);

(2) A video tape service provided may disclose personally identifiable information concerning any consumer -

(A) to the consumer;

(B) to any person with the informed, written consent of the consumer given at the time the disclosure is sought;

(C) to a law enforcement agency pursuant to a warrant issued under the Federal Rules of Criminal Procedure, an equivalent State warrant, a grand jury subpoena, or a court order;

(D) to any person if the disclosure is solely of the names and addresses of consumers and if -
(i) the video tape service provider had provided the consumer with the opportunity, in a clear and conspicuous manner, to prohibit such disclosure; and
(ii) the disclosure does not identify the title, description, or subject matter of any video tapes or other audio visual material; however, the subject matter of such materials may be disclosed if the disclosure is for the exclusive use of marketing goods and services directly to the consumer;
(E) to any person if the disclosure is incident to the ordinary course of business of the video taper service provider; or

(F) pursuant to a court order, in a civil proceeding upon a

showing of compelling need for the information that cannot be accommodated by any other means, if -

(i) the consumer is given reasonable notice, by the person seeking the disclosure of the court proceeding relevant to the issuance of the court order; and

(ii) the consumer is afforded the opportunity to appear and contest the claim of the person seeking the disclosure. If an order is granted pursuant to subparagraph (C) or (F), the court shall impose appropriate safeguards against unauthorized disclosure.

(3) Court orders authorizing disclosure under subparagraph (C) shall issue only with prior notice to the consumer and only if the law enforcement agency shows that there is probable cause to believe that the records or other information sought are relevant to a legitimate law enforcement inquiry. In the case of a State government authority, such a court order shall not issue if prohibited by the law of such State. A court issuing an order pursuant to this section, on a motion made promptly by the video tape service provider, may quash or modify such order if the information or records requested are unreasonably voluminous in nature or if compliance with such order otherwise would cause an unreasonable burden on such provider.

(c) Civil Action -

(1) Any person aggrieved by any act of a person in violation of this section may bring a civil action in a United States district court.

(2) The court may award -

(A) actual damage but not less than liquidated damages in an amount of $2,500;

(B) punitive damages;

(C) reasonable attorneys' fees and other litigation costs reasonably incurred; and

(D) such other preliminary and equitable relief as the court determines to be appropriate.

(3) No action may be brought under this subsection unless such action is begun within 2 years from the date of the act complained of or the date of discovery.

(4) No liability shall result from lawful disclosure permitted by this section.

(d) Personally Identifiable Information - Personally identifiable information obtained in any manner other than as provided in this section shall not be received in evidence in any trial, hearing, arbitration, or other proceeding in or before any court, grand jury, department, officer, agency, regulatory body, legislative committee, or other authority of the United States, a State or a political subdivision of a State.

(e) Destruction of Old Records - A person subject to this section shall destroy personally identifiable information as soon as practicable, but no later than one year from the date the information is no longer necessary for the purpose for which it was collected and there are no pending requests or orders for access to such information under subsection (b)(2) or (c)(2) or pursuant to a court order.

(f) Preemption - The provisions of this section preempt only the provisions of State or local law that require disclosure prohibited by this section.

¶ 2711. Definition for chapter

As used in this chapter-

(1) the terms defined in section 2510 of this title have, respectively, the definitions given such terms in that section; and

(2) the term "remote computing service" means the provision to the public of computer storage or processing services by means of an electronic communication system.

Glossary

3DES (Triple DES) – An encryption algorithm used in many VPN devices for the purpose of data privacy that encrypts, decrypts, and re-encrypts data using DES encryption and two secret keys. 3DES is used by the US Federal Government for FIPS (Federal Information Processing Standard) compliance.

802.1x – An IEEE standard for port-based access control, completed in 2001, used in wired networking that has been adapted for use in wireless LAN networking using virtual ports instead of physical ports. 802.1x is used for adding user-based authentication with RADIUS and EAP support to wireless LANs for added security.

802.1q VLAN tagging – An IEEE standard that establishes a method for inserting virtual LAN (VLAN) membership information into Ethernet frames. The standard was developed to address the problem of how to break large networks into smaller parts so broadcast and multicast traffic would not take more bandwidth than necessary. The standard also helps provide a higher level of security between segments of internal networks.

802.3 – IEEE standard that specifies a carrier sense and medium access control mechanisms and physical layer specifications for wired LANs. 802.3 is generally considered Ethernet.

802.5 – IEEE standard that specifies a token-passing ring access method and physical layer specifications for wired LANs. 802.5 is generally considered Token Ring.

802.11 – IEEE standard that specifies medium access and physical layer specifications for 1 Mbps and 2 Mbps spread spectrum wireless connectivity between fixed, portable, and moving stations within a local area. 802.11 is generally considered wireless LAN technology, and equipment operation is specified for the unlicensed 2.4 GHz ISM band.

802.11b – A revision to the IEEE 802.11 standard that addresses changes in direct sequence spread spectrum (DSSS) wireless LANs in order to enhance speed. 802.11b products support 1, 2, 5.5, and 11 Mbps DSSS connectivity in the unlicensed 2.4 GHz ISM band.

802.11a – An IEEE 802.11 standard that specifies equipment operation in the unlicensed 5 GHz bands (UNII bands). 802.11a products have data rates up to 54 Mbps and must support 6, 12, & 24 Mbps using OFDM technology.

802.11f – An IEEE standard that addresses many aspects of client roaming within the 802.11 series of wireless LAN standards. The original 802.11 standard did not specifically address the technical aspects of client mobility, so the 802.11f draft (soon to become a standard) acts as a supplemental standard to address this important feature.

802.11i – An IEEE standard that addresses many security mechanisms for wireless LAN networks. The original and subsequent standards have not addressed adequate security mechanisms, so the 802.11i Task Group has been steadily developing the 802.11i standard for this purpose. Currently IEEE 802.11i is in draft form.

802.11g – An IEEE 802.11 standard that specifies equipment operation in the unlicensed 2.4 GHz ISM band at rates of up to 54 Mbps using OFDM technology. Backward compatibility with 802.11b technology using DQPSK/CCK technology at 5.5 and 11 Mbps speeds is specified.

encryption/decryption accelerators – Many computer hardware devices have separate processing units that perform only the tasks of encryption and decryption so that the main CPU is not busied with these added tasks. This allows higher throughput when using strong encryption for data privacy.

access control lists (ACLs) – A security mechanism used to allow or deny particular types of traffic onto and out of a network segment based on criteria such as source and destination IP addresses. Routers and firewalls typically implement ACLs. ACLs can be time-consuming to configure because they are often command line driven.

Access Control Server (ACS) – An ACS can be either a software application or an appliance. The purpose of an ACS is to control access onto a network via authentication methods such as passwords, certificates, or tokens. An ACS may perform added functions such as AAA and remote configuration of network infrastructure nodes.

access point (AP) – A layer-2 connectivity device that serves as a portal between the wireless network and a wired network. Access points typically have one or more layer 3 management interface types such as TELNET, HTTP, HTTPS, and SNMP. Clients associate (connect) to the access point in order to gain access to the wired network resources. Access points combined with a distribution system (e.g. Ethernet) support the creation of multiple radio cells that enable roaming throughout a facility.

active scanning – A method by which stations broadcast a probe request frame, and all access points within range respond with a probe response frame. Similar to passive scanning using beacon management frames, the station will keep track of the probe response frames in order to make a decision on which access point to authenticate and associate with based on the probe responses having the strongest signal level, best quality, and other factors.

Address Resolution Protocol (ARP) – A TCP/IP protocol that binds network layer IP addresses to physical addresses (MAC).

Ad Hoc network – A wireless network composed of only stations and no access point. The IEEE 802.11 standard calls for an Ad Hoc networking mode for quick, inexpensive network setup.

Advanced Encryption Standard (AES) – A standard for data encryption that uses the Rijndael (pronounced "Rine Dale") algorithm and was chosen by the National Information and Standards Institute (NIST) as the Federal Information Processing Standard (FIPS); it is considered uncrackable. AES is now being used in Enterprise Wireless Gateways, VPN servers, and soon to be used in wireless infrastructure hardware.

anomaly detection – Refers to detecting changing in the existing network or network environment due to external influences. Intrusion Detection Systems (IDS) are designed to notice changes like this when humans could not.

Application Layer – The highest layer of the OSI model. Establishes communications with other users and provides services such as file transfer and electronic mail to the end users of the network.

authenticated DHCP – An application used for forcing client devices to authenticate to the network prior to receiving an IP address. Clients and the DHCP mutually authenticate using a counter and a message authentication code (MAC).

authentication – The process a station uses to announce its identity to another station or to a server device. The IEEE 802.11 standard specifies two forms of authentication: Open System and Shared Key. 802.1x/EAP types define various types of authentication, many types of authentication servers are now in use, and multi-factor authentication has recently become available in the market.

authentication header (AH) – An IP Security (IPSec) protocol that verifies the authenticity of an IP packet by performing a calculation against the IP header. The AH protocol provides no data payload encryption.

authentication service (AS) –A service that verifies the identity of a network user. An authentication service is used to keep intruders from accessing the network.

basic service set identifier (BSSID) – A six-byte address (the first half of the MAC address) that distinguishes a particular access point from others.

biometrics – A term used to describe the unique attributes of a user's body. Biometrics are used for unique identification by an authentication service.

Bluetooth – A part of the 802.15 standard for WPANs (Wireless Personal Area Networks). Bluetooth is a close-range networking protocol primarily used for mobile devices, utilizing FHSS in the 2.4 GHz ISM band at around 1600 hops/second. Because of the high hop rate, Bluetooth devices may interfere with other devices operating in the 2.4 GHz band at close range.

broadcast SSID – A blank service set identifier field found in many types of wireless LAN management frames. The "broadcast SSID" is a term used to describe when any node is allowed to see or authenticate to the network.

Carrier Sense Multiple Access / Collision Avoidance (CSMA/CA) – A protocol used with IEEE 802.11 wireless LANs where the exponential random backoff process happens before traffic is transmitted instead of after a collision occurs (as with CSMA/CD).

Category 5 UTP data cable (Cat5) – Data cable certified for data rates up to 100 Mbps, which facilitates 802.3 100BaseT (Ethernet) networks.

Challenge Handshake Authentication Protocol (CHAP) – A type of authentication in which the authentication agent (typically a network server) sends the client program a key to be used to encrypt the username and password. This enables the username and password to be transmitted in an encrypted form to protect them against eavesdroppers.

Cisco Discovery Protocol (CDP) – A proprietary Layer 2 discovery protocol used by Cisco infrastructure devices for the purpose of network device discovery and management. CDP is unauthenticated and gives a plethora of information to anyone that can read its format.

class of service (CoS) – A term used to describe a situation configured by a network administrator to group users into categories, each having a different set of parameters and network use privileges. CoS is often used on Enterprise Wireless Gateways to distinguish between guest, authorized user, and network administrator access levels.

closed system – A term used to describe a wireless network configured to not announce its service set identifier (SSID).

Data Encryption Standard (DES) – A cryptographic algorithm that protects unclassified computer data. DES is a National Institute of Standards and Technology (NIST) standard, and is available for both public and government use. Most of today's leading edge cryptographic solutions include DES support because of its relative strength and wide popularity.

data flooding – The process of sending or receiving so much data to or through a device that its capacity is exceeded and the network slows. Sometimes devices simply drop much of the data sent to it for this reason. Data flooding may be intentional or unintentional, but the result is the same – a significant network throughput decrease.

Data Link Layer – The second layer of OSI model that performs the assembly and transmission of data frames using hardware source and destination addresses.

decryption – The process of extracting the original data out of an encrypted data packet or file for the purpose of reading it in its original form.

demilitarized zone (DMZ) – An area on a network where limited public access is granted inbound, and often unlimited outbound access is provided to locally attached workstations. A network's DMZ is often used to host publicly available services such as web servers, email servers, and FTP servers. The DMZ is always located outside of a segmentation device such as a firewall, VPN server, or similar. In a wireless network, it usually refers to the segment of the network housing the access points and wireless users, which is separated from the network backbone by a segmentation device.

denial of service (DoS) attacks – A type of network attack where the attacker's goal is to limit or prevent an authorized user from accessing network services.

dictionary attacks – An attack against a device performing password authentication where a long pre-configured list of words or character strings are tested in order to bypass the password authentication and to gain network access.

digital certificates – A digital file created and used for the purpose of identification. Certificates are placed onto a computer (such as a laptop or PDA) for the purpose of identifying the owner to the network. Certificates are protected by passwords or passphrases and offer a very strong method of identification.

Direct Sequence Spread Spectrum (DSSS) – Combines a data signal at the sending station with a higher data rate bit sequence, which many refer to as a chipping sequence. A high processing gain ratio of data bits to chipping bits) increases the signal's resistance to interference. The IEEE specifies a minimum processing gain of 11 and most products operate under 20. Until May 2002, the FCC limited processing gain to a minimum 10, however this is no longer the case. DSSS uses up to 14 channels worldwide, 11 in the United States, for data transmission. There can be only 3 non-overlapping channels in any one physical area.

dumpster diving – A slang term for a method of finding useable information when performing network or facility intrusion. An individual goes through a person or company's garbage in order to find private information that would lead to an easier network penetration.

Dynamic Host Configuration Protocol (DHCP) – A network service that may run on any layer 3 aware device such as a router, server, or even an access point. DHCP issues IP addresses automatically when requested by a client device. IP addresses are issued within a specified range. Client devices retain use of the IP address for a specific license period that the system administrator may define.

Electronic Communications Privacy Act – An act of Congress whereby eavesdropping and gaining access to electronic communications (including data communications) is deemed unlawful.

Enterprise Encryption Gateway (EEG) – A device that implements encryption at layer 2 of the OSI (similar to WEP) and acts as a gateway device for segmentation of the wireless network segment. Client software is necessary, and no routing is performed on the EEG.

Enterprise Wireless Gateway (EWG) – A layer 3 device used for wireless network segmentation that may include routing, NAT, CoS, RBAC, VPN services, firewall services, and more.

Ethernet hub – A layer 2 device that allows half-duplex communications across a wired Ethernet network. Ethernet hubs generally have no inherent intelligence, and perform only the most basic connectivity functions.

Ethernet switch – An Ethernet connectivity device more intelligent than a hub, having the ability to connect the sending station directly to the receiving station in full duplex. Additionally, switches may have filtering, learning, and loop-free topology capabilities.

Extensible Authentication Protocol (EAP) – The Extensible Authentication Protocol (EAP) is a general protocol for PPP authentication that supports multiple authentication mechanisms. EAP does not select a specific authentication mechanism at the link control phase, but rather postpones this until the authentication phase. This allows the authenticator to request more information before determining the specific authentication mechanism. This also permits the use of a "back-end" server, which actually implements the various mechanisms while the PPP authenticator merely passes the authentication exchange through to each side (supplicant & authentication server).

EAP-MD5 – EAP-Message Digest 5 Challenge Handshake Authentication Protocol (EAP-MD5 CHAP) is a required EAP type that uses the same challenge handshake protocol as PPP-based CHAP, but the challenges and responses are sent as EAP messages. A typical use for EAP-MD5 CHAP is to authenticate the credentials of remote access clients by using user name and password security systems. You can also use EAP-MD5 CHAP to test EAP interoperability. Uses static WEP keys, does not support mutual authentication, and does not support rotation and distribution of WEP keys.

EAP-RADIUS – is not an EAP type, but the passing of EAP messages of any EAP type by an authenticator to an authentication server. EAP-RADIUS is used in environments where RADIUS is used as the authentication server.

EAP-TLS – EAP-Transport Layer Security is used in certificate-based security environments. It provides a strong authentication and key determination method. EAP-TLS provides mutual authentication, negotiation of the encryption method, encrypted key determination between the client and the authenticator, and dynamic key rotation and distribution. Server and client side certificates are required.

EAP-TTLS – EAP-Tunneled Transport Layer Security provides the same features as EAP-TLS with the added benefit of using a server-side certificate and client-side password authentication while not degrading the security level. An encrypted channel is built between the client and authentication server before the client's username and password are sent to the authentication server for authentication.

eavesdropping – The act of listening to and possibly capturing data transmissions in an unauthorized manner.

Federal Communications Commission (FCC) – The Federal Communications Commission (FCC) is an independent United States government agency, directly responsible to Congress. The FCC was established by the Communications Act of 1934 and is charged with regulating interstate and international communications by radio, television, wire, satellite, and cable. The FCC's jurisdiction covers the 50 states, the District of Columbia, and U.S. possessions.

Federal Information Processing Standard (FIPS) – Under the Information Technology Management Reform Act (Public Law 104-106), the Secretary of Commerce approves standards and guidelines that are developed by the National Institute of Standards and Technology (NIST) for Federal computer systems. These standards and guidelines are issued by NIST as Federal Information Processing Standards (FIPS) for use government-wide. NIST develops FIPS when there are compelling Federal government requirements such as for security and interoperability and there are no acceptable industry standards or solutions.

File Transfer Protocol (FTP) – A TCP/IP protocol for file transfer that has independent client and server software pieces.

firewall – A device that interfaces the network to external networks (such as the Internet) and shields the network from unauthorized traffic and traffic types. For example, some firewalls may permit only electronic mail and web browser traffic to enter the network from elsewhere. This helps protect the network against attacks made to other network resources, such as sensitive files, databases, and applications.

free-space path loss – A reference to the loss incurred by an RF signal due largely to "signal dispersion" which is a natural broadening of the wave front as the wave traverses a medium. The wider the wave front, the less power can be induced into the receiving antenna. This loss of signal strength is primarily a function of distance and becomes a very important factor when considering link viability.

Frequency Hopping Spread Spectrum (FHSS) – Takes the data signal and modulates it with a carrier signal that hops from frequency to frequency as a function of time over a wide band of frequencies. For example, a frequency-hopping radio will change the carrier frequency over the 2.4 GHz frequency band between 2.402 GHz and 2.4835 GHz at 1 MHz intervals. A hopping pattern called a channel determines the frequencies the transmitter will use and in which order. To properly receive the signal, the receiver must be set to the same hopping pattern and listen to the incoming signal at the right time at the correct frequency

Fresnel Zone – An elliptical area around the straight line of sight path between two wireless antennas that must be at least 60% clear for a reasonable RF data path to be established.

forced roaming – A situation caused by a wireless hijacker wanting to gain control of an unsuspecting authorized user's wireless connection where a narrowband RF jamming device is used to force the authorized user to roam to another DSSS channel hosted by the hijacker's rogue access point.

Foreign Agent (FA) – A mobile IP node type specified by RFC 2002 that assists mobile stations in establishing an IP connection with the Home Agent node.

forgery attacks – Attacks performed by intruders where packets are made to look like they came from an authorized node when they did not.

full-duplex – Refers to a type of communication in which devices can communicate in both directions at the same time; devices can transmit and receive simultaneously.

gain – There are two types of gain – passive and active. Passive gain describes the process of focusing the lobes of an antenna in a specific direction in order to extend the signal's reach and to lessen the impact of environmental RF interference. Active gain describes use of amplifying devices to boost the RF signal's amplitude while in the coax cable.

Generic Attribute Registration Protocol VLAN Registration Protocol (GVRP) – allows a LAN device to signal other neighboring devices that it wishes to receive packets for one or more VLANs. The main purpose of GVRP is to allow switches to automatically discover some of the VLAN information that would otherwise have to be manually configured in each switch. This is achieved by using GARP to propagate VLAN Identifier attributes across a bridged LAN.

half-duplex – Refers to a type of communication in which devices can communicate in only one direction at a time; devices can either be transmitting or receiving, but not both simultaneously. Ethernet hubs function in half-duplex mode.

hijacking – A type of attack where an authorized user's layer 2 (wireless LAN) and/or layer 3 (Internet Protocol) connections can be removed from the authorized network and placed on a rogue network. The rogue network is typically a mobile computer, such as a laptop, simulating a larger network environment.

Home Agent (HA) – A mobile IP node type specified by RFC 2002 that hosts each mobile node's home network IP address and establishes an IP connection with the mobile node (client) directly or through an FA as the mobile node roams.

honey pot – A device used to deceive network intruders. Honey pots typically simulate one or more servers of many types and can report attack statistics. Some honey pots can scan the attacker and provide crucial information for their location and attack patterns to the network administrator.

Hotspot – An area enabled with wireless LAN technology for the purpose of local wireless Internet connectivity. Hotspots are typically indoors in areas that would already have a large group of people, such as an airport, coffee shop, or hotel.

identity theft – The act of stealing someone's identity information so that it can be used for false identification. Identity theft has reached staggering proportions, and must be guarded against vigorously.

impact analysis – A process of analyzing what the financial or legal repercussion might be when a given level of network intrusion happens. Since using wireless LAN technology opens an organization to another realm of network attacks, it is important to assess the consequences of a network break-in.

Industrial Scientific Medical (ISM) bands – Radio frequency bands that the Federal Communications Commission (FCC) has authorized for wireless LAN use. The ISM bands are located at 915 +/- 13 MHz, 2450 +/- 50 MHz, and 5800 +/- 75 MHz.

Institute of Electrical and Electronic Engineers (IEEE) – A United States-based standards organization participating in the development of standards for data transmission systems. IEEE has made significant progress in the establishment of standards for LANs, namely the IEEE 802 series of standards.

Internet Key Exchange (IKE) – A key management protocol standard that is used in conjunction with the IPSec standard. IPSec can be configured without IKE, but IKE enhances IPSec by providing additional features, flexibility, and ease of configuration for the IPSec standard. IKE automatically negotiates IPSec security associations (SAs) and enables IPSec secure communications without costly manual preconfiguration. IKE is a hybrid protocol which implements the Oakley key exchange and Skeme key exchange inside the Internet Security Association and Key Management Protocol (ISAKMP) framework. (ISAKMP, Oakley, and Skeme are security protocols implemented by IKE.)

Internet protocol (IP) – A network layer (layer 3) protocol that allows the assignment of logical addresses to devices in a network for routing purposes.

intrusion detection systems (IDS) – A system composed of a central processing computer or cluster of computers and various types of sensors that continuously scan for network anomalies, misconfiguration, and attack signatures for the purpose of warning the network administrator that a network attack is under way. IDS systems log attack events, and may notify the network admin in one of many ways.

IPSec – Internet Protocol Security is a layer 3 data integrity and security protocol used in VPN devices. Since VPN equipment is often used in wireless environments, IPSec is commonly seen protecting wireless client devices. Data can be encrypted and packets and users authenticated using IPSec technology.

Key Distribution Center (KDC) – The central component of the Kerberos secure authentication protocol. The KDC is responsible for maintaining all nodes' encryption keys, authenticating nodes, and distributing tickets to clients.

Kerberos – A secure authentication protocol devised by MIT. Uses DES encryption, a ticket-based authentication scheme, and is the default authentication method for Windows 2000/2003 with Active Directory enabled.

Kerberos Setup Service (KSS) – A proprietary application by Symbol Technologies used as a registration and management utility for Symbol Spectrum24 access points when using Kerberos authentication. The KSS acts as a go-between for the access points and the Windows 2000/2003 Active Directory.

Layer2 Tunneling Protocol (L2TP) – A VPN protocol that combines advantages from Microsoft's PPTP and Cisco's L2F protocols. L2TP is supported in Windows 2000/XP, many VPN server devices, and often used with IPSec for data encryption. L2TP is a well-suited VPN protocol for wireless networks because of its authentication and encryption mechanisms.

Layered security solution – There are many categories of wireless security solutions on the market. OSI layers used vary between solution types. For added security, solutions may be layered, but it is essential to use solutions that do not conflict at a given OSI layer.

Lightweight Directory Access Protocol (LDAP) – A protocol for accessing information directories and a method of configuring an information directory.

Lightweight Extensible Authentication Protocol (LEAP) – Another term for EAP-Cisco Wireless which is Cisco's proprietary version of the Extensible Authentication Protocol. Cisco's LEAP supports mutual authentication, and uses password authentication.

malicious insertion – A term used to describe putting unlawful or unethical data onto a network through an unsecured connection such as wireless.

Message Authentication Code (MAC) – A one-way hash of a message that is then appended to the message. This is used to verify that the message is not altered between the time the hash is appended and the time it is tested.

Message Integrity Check (MIC) – A one-way hash of a message that is then appended to the message. This is used to verify that the message is not altered between the time the hash is appended and the time it is tested. Same as Message Authentication Code.

Mobile IP – A protocol developed by the Internet Engineering Task Force (RFC 2002) to enable users to roam to parts of the network associated with a different IP address subnets than what's loaded in the user's appliance.

Microsoft Point-to-Point Encryption (MPPE) – A method of encrypting data transferred across Point-to-Point Protocol (PPP)-based dial-up connections or Point-to-Point Tunneling Protocol (PPTP) virtual private network (VPN) connections. MPPE uses the RSA algorithm for encryption and supports 40-bit and 128-bit session keys, which are changed frequently to ensure security. MPPE does not compress or expand data.

Network Address Translation (NAT) – A method of translating node's IP addresses from one address to another. Four types of NAT are static, dynamic, overloading, and overlapping.

Network Address Port Translation (NAPT) – A method of translating multiple IP addresses into a single IP address by mapping each node to a port number and maintaining a translation table.

Network Layer – A layer of the OSI model that provides logical separation of local network segments and provides a means for addressing across many such network segments.

Open System authentication – The IEEE 802.11 default authentication method, which is a very simple, two-step process. First the station wishing to authenticate with an access point sends an authentication request frame containing the sending station's identity. The access point then sends back an authentication response frame alerting the authenticating station that it is associated. Open System authentication running on an access point is essentially a null authentication process – allowing any station to associate that is also using Open System authentication.

Orthogonal Frequency Division Multiplexing (OFDM) – A method of digital modulation in which a signal is split into several narrowband channels at different frequencies.

OS fingerprinting – A method of deducing what operating system is running, what services are running, and what vulnerabilities exist. This is typically accomplished using vulnerability scanning software running on a laptop or workstation computer.

packet – A basic message unit for communication across a network at the network layer (layer 3). A packet includes logical and data link (MAC layer) addresses plus the data payload of all higher OSI layers.

packet generator – An application or hardware device capable of creating packets with random or meaningless data for the purpose of throughput testing or network attacks.

password authentication protocol (PAP) – The most basic form of authentication in which a username and password are transmitted over a network in clear text and compared to a database of authorized users to allow network access.

peer-to-peer attack – An attack originating at one client node targeting another client node for the purpose of gaining access to valuable information or functional manipulation of the target machine.

Protected EAP (PEAP) – A protocol used in wireless networking co-developed by Cisco, Microsoft, and RSA for the purpose of stronger data encryption and authentication than previously available. Works similarly to EAP-TTLS, supports mutual authentication, and encrypted exchange of credentials.

Physical Layer – As the lowest layer of the OSI model, the Physical layer defines electrical, mechanical, and procedural specifications for providing the transmission of bits through a physical medium.

Point-to-Point Protocol (PPP) – A protocol that provides router-to-router and host-to-network connections over both synchronous and asynchronous circuits. PPP is the successor to SLIP and supports user authentication.

Point-to-Point Tunneling Protocol (PPTP) – A widely adopted, Microsoft proprietary VPN technology that is available as part of almost all Microsoft operating systems and implemented in many Linux software packages and appliances. PPTP forms a tunnel between two PPP endpoints and has optional encryption using MPPE.

polarization – The orientation of the electric field of an antenna element in reference to the Earth's surface.

Port Address Translation (PAT) – A term used to describe many-to-one Network Address Translation where the private IP addresses of many nodes are translated to a single public IP address. The translating device (a router) tracks the sessions in a NAT table in order to return each node's traffic to the proper device.

port scanning – The act of probing an IP node's layer 4 ports in order to determine what services are running on the node. This is accomplished through a software application on a diagnostic device (such as a laptop computer).

Power over Ethernet (PoE) – A method of injecting DC current into the unused pairs in Cat5 cabling to power access points and bridges in remote locations (<100 meters from the data switch); reduces the need to install separate power runs to power wireless infrastructure devices.

Pre-Shared Key (PSK) mode – The Wi-Fi Alliance has recently introduced WPA 1.0 which will have a mode called PSK that will be somewhat similar to static WEP, but with enhanced security mechanisms.

protocol analyzers – An application or appliance that captures, decodes, and analyzes frames, packets, or datagrams for the purposes of network intrusion, troubleshooting, and design.

Public Key Infrastructure (PKI) – A Public Key Infrastructure is a Cryptographic key and Certificate delivery system that makes possible secure financial electronic transactions and exchanges of sensitive information between relative strangers. A PKI will provide Privacy, Access control, Integrity, Authentication, and Non-repudiation support to information technology applications and electronic commerce transactions. A PKI will: manage the generation and distribution of Public/Private Key pairs; and publish the Public Keys with the user's identification as "certificates" in open bulletin boards (i.e., X.500 Directory Services). A PKI provides a high degree of confidence that: Private Keys are kept secure; specific Public Keys are truly linked to specific Private Keys; and the party holding a Public/Private Key pair is who the party purports to be.

Quality of Service (QoS) – Refers to the capability of a network to provide better service to selected network traffic over various technologies that may use any or all of these underlying technologies. The primary goal of QoS is to provide priority including dedicated bandwidth, controlled jitter and latency (required by some real-time and interactive traffic), and improved loss characteristics. Also important is making sure that providing priority for one or more flows does not make other flows fail. QoS technologies provide the elemental building blocks that will be used for future business applications in campus, WAN, and service provider networks.

Remote Access Dial-In User Service (RADIUS) – A network authentication protocol and service that has many implementations. RADIUS servers are used extensively in wireless networks due to VPN and 802.1x/EAP technologies.

rate limiting – The process of limiting or specifically defining the throughput of a particular user or group across a network device such as a router or switch. Rate limiting may be implemented at layer 2 or layer 3 of the OSI model.

replay attacks – Attacks against a network host that replays information previously captured from an authorized node transmission. The replayed information may be a financial transaction such as a bank deposit or an authentication conversation between client and server. Packet sequence numbers are a method of preventing this type of attack.

RF jamming – Interrupting authorized, useful RF transmissions using a high-powered RF transmitter on the same frequencies in use by the data transmission system.

RF Signal Generator – A device capable of transmitting RF signals, whether narrowband or spread spectrum, on a single or multiple RF frequencies at a designated amount of output power.

Rijndael algorithm – The encryption algorithm specified by NIST for the Advanced Encryption Standard (AES).

risk assessment – The process of determining the amount of risk associated with a given level of network security through a series of tests and calculations.

Role Based Access Control (RBAC) – A feature implemented in some Enterprise Wireless Gateways that provides for roles that are assigned network privileges. Users or user groups are assigned to the roles and have the level of network access assigned to their role. Role attributes may include access to certain network services and bandwidth controls.

rogue device – An unauthorized device attached to the network. Rogues placed by employees are typically on the network to facilitate convenient network connectivity. Rogues placed by intruders are typically on the network to facilitate bypassing security measures and gaining access to valuable network resources.

Remote Authentication Dial-In User Service (RADIUS) – an authentication service specified by the IETF that utilizes a computer-based database (RADIUS server) to compare usernames and passwords to allow access to a network.

router - A network layer device that moves packets between subnets across LAN and WAN connections.

Routing Information Protocol (RIP) – A routing protocol that bases its routing criteria on the distance (number of hops) to the destination. RIP maintains routing table information by sending out periodic routing updates to neighboring routers. RIP has two versions: version 1 and version 2. Version 1 is a classful protocol with a distance limitation of 15 hops. Version 2 is a classless protocol that sends only updates instead of the entire routing table. Version 2 supports authentication.

Secure File Transfer Protocol (SFTP) – FTP by itself passes usernames and passwords in clear text format – easily readable by anyone with a protocol analyzer. SFTP typically uses SSL or SSH to secure the both the authentication and the data transfer from eavesdropping.

Secure Sockets Layer (SSL) – A secure authentication and data transmission protocol developed by Netscape for transmitting private documents via the Internet. SSL works by using a public key to encrypt data that's transferred over the SSL connection.

Secure Shell (SSH) – An application used to log into another computer over a network, to execute commands on a remote machine, and to move files from one machine to another. It provides strong authentication and secure communications over insecure channels. It is a replacement for telnet, rlogin, rsh, rcp, and rdist.

segmentation devices – Devices used to separate unsecured and secured network segments and to provide authentication, data encryption, and network access control for users on the unsecured segment. Segmentation devices can be routers, layer 3 switches, SSH servers, firewalls, enterprise wireless gateways, enterprise encryption gateways, and others.

Shared Key authentication – A type of IEEE 802.11 authentication that assumes each station has received a secret shared key through a secure channel independent from the 802.11 network. Stations authenticate through shared knowledge of the secret key. Use of Shared Key authentication requires implementation of the 802.11 Wireless Equivalent Privacy algorithm and dictates a 4-way handshake process.

Simple Mail Transfer Protocol (SMTP) – A protocol for sending email messages to and between email servers

Simple Network Management Protocol (SNMP) – A network management protocol used for controlling and monitoring network devices through use of Management Information Bases (MIBs) located on the client devices and network management software located on a network management computer.

site survey – The act of surveying an area or a facility to determine the contours of RF coverage, interference, and equipment placement for optimum RF coverage and wireless LAN operation.

SNMP community strings – Serve as SNMP device passwords for network management stations to use in managing network nodes. There are two types of community strings that are of significant importance: read-only and read-write. Read-only community strings allow the administrator to view network device statistics whereas the read-write string allows the administrator to change configuration parameters in addition to viewing statistics.

Spanning Tree Protocol (STP) – A link management protocol that is defined by the IEEE 802.1d standard. STP provides path redundancy while preventing undesirable loops in a network.

social engineering – The act of deceiving authorized personnel into giving out information that should be given only to authorized personnel.

spectrum analyzer – An instrument that identifies the amplitude, characteristics, and frequency of RF signals.

Subnetwork Access Protocol (SNAP) – While the original 802.3 specification worked well, the IEEE realized that some upper layer protocols required an Ethertype to work properly. For example, TCP/IP uses the Ethertype to differentiate between ARP packets and normal IP data frames. In order to provide this backwards compatibility with the Version II frame type, the 802.3 SNAP format was created. The SNAP Frame Format consists of a normal 802.3 Data Link Header followed by a normal 802.2 LLC Header and then a 5 byte SNAP field, followed by the normal user data and FCS.

Terminal Access Control Access Control System (TACACS+) – A protocol that has been widely implemented across Cisco devices, including routers, switches, VPN concentrators, etc. The TACACS+ protocol provides a means to authenticate and authorize user and administrative access to Cisco devices. TACACS+ provides for fine-grained access control of administrative logins.

target profiling – The act of thoroughly researching and gathering information on a specific person or network for the purpose of facilitating intrusion.

Temporal Key Integrity Protocol (TKIP) – A Cisco proprietary protocol that repairs many of the weaknesses associated with static WEP as a wireless LAN security solution.

ticket-granting service (TGS) – A sub service running on the Kerberos KDC that grants tickets to client devices for the purpose of authentication.

TGT forwarding – The process of server #1 proving to server #2 that a client has been authenticated by forwarding the client's TGT to server #2.

Ticket Granting Ticket (TGT) – A ticket issued by the KDC's TGS to a client for the purpose of obtaining service tickets at a later time.

trace route – The process of identifying reachability, hops in the path between two points, and latency at each hop. Most operating systems have commands for trace routing.

Trivial File Transfer Protocol (TFTP) – A simple form of the File Transfer Protocol (FTP). TFTP uses the User Datagram Protocol (UDP) and provides no security features. Often used by servers to boot diskless workstations and to upgrade routers, switches, wireless bridges, and access points.

Unlicensed National Information Infrastructure (UNII) bands – A set of RF frequencies allocated by the FCC for unlicensed data communications and adopted by the IEEE 802.11a standard for wireless LANs; the three bands are: 5.15 to 5.25 GHz, 5.25 to 5.35 GHz, and 5.725 to 5.825 GHz

Virtual Local Area Network (VLAN) – Layer-2 functionality used in switch software to logically segment a switch or switched network into smaller units for the purpose of isolation.

Virtual Private Network (VPN) – An authenticated and encrypted link between two endpoints over a public network medium such as a wireless network or the Internet.

VPN concentrator – The server-side device in a VPN that authenticates client devices and builds encrypted tunnels to them.

war chalking – The act of marking on sidewalk, wall, or other medium near an unsecured wireless network for the purpose of documenting the network status for others or yourself for a later visit.

war driving – The act of driving around an area looking for an unsecured wireless network.

warez – Pronounced 'wares' where the 's' is pronounced as a 'z', this is a slang term for unlawfully copied software.

Wi-Fi Protected Access (WPA) – A subset of the Wi-Fi Alliance's equipment interoperability certification called Wi-Fi. WPA focuses specifically on the security features implemented within wireless infrastructure equipment. WPA 1.0 (the first level of implementation) is a subset of the forthcoming 802.11i standard. WPA 2.0 will be a full implementation of 802.11i when it is ratified as a standard.

Wired Equivalent Privacy (WEP) – An optional IEEE 802.11 authentication and encryption feature that offers frame transmission privacy similar to a wired network. WEP uses the RC4 encryption algorithm and can be used with Open System and Shared Key authentication methods.

Wireless bridge – A data link layer device used to connect multiple wired LAN segments wirelessly.

Wireless Network Management Protocol (WNMP) – A Symbol Technologies proprietary network management protocol used for wireless LAN infrastructure device management in a similar manner to SNMP. Many Symbol devices support both SNMP and WNMP.

Wireless VLAN – A method of segmenting wireless LAN users logically by assigning SSIDs or VLAN tags to users or their network connection through use of RADIUS attributes.

The Wi-Fi Alliance – Founded in 1999, this organization's charter is to certify interoperability of IEEE 802.11b products and to promote Wi-Fi™ as the global wireless LAN standard across all market segments.

Wireless Fidelity (Wi-Fi®) – The Wi-Fi Alliance certification standard signifying interoperability among 802.11b products

INTERNATIONAL CONTACT INFORMATION

AUSTRALIA
McGraw-Hill Book Company Australia
Pty. Ltd.
TEL +61-2-9900-1800
FAX +61-2-9878-8881
http://www.mcgraw-hill.com.au
books-it_sydney@mcgraw-hill.com

CANADA
McGraw-Hill Ryerson Ltd.
TEL +905-430-5000
FAX +905-430-5020
http://www.mcgraw-hill.ca

GREECE, MIDDLE EAST, & AFRICA
(Excluding South Africa)
McGraw-Hill Hellas
TEL +30-210-6560-990
TEL +30-210-6560-993
TEL +30-210-6560-994
FAX +30-210-6545-525

MEXICO (Also serving Latin America)
McGraw-Hill Interamericana Editores
S.A. de C.V.
TEL +525-117-1583
FAX +525-117-1589
http://www.mcgraw-hill.com.mx
fernando_castellanos@mcgraw-hill.com

SINGAPORE (Serving Asia)
McGraw-Hill Book Company
TEL +65-863-1580
FAX +65-862-3354
http://www.mcgraw-hill.com.sg
mghasia@mcgraw-hill.com

SOUTH AFRICA
McGraw-Hill South Africa
TEL +27-11-622-7512
FAX +27-11-622-9045
robyn_swanepoel@mcgraw-hill.com

SPAIN
McGraw-Hill/Interamericana de España,
S.A.U.
TEL +34-91-180-3000
FAX +34-91-372-8513
http://www.mcgraw-hill.es
professional@mcgraw-hill.es

UNITED KINGDOM, NORTHERN,
EASTERN, & CENTRAL EUROPE
McGraw-Hill Education Europe
TEL +44-1-628-502500
FAX +44-1-628-770224
http://www.mcgraw-hill.co.uk
computing_neurope@mcgraw-hill.com

ALL OTHER INQUIRIES Contact:
Osborne/McGraw-Hill
TEL +1-510-549-6600
FAX +1-510-883-7600
http://www.osborne.com
omg_international@mcgraw-hill.com